EMPOWERING CHILDREN

Play-Based Curriculum for Lifelong Learning

CAROL DALE SHIPLEY
Algonquin College

Nelson Canada

© Nelson Canada,
A Division of Thomson Canada Limited, 1993

Published in 1993 by
Nelson Canada,
A Division of Thomson Canada Limited
1120 Birchmount Road
Scarborough, Ontario M1K 5G4

Distributed in the United States by
Delmar Publishers Inc.,
3 Columbia Circle Drive
P.O. Box 15015
Albany, New York 12212

Canadian Cataloguing in Publication Data

Shipley, Carol Dale, 1945–
    Empowering children: play-based curriculum
for lifelong learning

Includes bibliographical references and index.
ISBN 0–17–603628–8

1. Play.   2. Early childhood education.   I. Title.

LB1140.35.P55S55 1993   372.21   C92–095042–6

Acquisitions Editor   Charlotte Forbes
Supervising Editor   Nicole Gnutzman
Developmental Editor   Bob Kohlmeier

Art Director   Bruce Bond
Cover and Text Design   Liz Nyman
Cover Photographer   Jeremy Jones

Printed and bound in Canada
1 2 3 4   WC   96 95 94 93

C O N T E N T S

Acknowledgments

This textbook represents the culmination of many years of striving to find a clear path through the diversity of values, opinions, research evidence, and theoretical viewpoints that abound about how young children develop and learn. Over the years, my students have provided inspiration and insight. Their sincerity and commitment have helped me maintain my vision for early childhood education and my belief that there is a way to move beyond the rhetoric to the implementation of viable, outcomes-oriented, developmentally appropriate practice in the education of children during the early years.

Writing a textbook is a project of considerable magnitude that cannot be accomplished alone. There are many persons whose influence I wish to acknowledge and whose support I greatly appreciate. Dr. Marilyn Segal, my professor of child growth and development at Nova University, was the first to encourage me to write for publication. The bright ideas and sensible publications of Dr. Chris Nash captured what I was feeling about early childhood education in the 1970s and motivated me to explore further in this field. The scholarly perspective of Dr. Evelyn Weber, my graduate school professor of early childhood education at Wheelock College in the 1970s, has guided me as a teacher and student for the past nineteen years.

I also want to thank Nelson editors, Charlotte Forbes and Nicole Gnutzman for their support and guidance throughout this lengthy endeavour. I am particularly indebted to my reviewers: Ingrid Crowther, Loyalist College; Anne Ellison, Ryerson Polytechnical Institute; Marie Goulet, George Brown College; Mabel Higgins, Lambton College; Barbara Marcus, Vanier College; Carol Paasche, Seneca College; Laurie Papas, Kwantlen College; Billie Shepherd, Mount Royal College; Alice Taylor, Holland College; Goranka Vukelich, Mohawk College; and Jennifer Wolfe, Grant MacEwan Community College. They have provided thoughtful advice throughout the drafts and have been instrumental in ensuring that the text would address diverse needs.

Karen Hunt, Director of the Orleans Cooperative Nursery School, managed the painstaking collection and editing of the photographs for this book. Parents of children at her school graciously permitted me to publish photographs she took of their children at play. Professor Steen Esbensen read Chapter 20, "Playgrounds for Learning," and offered sound advice and support. Carol Garceau and Deborah Lihou assisted in the preparation of the drawings.

I owe most to Pierre Giroux whose encouragement, generosity, and support made all the difference in my turning this project from a dream into a reality. My children, Lyle and Dee, have been a source of inspiration and continue to reinforce my belief in the lifelong impact of children's early learning experiences.

This early childhood education textbook is dedicated to the memory of my grandmother, Brydah Rose Rattle, who knew intuitively that children need stimulation and challenge as well as acceptance and love.

About the Author

Carol Dale Shipley, Ed.D., has been a teacher at all levels in the education system and has taught in Canada, England, and the United States. For the past fifteen years, Dale has been a professor in the Early Childhood Education Program at Algonquin College, Ottawa, Ontario. She is a graduate of McMaster University, Hamilton, Ontario; Wheelock College, Boston, Massachusetts; and Nova University, Fort Lauderdale, Florida.

INTRODUCTION

Educational reform has become a watchword of the 1990s, with theories and practices related to education and learning at all levels being debated by the general public, politicians, parents, and early childhood educators. In the midst of this debate the credibility of early childhood education has made impressive gains. There is growing recognition that the early childhood education profession represents values, practices, and standards held by well-trained early childhood educators. Politicians, educational administrators, and policy analysts, as well as the general public, are increasingly aware that specialized skills, knowledge, and understanding are required of early childhood educators who practise in programs that meet legislated standards and licensing requirements (Doherty, 1991).

The vast amount of public funds devoted to education in a period of profound economic change is prompting closer examination of education systems as well as growing demands for accountability and rigour in the education of our young. More and more North Americans are looking to child care programs and kindergartens to assume greater responsibility for the education of children at the early end of the lifelong learning continuum. Added professional recognition carries obligations as well as privileges for early childhood education professionals. The present challenge is for the early childhood education profession to deliver on the many claims it has made about the importance of high-quality early childhood education in children's lives.

One aspect of this challenge is the need for early childhood educators to be more specific about the factors that contribute to quality caregiving and **developmentally appropriate practice** in early education. Developmentally appropriate practice is the planning and implementation of child-centred programs that address the needs and interests of children at each developmental stage (Bredekamp, 1987). The focus of the past three decades on developmental goals and objectives, nurturing, comfortable environments with responsible, warm caregivers, and emphasis on open-ended play environments continues to provide an important framework for early childhood education. The demands of the present, however, are that more attention be paid to the developmental and learning outcomes of the years children spend in child care programs and kindergartens. These outcomes have to be observed in children individually and be directly attributable to the educators and programs that promote the health, development, learning, and progress of each child. This textbook describes the many factors present in early learning environments that facilitate these developmental and learning outcomes in young children.

■ FOCUS ON PLAY

The role of play in children's lives has dominated discussion about the optimal conditions under which children develop and learn. Children's inner lives are enriched through their daily interactions with events, people, and things, and play is clearly linked to children's progress in the social, emotional, cognitive, and physical domains. The pivotal role of play is clear. Children play in order to know and understand the world around them, to express themselves, and to practise new skills. Play is engaged in for its own sake. It contributes to children's physical and social knowledge, logical understanding, and sense of self.

Developmental early childhood education puts play at the centre of the learning process in early childhood. The belief is that through play children actively explore, manipulate, act upon, and respond to the stimuli, events, objects, and experiences they encounter daily. Through this interaction with the concrete environment, children develop intellectually and acquire abilities in the social, emotional, and physical domains as well.

From the 1940s to the 1970s, a child's environment was considered to be relatively unimportant since development was believed to occur in almost any setting. Play was viewed as a vehicle for the child's physical involvement, an avenue for self-expression, and an opportunity to acquire social experience through playful interaction with others. The belief in the 1940s and 1950s, in particular, was that no matter what environmental conditions were present, the tendency towards development predetermined by each child's genetic inheritance was so dominant that their environment played an accidental role rather than an active one. It was thought that children mainly needed opportunities to play and be social, and that the healthy functioning of the child at each stage was most important. The particular contexts and characteristics of play—in other words, whether it was social, group-oriented, solitary, task-oriented, planned, spontaneous, or expressive—were judged to be less important than heredity in terms of the child's eventual adaptation and success.

Piaget's belief that the child's environment plays a key developmental role as it responds to the child's actions revolutionized thinking in early childhood education in North America in the 1960s and 1970s. His cognitive developmental theory supported the view that play is the child's vehicle for development and learning. An idea that gained general acceptance as a result was that *children need a wide range of developmentally appropriate play opportunities, planned and set up by teachers in a well-organized environment that promotes the children's hands-on, self-directed, experiential learning.* These planned play experiences came to be seen as an important link between learning, environment, and development in all domains—physical, social, emotional, and cognitive.

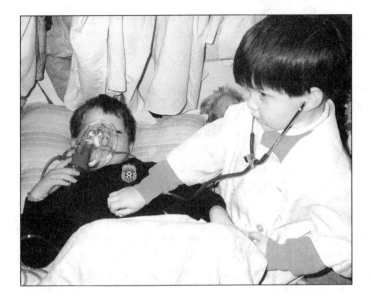

ACTIVE LEARNING

Information processing theory of the 1980s and 1990s has much in common with Piaget's cognitive development theory but focuses more on how children use information and integrate knowledge and concepts with what they already understand. Information processing psychologists view the mind as being much like a computer and attempt to describe in great detail the steps used by a child in solving a problem or learning a skill. Like Piaget, information processing theorists are interested in underlying mental processes. Piaget emphasized that children need plenty of opportunity to reflect on what they are actively engaged in doing, a process he termed "reflective abstraction," and that **cognitive development** consists of passages from one set of logical structures to another. Information processors assign much more importance to the memory, particularly to strategies for remembering, and information storage and retrieval; attending skills and learning-to-learn strategies are considered central to cognitive development. Information processing theory, according to Skolnik (1986) is not so much anti-Piagetian, as neo-Piagetian.

These theoretical perspectives gained credibility in early childhood education during the 1980s and are becoming more influential. Both support the importance of purposeful planning by teachers to ensure that a wide range of play opportunities are available to children. Planning play experiences that will result in observable learning outcomes is an essential component of high quality early childhood education (Walsh, 1991; Jipson, 1991; Kessler, 1991). This concept has reinforced the importance of the trained professional as a knowledgeable and purposeful planner, implementer, observer, and evaluator of effective early childhood education programs.

■ THE PURPOSE OF THIS TEXTBOOK

This textbook attempts to explain and show how to put into practice the relationships that exist among child development theories, play, and learning. The challenge for early childhood educators is to create an educational setting and plan experiences for young children that will encourage play, guide it in profitable directions, support the child's free choices of play activities, foster self-expression, and facilitate the acquisition of skills, knowledge, and understanding. The well-planned environment will be the catalyst for development and learning.

This textbook emphasizes links among the meaning and function of play, types of play, social contexts of play, the learning environment, child development and learning theory, principles for the planning of learning centres, and specific play and learning experiences. All of these factors need to be examined in relation to one another to ensure that early childhood education in general, and children's play experiences in particular, lead to the optimal progress and well-being of the child at each stage and in all developmental domains.

The organization and design of learning centres is highlighted in order to help teachers make efficient use of space and resources, and to facilitate children's largely self-directed play and learning experiences, which together promote growth and progress. Developmental principles are linked with suggestions for the design of learning centres and the choice of equipment, materials, and supplies. Play and learning experiences intended to make effective use of all facets of the environment are also included.

Philosophical Bias

The overriding assumption in this textbook is that the simplest activities—those using basic, exploratory play materials—are always best for young children. It is important, however, not to equate the simplicity of play materials with an oversimplification of learning opportunities. The best play and learning experiences are those that permit children to have their own ideas (Duckworth, 1991). They should be permitted to acquire new concepts through their hands-on investigation of the complexities inherent in things, phenomena, and events. Play experiences which encourage the child's self-directed and freely chosen action on concrete objects and events facilitate development in all domains. This kind of learning through play leads to sharper perceptions, increased knowledge, and enhanced understanding of progressively complex concepts. Children gain a feeling of mastery over their environments and an enhanced sense of self as they transform their world through play.

The Textbook as a Learning Tool

Empowering Children: Play-Based Curriculum for Lifelong Learning assumes that student teachers in early childhood education benefit when clear links are made for them between theory and practice. Many textbooks describe what "should be" in early childhood education. This textbook reinforces the values and beliefs with which most teachers and students already identify and shows how to put them into practice. It is intended to be a "how to" book that students and practising teachers may follow as they plan, implement, and evaluate play experiences and learning environments for children.

The book's step-by-step approach is intended to make it as useful to the student teacher, practising graduate, or supervisor as any guidebook that seeks to bring about concrete, observable outcomes would be. The belief represented here is that children in programs that adopt a clearly formulated set of planning principles and strategies will make developmental progress in all domains no matter what their particular strengths, weaknesses, or disabilities. Early childhood educators facilitate this developmental progress by observing children, planning environments and learning experiences that address children's observed developmental needs, and evaluating activities and programs. It will be a bonus if early childhood educators-in-training gain also an enhanced sense of the importance of their professional roles in the creation of developmentally appropriate play and learning environments from this textbook.

References

Bredekamp, S. (1987). *Developmentally Appropriate Practice in Early Childhood Programs Serving Children From Birth Through Age 8*. Washington, D.C.: National Association for the Education of Young Children.

DeVries, R. and Kohlberg, L. (1987). *Constructivist Early Education*. Washington, D.C.: National Association for the Education of Young Children.

Doherty, G. (1991). *Factors Related to Quality in Child Care*. Toronto: Ministry of Community and Social Services.

Duckworth, E. (1991). Twenty-four, Forty-two, and I love you: keeping it complex. *Harvard Educational Review* 61 (1):1–24.

Forman, G., and Kuschner, D.S. (1983). *The Child's Construction of Knowledge: Piaget for Teaching Children*. Washington, D.C.:

National Association for the Education of Young Children.

Jipson, J. (1991). Developmentally-appropriate practice, culture, curriculum, connections. *Early Education and Development* 2 (2):120–36.

Kessler, S. (1991). Early childhood education as development: critique of the metaphor. *Early Education and Development* 2 (2): 137–52.

Ministry of Education, Ontario. (1991). *The Early Years: Restructuring Education*. A consultation paper. Toronto: June, 1991.

Skolnick, A.S. (1986). *The Psychology of Human Development*. New York: Harcourt Brace Jovanovich.

Walsh, D.J. (1991). Extending the discourse on developmental appropriateness: a developmental perspective. *Early Education and Development* 2 (2):109–19.

HISTORY AND THEORY OF PLAY AND LEARNING

Chapter 1 reviews the historical development of play theory and introduces several of the principles underlying the centuries-old relationship between play and learning. The various categories and criteria that are used to define and describe stages of play, types of play, and social contexts of play are addressed in Chapter 2. Some of the issues from the past that have influenced present understanding about the role of play in learning and the impact of recent research on current play theory and acceptable practice are discussed in Chapter 3.

Section 1 addresses the following topics:

- historical antecedents of play theory
- contemporary play theory
- relationship between play and learning
- stages in children's play
- types of play
- social contexts of play
- function of play
- current issues with respect to play and learning
- philosophy of play and learning for young children

C H A P T E R 1

CHILDREN LEARN
THROUGH PLAY

■ IMPORTANCE OF PLAY TO CHILDREN

Play is an absorbing, satisfying, and sometimes joyful experience for children. Observing children at play often causes longing in adults who recollect times from their own childhoods in which they were able to abandon themselves totally to the interests of the moment. Any adult who has watched a young child hover over an insect or try to make intricate pathways with a stick in the earth has witnessed how all-consuming play can be for a child. In play the rest of the world is often shut out and the child's senses gravitate to the object of play. Total immersion is evident as the child moves to the beat of her own drummer. She re-enters the real world when someone or something from outside her play cocoon commands her attention.

Play provides respite from the world and opens up the world to a child. No matter how eager we may be as early childhood educators to provide purposeful play opportunities for children that will enhance development and lead to learning, we must never forget that one of the greatest gifts of childhood is the ability to pursue seemingly insignificant interests and to explore tiny details to one's heart's content. It is a marvellous, renewable resource in the life of a child that can be resumed at any moment. Play may follow any path the child desires and will end when the child decides to move on to something else or when the demands of living in the world intrude on the child's own agenda.

Childhood is a time when "children are shielded so that they can play, and this play is quintessentially human" (Garbarino, 1989:17). Children need opportunities for uninterrupted, spontaneous, freely chosen, absorbing play. The ability to release oneself to the pleasure, challenge, and fascination of the moment, to focus on details or tasks, however minor by adult standards, is a child's right. Children who are not given the opportunity to play may be forced much too soon into the world of immediate demands, anxiety over things they cannot control, and experiences they are unable to comprehend.

Most children play without prompting, without direction from adults, and without a plan. For generations children have played and developed and learned through their spontaneous play. Why then, as early childhood educators, do we spend so much time and energy trying to find ways to guide play in more fruitful directions? That question will be addressed in this book.

■ HISTORY OF PLAY

Play has been a significant part of human life since the beginning of recorded history and likely also before that. Centuries ago, peoples' lives were directed towards survival and the satisfaction of basic human needs. Even so, evidence suggests that games, rituals, and dances were devised to help people understand some of the unknown forces and actions in the world which seemed to control them. In ancient civilizations (500 BCE (Before Common Era)–500 CE (Common Era) philosophers such as Plato, Aristotle, and Cicero promoted the importance of children's play and the relevance of play activities to later development. Plato, for example, listed the toys households should provide for their children such as balls, hoops, rattles, and swings. He also emphasized the importance of observing children at play. Excavations in Egypt and Asia uncovered toys used in ancient civilizations. From ancient times to the Middle Ages, Renaissance, the beginning of the modern period, and right through to the present, there is evidence that play has been experienced in childhood, to varying degrees in all known civilizations.

Until modern times, however, families were more concerned about the survival of their children than about their play. Infant mortality was high, and children who survived were often relied upon for labour and service in adult society. During the Middle Ages (900 CE–1200 CE) and even into the Renaissance (1200–1500), whatever play pastimes were available to children were generally interwoven with those of adult society. Adult games, playthings, and pleasures were available to children as well as adults. Children were hurried into the adult world as quickly as possible (Ariès, 1962). Some historians have cited evidence that children themselves were frequently used as playthings for adults. These accounts have described scenes of drunken courtiers tossing swaddled infants from one to another, and even between the open windows of adjacent buildings. Several historical accounts described the frequent use of children as sexual playthings by adults (DeMause, 1974).

Historical evidence shows that during the late Renaissance, greater attention was paid to the role of childhood in the formation of the adult. Michel de Montaigne, a French essayist of the sixteenth century, referred to the seriousness of children's play: "It should be noted that children at play are not playing about; their **games** should be seen as their most serious-minded activity." He believed that if children were encouraged to be fully involved in their play, they would grow up to be vigorous, productive adults. Montaigne, and the seventeenth-century Moravian bishop Comenius were among the earliest philosophers to proclaim the importance of play in learning. Montaigne believed that children would desire learning if learning were made pleasurable. Comenius promoted the use of toys in learning and urged mothers to encourage their children to play.

It wasn't until the beginning of the modern era in 1700 that adults began to segregate children from adult pastimes. British philosopher John Locke, writing in the latter part of the seventeenth century, said that " ... because there can be no Recreation without Delight which depends not always on Reason, but oftener on Fancy, it must be permitted Children not only to divert themselves, but to do it after their own fashion." The eighteenth-century French philosopher, Jean Jacques Rousseau believed that play experiences and freedom in childhood were fundamentally important to development and a desire to learn. A generation later the Swiss educational reformer Heinrich Pestalozzi emphasized the importance of sensory experiences in early learning and advocated freely chosen play activities in order to promote childhood learning.

During the seventeenth and eighteenth centuries in North America, play tended to vary according to location, ethnic origin, and vocation of the population. The Puritan ethic emphasized work-related play activities such as quilting bees and barn-raising parties. In England and the United States play was suppressed longer than it was in other European countries (Butler, Gotts, & Quisenberry, 1978). By the nineteenth century, however, words for a special literature, organized games, and sporting activities for children had evolved in the English language.

The German founder of the kindergarten Friedrich Froebel was instrumental in supporting the role of play in the early formation of children's minds and souls, and called play "a natural unfolding of the germinal leaves of childhood." The early Froebelian kindergarten, which originated in Germany in 1837, used specialized play materials, games, and activities to promote specific kinds of learning.

The nineteenth century and the early part of the twentieth saw renewed restrictions on children's play particularly in the newly industrialized nations of Britain and the United States. Children often had to perform heavy labour in factories and on farms, and were known to have worked twelve-hour days, seven days a week. For these children, play involved imitation of the adults around them. Adults sought to instil in children a strong sense of responsibility and obligation to work, which stifled children's needs for self-expression and self-fulfilment, and severely curtailed their opportunities for age-appropriate play.

Only in the 1920s did the role of play in childhood development and learning begin to regain its credibility. Champions of early development and play such as G.

Stanley Hall (1844–1924) promoted the belief that play allowed children to channel primitive instincts, and achieve self-control and maturity. During the same period Freud's psychoanalytic theories of human development reinforced the importance of play as a means of acting out painful and mysterious experiences and dealing with emotional stress.

EXPLORING SAND AND MEASUREMENT

The expansion of psychology and widespread interest in childhood development and early childhood education have characterized the decades from the 1940s to the present one. These years have seen renewed interest in protecting the special nature of childhood, segregating children from the rigours and abuses of adult society, and preserving the rich qualities of children's play.

From the 1940s to the 1970s preschool teachers, supported by the psychoanalytic view of the inner-directed child, advocated freedom for children from nearly all constraints in their play, believing that adult intervention infringed on their freedom of expression. During these decades the contributions of Maria Montessori fell into disrepute, particularly among traditional nursery school educators. Montessori's specialized, structured materials, the purposes of which were often misunderstood, were seen during this period as too interventionist and rigid. They were frequently viewed as an infringement on the child's right to be creative and use open-ended playthings and supplies instead. Play materials that encouraged open-ended exploration, sensory awareness, and self-expression, such as the unit blocks designed by Caroline Pratt at the turn of the century, were considered better by those who had a strong belief in the value of spontaneous, uninhibited free play.

Susan Isaacs (1885–1948), a twentieth-century educator and psychiatrist, reinforced the belief that play is instrumental in promoting all aspects of child development. She encouraged teachers to let children use their toys in their own ways because she believed that free exploration would promote emotional stability, creative self-expression, and social maturity.

Other neo-Freudian thinkers such as psychiatrist Anna Freud and play therapist Virginia Axline capitalized on the belief in play as a vehicle to promote emotional health. Axline (1947) went further and proposed that play could provide evidence of children's emotional disturbance and could also be used to help children gain understanding and mastery of their feelings.

Erik Erikson supported and elaborated on these psychoanalytic beliefs. His influential work promoted the idea that play is the child's way of coming to terms with the developmental tasks and crises of childhood (Erikson, 1968). The psychologist Bruno Bettelheim also stressed the importance of play in helping children achieve a sense of mastery over their environment and was a particular champion of the role of play in the development of the child's "rich inner life" (Bettelheim, 1987).

From the 1960s on, new understanding about children's cognitive development emerged in the work of Jean Piaget. His followers and interpreters impressed upon educators and psychologists the view that through their own self-initiated play activities young children are laying the foundation for their later learning by developing understanding, concepts, and learning styles that will last a lifetime.

Piaget saw play as a continuation of assimilation or the child's attempt to alter her world in order to fit new experiences with what she already knows. David Elkind, a Piagetian disciple, described play as

> ... *first and foremost, an individual's way of dealing with the stress of life. By transforming reality, play makes unmanageable situations manageable at the same time that it provides socially acceptable outlets for stress. Accordingly, children need to play for the same reasons adults do—to enable them to go on with the difficult task of adapting to an ever more complex and bewildering society.*

■ HISTORICAL INTERPRETATIONS OF "CHILDREN LEARN THROUGH PLAY"

"Children learn through play" is a sentence that has guided early childhood educators for decades. In the nineteenth century Montessori suggested that play is the work of childhood and that it is important for learning and development. Exactly how children learn through play has been a subject of some controversy in the past and continues to generate debate in educational circles even today. Educators and lay persons have for years considered the value of self-directed, open-ended play to be greater than the structured play prescribed and led by teachers. There have been many attempts to explain what it is that children learn through play and how they learn it. Volumes have been written about how to stimulate more efficient and more durable learning by altering the content and quality of children's play.

During the 1950s and 1960s educators believed that children learned through free play. It was thought that environments and learning methods were best left unstructured and open to children's spontaneous investigations. Interference from teachers or other adults who might try to direct children's explorations and predict the outcomes of their learning was frowned on. The watchword of this period was "follow the child." It promoted the value that the healthy functioning of the child at his chronological age level was most important. The child should be as free as possible to choose and to play without interference from adult figures in his environment.

Many prominent early childhood educators such as Margaret and Rachel Macmillan, Lawrence Frank, and Evelyn Pitcher were associated with this tradition. It found much of its theoretical foundation in the work of G. Stanley Hall, the father of child study; Arnold Gesell, who believed that genetic inheritance and maturation are the prime motivators of development; and Sigmund Freud, who emphasized the profound impact of early emotional experiences on the formation of the adult personality.

Bank Street College in New York was among the first institutions in North America to introduce progressive ideals into early childhood education during the 1960s and 1970s. The progressive educational philosophy of John Dewey was embedded in the Bank Street College approach to play and learning. This approach was articulated by Harriet Johnson (1928), Lucy Sprague Mitchell (1950), and Caroline Pratt (1948). The important relationship of active play and direct experience with learning and the stimulation of thinking through play became the cornerstones of Bank Street's child-centred philosophy and practice. Biber (1971) underlined the deep commitment of Bank Street to psychoanalytic/humanistic values; for example, she held that play allows children to release unconscious anxiety and express feelings. The central aims of the Bank Street programs were to provide play opportunities that would enhance competence, individuality, socialization, and the ability to use a variety of modes of self-expression.

The theories of Piaget gained a following in the United States and Canada from the late 1960s on and touched off years of debate about the kind of learning environment needed to foster optimal development in the cognitive as well as the physical, social, and emotional domains. Interpreting Piaget's theories became one of the main preoccupations of early childhood education and child development specialists during the 1970s. These years coincided with the American preoccupation with winning the space race and outstripping the Russians in science and mathematics. The "American question," as Piaget himself called it, became, "how can we accelerate the cognitive development of children?" For a time during the early 1970s it seemed that the importance of play, as well as Piaget's consistent assertion that children learn through self-directed play, might become lost or misinterpreted in the zealous campaign to beat the Russians and accelerate cognitive development.

The painstaking work of many British, American, and Canadian educators and developmental psychologists to accurately interpret Piaget's theories of cognitive development reinforced the importance of play in the cognitive development of children. Early childhood education and child development specialists such as Lawrence Kohlberg (1972, 1987), Margaret Donaldson (1978), Alice Yardley (1989), Constance Kamii (1976, 1980, 1982), David Elkind (1976, 1987), Rheta DeVries (1976, 1987), David Weikart (1971, 1984), Eleanor Duckworth (1973, 1987, 1991), Chris Nash (1975, 1989), and others, underlined the importance of children's active experience with concrete objects in the environment and revived the credibility of play as the key agent in children's intellectual development. The debate during the latter half of the 1970s centred on the importance of play in the learning and development of the whole child in the cognitive, physical, and affective domains (Hendrick, 1975). Piaget himself wrote in a foreward to *Group Games in Early Education* (Kamii & DeVries, 1980: vii) "Play is a particularly powerful form of activity that fosters the social life and constructive activity of the child."

DECORATING FOR SPRING

The 1980s witnessed the widespread expansion of cognitive-developmental theories that supported the idea that the quality of children's play at each stage has a significant impact on development. Educators began to seek new ways of creating child-centred environments in which children could engage in self-directed learning that would enhance their developmental capabilities in all domains. Even the Head Start programs for disadvantaged children that originated in the mid-1960s and generally followed the direct teaching approaches of behavioural science began to move towards a play-oriented philosophy. The encouraging results of one such Head Start program of the 1970s, the Perry Preschool Project, supported the importance of play as a vehicle for learning and development. Longitudinal studies of adolescents who had participated in the play-oriented preschool programs in Ypsilanti, Michigan, as children showed reduced frequency of dropping-out of school, juvenile delinquency, and teen pregnancy, and more positive socialization and adaptation in general (Schweinhart & Weikart, 1984).

The simple sentence "children learn through play" provided the rationale for numerous models for the delivery of early childhood programs and a multitude of theoretical approaches, and became a way of explaining almost anything that a teacher does to keep children occupied in the classroom. By the mid-1980s the idea that children construct their own intelligence through freely chosen, self-directed play with responsive, transformable objects in their environments became an important belief in early childhood education. It provided the theoretical framework for the landmark position paper of the National Association for the Education of Young Children, *Developmentally Appropriate Practice in Early Childhood Programs Serving Children From Birth Through Age 8* (Bredekamp, 1987). Since the publication of this paper several attempts have been made to further define developmentally appropriate practice, among them, a paper entitled, "Myths Associated with Developmentally Appropriate Programs" (Kostelnik, 1992). This article wisely points out that many variations in teaching and learning can be accommodated in developmentally appropriate practice, that the approaches used should build on teachers' prior knowledge and experience, that a balance of structure and open-ended activities should be present, and that effective teaching includes purposeful planning of curriculum, the learning environment, and daily program.

Signs are that in the 1990s, the emphasis on learning through play will continue. That children are active learners who construct their knowledge and understanding of the world through play experiences has become a cornerstone of early childhood education in North America. Educators are increasingly ready to relinquish to children more of the responsibility for their own learning in well-planned environments that include expectations for progress based on the developmental levels and abilities of each individual child.

The increasing importance attached to individual learning styles and types of intelligence is another factor that is changing early childhood education (Gardner, 1982, 1989). Fewer educators believe that children should learn the same body of knowledge at the same time in their school careers. Understanding of basic concepts and practice of learning-to-learn skills has come to be seen as more important during the early years than the acquisition of prescribed facts and information. The stranglehold of "back to basics" movements and behaviourist learning theories that have shaped early primary education in Canada and the United States for decades is loosening. There are signs that increased interest in early childhood education will lead to demands by teachers for greater knowledge and understanding of how children learn through play.

As individuals we have values that we should foster and that should direct our choices for young children as early childhood education in North America continues to be redefined. The system of early childhood education that we adopt for our young children will have to compare favourably with the systems followed by other nations of the world that have been providing developmentally based educational programs for young children for much longer than we have. A better understanding of how children learn through play is necessary at a time when we are feeling pressure to equip our children with the skills, knowledge, and understanding they will need to adapt and succeed in a rapidly changing and more sophisticated world. It is important that our children acquire the cognitive, physical, social, and emotional skills that will enable them and North America as a whole to compete effectively. Our collective and individual security depends heavily on the provision of excellent early childhood programs that provide a developmentally sound foundation and meet the needs of young children and of society as a whole.

■ CONDITIONS NEEDED FOR CHILDREN TO LEARN THROUGH PLAY

Play is a legitimate, viable, and highly recommended educational endeavour for young children who are gaining much of their knowledge about the world through the senses. The younger the children, the more dependent they are on sensory learning and physical contact with their environment in order to learn and to know. When play is sensory-based, it encourages children's active involvement and is relevant and meaningful to them since they find it easier to attend and remain interested. We also know that the more children's emotions are involved in play situations, the more open they are to the sensory information they receive. The more active children are able to be in their play, the more easily learning will take place.

Play helps children find new ways of dealing with reality. As children play, they explore the properties of things and extract information about their environments. They imitate, recreate, and rehearse roles that help them understand and solve problems related to everyday living. They form relationships, share, cooperate, master their feelings, extend the range of their experience, test ideas, and form associations between things, events, and concepts.

Teachers must consider many questions when thinking about the kinds of play and learning environments they will provide for children. They should also think through their own roles in these environments. What are the *right* conditions for play? What is the proper balance between spontaneous and structured or child-centred and adult-led play? Should the teacher plan specific play experiences that lead to predictable outcomes? How important is the identification of specific developmental objectives in planning for play? To what extent should the individual developmental needs of each child determine the daily agenda of play and learning experiences? What is the role of developmental norms (milestones) in determining how the environment will be planned and set up for children? These questions, and others, will be considered in the following chapters, which address specific dimensions of the play and learning environment for young children.

■ WHAT IS PLAY?

There are almost as many definitions of play as there are experts on play. Historically, early childhood educators have moved away from earlier beliefs that play is what happens when energy is left over after work has been finished, or that play is a way of generating energy needed for work. More recently, play has been seen as a largely therapeutic activity that helps children deal with complex emotions and difficult real-life situations. These dynamic theories have gradually given way to developmental theories of play. Although in recent years our understanding of play has evolved, there is still no one definition of play on which all experts can agree.

Garvey (1977) claims that it is impossible to define play as a particular type or set of actions. She suggests that it is often best understood by a consideration of what is "not play." The key distinction between play and not-play lies in the intentions behind the behaviour. Garvey believes that play has no external goals and is undertaken more for the process involved than for any particular purpose or end. It must be freely chosen by the player, and be spontaneous, enjoyable, and valued in and of itself.

An important characteristic of play is active involvement by the player, a factor which rules out passive behaviours such as daydreaming or watching television. In determining what is play and what is not-play, Garvey explains that one must examine the behaviour in terms of causes, motivations, and consequences of the behaviour. She refers to *literal* versus *non-literal behaviours,* terms that reflect our tendency to attribute meaning or intention to our own actions and those of others (Garvey, 1977:7).

COOPERATIVE PLAY

One of the criteria of play is the ability of the player to pretend or behave as if something is so. Behaviour that is non-literal, or pretend, is immune to consequences, and the players understand that what is done is not what it appears to be (Garvey, 1977). It is important to recognize, however, that although play may be *non-literal*, we must avoid any tendency to treat children's play as *unreal* (Bettelheim, 1987). Play is very real to the child and is in many ways the child's true reality.

Rubin, Fein, and Vandenberg (1983) have found six factors to use in separating play from what is not-play:

1. Play is intrinsically motivated; that is, it comes from inside the child and is motivated neither by competition nor by social demands.

2. Play focuses on means not ends; it is process-oriented rather than product-oriented.

3. Play occurs when objects are familiar; exploration occurs when objects are unfamiliar or poorly understood.

4. Play involves pretending, that is, engaging in activities that have an "as if," representational, or non-literal quality.

5. Play is free of the externally imposed rules that distinguish play from games.

6. Play is characterized by the active involvement of the participant and, therefore, does not include daydreaming, flitting about, and mindless exploration.

References

Ariès, P. (1962). *Centuries of Childhood.* New York: Alfred A. Knopf.

Axline, V. (1947). *Play Therapy.* New York: Ballantine.

Bettelheim, B. (1987). The importance of play. *The Atlantic* 262 (3):35–46.

Biber, B., Shapiro, R., and Wickens, D. (1971). *Promoting cognitive growth from a developmental-interaction point of view.* Washington, D.C.: National Association for the Education of Young Children.

Bredekamp, S. (1987). *Developmentally Appropriate Practice in Early Childhood Programs Serving Children from Birth to Age 8.* Washington, D.C.: National Association for the Education of Young Children.

Butler, A.L., Gotts, E.E., and Quisenberry, N.L. (1978). *Play as Development.* Columbus: Merrill.

DeMause, L. (1974). *History of Childhood.* New York: Psychohistory Press.

DeVries, R. (1976). (See Kamii, C., and DeVries, R. (1976).)

DeVries, R., and Kohlberg, L. (1987). *Constructivist Early Education: Overview and Comparison with Other Programs.* Washington, D.C.: National Association for the Education of Young Children.

Donaldson, M. (1978). *Children's Minds.* London: Fontana.

Duckworth, E. (1973). The having of wonderful ideas. In *Piaget in the Classroom,* ed. M. Schwebel and J. Raph. New York: Basic Books.

Duckworth, E. (1987). *The Having of Wonderful Ideas and Other Essays on Teaching and Learning.* New York: Teachers College Press, Columbia University.

Duckworth, E. (1991). Twenty-four, Forty-two, and I Love You: Keeping It Complex. *Harvard Educational Review* 61 (1): 1–24.

Elkind, D. (1976). *Child Development and Education: A Piagetian Perspective.* New York: Oxford University Press.

Elkind, D. (1979). *The Child and Society.* New York: Oxford University Press.

Elkind, D. (1987). *Miseducation—Preschoolers at Risk.* New York: Alfred A. Knopf.

Erikson, E. (1968). *Identity, Youth and Crisis.* New York: W.W. Norton.

Garbarino, J. (1989). An ecological perspective on the role of play. In *The Ecological Context of Children's Play,* ed. M.N. Bloch and A.D. Pelligrini. Norwood, NJ: Ablex.

Gardner, H. (1983). *Frames of Mind.* New York: Basic Books.

Gardner, H. (1989). *To Open Minds.* New York: Basic Books.

Garvey, C. (1977). *Play.* Cambridge: Harvard University Press.

Hendrick, J. (1975). *The Whole Child: New Trends in Early Education.* St. Louis, MO: C.V. Mosby.

Isaacs, S. (1933). *Social Development in Young Children: A Study of Beginnings.* London: Routledge & Sons.

Isaacs, S. (1935). *Intellectual Growth in Children.* London: Routledge & Sons.

Johnson, H. (1928/1972). *Children in the Nursery School.* New York: Agathon Press.

Kamii, C. (1982). Autonomy. The aim of education envisioned by Piaget. *Phi Delta Kappan* 65 (6):410–415.

Kamii, C., and DeVries, R. (1976). *Piaget, Children and Number.* Washington, D.C.: National Association for the Education of Young Children.

Kamii, C., and DeVries, R. (1980). *Group Games in Early Education.* Washington, D.C.: National Association for the Education of Young Children.

Kohlberg, L., and Mayer, R. (1972). Development as the aim of education. *Harvard Educational Review* 42 (4): 449–96.

Kostelnik, M.J. (1992). Myths associated with developmentally appropriate programs. *Young Children* 47 (4): 17–23.

Nash, C. (1975, 1989). *The Learning Environment: A Practical Approach to the Education of the Three-, Four-, and Five-Year-Old.* Toronto: Collier-Macmillan.

Pratt, C. (1948). *I Learn from Children.* New York: Simon & Schuster.

Rubin, K., Fein, G., and Vandenberg, B. (1983). Play. In *Handbook of Child Psychology: Vol. 4. Socialization, Personality and Social Development,* ed. P.H. Mussen and E.M. Hetherington, pp. 693–774. Copyright © 1983. Reprinted by permission of John Wiley & Sons, Inc.

Schweinhart, L.J., and Weikart, D.P. (1984). *Changed Lives: The Effects of the Perry Preschool Program on Youths Through Age 19.* Ypsilanti, MI: High/Scope.

Weikart, D. (1971). The Cognitively-Oriented Curriculum: A Framework for Preschool Teachers. Urbana, IL: University of Illinois.

Weikart, D. (1984). (See Schweinhart, L.J., and Weikart, D.P. (1984).)

Yardley, A. (1989). *Young Children Learning.* Oakville, Ontario: Rubicon Press.

C H A P T E R 2

THEORIES AND CATEGORIES OF PLAY

■ EVOLUTION OF PLAY THEORIES

Major ideas about play and its role in childhood fall broadly into two categories of play theories: classical and dynamic. J. Barnard Gilmore (1966) defined these two categories by concluding that the older classical theories tried to explain why people play, and the modern, dynamic theories focus on the processes of play.

Classical Theories

Classical theories, from the seventeenth to the late nineteenth century, include the surplus energy theory, the relaxation theory, the pre-exercise theory, and the recapitulation theory.

The **surplus energy theory** suggests that when people have more energy than is needed for work, the excess is used in play. What people do when they play was considered less important by these theorists than the fact that the play activity has no goals. The idea was that the energy people have must be used somehow, and if it is not used in work it will be used in play.

The **relaxation theory** expresses an opposite view by claiming that play is used to generate the energy needed for work. This theory was less applicable to children's play as it was obvious that children did not use play to replenish energy.

The **pre-exercise theory** was based on the idea that children play to practise future roles in society. For example, little girls playing with dolls were seen as rehearsing their future roles as mothers. Children were believed to be instinctively drawn towards play that prepares them for mature adult behaviours.

The **recapitulation theory**, proposed by G. Stanley Hall, contradicted the pre-exercise theory. Hall believed that children's play resembled the behaviours of primitive peoples more than those of mature adults. In play, children were believed to be re-enacting the activities of each successive period in the evolution of the human race. He used the examples of children playing with bows and arrows, and making crude forts to prove his point. Both the pre-exercise theory and Hall's recapitulation theory of play were based on Darwin's theory of the evolution of the human race from primates (Butler, Gotts, & Quisenberry, 1978). The phrase associated with Hall, "ontogeny recapitulates phylogeny," implied that the development of the human being from infancy to adulthood parallels and repeats the origin and development of the human race as a species.

Dynamic Theories

Classical theories were replaced in the twentieth century by the more modern dynamic theories of which there are two categories: psychoanalytic and developmental theories (Gilmore, 1966).

Psychoanalytic Theories

Psychoanalytic theories maintain that play allows children to express themselves and provides opportunities to act out inner feelings that children are unable to verbalize. Play facilitates children's understanding and ability to deal with real-life experiences and unfamiliar roles (Butler, Gotts, & Quisenberry, 1978). Creativity and appreciation of beauty and harmony were believed to be fostered through play (Rogers & Sawyers, 1988). The value of play as a mode in which children could practise socialization skills and learn to channel emotions has been an important principle in early childhood education for decades. Much of the literature of the 1950s and 1960s focused on the usefulness of play as a way of helping children release pent-up anxieties and deal with traumatic events (Fein, 1985).

The therapeutic value of play is a primary preoccupation of psychoanalytic theorists who believe that play helps children cope with reality, particularly when their reality is painful, confusing, or oppressive. Play therapy emerged as a way for disturbed or emotionally burdened children to unravel complex feelings and deal with confusion, hostility, and fear present in their everyday world (Axline, 1947).

For example, in the days immediately following the explosion of the space shuttle in 1986, several preschool teachers reported instances in which children attempted to recreate the event through play with a variety of construction materials, especially blocks. By building a high tower, hitting it, and watching it crash down to the floor, while supplying sound effects of their own, children seemed to be trying to understand and unravel some of the mystery and their own anxiety surrounding the awful event.

Developmental Theories

The evolution of play theory has, for the most part, corresponded with our understanding of child development. The nature of children's play is believed to be influenced by the child's developmental level as well as by social, historical, and cultural factors. Most developmental theories of play attempt to describe characteristics of play, show how positive play experiences facilitate intellectual growth, and relate play to periods of change and developmental progress (Garvey, 1977).

Developmental theories of play have emerged largely from the pioneering work of Jean Piaget in cognitive development. Although some of the cognitive developmental milestones that Piaget described have been observed in more recent research to occur earlier in children, his developmental theory and sequence of stages have stood the test of time quite well. Piaget believed that through play children organize their experiences in the world, thereby achieving higher levels of adaptation to their environments. He spoke of play as assimilation and imitation as accommodation (Piaget, 1970). The processes of assimilation and accommodation are followed by equilibration, in which children build mental structures and add to their intelligence. These cognitive processes are described in greater detail on page 57.

Piaget described four stages of children's play, which correspond closely to his developmental stages of cognitive development in childhood, the sensorimotor, preoperational, and concrete operational periods. The play stages are: sensorimotor play, symbolic play, reproductive play, and games-with-rules play.

Sensorimotor Play Stage   Sensorimotor play characterizes play during the first two years of life in particular and is largely physical and sensory in nature. Sensorimotor children are busy gaining control over their movements, gathering information by way of the senses, learning to coordinate physical actions, and responding to the effects they have on "things." Infants gain pleasure from mastery of motor skills; therefore, much of their play involves repeated actions, called **practice play**, in which they appear to practise a newly acquired skill. The infant who repeatedly drops objects from the high chair, for example, and watches the effect of these actions, enjoys playing pat-a-cake over and over again, or, after having done so once, repeats the action of stacking cups, one inside the other, is engaging in sensorimotor play. It is the kind of play that involves the child's physical interaction with concrete objects in the environment in order to explore and discover the physical properties of things.

Symbolic Play Stage   Symbolic play coincides with the preoperational stage of development that occurs approximately between two to six or seven years of age. In symbolic play the child learns to use symbols, making one object stand for another, as in using a wooden block to represent a car. At this stage children generally use play materials to satisfy their own purposes rather than to conform to any external standards imposed by adults. This **productive play** is usually character-ized by very involved activity in which children's play outcomes are increasingly recognizable to adults. Children at this stage may engage in dressing and undress-ing a teddy bear, loading and unloading a dumptruck, and filling a pail with sand and emptying it repeatedly, seemingly happy to be performing these actions for their own ends. As children begin to construct things, such as using blocks to build a house, their play outcomes and products become more lifelike and therefore more recognizable.

Reproductive Play Stage   Reproductive play is a more advanced type of symbolic play that occurs between the ages of four to seven when children are able to represent remembered events, images, and actions using a variety of representa-tional media. This type of play is increasingly representative of what children understand or want to understand about their environments and experiences. Ini-tially, children may use art media to represent a remembered image; later, they might engage in pretend, dramatic, or sociodramatic play. Towards the latter end of the symbolic play stage, children become increasingly adept at using a range of media—art, drama, music, language—to represent the real world and their experi-ences in it.

Games-with-Rules Play Stage   Games with rules play appears as the child reaches the **concrete operational period** of development about the age of seven. At this stage children begin to accept certain external limitations on their play such as rules made by someone else. Their increasing ability to think and behave objec-tively allows them to participate in group projects, become team members, and sub-mit to the structure imposed by limits and rules. Children also begin to make their own rules and to question existing ones. They collaborate in the amending of rules and accept the binding nature of group-adopted rules for the duration of a game or project.

■ CATEGORIES OF PLAY

The multitude of ways in which children play alone or together is difficult to cap-ture in discrete classification systems. Play may be described according to the ways in which children interact with materials (types of play), according to the various social contexts in which play occurs, and according to the developmental stages of play mentioned above. The boundaries between types of play are often blurred since children can be engaging in several types of play at the same time. Also, as children's play styles progress developmentally, the children do not forsake earlier types, but continue with them throughout childhood.

It is necessary to define the terms used to describe play styles and types in order to help clarify for teachers what types of play they are seeing when observing children at play. What follows here is a brief description of types of play and the social contexts in which play occurs.

Types of Play

Functional Play

Functional play consists mainly of simple, repetitive movements with or without concrete objects (Rubin, Fein, & Vandenberg, 1983). This type of play dominates the sensorimotor stage of development during the first two years of life. Functional play continues throughout childhood, but it largely characterizes the play of the infant and toddler who explore objects physically, using their senses. It becomes their way of understanding the properties of things in their world and testing the reactions of objects to various forms of physical manipulation.

Repetitive or **practice play** is a form of functional play and usually involves the repetition of physical behaviours that have already been mastered. Practice play is the earliest form of **exploratory play** and is characterized by the infant's sucking on objects, making sounds, listening, gazing, and following moving objects visually. Exploratory activities in infancy and toddlerhood include tasting, emptying, filling, inserting, pulling, stacking, pushing, rolling, and climbing into and under things.

During the two- to three-year-old stage, exploratory play involves arranging, heaping, combining, sorting, spreading, and transforming things in the environment. At a later stage, children engage in verbal exploratory play, including the putting of words and sounds together in new and often funny combinations. The

TYPES OF PLAY

FUNCTIONAL PLAY

- repetitive or practice play
- exploratory play
- testing play

CONSTRUCTIVE PLAY

- productive play
- creative play

SYMBOLIC PLAY

- imitative play
- pretend/dramatic play
- sociodramatic play
- fantasy play

GAMES-WITH-RULES PLAY

- rule-bound play
- competitive play

presence of interlocking materials such as Lego; modular materials such as small blocks; materials like balls, rattles, keys, and drums; and stacking or nesting toys facilitate functional play that can be repeated with objects that are made to be manipulated in many ways.

Testing play is another form of functional play and appears early, from the time the child engages in motor testing by crawling into and out of small places. Later on, children engage in testing play when they challenge their own ability to climb to the top of the climber and when they explore the capacity of the unit blocks to sustain their gigantic tower shape without falling over.

Constructive Play

Constructive play begins with productive play. **Productive play** involves recognizable play with materials that produce results the child intends. It occurs from about two years of age, when children learn the uses of simple play materials and play with them to satisfy their own purposes.

Constructive play includes creative play such as block-building, constructing with Tinker Toy and other interlocking materials such as Lego, **malleable materials** such as play dough or plasticene, and creating patterns or designs with **modular materials** such as parquetry and Lego. Children have to practise achieving their own goals in play before they are ready to adapt to externally imposed goals (Butler, Gotts, & Quisenberry, 1978). In constructive play, children interact with the play materials for their own purposes often without any particular plan or strategy to produce a specific outcome. Rubin, Fein, and Vandenberg (1983) state that constructive play is the most common form of play in preschools and kindergartens.

Symbolic Play

Symbolic or **representational play** involves the ability to use symbols. For example, the child may make one object stand for another, as in using puppets to represent the other children in the group or pretending that the table is a house. Being able to transform objects and events by imagining that they are different from the original meanings conveyed by the object or event lies at the heart of cognitive development and communication (Nourot & Van Hoorn, 1991).

Symbolic play occurs during the preoperational stage of development, which lasts from two to six or seven years. About two years of age, the child's newly acquired ability to use objects as symbols begins to predominate over practice play. There are several kinds of symbolic play: imitative play, pretend/dramatic play, sociodramatic play, and fantasy play, each of which involves "progressively symbolic distancing" from the object or event being represented (Nourot & Van Hoorn, 1991: 40–50). These forms of symbolic play will be discussed in detail in Section 4.

Imitative Play

Imitative play is a form of symbolic play that occurs during the first year of life and refers to the child's simple imitation of the parent or caregiver. The child enjoys games like pat-a-cake, making cooing or gurgling sounds along with her mother, or mimicking some of her actions such as hitting a cushion. Right from the early months of life, the infant can imitate other people, and is particularly attentive to other children's actions. Early imitations resemble very closely the actions of the adult or older child.

Pretend Play

Towards the end of the sensorimotor period, the child begins to engage in **pretend** or **dramatic play** in which they practise their own versions of adult behaviours rather than imitating only what they have seen (Rogers & Sawyers, 1988). At this stage, the child delights in pretending to be mummy or daddy by taking a doll for a stroll in a carriage or pretending to push the stroller like a shopping cart in the supermarket. The dramatic/pretend play of three-year-olds in the early stages of the preoperational period is fairly predictable, and the representations are very simple. Much of this early dramatic play tends to be solitary. Children at this stage generally prefer props that are familiar to them and very similar physically to he objects and events being imitated. For example, they enjoy playing with child-sized replicas of household equipment, cars, trucks, toy telephones, and cash registers.

As children mature and social play becomes predominant, considerable social interaction and cooperative play are incorporated into pretend play. It also becomes less predictable as more variables are involved. This is the stage at which sociodramatic play begins.

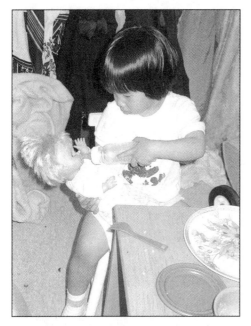

PRETEND PLAY

Sociodramatic Play

Sociodramatic play is a more social and complex form of symbolic play that appears about four years of age. During the intuitive period, which lasts from ages four to seven, children's role play becomes more realistic and accurate. Sociodramatic play involves more than one child collaborating in the dramatization of experiences from their physical and social environments. It differs from fantasy play in that it involves dramatization of remembered experiences that are common to the children playing, such as going to the hospital emergency room or having lunch at a restaurant. It is generally important to children older than four or five that their sociodramatic play be as close to reality as possible.

Along with the child's sharper perception of reality comes a desire to reproduce actions, events, and behaviours that are as close as possible to the adult world. Children at this stage enjoy assuming adult roles, as if practising for the future or trying to understand what it feels like to be someone else. As with dramatic play, which involves one child engaged in solitary play, sociodramatic play, in which two or more children participate, provides an opportunity for children to express feelings, solve problems related to their emotional lives, understand the conflicts of others, and experiment with new behaviours. At this stage, children prefer unstructured, more abstract props that can become whatever the child wants them to become in their symbolic play (Curry & Arnaud, 1984). Cardboard boxes, hollow blocks, blankets, sticks, and furniture are examples of such abstract props. With time, children abandon the use of props in their sociodramatic play and rely more on verbalizing what they are doing, using, and thinking.

Sociodramatic play helps children learn to take turns and understand that certain behaviours are important in specific social situations. The ability to cooperate socially when assuming interdependent roles and to maintain a common "script" requires considerable cognitive and social sophistication. Children need to be aware of typical roles in the social world. They have to be sensitive to the complexities of relationships. They must also be aware of social networks and are required to communicate, negotiate, and follow commonly understood sequences of social events. Many studies have also linked symbolic play to language development and literacy skills (Nourot & Van Hoorn, 1991). Pelligrini (1980) found that literacy skills in early primary children are related to their ability to assume complex roles and use symbols.

Several cognitive capabilities are required in order for children to maintain a sociodramatic play script or pantomime. Studies have shown that sociodramatic play is vital to children's cognitive development and that sociodramatic play promotes cognitive skills. Children have to be able to take a perspective other than their own, separate fantasy from reality, take turns, share, cooperate, negotiate, and pretend without the presence of realistic props. They also have to remember the directions that are generally established by the group at the beginning of the sociodramatic play episode. Frequently, children embarking on a sociodramatic play situation will be heard negotiating roles such as "you can be the daddy, she'll be the mummy and I'll be the baby." Another scene may see children establishing the ground rules such as "let's pretend that we've already done our shopping and have unpacked the groceries and now it's time to get dressed for the party."

Children also develop the capacity to remove themselves temporarily from the script or mime to re-negotiate a role or alter the plot. Sometimes children will step out of their roles to prompt another child who has "lost" the script he holds in his head, whispering something like "now go and answer the telephone and pretend you're talking to Leonardo." Several studies have found that sociodramatic and fantasy play significantly increase children's abilities to take a perspective other than their own and to understand the thoughts and feelings of others (Rubin & Howe, 1986).

Children whose social experiences are limited, who lack communication skills, and who have low self-esteem generally shun sociodramatic play opportunities altogether or drop out very soon after the play has begun. The richness of this type of play as a vehicle for learning cognitive and social skills makes it imperative that teachers try to find ways to help all children become full participants in sociodramatic play situations.

The sophistication and complexity of sociodramatic play make it an excellent vehicle for learning a wide range of developmental skills. Most play experts agree that opportunities for sociodramatic and fantasy play are very important to the development of representational abilities, which permit children to project themselves out of their immediate context into a pretend or fantasy world.

Fantasy Play

Fantasy play is a variation of dramatic and sociodramatic play that usually begins to appear in the third year as soon as children are able to use symbols. It is a "particular type of social pretend play that involves fantastic rather than realistic characters and situations," such as Superman, Goldilocks, Ninja turtles, and Batman (Saltz & Saltz, 1986:159).

Successful experiences in make believe or fantasy play depend on privacy, time to oneself, and an unstructured environment that permits flexible use of a wide range of materials and equipment in interesting ways. Fantasy play requires the ability to concentrate and lose oneself in play, and positive attitudes, healthy self-esteem, and a rich imagination. Often more than one child is involved in trying to dramatize remembered themes from a fairy tale or television program and to assume the roles of characters in these stories. Sometimes roles are assigned by children and attempts are made to stay close to the plot, which all players recognize or remember. The element of fantasy remains as children see themselves as the character in the story they are representing and pour themselves wholeheartedly into becoming their fantastical character.

Games-with-Rules Play

Play is activity that is characterized by freedom from all but self-imposed rules, which may be changed at will, by open-ended fantasy, and by the absence of any goals beyond the activity itself. Games often involve competitive play, with agreed-upon, often externally imposed rules, and require the use of materials in the manner in which they are intended for the game, and have a goal or a purpose outside the activity, such as winning the game. Play is usually regarded as pure enjoyment, whereas games are considered to be demanding and sometimes stressful.

Games-with-rules play is play according to prearranged rules that children can accept and to which they are able to adapt. It requires that children be able to control their behaviour within the limits established (Rogers & Sawyers, 1988). When children achieve the concrete-operational stage of development at about seven years of age, **rule-bound play** or **games with rules** predominate, and school-age children are usually able to understand the significance and stability of rules for the duration of the game or activity.

From seven to twelve, making and accepting rules become an important part of children's play. Children in this concrete operational period are able to delay gratification, accept external limitations and authority, and challenge existing social expectations and rules in a reasonable manner. During the early stages of this period, children normally engage in board games, physical activities, and games with straightforward externally imposed rules.

Competitive play provides opportunities for children to develop and improve their abilities, gain a clearer sense of their own levels of competence, and learn skills of sportsmanship such as the ability to win and lose graciously (Weininger, 1979). Children's increasing ability to negotiate, form social contracts, question existing rules, collaborate in the amending of rules, and behave objectively prepares them for engaging in group projects and becoming team members.

■ SOCIAL CONTEXTS OF PLAY

Parten (1933) was the first to classify children's play in her classic study of the social interactions of two- to five-year-old children. In it, she defined six increasingly complex levels of social play; she also found that children do not lose the ability to engage in earlier forms of social play as they get older and that during the years from four to six, all social contexts of play may be observed at different times.

Several studies have shown that considerable learning in all developmental domains occurs as a result of social play (Parten, 1933; Smilansky, 1968, 1990). Language, communication, physical, and cognitive abilities are fostered when children play together in either mixed-age or age-graded groupings. A wide range of social and emotional skills also depend on children's play with each other in a variety of social groupings. Learning to listen, take turns, cooperate, share, empathize, show affection, be responsible, channel and communicate emotion acceptably, exercise restraint, delay gratification, and a host of other affective abilities are addressed in the context of social play.

SOCIAL CONTEXTS OF PLAY

- onlooking play
- solitary play
- parallel play

- associative play
- cooperative play/competitive play

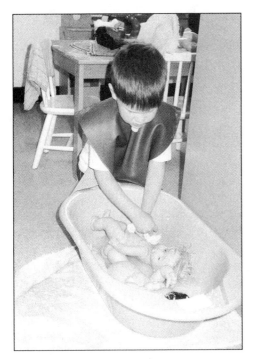

SOLITARY PLAY

Types of Social Play

Onlooking Play

In **onlooking play**, a child observes children playing but does not physically participate. In this type of play, which is sometimes called spectator play, the child remains on the periphery of the group and may later imitate the play behaviours witnessed. Onlooking play is found in the play of children at all stages.

Solitary Play

One child plays alone, in **solitary play**, although she is in a room where other children are playing. Solitary play may be egocentric in that the child focuses on satisfying her own needs. Children at all stages engage in solitary play.

Parallel Play

In **parallel play** two children play side-by-side, each occupied by his own activity and not really interacting, even though each may talk in monologue. There is usually no exchange of conversation or play materials. The child is involved in his own play and is aloof from actual interaction with another child or a group. Parallel play is particularly prevalent among older toddlers and young three-year-olds.

PARALLEL PLAY IN THE SAND

Associative Play

Associative play is loosely organized play in which children participate in a similar activity and may even exchange ideas or play materials but do not subordinate their individual interests to those of the group. For example, they may add their contributions to the making of a mural without particular reference to what the other children may be adding. A child may imitate the play behaviours of another child, but does not engage in mutually interdependent play activity. Associative play is common among three- to four-year-olds.

Cooperative Play

Cooperative play is paired or group social play that involves children with common goals who assume different roles or tasks where there are usually one or two leaders. An example is that of two children cooperating in an art activity or science project. Another instance is intergroup play in which two or more groups cooperate towards a common end, such as making a mural or planning a puppet show. Play continues for a relatively long time and at a fair level of complexity. Cooperative play begins when children are about four and continues to the onset of the concrete operational period and beyond. Children generally become progressively more capable in their cooperative play between four and seven years of age and should be encouraged in cooperative endeavours.

ASSOCIATIVE PLAY

Competitive Play

Competitive play may describe two or more children playing in a group or two or more groups of children competing to win, for example, in team sports, relays, and other competitive challenges (Weininger, 1979). Children aged six and up are generally ready for competitive play activities.

■ PRINCIPLES OF PLAY AND LEARNING ASSOCIATED WITH DEVELOPMENTAL THEORY

Piaget's outline of the cognitive stages of development in childhood has provided a framework for developmental theories of play. As Piaget's developmental theory has been elaborated on by contemporary educators and further research, a **constructivist theory** of play has emerged. The constructivist view of play and learning has been described by DeVries and Kohlberg (1987), Kamii and DeVries (1976, 1980), Forman and Kuschner (1983), and Duckworth, (1987, 1991). Two important principles for early childhood education associated with constructivist theories are described below.

1. Hands-on Learning

Children learn largely through their active interaction with concrete objects in their environment. This principle comes from the knowledge that preoperational children, those approximately two to six years of age, are largely physical beings for whom most learning occurs through the senses. Interaction with the environment through play is seen as essential to the child's ability to construct her own intelligence. Much of what children know and learn is also perceptually bound in that what they see is what they believe. Through active interaction with their environment, in other words, hands-on play, children acquire new knowledge and understanding. Manipulation of things and their direct experience added to their existing knowledge and understanding brings this new learning about. Through this **hands-on learning**, children increase the complexity of their mental structures. As the concepts they understand and the knowledge they gain from active experience increase, children make progress by achieving a higher level of development.

2. Informal Teaching and Learning Methods

For almost two decades, developmental educators have advocated informal teaching and learning methods for young children. David Elkind differentiated between formal and informal education in the 1970s when he described the "active classroom." He referred to **informal education** as comprising those educational activities that are used "for the purpose of structure formation" and are generally initiated by the child for his own sake. **Formal education** he called "structure utilization," and this term referred to activities that are suggested or initiated by the teacher, sometimes for some sort of reward, and that make use of structures already formed (Elkind, 1977:20–21).

In spite of the developmental relevance of informal methods of learning for children under six, some educational administrators, trustees, and a large segment of the general public have continued to advocate a "back-to-basics," knowledge-based curriculum broken into subject areas, along with rote learning, external reward systems, and standardized testing—and believe it should begin as early as kindergarten. This reactionary approach, which is sometimes touted as the answer to needed educational reform in North America, flies in the face of what we know in the 1990s about how young children learn. In the preoperational stage, children are laying the foundation for later learning and building mental structures through their active interaction with their environment. Informal, active, child-centred, and individualized learning practices are essential to children's healthy growth and development at the preoperational stage. Rushing young children prematurely into formal learning methods that are oriented towards knowledge-based, academic, and standardized learning outcomes leads to the "miseducation" of children (Elkind, 1987).

References

Axline, V. (1947). *Play Therapy.* New York: Ballantine.

Bettelheim, B. (1987). The importance of play. *The Atlantic* 262 (3):35–46.

Butler, A.L., Gotts, E.E., and Quisenberry, N.L. (1978). *Play as Development.* Columbus: Merrill.

Curry, N., and Arnaud, S. (1984). Play in developmental preschool settings. In *Child's Play: Developmental and Applied,* ed. T. Yawkey and A. Pellegrini, pp. 273–90. Hillsdale, NJ: Erlbaum.

DeVries, R., and Kohlberg, L. (1987). *Constructivist Early Education: Overview and Comparison with Other Programs.* Washington, D.C.: National Association for the Education of Young Children.

Duckworth, E. (1987). *The Having of Wonderful Ideas and other Essays on Teaching and Learning.* New York: Teachers College Press, Columbia University.

Duckworth, E. (1991). Twenty-four, Forty-two, and I Love You: Keeping It Complex. *Harvard Educational Review* 61 (1):1–24.

Elkind, D. (1977). The early years: the vital years. *Journal of the Canadian Association for Young Children.* 3 (1): 20–21.

Elkind, D. (1987). *Miseducation: Preschoolers at Risk.* New York: Knopf.

Elkind, D. (1988). Play. *Young Children* 43 (4): 2.

Elkind, D. (1989). Developmentally appropriate education for 4-year-olds. *Theory into Practice* 28 (1):47–52.

Elkind, D. (1989). Developmentally appropriate

practice: philosophical and practical implications. *Phi Delta Kappan* 71 (2):113–17.

Fein, G. (1985). The affective psychology of play. In *Play Interactions: The Role of Toys and Parental Involvement in Children's Development,* ed. C.C. Brown and A.W. Gottfried, pp. 19–28. Skillman, NJ: Johnson & Johnson.

Forman, G.E., and Kuschner, D.S. (1983). *The Child's Construction of Knowledge: Piaget for Teaching Children.* Washington, D.C.: National Association for the Education of Young Children.

Garvey, C. (1977). *Play.* Cambridge: Harvard University Press.

Gilmore, J.B. (1966). Play: a special behavior. In *Current Research in Motivation,* ed. R.N. Haber, pp. 343–55. New York: Holt, Rinehart & Winston.

Kamii, C., and DeVries, R. (1976). *Piaget, Children and Number.* Washington, D.C.: National Association for the Education of Young Children.

Kamii, C., and DeVries, R. (1980). *Group Games in Early Education.* Washington, D.C.: National Association for the Education of Young Children.

Nourot, P.M., and Van Hoorn, J.L. (1991). Symbolic play in preschool and primary settings. *Young Children* 46 (6):40–50.

Parten, M. (1933). Social participation among preschool children. *Journal of Abnormal and Social Psychology* 28:136–47.

Pelligrini, A.D. (1980). The relationship between kindergartners' play and achievement in pre-reading, language and writing.

Psychology in the Schools 17 (4):530–35.

Piaget, J. (1970). *The Science of Education and the Psychology of the Child*. New York: Viking Compass.

Rogers, C.S., and Sawyers, J.K. (1988). *Play in the Lives of Children*. Washington, D.C.: National Association for the Education of Young Children.

Rubin, K., Fein, G., and Vandenberg, B. (1983). Play. In *Handbook of Child Psychology: Vol 4. Socialization, Personality, and Social Development,* ed. P.H. Mussen and E.M. Hetherington, pp. 693–774. New York: Wiley.

Rubin, K.H., and Howe, N. (1986). Social play and perspective-taking. In *The Young Child at Play,* Vol. 4., ed. G. Fein and M. Rivkin. Washington, D.C.: National Association for the Education of Young Children.

Saltz, R., and Saltz, E. (1986). Pretend play training and its outcomes. In *The Young Child at Play: Reviews of Research*, Vol. 4, ed. G. Fein and M. Rivkin, pp. 155–73. Washington, D.C.: National Association for the Education of Young Children.

Smilansky, S. (1968). *The Effects of Sociodramatic Play on Disadvantaged Preschool Children*. New York: Wiley.

Smilansky, S., and Sheftaya, L. (1990). *Facilitating Play: A Medium for Promoting Cognitive, Socio-Emotional and Academic Development in Young Children*. Gaithersburg, MD: Psychosocial & Educational Publications.

Weininger, O. (1979). *Play and Education*. Springfield, IL: Chas. C. Thomas.

Wright, M. (1983). *Compensatory Education in the Preschool : A Canadian Approach*. Ypsilanti, MI: High/Scope.

C H A P T E R 3

ISSUES AND PRINCIPLES RELATED TO PLAY AND LEARNING

Early childhood educators need to understand the issues that challenge and sometimes divide the profession and tend to consume precious energy. Generally, there seems to be more agreement than difference of opinion among early childhood educators and administrators when the issues are clearly understood. Coherent policies are more likely to emerge when there is a well-articulated philosophy of early childhood education based on commonly held values, proven practices, clearly defined learning outcomes, and attainable standards.

Some of the issues relate to perceptions of the function of play, the importance of spiritual development, freedom versus structure in play, the relationship between play and child guidance, and whether to teach academic subjects in preschool. This chapter addresses these issues and some of the values, practices, and standards relevant to early childhood education in the 1990s.

■ ISSUES RELATED TO PLAY AND LEARNING

Function of Play

Play encourages children to find out for themselves, explore, investigate, discover, create, and invent with both new and familiar materials. The spontaneous nature of play, which allows children to choose freely, experiment, and discover, motivates children to try, take risks, and keep adding to their experiences and understanding of the world. Play also helps to reduce stress in children, allowing them be more effective and happier learners.

Play enables children to understand concepts and phenomena through their hands-on interaction with concrete objects. Through their sensory involvement with things, children manipulate and alter what is "out there" and try to fit new experiences with what they know and understand already. The ways in which play materials and props respond to children's actions on them lead to their greater understanding of the things and events in their world, as well as the ways in which they interconnect. For example, as children play with blocks, stacking and aligning them, the blocks respond and take the shape the child intends. Their new shape encourages further actions by the child. Responsive media like blocks have very rich play value, promoting both physical knowledge and understanding of concepts.

Psychoanalytic theorists, whose work is based on the theories of Sigmund Freud, believe that play serves children's emotional well-being by providing opportunities for self-expression, pretending and assuming roles, rehearsing new experiences, and fantasizing about unknown worlds. Open-ended materials such as blocks and paint allow children to express themselves in a manner unhindered by adult expectations or pressures to produce a predefined outcome. Such play is accompanied by a sense of emotional release as the materials are used to convey their deepest feelings and perceptions. When children are able to explore materials freely and use them to fulfil their own purposes, they feel a sense of mastery over their world.

Likewise, when children play with more structured, specific-purpose materials that are developmentally appropriate, they experience feelings of success when they are able to master the tasks inherent in the materials. Feeling self-satisfaction and fulfilment in meeting challenges motivates children to set higher goals. Play with open-ended and specific-purpose materials promotes self-confidence. Self-esteem is realized through successful experiences with appropriate materials in meaningful contexts.

The function of play is recognized by teachers who allow children to finish their paintings and the block structures they are making. The teacher who responds to a child's request to come and see what he has made even though the teacher must leave what she is doing temporarily is also acknowledging the importance of the child's play.

Play is so important to children's development that programs should be planned around the blocks of time during the day when children are encouraged to play. The early childhood program that schedules routines (i.e., mealtimes, washroom times, naptimes) around children's playtime, rather than wedging some playtime between the routines, is doing more than paying lip-service to the function of play in development and learning.

Play and Spiritual Development

Spiritual development is sometimes confused with religious education. In our multicultural society with its diverse values, attempts are being made to reduce or eliminate all forms of racial, religious, class, age, and gender prejudice. As a result, spiritual development has been neglected partly out of the fear of infringing on the rights of individuals to adhere to their own religious beliefs.

Bruno Bettelheim was concerned about the spiritual development of the child throughout his long career. He believed that a "child, as well as an adult, needs plenty of what in German is called spielraum." **Spielraum** means more than simply a "room to play in" (Bettelheim, 1987b:37). It implies space to grow spiritually and emotionally as well as physically. Bettelheim believed that the development of "an inner life, including fantasies and daydreams, is one of the most constructive things a growing child can do" (Bettelheim, 1987a:177). Play that is freely chosen encourages a child to lose himself in play, to become absorbed, and to experience fully. Children who lose themselves in play gain an enhanced sense of themselves as human beings. An important element of play is its capacity to provide an avenue to the soul, promote a deepening of the spirit and a fuller understanding of self. Play that is absorbing provides escape into an inner world of imagination, dreams, and ideals. Environments that provide "spielraum" respect the importance of children's play at its deepest level.

A rich inner life is not achieved through imposed participation in a packed schedule of routines, group activities, and teacher-centred, direct instruction. Some of us remember from our early childhood the broad expanses of unplanned days at home. We can recall times when we were able to listen to the sounds of leaves in the trees, chase butterflies, wade in a muddy stream, and collect all sorts of objects like acorn tops, milkweed blossoms, and shiny stones. It is in contact with the natural world of the outdoors that play offers the greatest opportunities for the development of the inner life of which Bettelheim speaks. A happy, playful childhood is a reservoir of dreams, ideals, sensory images, fond remembrances, moments of keen insight, and other treasures usually gathered when one is lost in doing something for its own sake.

Robert Coles (1990) has concerned himself with the spiritual life of children and has found it to be remarkable, thoughtful, and deep, even to the extent of their trying to understand the meaning of life and death. Although children tend to glean what they need from their environments, their spiritual development depends very much on the wholesomeness, variety, and spontaneity of their everyday worlds.

It may be easier to identify the effects of the absence of a rich spiritual life than to describe the benefits of its presence. Bettelheim claims that the absence of opportunities to spend energy on an inner life causes a child to turn to readily available stimuli such as television or video games. When children depend increasingly on television and other modern media to fill a void not filled by spontaneous contact with nature, large elements of childhood disappear, including distinctions between adulthood and childhood (Postman, 1982). Children become exposed too early to the interests, anxieties, stresses, and preoccupations of adults.

Freedom and Structure in Play

An important principle in early childhood education is freedom of choice for children in their play. Freedom for children as an ideal goes back to the writings of Rousseau and has been echoed as a guiding principle in early childhood education ever since. The Psychoanalytic School reinforced the importance of freedom through their emphasis on self-expression, individual self-realization, and autonomy (Erikson, 1963; Rogers, 1969).

ABSORBED IN PLAY

The concept of freedom appeared in the early childhood education field as early as the turn of the century with the familiar term "free play," which was defined by Patty Smith Hill as follows: "In free play the self makes its own choices, selections and decisions, and thus absolute freedom is given to the play of the child's images and volition in expressing them" (cited in Weber, 1984:96).

The idea of activity in learning, expressed by Dewey in the nineteenth century, also supported the principle of freedom. He advocated freeing the child from the constraints of desks, workbooks, and formal learning, offering instead opportunities to move about in the classroom, learn through active projects, set one's own goals and determine the method for achieving them (Weber, 1984).

Caroline Pratt wrote in 1948, "Was it unreasonable to try to fit the school to the child, rather than—as we were doing with indifferent success—fitting the child to the school?" (quoted in Goffin, 1991:63). Even then, nursery school teachers were feeling pressure to force formal, academic learning on young children before they were developmentally ready.

Patty Smith Hill's concept of free play was often represented during the 1950s, 1960s, and even into the 1970s as non-interference and non-involvement with children in their play. This interpretation frequently led to an overemphasis on open-ended materials in order to promote self-expression in the play and learning environment. It also suggested that planned activities using specific-purpose materials to address sequenced developmental objectives would somehow inhibit children's freedom.

In the 1970s, freedom to express oneself became closely associated with the development of self-esteem. During the 1980s and into the 1990s, school systems began to include self-esteem as an explicit goal to be addressed by the curriculum (Leo, 1990). Linking freedom in education to the development of self-esteem in children made it difficult for cognitive-developmental educators to argue for more structure in the design of play and learning environments. Some educators began to favour removing the link between freedom and self-esteem. They advocated, instead, linking self-esteem to any society or culture that respects humanity, provides opportunity for meaningful challenge and success, and supports the dignity of the individual (Beane, 1991).

In the 1990s, the issue of freedom and structure in early childhood education is being clarified by educators who are committed to providing planned environments and purposeful programs that will promote higher levels of development and learning in all domains (Elkind, 1989; Katz & Chard, 1989; Bredekamp, 1987; Gardner, 1989; Walsh, 1991; Jipson, 1991). Advocates of developmental education assume that children are capable of making wise choices when a meaningful array of carefully planned play opportunities and appropriate materials are presented to them. Freedom and structure are now being seen as natural partners. "There is no effective knowledge which does not have structure, whether derived through spontaneous interaction with an environment or through a teacher ordering and explaining patterns to facilitate discovery and learning on the part of the child" (Fowler, 1971:30). Structure refers to the extent to which teachers develop an instructional plan, then organize the physical setting and social environment to support the achievement of educational goals (Kostelnik, 1992:18).

Freedom is a measure of the extent to which the children have a degree of control over the play situation. When they are allowed to decide whether to play, when to start and stop, and when to switch to another play activity, the freedom to determine their own pursuits generally motivates them to act.

In order to promote learning, play should be interesting, chosen and engaged in freely by children, and provide opportunities for them to be successful. Children learn through play that is a balance of open-ended and more structured learning opportunities that together promote development in all domains. That the development of the whole child "just happens" and that self-expression is a simple matter of "messing about" with open-ended things indiscriminately are ideas that impede progress. Early childhood educators have a definite role to play in ensuring that children's play experiences are meaningful, rich, and varied.

Play Versus Work

Many attempts have been made to differentiate play from work. Play is generally believed to be activity done for its own sake, while work is done for some form of external reward. Montessori believed that play is the work of children. Dewey introduced the notion that play may induce a desire for work that requires more thought and effort than self-gratifying play.

Elkind (1988) distinguishes between work and play in Piagetian terms, calling work "accommodation," and play "assimilation." Work takes place when the child has to alter her concepts or behaviour to better adapt to the demands of the world. For example, when we have to show a child how to tie her shoelaces, hold a fork, or hit a ball with a bat, this is accommodation or work. On the other hand, when a child uses a ball of clay or a paint brush and paint to represent a thought, a remembered image, or a message, or pretends that a swing is an airplane, we are witnessing "assimilation" or play. Elkind believes that when adults say that play is the child's work and equate the two, they are really doing the child and play a disservice. It is the nature of the activity in which they are engaged that determines whether children are working or playing.

Play and Child Guidance

The goals of child guidance are self-control and self-discipline. Self-control involves the ability to channel emotions and restrain one's impulses appropriately. Children develop self-discipline by making their own choices and learning the consequences of those choices. Part of self-discipline is learning to be responsible for one's decisions. Therefore, children need plenty of opportunities in their play to choose among real alternatives and to follow through with their decisions.

The main question in child guidance is "what does a teacher do when children do not respect the limits that have been clearly established?" In early childhood education, all forms of punishment are unacceptable, and reward systems are inappropriate ways of controlling or manipulating behaviour. Attempts to extinguish undesirable behaviours by ignoring them often increase the behaviours or give messages to children that they have no value within a world that is manipulated by adults. A delicate balance has to be struck between the teachers and children that allows both to have power while respecting the rights of all members of the classroom society.

Children need to feel that they are able to affect what happens in their environments. Katz (1974) claims that children feel psychologically safe when they perceive that what they do really matters to others. Teachers sometimes think that children

PLAY AND WORK

do not understand behaviours that convey messages about who has the power. But children do pick up on these cues, and become resentful and act out when they discover that the teacher has all the power.

An environment that provides real choices to children and encourages them to exercise choices safely and with consideration for the rights of others fosters industry and respect. Children's appreciation of fairness makes them willing to comply in situations that demand it. For the well-being of the group, they will also listen to the teacher when she exercises her authority. Children want adults to assume their authority appropriately and establish clear boundaries. Teachers need to do so with kindness, warmth, sensitivity, and concern for the developing ego and spirit of each individual. Clear limits, interesting things to do, activities that they can do for themselves, opportunities for meaningful self-expression, and a climate in which children are redirected and supported when they make mistakes all serve to guide children without imposing manipulative strategies, punishment, or guilt.

When children cross limits that have been clearly established, clarified, and repeated many times, they should be dealt with firmly and immediately. Redirecting a child from the scene of his misbehaviour to another activity while explaining verbally the reason for the action is one guidance technique. Removing a child from play with peers but allowing him to play alone is also often effective. This "renewal time" conveys the message that the child can return to play with others when he has calmed down, thus giving the child more control over his own recovery (Cherry, 1983).

Above all, teachers have to plan and set up an environment that will establish the limits and norms of the classroom society. The need for enforcement strategies is often reduced when learning centres are organized and communicate clear messages about the behaviours expected there. Children are guided positively when teachers provide meaningful, developmentally appropriate choices for children, when there is enough to do, adequate space in which to do it, and interesting things to play with, and when a climate of respect for all individuals prevails.

Teaching Academic Subjects in Preschool

Child-centered early childhood education is *not* open-ended, goal-less, and value-free activity in an environment without standards or structure. An obstacle to developmentally appropriate practice in early education is the widespread belief that developmental education lacks the definition and specific learning outcomes of so-called back-to-basics traditional educational styles.

Most parents want assurances that their children will acquire knowledge, skills, and attitudes that will lead to happy, successful, and healthy lives. This desire often translates to a call for a return to schools like the ones they knew, where outcomes were believed to be measurable and easily recognized. They believe that this is all that is needed to improve educational standards, and they link standardized curriculum, teaching methods, and tests to higher standards in education. Some also believe that developmental education lacks backbone and a clear philosophical framework.

In order to achieve greater acceptance of the developmental approach, the general public will have to be convinced of the validity of its philosophical principles and goals. The *values* upon which developmental theory is based, the *practices* that implement these values, and the *standards* upon which programs and children's progress can be evaluated and assessed must be clearly stated and publicized. What is needed in early childhood education, and at all levels in our educational system, is "a different kind of theory, one which focuses on the educational aspects of development, learning and motivation and which directly yields principles for engaging children in learning" (Egan, 1986:6).

It is counterproductive to the aims of developmentally appropriate practice to view the teaching of academic skills in early childhood education programs as detrimental to the cause and harmful to young children. What is needed is a clearer understanding of the critical relationship between sound developmental practice and the promotion of academic learning. Programs that "emphasize concepts and processes, that utilize small group instruction, active manipulation of relevant, concrete materials, and interactive learning provide a solid foundation for academics within a context of meaningful activity" (Kostelnik, 1992:22).

■ DEVELOPING AN EDUCATIONAL PHILOSOPHY FOR YOUNG CHILDREN

Values

Values are beliefs that motivate behaviour. Developmentally appropriate practice is based on the belief that children are motivated largely from within. It also assumes that children pass through distinct stages in a given sequence. Each stage is characterized by specific cognitive styles and abilities that are very different from those of an adult. Since cognitive development in early childhood is largely sensory and physical, children's knowledge of the world around them depends on the freedom to explore, manipulate, and be physically active.

According to cognitive-developmental theory, early learning must be individualized and child-centred since no two children learn at the same rate, to the same level, and in the same way. Children need freedom to engage in learning that is interesting and matches their needs and abilities. Real learning occurs when children integrate new understandings from their concrete experiences. This learning process takes time and patience. It also assumes that children are capable of building frameworks that will accommodate new and more complex learning challenges leading to higher levels of development during childhood and after. An important value of the cognitive-developmental approach is the achievement of higher levels of functioning by adults as a direct result of a strong foundation in development and learning in childhood.

Practices

Teaching practices are generally derived from values that guide our behaviours and choices. Some of the practices associated with child-centred early childhood education are:

1. Children should be free to choose their own play experiences.
2. The environment should offer play alternatives that are meaningful and accessible to children.
3. Play experiences should be based on objectives derived from observations of children in order to facilitate developmental progress from their present level to a higher level of development. Unplanned, randomly selected activities not based on assessments of the developmental levels and needs of individual children often amount to little more than busy work.

4. Teachers should plan a range of play experiences from the simple to the complex and begin with very concrete learning challenges in which the concepts or skills to be mastered are clear and observable to the learner. These simple activities should be followed by more abstract learning tasks that gradually challenge the child to move beyond sensory exploration and physical manipulation to thinking and problem solving. More complex activities may involve skills such as matching, comparing, classifying, predicting, estimating, and communicating.

5. A balance of structured (convergent) and open-ended (divergent) activities should be provided. Structured experiences with specific-purpose materials such as puzzles and stacking toys provide built-in cues regarding what is to be done and learned with the materials. The tasks to be accomplished in structured play experiences are clear to the teacher and the child. Open-ended activities such as easel painting, sociodramatic play, and block play offer opportunities for children to explore materials, invent plans and procedures, try several alternatives, make decisions, and achieve outcomes decided by the child.

6. A balance of individual and group activities to allow for children's unique learning styles should be provided.

7. Equipment, materials, and supplies should be organized into well-defined learning centres that ensure children's receipt of messages from their environment about what they should be doing and learning in each learning centre.

Early childhood educators need to be designers and planners of the learning environment, skilled observers and assessors of children's developmental levels and needs, and facilitators of children's learning while the children are engaged in largely self-directed play. The developmental educator plays a supportive rather than a leadership role during children's playtime. The learning environment should also provide clues to the children about the kind of play possible in each area of the classroom.

Standards

The standards in a developmental program are developmental and learning outcomes identified for play experiences. Children's developmental progress is determined by their mastery of objectives that are sequenced from simple to complex and require progressively higher levels of skill, knowledge, and understanding. The standards in developmental early childhood education are the indicators of developmental progress made by individual children. These indicators are often obtained through observation.

Teachers need to observe children's entering behaviours, make assessments of their developmental levels, monitor the developmental skills they are able to master in various activities, and make some assessment of their progress from the point at which the learning process began. Assessment is a sophisticated skill which requires knowledge of child development, and well-developed observation and recording skills. It also relies on the teacher's ability to correctly match activities and materials to children's developmental levels for both individual and group play.

When the standards of the program have been met, children have generally made progress on a number of developmental objectives from the point at which they entered the learning environment. When children do not demonstrate progress, there is something wrong, either with the environment or with the teaching and learning methods. The same principle applies to children with special needs. Regular and systematic program evaluation strategies that look carefully at all components of the play and learning environment, including the teachers, will usually reveal problems and weaknesses that can be addressed and helped.

Promoting developmental progress should not be confused with attempting to accelerate children's development. Effective developmental programs promote children's progress at their own rate, in their own ways, following their unique learning styles and interests. The level of skill, knowledge, or understanding to be achieved by all children within a given time frame is not stated in advance. Observable evidence that each child is progressing developmentally from the point at which she began is what is important.

■ PLAY AND THE CHILD WITH DISABILITIES

Play is a universal experience in childhood. All children, whether disabled or not, learn through play. The integration of the special child who experiences physical, cognitive, or affective problems, or a multitude of problems that cross developmental domains, is based on the assumption that children with disabilities are more similar to all children than they are different. Teachers have to ensure that the child with disabilities learns and grows in spite of the disability. This goal is met by providing materials, a play environment, and interpersonal support that minimize the effect of the disability while maximizing the child's strengths. In well-planned integrated programs, opportunities exist for the child with disabilities to make developmental progress, just as they do for the non-disabled child.

Sometimes the challenges for teachers are very great. Learning centres often have to be rearranged in order to provide wider pathways for a wheelchair or a child on crutches. A broader range of developmental activities are frequently needed to address the capabilities and interests of the child with disabilities. Special materials and media, such as computers or symbol boards (Blissboards), allow a child to minimize the effects of the disability in order to achieve the objectives of play. Whatever accommodations have to be made, the teacher should ensure that the child is able to learn through play with things that she can manage successfully. Placing children with disabilities in structured, prescriptive educational settings robs them of their right to learn through play. Programs that depend on direct teaching and try to compensate for children's disabilities by manipulating their behaviour are inconsistent with the philosophy of early childhood education.

■ MAKING DECISIONS AND PLANNING FOR PLAY

The usefulness of an educational philosophy lies in its ability to guide decision making, planning, and practice. Purposeful planning for play by teachers involves thinking through the elements that are necessary for a child to experience a good day in a preschool or kindergarten. Facilitating children's development implies an understanding of the developmental tasks of early childhood and knowledge of the sequence of developmental learning. Developmental goals and objectives are the basis of developmental planning. Creative use of resources and physical space will lead to satisfying play and positive learning experiences for children.

Planning for play is based on the following assumptions about play:

- play activities should be freely chosen by the child
- flexible use of play materials and accessibility of resources to children is essential to self-expression
- schedules and routines should take second place in the planning and management of the child's day in order to ensure that children's play is accorded its rightful importance
- the child's spiritual development takes place largely in unstructured natural environments, often outdoors, where he has the privacy and individual freedom to explore physically and cognitively the things that are of interest to him
- children's learning through play depends primarily on the quality and accessibility of a wide range of concrete objects in the environment that are responsive to their actions on them
- the environment should provide sufficient space and accessibility to a range of equipment, materials, and supplies that may be used in flexible ways
- the environment should offer *real* choices of play activities to children in learning centres where planning is based on specific developmental objectives
- the learning environment should provide messages to children that are consistent with the teacher's verbal messages
- the child's right to privacy should be respected—this includes letting children play alone when they choose to
- children learn through play outdoors as well as indoors; therefore, planning the learning environment involves planning both the outdoor and the indoor space

References

Almy, M. (1984). A child's right to play. *Young Children* 39 (4):80.

Beane, J.A. (1991). Enhancing children's self-esteem: illusion and possibility. *Early Education and Development* 2 (2):153–160.

Bettelheim, B. (1987a). *A Good Enough Parent.* New York: Random House. Copyright © 1987 by Bruno Bettelheim. Reprinted by permission of Alfred A. Knopf, Inc.

Bettelheim, B. (1987b). The importance of play. *The Atlantic* 262 (3):35–46.

Bredekamp, S. (1987). *Developmentally Appropriate Practice in Early Childhood Programs Serving Children From Birth to Age 8.* Washington, D.C.: National Association for the Education of Young Children.

Cherry, C. (1983). *Please Don't Sit on the Kids.* Belmont, CA: Pitman.

Coles, R. (1990). *The Spiritual Life of Children.* Boston, MA: Houghton-Mifflin.

DeVries, R., and Kohlberg, L. (1987). *Constructivist Early Education: Overview and Comparison with Other Programs.* Washington, D.C.: National Association for the Education of Young Children.

Dewey, J. (1916/1966). *Democracy and Education.* New York: Free Press.

Egan, K. (1986). *Individual Development and the Curriculum.* Melbourne, Australia: Hutchinson Education.

Elkind, D. (1981). *The Hurried Child.* Reading, MA: Addison-Wesley.

Elkind, D. (1988). Play. *Young Children* 43 (4):2.

Elkind, D. (1989). Developmentally appropriate practice: philosophical and practical implications. *Phi Delta Kappan* 71 (2):113–17.

Ellis, M. (1973). *Why People Play.* Englewood Cliffs, NJ: Prentice-Hall.

Erikson, E. (1963). *Childhood and Society.* 2d ed. New York: Norton.

Fowler, W. (1971). On the value of both play and structure in early education. *Young Children* 27 (1):24–36.

Gardner, H. (1989). The study of intelligences. Speech delivered to the Annual Conference of the Canadian Association for Young Children. Kingston, Ontario: Queen's University, October, 1989.

Goffin, S. (1991). We are not champions of a newly discovered cause: remembering the heroines of early childhood education. *Young Children* 47 (1):62–64.

Halman, P.E. (1991). Developing a sense of wonder in young children: there is more to early childhood education than cognitive development. *Young Children* 46 (6):53.

Hartley, R., Frank, L., and Goldenson, R. (1957). *Understanding Children's Play.* New York: Columbia University Press.

Jipson, J. (1991). Developmentally-appropriate practice: culture, curriculum, connections. *Early Education and Development* 2 (2):120–36.

Johnson, H. (1936). *School Begins At Two.* New York: New Republic.

Katz, L. (1974). *Talks with Teachers.* Washington, D.C.: National Association for the Education of Young Children.

Katz, L., and Chard, S. (1989). *Engaging Children's Minds: The Project Approach.* Norwood, NJ: Ablex.

Kessler, S.A. (1991). Alternative perspectives on early childhood education. *Early Childhood Research Quarterly* 6 (2):183–97.

Kessler, S.A. (1991). Early childhood education as development: critique of the metaphor. *Early Education and Development* 2 (2):137–52.

Kostelnik, M.J. (1992). Myths associated with developmentally appropriate programs. *Young Children* 47 (4):17–23.

Leo, J. (1990). The trouble with self-esteem. *U.S. News and World Report,* April 2, 16.

Piaget, J., and Inhelder, B. (1969). *The Psychology of the Child.* New York: Basic.

Piaget, J. (1970). *The Science of Education and the Psychology of the Child*. New York: Viking Compass.

Postman, N. (1982). *The Disappearance of Childhood*. New York: Delacorte Press.

Rogers, C. (1969). *Freedom to Learn*. Columbus, OH: Merrill.

Walsh, D. (1991). Extending the discourse on developmental appropriateness: a developmental perspective. *Early Education and Development* 2 (2):109–19.

Weber, E. (1984). *Ideas Influencing Early Childhood Education: A Theoretical Analysis*. New York: Teachers College Press, Columbia University.

PLANNING FOR PLAY AND LEARNING

Understanding the relationship between play and developmentally appropriate practice in early childhood education is the first step in planning environments and programs that will meet children's individual needs. Section 2 emphasizes three components involved in planning developmentally appropriate environments for young children: Chapter 4 looks at the creation of a positive social and emotional (affective) climate; Chapter 5 discusses the organization and use of space; and Chapter 6 outlines the function, location, design, and organization of learning centres.

Section 2 addresses the following topics:

- creating a climate that supports play and learning
- review of Piaget's cognitive-developmental theory
- principles of learning for young children
- role of the schedule
- ingredients of a positive play and learning climate
- locating the learning environment
- use and organization of space
- units of play
- creating play zones
- locating learning centres
- function of learning centres
- storage units

C H A P T E R 4

CREATING A CLIMATE
FOR PLAY

■ DEFINITION OF CLIMATE

Climate refers to the affective (social and emotional) conditions present in an environment. These conditions contribute to the overall social and emotional mood and culture. Factors such as emotional warmth, friendliness, a sense of physical and psychological safety, and social acceptability are some elements of climate that foster the happy play settings that contribute to learning and growth.

The climate of a play and learning environment affects children's development and learning. When children are encouraged to explore, have access to materials they can manipulate, and pursue individual interests at their own pace, they are likely to learn. Children need to be able to make mistakes, but be accepted and supported. They will forget rules and should be able to trust that they will be reminded of them when they do. A healthy climate for play and learning accepts children's need to be secure in order to take risks and is also sensitive to their frailty and inexperience.

■ CLIMATE AND LEARNING

Children learn in environments that are planned and set up to meet their developmental levels and interests. In order for children to learn through play, their environment should give messages to them that this is their place to roam, explore, and discover. Too many rules and boundaries tell children that they have very few opportunities to influence what happens in the classroom. A healthy social and emotional climate assures children that who they are and what they do is important, and that adults care about their interests and motivations. When children are able to affect what happens in the environment, they feel that they share power with their teachers.

A classroom for the early years is a microcosm of the world beyond (Nash, 1989). A rich environment for children is a capsule of the many physical, sensory, emotional, social, and intellectual dimensions of daily life. The environment should provide many two- and three-dimensional concrete objects to explore and manipulate, as it is through sensory exploration that young children learn best.

Creative, stimulating play is fuelled by the imagination and by messages received through the senses. A play environment that provides space for dreaming and contemplation, is unhurried and flexible, and offers many kinds of sensory experiences facilitates self-expression and experimentation. Children's inner lives are developed in an environment in which they have opportunities to experience the same things in a variety of contexts. A learning environment that is rich in materials encourages children to invent new ways of combining and using concrete objects.

■ CLIMATE AND THE NEED FOR ACTIVE AND QUIET PLAY

Children have physical needs for both active and quiet play. Learning centres and activities in the classroom should be planned to provide a balance of active and quiet play, just as they allow for individual and group play (NAEYC, 1991). Child care programs, which some children attend for as many as ten hours a day, five days a week, and sometimes fifty weeks a year, constitute a major part of children's lives in the early years. Being expected to maintain a consistent and sometimes rigorous daily routine is tiring for teachers and can be very stifling for children. When children are expected to remain in groups for most of these long periods, it is no wonder that they sometimes become competitive, manipulative, anxious, aggressive or resentful.

Planning spaces where children can be alone for a while during the day, and enjoy some privacy and relief from the mainstream is essential for their mental health. A healthy climate for children in group care is one that respects their need for some privacy, provides for some "down time" during the day when not much is expected of them, and allows frequent opportunities to remove themselves from the presence of other children when they feel a need to do so.

■ CLIMATE AND THE INFLUENCE OF PHYSICAL CHARACTERISTICS

Child-sized furniture, shelves, and cupboards placed at children's levels make the environment accessible to children and contribute to a feeling of belonging and a sense that they are important.

Natural flowers and leaves placed on low tables that children can touch and smell, stir their appreciation of nature's beauty. Accessories such as placemats, curtains and cushions that are pretty and soft are appreciated by children and teachers alike, creating a homelike atmosphere and reducing the institutional feeling often present in an environment composed mostly of hard surfaces and geometric shapes. Pictures hung at a child's-eye view reinforce the message that children are important. A classroom arranged so that children can touch and explore the beautiful things placed within their reach or view conveys the message, "this is your place to discover and enjoy."

Successful play environments provide abundant sensory stimulation and appeal. Soft or hard, and rough or smooth textures, complementary colours, curved as well as sharper contours, and natural as well as artificial materials create an environment of contrast and variation. Sharp, rigid contours seem to prevail in many early childhood classrooms. Tables with perpendicular instead of round edges, hard instead of cushioned chairs, tile floors instead of carpeting, are often the rule. A cushioned rocking chair or a comfortable sofa in a quiet corner are commonly children's favourite places because they provide sensory relief from hard surfaces and offer comforting reminders of home.

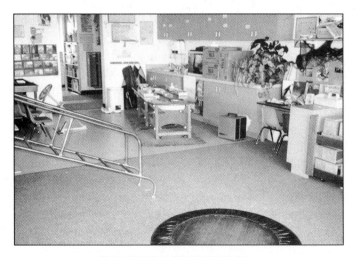

CLIMATE IS INFLUENCED BY
PHYSICAL CHARACTERISTICS

We know that smooth, hard surfaces make more practical and durable toys, equipment, and furnishings. For similar reasons, plastic, vinyl, ceramic, and arborite are more prevalent than wood, textiles, cork, and rubber building products and accessories in child care programs and kindergartens. Most amenities look as if they could be hosed down without a change in their physical properties. In some environments, practical and utilitarian features replace the comfortable, homelike, and aesthetically pleasing amenities that most of us need and enjoy.

It would be foolish to argue against the obvious advantages of building products and materials that are easy to maintain, sanitary, and durable. However, such functional classroom environments do not invite cuddling up in a chair with a stuffed animal, learning to wipe the paint off one's hands before touching the flowered cushion, rubbing one's face against the knubby, woven curtains, or feeling the soft texture of the quilted placemats when helping to set the table for lunch. Children are at a stage when sensory impressions contribute to the formation of habits, values, and choices that affect the quality of life later on. Arguments may be made that the aesthetic and sensory characteristics of an environment are as important as its functional and practical aspects.

Climate also affects spiritual development. Children need authentic environments that include properties of the natural world. Comfortable surroundings and private spaces contribute to intellectual and physical "meanderings" that nourish the spirit. Natural objects and materials such as wood, cork, plants, earth, leaves, flowers, water, wool, and stones add authenticity and natural content to classrooms which are mostly utilitarian. Our play and learning environments should reflect the abundance of beautiful, natural, building products that North America enjoys.

■ THE HEALTHY, MULTICULTURAL CLIMATE

The ideal climate for a play and learning environment is also multicultural. Children respond to pictures, artifacts, clothing, implements, and foods that represent the cultural heritage of their families and provide reminders of home. Stimulating environments are those to which all children in the group can relate.

Multicultural elements should not be singled out for special attention only at times when traditional festive occasions occur. A truly multicultural environment is one in which concrete evidence of the various cultural and ethnic groups represented in the program's child population is present all the time (Mock, 1984; Cech, 1990). Without being reminded, children recognize and identify with the pita bread served for lunch, the sitar a child's mother played in the morning group time, the traditional Chinese fan decorating the wall, soft leather moccasins to wear, chanukkah candles along with evergreen boughs in December, bocce balls in the playground, the poster of windmills and tulips on the wall, and the hand-painted Ukrainian egg cups in the housekeeping area.

■ CLIMATE AND TECHNOLOGY

The presence of technology in the early childhood classroom represents North American reality and culture, as do the fish tank, model cars, and telephone. Type-writers, tape players, and microcomputers, where they can be made available, add features of today's world that are almost as familiar as the child-sized stove and refrigerator. When integrated into the program at a child's level of development and understanding, technology adds to the authentic, culturally relevant climate of the learning environment.

■ CLIMATE AND CLEANLINESS

The cleanliness of the play and learning environment also contributes to the climate. Attention paid by teachers to keeping environments clean by washing dirty tables, cleaning and disinfecting toys frequently, having children wipe or remove shoes before entering the centre or school and wash their hands often are all practices that encourage clean behaviours in children. Consistent attention to cleanliness by teachers reinforces the importance of the role of custodian of the environment that must be assumed by everyone in it (Nault, 1991).

An important element of freedom and enjoyment for children is being able to play with messy, sensory materials, as well as blocks that they sometimes like to strew over wide areas. A climate that permits children to make a mess but also assume responsibility for helping to tidy up teaches children the importance of using an environment and the things in it freely and creatively. It also reinforces the need to return things to their original places in the playroom and re-establish order when it is time to move on to something else.

■ LEARNING THROUGH PLAY AS A RATIONALE FOR PLANNING ENVIRONMENTS

The learning environment should ensure that children have space to move freely and access to a wide range of developmentally appropriate materials, supplies, and equipment. Clearly stated limits and boundaries within which children feel secure and able to take risks allows them greater independence in their play and contributes to a sense of mastery. Children also need teachers who trust them to do their own learning within a planned setting.

Learning through play does not happen in just any play environment. The climate is a key factor. In some environments children regularly meander, engage in repetitive activity, or while away the time. In others, they are tightly organized into an endless round of teacher-led activities. Sometimes, play is simply "messing about." Not all play involves learning; some can be described as simply being.

Learning through play does not even necessarily define the best kind of play. The phrase does, however, endorse the fact that play can be a powerful vehicle for learning when that is the stated and practised intention of the play environment.

■ DEVELOPMENT AND LEARNING DEPEND ON A CLIMATE THAT SUPPORTS GROWTH

The optimal development of the child at each stage is an important goal of early childhood education. Interaction between the child and the environment facilitates development, particularly in the physical and cognitive domains. A review of Piaget's theory of how children come to know and understand may help explain the important role of the social and emotional climate in children's learning.

Cognitive-Developmental Theory

Piagetian developmental theory states that learning involves the building of mental structures acquired through the joint processes of assimilation and accommodation. **Assimilation** is the change that occurs when children try to fit the new learning experience to their existing mental structures. **Accommodation** occurs when children alter their existing mental structures to make a fit between what they already know and the new experience that unseats or challenges the existing state of their understanding. **Equilibration** is the motivational factor for the learning that occurs as a result of these joint processes of assimilation and accommodation. When children achieve equilibration, they reach a new state of balance and a higher level of

MESSY PLAY

development. It is through the joint processes of assimilation and accommodation that children become intelligent. One aspect of becoming intelligent means that children develop the thinking abilities they need to solve new problems and originate new ideas (Piaget, 1972).

Children construct their own intelligence largely through active interaction with concrete objects in the environment (Piaget, 1969). Real learning occurs when children are able to transfer concepts gained in one play context to another play context. The quality of the play materials and the context in which they are presented to children often determine what children will learn. It is the role of teachers to set up concrete play materials in a physical context where they will provide messages to children about what they are to learn and how they are to learn it.

For example, placing measured beakers, jugs, and measuring cups of different shapes in the water table provides cues to children that pouring and comparing are planned for play in the water table that day. Children may, however, simply fill and empty each of the containers without comparing, just for the pleasure of watching the water swoosh from one container to the other. They may pour water from a tall thin beaker into a stubby measuring cup without necessarily comparing or determining that the same amount of water will fill each container. Sooner or later, even without teacher intervention, play materials such as these, that have been carefully selected by the teacher will provide concrete clues to children that promote the learning of concepts, in this case, the concept of volume. Understanding is most likely to occur in a learning climate that gives children optimal freedom to choose activities that interest them and to pursue learning at their own pace, with materials that help them uncover concepts for themselves.

Types of Knowledge

Piaget differentiates among physical, social-conventional, and logical-mathematical knowledge. The climate of the classroom influences the type of learning children actively pursue and affects the learning outcomes of play.

Physical Knowledge

Physical knowledge is largely sensory learning about the concrete, physical properties of objects. It refers to learning about shape, size, colour, texture, and other observable characteristics of things. Infants begin to acquire physical knowledge right from birth. The entire sensorimotor period up to eighteen or twenty-four months of age is primarily directed towards the acquisition of physical knowledge of the objects, people, and events in the child's immediate surroundings.

Children acquire physical knowledge through physical and sensory exploration of things. The learning climate that fosters the acquisition of physical knowledge is one in which children have ample opportunity to explore, move freely, test, and compare the physical properties of things.

Social-Conventional Knowledge

Social-conventional knowledge refers to facts and information that are socially and culturally transmitted and may be arbitrarily assigned, such as rules, proper names, conventions, and customs. Knowledge of street names, important dates, safety rules, manners, social conventions, the functions of social institutions, and historical data are examples. During the preoperational years, from two to six or seven, this kind of knowledge is usually acquired through verbal and cultural transmission from parents and other adults to children. Later, school-age children, who are concrete-operational, also acquire social-conventional knowledge in formal learning contexts from textbooks and other academic learning materials.

Effective climates for learning promote positive social interaction between teachers and children and among children. Visitors representing the community bring the outside world into the classroom and are important resources for social-conventional knowledge. Welcoming parents into the classroom gives messages to children that their parents and the values and customs they learn at home are valid, worthwhile, and accepted.

SOCIAL-CONVENTIONAL KNOWLEDGE

Logical-Mathematical Knowledge

Logical-mathematical knowledge involves understanding universal concepts and principles that do not change from culture to culture. It includes the ability to understand the largely abstract relationships that exist between concepts. For example, young children recognize the physical properties inherent in two red circles of equal size. They can perceive that each one is red and round. They may even know that each is a circle if they are able to identify the shape by its label, "circle." What they may not understand is the quality of two-ness that is created by putting the two red circles together, for that involves creating a relationship between the two objects that is not observable but exists largely in the mind. The quality of two-ness is inherent only in the *relationship* that one attaches to the two red circles. By understanding that the circles are the same, children are beginning to see one kind of relationship that exists between the two when they are put together. The quality of their two-ness is also a concept that is known only as a result of the relationship. Take away one red circle and the quality of two-ness vanishes from both circles, while the redness and circular shape of each remain visible and the noun (circle) which describes them is unchanged.

Arriving at an understanding of abstract concepts takes time and the right learning climate which promotes investigation, inquiry, testing, trial and error, and plenty of opportunity to interact with concrete materials. The old saying, "What I hear I forget; What I see I remember; What I do I understand," captures the essence of the relationship between a climate which promotes inquiry and the acquisition of logical-mathematical knowledge.

Social-Emotional Climate and Informal Learning

ICE-CREAM STORE

Learning that provides for the acquisition of physical, social-conventional, and logical-mathematical understanding occurs in informal learning settings. Informal settings promote children's freely chosen activity within carefully designed environments that allow for hands-on experience with things, events, and people (Elkind, 1977). The building of a strong foundation of mental structures that facilitate formal learning during the school years is a fundamental developmental task of early childhood.

A healthy climate for learning recognizes that children develop at different rates. The provision of a choice of child-centred learning activities they can pursue as they are ready respects children's individual pace and learning styles (Bredekamp, 1987).

Childcentred means that children will select activities themselves, pursue them in their own ways, set their own goals, decide when they have finished, and sometimes communicate what they have done. To individualize activities and programs for children means that teachers purposely plan and set up activities that meet the developmental needs and interests of each child in the group.

Small-Group Versus Large-Group Learning

Children learn at different rates and employ unique learning styles for each learning task. Therefore, small-group or individual play activities are more effective than large-group, teacher-centred activities for the acquisition of physical knowledge and the mastery of abstract concepts (logical-mathematical understanding) during early childhood. Individual and small-group activities also allow for greater hands-on involvement with things in the environment.

Large-group activities are useful for some physical activities, and for music and movement activities. They promote social skills as well as specific knowledge and opportunities to practise physical skills. Children find it easier to feel a part of the larger group when large-group activities are planned. An appropriate balance of small-group, large-group, and individual play activities is an important element of a positive learning climate.

■ ROLE OF THE SCHEDULE

The daily schedule of routines and playtime in a child care program/early years classroom will either undermine or promote the effectiveness of children's play opportunities. It is important that the schedule support a positive climate for play and learning.

Playtimes are often undermined by the scheduling of routines that keep interrupting children's activities and learning. This happens when teachers believe that the pace, daily agenda, and routines should provide frequent changes of activity. Sometimes small blocks of time are scheduled for specific kinds of play, such as "free play," circle time, outdoor play, organized games, and quiet playtime. Interspersed in these allocations of playtime are washroom routines, snacktimes, naptimes, mealtimes, and the inevitable transition periods intended to form smooth bridges from one type of activity to another. In following schedules like this, children often barely manage to have one full hour of uninterrupted playtime in a whole day. They are bombarded with reminders that it is time to tidy up, or get dressed, or prepare to go to the washroom, or move to another area of the school or centre.

Program schedules that assume children have short attention spans foster play that is product-oriented. Short intervals of play interspersed with frequent routines encourage children to choose activities that can be completed in one short "sitting." Projects and two- or three-stage activities are often unfinished by the time children have to move on to something else. In programs like these, the schedule becomes the master of the day. It is invested with the power to disrupt, interrupt, alter, and disengage the attention and involvement of children in their play. Consequently, play loses its meaning and much of the potential it might have had to motivate and provide feelings of success and mastery. One study showed that schedules that provide short intervals of play actually decrease children's attention spans (Nash, 1975).

Scheduling Time for Teachers

Teachers, who have so many responsibilities, need time to sit down, or to have something to drink and eat, as well as time to plan or set up activities. Early childhood programs are not like retail stores or factories where staff check in and out for ten-minute breaks and lunch periods. Ratios of children to adults are affected every time a teacher leaves "the floor." The common assumption is that in order to ensure that legal ratios are always maintained, teacher breaks should not interfere with clearly defined routine periods. The schedule is sometimes planned so that teachers can be observed performing their duties in the manner outlined by the regulations. Play and learning are sacrificed when the schedule dominates the lives of the teachers and children.

Teachers need "down time"—allotments of time when they may do some thinking for the next day, nave a cup of tea, and rest for a few minutes. When supervisors and teachers see their role as that of standing guard when they are "on the floor," they become tired very quickly and require scheduled breaks when they can move away from the children. Being "professional" does not always mean assuming a supervisory stance in the classroom. In another sense, teachers are never "off duty" when they are in the school or centre. Schedules should recognize and acknowledge teachers' humanity and needs; doing so will help them meet children's needs with greater energy and sincerity.

Scheduling Routines

The approach to scheduling recommended in Table 4.1 assumes that children are able to use the washroom largely on their own. This approach generally means that the toilets and sinks are located just off the playroom and can be supervised by teachers through glass enclosures or over half-walls enabling them to give children the usual encouragement and reminders. Two-year-olds naturally require more direct attention and assistance, and the regularity and consistency of the routine becomes part of the learning agenda for each day.

T A B L E   4 . 1

EXAMPLE OF A DAILY SCHEDULE FOR A CHILD CARE PROGRAM OR FULL-DAY KINDERGARTEN

7:30	arrival; greeting; warm drink or snack; early arrivals play in the learning centres
8:30	morning group planning time with the teacher to talk about the day ahead
8:45	playtime in learning centres
10:00	snack brought to snack table for children to help themselves; four chairs at the table to accommodate four children at a time; children should wash their hands at a sink with soap before they sit at the table
10:30	reminder regarding washroom; planned physical program in the gymnasium, psychomotor room, or outdoors; some group physical activities may be led by the teacher
11:45	preparation for lunch; washroom; lunchtime
12:45	naptime; quiet play in learning centres for children who do not require more than an hour of rest
14:15	storytime with teacher in small groups
14:45	playtime outdoors or indoors in learning centres, depending on whether children were outside for a morning a physical program and depending on the weather
16:00	playtime continues indoors depending on the weather; snack offered at snack table indoors or outdoors depending on weather and presence of insects
16:30	group time with teacher to discuss the day, share plans for the next day, work on a group project, or perhaps make some play materials for the next day
17:00	preparation for home, while some children continue to play in learning centres

The schedule in Table 4.1 omits many events that will inevitably occur during the course of the day. Time for dressing and undressing before and after outdoor play, for example, is not listed. Children are assumed to be capable of using the washroom independently, although teachers may remind individual children to use the washroom. An informal approach to the management of children's need to use the washroom frequently is less disruptive to their play and less institutional.

▪ PRINCIPLES OF SCHEDULE PLANNING TO MEET CHILDREN'S NEEDS

The daily schedule should coincide with the natural rhythms of children and contribute to their physical and emotional well-being. It should also reflect the goals of the program. Programs that state, for example, that the goals for children are independence, freedom to choose, decision-making abilities, and attending skills should not implement schedules that rigidly insist children remain in bed for the whole naptime even though they cannot sleep, or that prevent a child from finishing an activity that requires just a few more minutes.

That teachers and children require time frames and limitations in order to accomplish necessary tasks in a day is a given. One question, however, remains: what needs to be done in a day? Children need to arrive, settle in, have frequent snacks and a meal, rest, and prepare for going home. They need to use the washroom frequently. For the rest of the day, children should be able to engage in self-directed play, with time set aside for organized group activities.

One study demonstrated that longer play periods promote more total play activity, group play, constructive play, and group-dynamic play, whereas during shorter play periods, children spend more time in unoccupied behaviour, functional play, and parallel-dramatic play (Christie & Wardle, 1992). They argue that longer, unstructured play periods promote more complex and productive play activities, and that the schedule should be adjusted in order to ensure that they occur every day. Routines such as getting dressed and undressed become natural transitions between going outside or coming inside, while other routines take place between lunch and naptime, or naptime and the resumption of play.

The daily schedule is the skeleton of the day upon which having a good day often depends. The quality of the affective climate and the effectiveness of the learning environment often depend on the emphases and flexibility within the schedule.

Principles of Schedule Planning

1. The schedule should be open and loose enough to allow for unexpected occurrences, changes in plan, and meeting children's spontaneous needs and interests.

2. The schedule should be regular but not inflexible. The order in which events occur during the day will remain fairly constant most days, but the times may vary, depending on a range of factors including weather conditions, special plans, and the needs of other groups to use facilities or equipment.

3. The schedule should generally provide for alternating periods of quieter and more active experiences. Moving from active to quieter activities will reduce the likelihood that excitement will escalate and tire children more quickly.

4. The schedule should provide for a variety of activities and outlets for children at any given time, whether indoors or outdoors. Children have different activity level requirements: some are able to play actively for longer periods without becoming overexcited or fatigued, while others can engage in seated or quiet activity for long periods without becoming restless or bored. Each play period should permit children to choose either more active or quiet pursuits. Quiet corners allow for privacy and individual play; active role play areas encourage social interaction and motor activity.

5. The schedule should provide a balance of indoor and outdoor play. Children generally love the outdoors. But on extremely cold days, no one enjoys being outside. Common sense usually prevails on days when it is too cold or damp for children to play comfortably outdoors and the schedule is usually adjusted accordingly. In climates where indoor-outdoor playtimes are possible and there are sufficient staff to meet ratios both inside and outside, schedules should permit freedom of movement from the playground to the indoor playroom and vice versa.

6. Schedules should account for seasonal changes in children's needs. The schedule planned for September may not suit the needs of children in December or May. Knowledge of the needs and rhythms of children will lead to changes in the schedule to accommodate changing climatic conditions and children's energy levels.

7. It is important to provide enough time for children to become deeply involved in what they are doing. Schedules requiring that children be continually herded from one place to another, or frequently interrupted in order to move to another set of activities, reduce children's powers of concentration and delay the development of attending abilities. Asking a child to leave an activity in which she is involved before she is finished exacts a cost in terms of the message received by the child. She may hear the teacher say on the one hand that it is important to

"finish what you start" and on the other, experience discomfort and frustration at being urged by the same teacher to leave what she is doing in order to have a snack, when a few minutes more would have allowed her to experience the satisfaction of completion and success.

8. Schedules should allow sufficient time for transitions from one activity to another, or from an activity to a routine. Children are notoriously poor at "hurrying," especially when they know you want them to. Transition times are not wasted times; when used well and understood by teachers, they allow valuable time for teachers to relate to children individually.

9. Schedules should provide for a suitable balance of playtime, when children can choose to play alone or in small groups, and time when children may be expected to participate in group learning and projects. Unstructured playtimes help children learn to make responsible choices, develop autonomy and initiative, and pursue their own interests and goals. Group learning times help children practise functioning as members of a group and allow teachers to relate to the group as a whole and instil in them a sense of group identity and belonging. Group times also promote a sense of common mission, especially when the teacher and the children together use the time to plan, develop, and carry out meaningful projects that arise from children's interests and choices (Katz & Chard, 1989). The periods of unstructured playtime when children may choose to play alone or with others, at activities of their own choosing, will generally assume a much larger portion of the day than the group learning times. This approach to scheduling recognizes that the child is primarily a physical being whose learning takes place mostly through physical, sensory involvement with concrete objects and events.

10. Schedules should also account for the needs of the adults who work with young children. While these needs should not supersede those of the children, it is important to recognize the demanding nature of the teacher's role. Teachers also need variety in their tasks and some opportunity for choice. The schedule should make the best possible use of human resources by encouraging teachers to do what they most enjoy doing. Teachers also need help with some of the tedious, time-consuming tasks involved in caring for children. They should be encouraged to share simple chores with children, such as helping to tidy the cupboard, cut collage materials, fold laundry, set the table, insert napkins in rings, and plan for the next day's activities. In these ways, children learn to use time well (Nash, 1989).

11. Schedules should also allow time for teachers to interact with parents in order to involve them as much as possible in the lives of their children and in the program. Schedules that do more than pay lip-service to the partnership between parents and teachers in the care and education of children ensure that teachers have comfortable periods of contact with parents at arrival and departure times.

■ SUMMARY

A healthy, affective climate includes positive relationships between adults and children that promote mutual respect and genuine affection. Children have to feel that what they believe and how they feel are important. Power is shared between teachers and children. The aesthetic appeal of the environment, including colour, textures, contours, cleanliness, and tidiness contribute to an atmosphere of order, safety, beauty, and harmony. Group times are used to foster a sense of belonging and identity in the group's members. Children are encouraged to choose from among a wide range of play and learning opportunities and are permitted to pursue activities at their own pace. Teachers' needs are addressed in order that they may minister more effectively to the needs of children. Schedules are based on children's natural rhythms and are flexible enough to allow for change. They provide for large blocks of playtime and minimize the importance of rigid, institutional routines in cases where they are unnecessary.

Together these ingredients of a healthy, affective climate will positively influence the effectiveness of the physical setting and the intellectual challenge children encounter there.

References

Bredekamp, S. (1987). *Developmentally Appropriate Practice in Early Childhood Programs Serving Children From Birth to Age 8.* Washington, D.C.: National Association for the Education of Young Children.

Cech, M. (1990). *Globalchild.* Toronto: Addison-Wesley.

Christie, J.F., and Wardle, F. (1992). How much time is needed for play? *Young Children* 47(3):28–32.

Elkind, D. (1977). The early years: the vital years. *Journal of the Canadian Association for Young Children* 3 (1):20–21.

Katz, L., and Chard, S. (1989). *Engaging Children's Minds: The Project Approach.* Norwood, NJ: Ablex.

National Association for the Education of Young Children. (1991). Position Statement: Guidelines for an appropriate curriculum and assessment in programs serving children ages 3 to 8. *Young Children* 46 (3):21–38.

Mock, K. (1984). Multicultural education in early childhood: a developmental rationale. In *Multicultural Early Childhood Education,* ed. K.A. McLeod. Toronto: Guidance Centre, University of Toronto.

Nash, C. (1975, 1989). *The Learning Environment: A Practical Approach to the Education of the Three-, Four- and Five-Year-Olds.* Toronto: Collier-Macmillan.

Nault, M. (1991). *William, Won't You Wash Your Hands?* Ottawa: Canadian Institute of Child Health.

Piaget, J. (1969). *Science of Education and the Psychology of the Child.* New York: Viking Compass.

Piaget, J. (1972). *To Understand Is To Invent.* New York: Grossman.

C H A P T E R 5

PLANNING PLAY SPACE

Indoor and outdoor play areas constitute the learning environment. This environment should include equipment, materials, and supplies that will promote specific kinds of play and represent some aspects of the adult world. For example, a well-designed housekeeping play area for three-year-olds may have miniature versions of household appliances and equipment such as a refrigerator, cupboards, tables, and chairs. Four- and five-year-olds need a more flexible pretend area which doesn't signal but does allow for relational role play and representation. Familiar miniature models of things found at home such as an ironing board and iron, a telephone, clothes racks, doll beds, a mirror, and a rocking chair contribute to the homelike setting of this play area. Play areas like this one, and others, are quite separate from the school or centre's kitchen, janitorial areas, office space, and staff and reception areas that are not considered part of the learning environment.

■ LOCATING THE LEARNING ENVIRONMENT

Decisions regarding the location of the learning environment within a child care program or kindergarten are usually the first and most important ones to be made in planning a program. Sometimes there are very few options, especially if a program is borrowing space from a school, using rooms in an old house, apartment block, church, or community centre.

Many factors should be taken into account when deciding where to locate the learning environment. Where are the access points (entrances and exits, gates, walkways, and parking spaces) of the building located? Easy entry and exit from the street, parking lot, and playground are important factors. Where does the natural light enter the play space? Where are the emergency exits? On what floor of the building is the program located, and how easily can the stairs be managed by children? Where are the washrooms, the gymnasium or active play area, and the cloak-room?

Ideally, an indoor learning environment for young children will be housed in a physical space that has one room large enough to accommodate all the children at one time. Where space is at a premium, a gross motor play area for active, physical play may have to be separated from the main playroom. Program planners who have to cope with several small rooms that will accommodate only two or three learning centres at a time should be particularly careful to ensure that the centres located in one small room are compatible.

■ ORGANIZING SPACE TO FACILITATE PLAY AND LEARNING

When children are able to move easily from one learning centre to another and from one activity to another that is nearby and has similar objectives but different materials, they begin to experience the possibility of testing ideas and practising skills using a variety of media and materials. This kind of organization contributes to the development of divergent thinking, which is the ability to see many possible solutions to a problem. This movement of equipment or materials and transferral of learning from one learning centre to another happens more naturally when play materials with similar developmental objectives are located close to one another and are easily seen by children. Their presence in the same room encourages

STORAGE UNITS

children's recognition of new possibilities for discovery that are related to those already acquired. An effective play and learning environment is a well-organized blend of resources and zones for play, which complement each other and represent many aspects of daily living.

Storage Units

Effective organization of space requires ease of supervision and efficient placement of storage units. The shape of the space and the distribution of things within that space should allow teachers to see and be seen easily. Materials and supplies should be stored close to where they will most likely be used. Movable equipment and furniture gives teachers more control over the physical setting. Similarly, portable storage is usually better than built-in or permanent storage as it allows for more flexible use and greater potential for variety in the environment. In the initial planning of classroom space, the placement of more permanent larger equipment such as swings and climbers, non-movable counters, and storage units requires careful consideration.

The quality and efficiency of storage units for materials and supplies are important to the smooth operation of the environment and have a significant impact on the morale and effectiveness of teachers. It is possible to purchase many types of customized storage units for art materials, puzzles, books, modular materials, graphic and construction supplies, and specific-purpose materials. These units usually have the added benefits of ensuring that materials and supplies are more accessible to children.

Effects of the Use of Space

The use of space affects the behaviours of persons who use the space. Spatial cues in the arrangement of play stations and learning centres stimulate specific kinds of behaviour, play, and learning.

Poorly organized space may lead to conflict between the goals of the program and the behaviours caused by the setting. When space is used carelessly, rules and various other forms of constraint such as locked cupboards and frequent teacher intervention are often needed to provide the cues for behaviour that the environment has failed to communicate. The presence of many rules and constraints reduces the freedom children have to explore, experiment, and choose, and thereby conflicts with the main aims of early childhood education programs.

Densely Organized Space

The organization of space also affects the quality and ease of social interaction in a program. In densely organized space where there is the least possible amount of space between play units, children are guided towards interactive play and the development of social skills becomes paramount. Programs whose goals emphasize social learning are more likely to encourage frequent social interaction and larger group play through densely organized space.

Loosely Organized Space

Loosely organized space provides more empty space per child and conveys a sense of openness. Open, spacious environments often contain more **potential units** of play and broader pathways. Kritchevsky & Prescott (1977:9) define potential units as "empty space which is surrounded in large part by visible and/or tangible boundaries." Potential units are useful for setting up props for sociodramatic play activities such as those that might take place in a hospital, restaurant, office, or beauty salon. But a potential unit may also be a small corner, an empty table, or space under an awning.

Environments with potential units and loose organization give the message to children that they are free to move, be active, spread out play materials, and play alone more often. Therefore, loose organization often suits the longer time frame of the full-day program. When children are involved in solitary, self-directed, and small-group play, teachers' time with individual children is often maximized.

Pathways

Effective organization of the learning environment depends on the presence of adequate empty space and **pathways** that are visible to children and help them move easily from one place to another. Kritchevsky and Prescott (1969:17) state that "a clear path is broad, elongated and easily visible...Paths are very difficult to describe in words, but when they are well-defined they are easily seen." Child-centred learning environments ensure that pathways are visible from a child's eye level and are easy to find.

Clear pathways in the learning environment lead children from one area of the classroom into another without their being distracted along the way by play equipment from learning centres that encroach upon the path. For example, a child who is outdoors may set out from the garden area and be headed towards the sandbox but may be enticed into climbing instead if the climbing equipment and surrounding play space intrudes on or obstructs the pathway. Sometimes a pathway is clear but does not lead to all learning centres. Some areas in learning centres may be hidden and therefore seldom used. In planning physical space, teachers need to ensure that pathways are clearly defined, that boundaries of learning centres and play spaces surrounding equipment are clearly visible, and that major pathways lead to and from all learning centres (Nash, 1989).

When major pathways converge in an open, unbounded space in the centre of a room, children may never find their way into a learning centre and will more likely be distracted by and remain in this area of "dead space." When active play areas are placed close to quiet, more individually oriented areas, noise and high levels of physical activity may distract the quiet play of children who are engaged in activities that require some concentration. Imposing rules in environmentally induced situations like these lessens the freedom and independence of the children in the program.

When there are clear pathways through space:

■ children playing at one unit cannot reach children in another unit
■ teachers and children do not need to pass through play units and their surrounding space to get from one place to another
■ no play units are permanently hidden
■ there is no dead space (Kritchevsky & Prescott, 1977)

Dead space is a large amount of empty space roughly square or circular in shape and without any visible or tangible boundaries (Kritchevsky & Prescott, 1977:19). It is sometimes found in the centre of a classroom or playground where the pathways and boundaries of play areas have not been clearly defined. Often out-of-bounds running or play develops and teachers have to intervene. Dead space can usually be eliminated by adding a play unit or moving some equipment or furniture.

Amount of Empty Space

An important criterion of good physical organization of space is the amount of empty versus covered space in the classroom. Kritchevsky and Prescott (1977:19) propose as a general rule of thumb that one-third to one-half uncovered surface in a room or yard will facilitate good organization of space. Larger groups of children need a larger proportion of empty space (i.e., closer to one-half uncovered surface). The total amount of space in a classroom is related to the number of children who would be using the room at one time. The ratios of total space available per child are regulated by provincial legislation in Canada and differ slightly among provinces. Similar jurisdictional differences occur in the United States.

■ CONTENTS OF PLAY SPACE

Kritchevsky and Prescott's book *Planning Environments for Young Children: Physical Space* (1977) has solved many space organization problems for early childhood educators. Their formulas for use of space and descriptions of play units are used frequently. Play space has two parts: the **contents,** which are the play units themselves, and **potential units** which, as previously mentioned, are empty spaces in a room or yard to which can be added a play material of one kind or another. The planning of space has to account for the fact that most equipment and play materials require surrounding space for children to play with them effectively, and this surrounding space should therefore be considered part of the play unit.

■ UNITS OF PLAY—SIMPLE, COMPLEX, AND SUPER UNITS

Kritchevsky and Prescott identify three types of play units: simple, complex, and super units. Each of these types varies in its relative capacity to keep children interested and in the number of children it can accommodate for play at one time.

EMOTIONAL WARMTH FOSTERS
HAPPY PLAY SETTINGS

Simple Units

A **simple unit** has one primary purpose in play and is generally used by one child at a time for the purpose intended (Kritchevsky & Prescott, 1977:11). Usually it does not have subparts. A child's drum, toy telephone, "corn popper" push toy, a spinning top, windup toy, and tricycle are examples of toys that are used in relatively fixed ways. Some simple units, such as a record player, a cash register with coins, and a rock-a-stack have component parts but still exist for one major play purpose. As play with a simple unit will usually accommodate only one child at a time, a simple unit is allocated *one play space* in calculating the complexity of the play environment.

Complex Units

A **complex unit** is "a play unit with sub-parts or a juxtaposition of two essentially different play materials which enable the child to manipulate or improvise" (Kritchevsky & Prescott, 1977:11). Complex units are allocated *four play spaces* in the calculation of complexity. A doll house with furniture, a doctor's kit, a water table with containers for pouring and measuring, and a puppet theatre with hand puppets are examples of complex units with built-in flexibility for various types of play. Complex units require sufficient space for a small group of children to work together using the same toy either cooperatively or independently. Complex units of play can be created by combining two or more simple units, or by adding simple units to one that is complex. When two or more simple units, such as a telephone and note pads, or a tape recorder and a few sets of earphones, are placed together, a complex unit has been created

Super Units

A **super unit** is "a complex unit which has one or more additional play materials, i.e., three or more play materials juxtaposed" (Kritchevsky & Prescott, 1977:11). Boxes, ramps, and boards added to a climber in the Active Role Play Centre, and the creation of a supermarket in a potential space by combining cash register, telephone, counter, shelves stocked with grocery boxes and tins, and paper bags are examples of super units. A super unit is allocated *eight play spaces* in calculating complexity, assuming that the space in which the super unit is set up can reasonably accommodate eight children.

SUPER UNIT

Adding blankets and tables to the playhouse area outdoors, or creating a post office in the technology centre by setting up a counter and desk with stamps, envelopes, and mail slot are examples of super units which may be created by teachers or by the children. Sometimes the best ideas for the creation of super units will come from the children themselves. A super unit accommodates the most children at once and usually holds their interest the longest. A climber with hollow blocks placed close to dramatic play props such as firefighters' hats, or a railroad and village accessories added to the unit blocks provide the potential for considerable flexibility and experience in play. Super units usually accommodate several children in either associative or cooperative play and are often the context for sociodramatic play opportunities.

UNITS OF PLAY	
SIMPLE UNIT	play unit that has one obvious use and does not usually have subparts—e.g., a ball, a doll, a telephone, a ball of clay. (1 play space each)
COMPLEX UNIT	play unit with subparts or a juxtaposition of two essentially different play materials that enable the child to manipulate or improvise—e.g., sand table with shovels and scoops; puppet theatre with puppets, doll house and furniture; single set of unit blocks. (4 play spaces each)
SUPER UNIT	complex unit having one or more additional play materials; i.e., two or more play units juxtaposed—e.g., climber with hollow blocks and blankets; supermarket with cash register, food containers, boxes, grocery bags, and counter space. (8 play spaces each)

■ VARIETY AND COMPLEXITY OF PLAY SPACE

Play units may be classified according to their variety and complexity. **Variety** is the potential of the play unit to accommodate different kinds of play activity such as digging, pouring, building, stacking, and twirling.

Variety also relates to the number of different kinds of play units in the classroom or playground that invite different kinds of activity. It is a measure of the capacity of the space to promote children's interest and involvement. When children are expected to play for long periods in an area and to make their own choices about what to play with, variety becomes an important factor in planning. A disproportionately large amount of one kind of play unit limits children's choices and reduces interest and participation. Teachers can evaluate the variety dimension of the environment by counting the kinds of play activity possible for each play unit and classifying the kinds of play activity available throughout the classroom.

Example:

A playground for preschoolers has twelve tricycles, a rocking boat, a tumble tub, a jungle gym with boxes and boards, a dirt area with scooper trucks, and a sand table with shovels. The teacher's task is to assess the variety present in the playground.

> **Analysis of variety:**   vehicles—riding, balancing, pedalling
> rocking boat—rocking, climbing, pretending
> jungle gym with boxes and boards—climbing, stacking, hauling, building
> dirt area with scooper trucks—digging, pushing, loading, scooping, emptying,
>   pretending
> sand table with shovels—digging, scooping, pouring, comparing, mixing

Variety present in the playground includes: riding, balancing, pedalling, rocking, climbing, pretending, stacking, hauling, building, digging, pushing, loading, scooping, emptying, pouring, comparing, and mixing. This would appear to be a sufficient number of kinds of things to do for twelve children. Whether there is sufficient variety will also depend on how long the children will be using the playground. Greater variety is required when children are expected to play in an area for a long period.

Complexity is the extent to which play units contain potential for active manipulation and alteration by children. It measures the capacity of the play environment to keep children interested for reasonable periods of time. It is calculated by determining the potential of each play unit for active manipulation by children. The addition of accessories or subparts to play units and combinations of play units produces greater complexity. Kritchevsky and Prescott have provided useful definitions and formulas for calculating the complexity of a learning environment, and these are outlined in the following section.

Measurements of the degree of complexity and variety in an environment are indicators of the extent to which children will find the environment interesting and involving. Sufficient complexity encourages children to make meaningful choices and to be continuously involved in the setting. Variety permits children to try a number of different kinds of activity, with the result that these activities hold their interest longer and expose them to the learning of a wider range of skills.

To summarize, well-organized space depends on sufficient complexity, variety, clear pathways, enough empty space and potential space, and accessibility of equipment, materials, and supplies. In space planning, it is important to identify the program goals and check all aspects of space against the goals to be achieved within that space. Play space evaluation should be carried out frequently to ensure that the close relationship between program goals and environmental design remains stable. (See Appendix A: A Learning Environment Audit, pages 81–84.)

■ CALCULATING COMPLEXITY IN THE LEARNING ENVIRONMENT

When preschool children are expected to play for more than twenty minutes in a playroom, a high degree of complexity adds to the amount of choice available to them and makes the environment more interesting. The degree of complexity will normally decrease for older children and increase for younger children. Older children tend to have more mature attending skills such as longer attention spans and greater abilities to concentrate. If an area is not sufficiently complex, teachers will often have to compensate, through their own active participation or intervention, for the failure of the space to provide sufficient play opportunities.

Kritchevsky and Prescott offer some approximate guidelines for determining the degree of complexity that is generally appropriate for various age groupings. According to them, groups of toddlers (up to thirty months of age) in an environment for twenty minutes or longer may require five or six play spaces per child. Three- and four-year-olds require approximately three to four play spaces each, while five- and six-year-olds require two to three play spaces per child.

RECOMMENDED NUMBER OF PLAY SPACES

18- to 30-month-olds	5–6 play spaces
3- and 4-year-olds	3–4 play spaces
5- and 6-year-olds	2–3 play spaces

The first step in calculating the complexity of a learning environment is to identify the play units in the playroom or playground as either simple, complex, or super units. Each unit is then assigned either one, four, or eight play spaces depending on whether it is a simple, complex or super unit. The number of play spaces are added up, and the total is then divided by the number of children in the play environment. The quotient indicates the *amount to do per child*, which is the measure of complexity of the play space.

Example:

A learning environment for eighteen 3-year-olds playing for one hour contains the following play units arranged in five learning centres:

- a one-metre-square water table with jugs and plastic bottles (1 complex = 4 play spaces)
- string painting at a round table for four (4 simple = 4 play spaces)
- 4 single-sided easels (4 simple = 4 play spaces)
- a small listening centre with 2 headsets (1 simple = 2 play spaces)
- a climber with slide, firefighter's pole, and helmets (1 super unit = 8 play spaces)
- a table and 4 chairs with a tea set (1 complex unit = 4 play spaces)
- one set of unit blocks with wooden accessories (1 complex unit = 4 play spaces)
- four hoops (4 simple = 4 play spaces)
- a bean bag target toss with four bean bags (1 complex = 4 play spaces)

CALCULATING COMPLEXITY

simple unit = 1 play space
complex unit = 4 play spaces
super unit = 8 play spaces

1. Identify play units as simple/complex/super.
2. Assign number of play spaces to each play unit.
3. Calculate total number of play spaces in the play and learning environment.
4. Divide the total number of play spaces by the number of children in the environment.
5. The quotient is the indicator of complexity.
6. Check the indicator of complexity against the recommended number of play spaces per child.

Calculation of Complexity

Calculate the number of play spaces by adding the bracketed amounts together:

4 + 4 + 4 + 2 + 8 + 4 + 4 + 4 + 4 = 38 play spaces.

To determine the complexity of the learning environment, divide the total number of play spaces (38) by the number of children who will be playing in the area at one time (18). The quotient, 2.1, provides the number of play spaces available per child. This is the measure of complexity.

Does 2.1 play spaces per child in this play environment represent sufficient complexity? The guidelines suggest that three-year-olds require between three and four play spaces per child. Therefore, one might conclude that there is insufficient complexity in this learning environment and additional play units will have to be added.

This kind of scenario is often seen in real-world learning environments. Frequently, the causes of aggressive or restless behaviour, or mindless flitting about can be traced to insufficient complexity in a learning environment. When the cause is discovered, teachers have to determine what other units of play to add and where to locate them, keeping in mind the need to adhere to guidelines with respect to pathways, amount of covered versus uncovered space, and so on.

Readers may have already noted that the guidelines with respect to the application of numbers of play spaces to units of play cannot always be taken too literally. They are intended as guidelines only. For example, a climber with ramps and hollow blocks may be located in a space large enough to accommodate only four or six children. A table with a doll house, furniture, and small dolls may be large enough to accommodate only three children. Using good judgement and the guidelines, teachers will be able to come up with an approximate indication of the degree of complexity in the environment. When there is too much or too little complexity, they will be able to make appropriate amendments by following the Kritchevsky and Prescott formulas.

■ SUMMARY OF PRINCIPLES FOR THE DESIGN OF A LEARNING ENVIRONMENT

- Children learn through play outdoors and indoors; therefore, planning the environment involves the careful and selective design and organization of indoor and outdoor space.
- The learning environment provides sufficient space for children to move freely from one learning centre to another and to play without obstructing the play of other children.
- A range of equipment, materials, and supplies that may be used in flexible ways is accessible to children.
- Children are offered real choices of activities in learning centres where program planning emphasizes specific developmental objectives.
- The learning environment gives messages to children that are consistent with the teacher's verbal messages. These messages imply respect for the privacy of a child who chooses to find a spot to be alone for a while and respect for physical boundaries around play stations that promote specific kinds of play.
- Flexible boundaries and use of space which can be altered to suit changing needs and priorities ensure that learning centres and activities will change as children progress.

References

Kritchevsky, S., Prescott, E., and L. Walling (1977). *Planning Environments for Young Children: Physical Space.* 2d ed. Washington, D.C.: National Association for the Education of Young Children.

Nash, C. (1989). *The Learning Environment: A Practical Approach to the Education of the Three-, Four- and Five-Year-Old.* Toronto: Collier-Macmillan.

Piaget, J. (1969). *Science of Education and the Psychology of the Child.* New York: Viking.

A LEARNING ENVIRONMENT AUDIT

1. Pathways

- clear at points of entry?
- visible from child's eye view?
- well-defined from end to end and unobstructed?
- learning centres separate from each other?
- reach all learning centres?
- lead children into and out of learning centres?

2. Use of Space

- how much surface is covered?
  more than 2/3? (tightly organized space)
  less than 1/2? (loosely organized space)
- is there any dead space (large amount of empty space roughly square or circular in shape without any visible or tangible boundaries)?
- is there enough space around each play unit?
- is there space for a potential unit (empty space surrounded by visible or tangible boundaries)?

3. Contents of Play Space

Variety

- how many kinds of things are there to do in the learning environment?
- is there a disproportionate amount of any one kind of thing to do?
- does the variety of the play units address the interests and developmental needs of all children individually?

Complexity

- identify the number of:
  simple units (x 1) =
  complex units (x 4) =
  super units (x 8) =
- calculate the total number of play spaces (add totals above)
- identify the number of children usually playing in the learning environment
- calculate the complexity of the play and learning environment (i.e., divide total number of play spaces by the number of children

playing in the learning environment)

complexity = amount to do per child

- is the proportion of things to do per child within the ranges deemed acceptable for the age group (i.e., 1–2 years = 5–6 play spaces 3–4 years = 3–4 play spaces; 5–6 years = 2–3 play spaces)?
- is there a need for:
  more simple units?
  more complex units?
  more super units?
- is there a need to combine units? list the play units which can be added to each learning centre to raise total number of play spaces:
  daily living
  active role play
  quiet thinking
  science discovery
  technology
  unit blocks
  creative arts
- total number of additional play units?
  calculate revised complexity using formulas:

total number of play spaces divided by number of children normally playing in a learning environment equals the complexity or amount to do per child

4. Noise

- can noisy and quiet activities take place without disruption?
- is space organized into quiet zones for play and noisy zones for play?

5. Orderliness

- is space organized so that tidy areas and messy areas for play are separate?
- is the learning environment simple and easy to maintain?
- does the environment convey a sense of order/organization?
- are storage units located close to learning centres where supplies and materials will be used?
- are materials/supplies accessible to children?
- do storage units and general organization of space convey the message to children that materials and supplies should be returned to their own places ready for use by another child?
- does the environment provide cues as to where materials and supplies should be used (e.g., wet or messy materials stored near tiled floor)?

6. Aesthetic Appeal and Comfort

- does the environment contain a variety of contours, textures, and natural as well as manufactured materials?
- is the environment attractive at the child's eye level?
- is children's artwork neatly displayed on special bulletin boards at children's eye levels?
- is carpeting used judiciously to soften noise, vary textures, and promote play on the floor?

- are colours used to decorate space?
- are the colours pleasing to the eye?
- is the area conducive to a relaxed and warm climate for play and learning?
- is it suitable for children?
- does the space include:
  multicultural pictures and artifacts?
  familiar reminders of children's home environments?
- is the environment:
  clean?
  easy to maintain?

7. Play and Learning Climate

- does the environment encourage industry and make it seem important to be involved and participate?
- does the environment discourage "flitting about" and mindless roaming?
- do the pathways lead to choices of play activities?
- is there a balance of areas for individual and group-oriented play?
- do the learning centres have an identity of their own (i.e., are they defined by dividers or storage units)?
- can children and adults see from one area to another in the playroom, yet still have some privacy?
- is there a balance of clearly indicated space/play areas for active and quieter play?

- are there sufficient work spaces (i.e., tables and chairs) for children to play comfortably either individually or with others?
- do the learning centres succeed in organizing equipment, materials, and supplies so that children understand what is expected of them in each learning centre?
- is the physical environment sufficiently organized and under control so that teachers can maximize the amount of time they have to observe children and facilitate play and learning (i.e., the closer the number of play spaces to the number of children playing, the greater the demands on the teacher to intervene and direct children's play)?
- does the learning centre provide opportunities for children to make real choices among activities?
  daily living?
  active role play?
  science discovery?
  quiet thinking?
  creative arts?
  technology?
  unit blocks?

8. Other Factors

- too much sun?
- too little natural light?
- broken or shabby equipment?
- broken or shabby materials?
- broken or shabby supplies?
- appropriate equipment size for children?

- temperature comfortable for children at play?
- easy access to washroom?
- easy access to outdoor play?
- non-toxic plants used to decorate and soften the environment?

- all learning centres visible to teachers from all areas of the learning environment?

C H A P T E R 6

FRAMEWORK FOR PLANNING LEARNING CENTRES

The organization of space in the learning environment builds upon the basic premises of a developmental approach to early childhood education. A theoretical framework helps teachers plan the environment: it provides direction, restricts the number of options available, and guides teachers towards philosophically consistent choices. Five steps in planning and designing the learning environment may be considered.

■ STEPS IN PLANNING

1. Determine Developmental Goals and Objectives

The statement of a set of *developmental goals* for children, based on the normal tasks of development of the early years is a first step. These goals become the goals of the curriculum and encompass all developmental domains—physical, social, emotional, and cognitive. Goals may be expressed as long-term aims for children such as: learn self-help skills, master basic fundamental movements, acquire a realistic concept of self, develop a sense of self-worth, develop friendship skills, develop age-appropriate language abilities, understand basic logical concepts. A statement of goals usually reflects a selected set of aims related to the commonly understood developmental tasks of each stage.

Objectives or short-term aims, are derived from goals. They are sometimes expressed as discrete skills that help children make step-by-step progress towards the attainment of the goals. Chapter 7 addresses activity planning according to developmental goals and objectives in detail. (See Table 7.1 on page 115 for examples of the relationships between goals and objectives.) When developmental objectives are clearly understood, it is easier to identify the actual behaviours within activities that will signify mastery of the objectives, such as locomotor skills: hopping three steps in a forward direction; classification skills: sorting beads according to colour/shape; visual discrimination: finding the mouse on the page, and so on. The objectives are the pivotal criteria upon which activity planning is based.

Teachers select the specific developmental goals and objectives to be addressed by children in play through their regular observations and assessments of children's developmental progress. The teacher's choice of a specific set of goals and objectives influences the design of the environment and the use of space.

2. Know Principles of Learning and Children's Learning Styles

An understanding of how young children learn should influence the planning and design of the play and learning environment. The box on pages 88–89 outlines some principles of learning based on the values, practices, and standards of the cognitive-developmental stream. Readers may refer back to Chapter 3 (pages 45–47) for a review of the philosophical basis for the principles of learning. Some discussion of learning styles may also add meaning to the principles of learning.

Learning style refers to each child's individual preference for learning in a certain way that is consistent with his developmental levels in each domain, his interest, and his approach to the environment and situations in it. An individual child may also employ different learning styles in different play situations. There is wide variation in the learning styles preferred by individual children (Gardner, 1989).

Gardner's *Frames of Mind* (1983) built upon Piaget's theoretical foundation and rejected the notion of unitary or general intelligence that had prevailed since the 1920s. The book describes seven independent intelligences, each with its own set of specific devices and each one responding to different challenges and tasks.

Gardner proposes that individuals have different blends of intelligences and different levels of intelligence in each area. These wide differences should be accounted for in play and learning environments, since the central task of early childhood education is to find out what "crystallizes" each child's learning. We can find out where children's aptitudes, interests, and particular talents lie by exposing them to a wide range of learning opportunities that address all of the intelligences and different styles of learning (Gardner, 1989). Later on, when children enter elementary school, programs and curriculum should guide them to courses, activities, and learning methods for which they have demonstrated special aptitudes.

Gardner's seven intelligences are linguistic, logical-mathematical, musical, spatial, bodily-kinesthetic, interpersonal, and intrapersonal. Each intelligence implies a different learning style and aptitude for learning some things more easily than others. Children differ from each other in their dominant learning styles, but each child also employs different learning styles, depending on the nature of the task in which she is engaged. Self-directed learning respects children's individual learning styles. Children will generally ask for direction, assistance, and leadership when they need it.

Gardner believes that early childhood educators should be "laid back" within a structured physical environment and "cue in" to the child's interests, aptitudes, and learning styles. When materials and tasks are clear and varied, children can be free to pursue them in an open, easy-going atmosphere in which the teacher is a resource person and facilitator. Teachers have to be able to match materials and children wisely and be ready to switch materials when children are not making progress with them. When activities and materials are clear, whether or not they are open-ended or specific-purpose, it is easier for teachers to assess children reliably and guide them profitably.

Some children are visual learners and need to be able to see a concept demonstrated before they are able to understand. Others learn better from auditory stimuli in which listening, interpreting, and acting upon auditory messages comes easiest. Tactile learners have to touch, feel, and interact physically with things in order to form concepts that endure. These children like to test, experiment, and manipulate materials in all manner of ways.

Some children are inclined to be observers and are relatively passive in their learning. Many children enjoy learning in social contexts by imitating, interacting, and collaborating with others. Others are solitary learners who prefer to work and play alone, pursuing their own objectives and interests, and arriving at their own understandings at their own pace. There are children who learn easily in a quiet, orderly environment where activity and noise are kept to a minimum and they are able to remain at a task for long periods of time, while others need plenty of activity, room to move, frequent breaks, and many opportunities to change from one activity to another. Activity planning for each learning centre should account for a wide variety of learning styles and aptitudes.

As children learn at their own rates, the speed with which they progress developmentally varies from child to child and within each child, depending on the nature of the learning experience. Learning occurs most readily when the new learning to be acquired contains elements of something that is already familiar to the child, in other words, when the distance between what is already known and the new learning to be achieved is optimal. Piaget describes the optimal discrepancy that should be present in any new learning experience for children. Optimal discrepancy means that the distance between what the child knows already and the new learning that has to occur on a specific task or problem should be optimal or "just right." Too little discrepancy between what is known already and what needs to be learned will fail to challenge or motivate the child. Too much discrepancy may frustrate the child and discourage learning.

Understanding involves internal change; change occurs more readily when children are able to experience for themselves. The best way for children to come to know and understand their world is to explore, experiment, and discover for themselves through their hands-on interaction with concrete objects in the environment. Teachers have to be aware of the teaching methods that accommodate children's typical learning styles and design the environment accordingly. Once a learning environment has been set up, the teacher can then support children's self-directed learning. This approach requires faith in children's abilities to make developmental progress in a well-designed environment.

PRINCIPLES OF LEARNING FOR YOUNG CHILDREN

1. Children are physical beings; their learning occurs largely through the senses. Therefore, they require plenty of opportunities for sensory involvement with their environment.
2. Children learn best when they can explore and experiment in an environment that allows freedom of movement, freedom of choice among real alternatives, and freedom to pursue an activity at their own pace, at their own level of developmental readiness, and according to their own learning styles (see section on learning styles, pages 86–88).
3. Children learn best by doing, in other words, through their active interaction with concrete objects in the environment.
4. Learning is most effective when children are interested in what they are learning and are able to choose and pursue activities in their own way.
5. Children are free to learn in an environment where they feel psychologically safe, where they are able to take risks, make mistakes, and receive encouragement for their efforts.
6. Preoperational children learn best in informal educational settings—those in which children engage in active, hands-on, experiential, and process-oriented learning using concrete objects. Informal learning is different from formal learning which focuses on the outcomes of learning and uses formal learning tools such as textbooks and worksheets and that emphasize the acquisition of knowledge. Formal learning is more appropriate to the operational child from age seven and up.
7. When the concept or the skill to be learned or mastered is inherent in the play materials themselves, children have an opportunity to uncover and discover the concept on their own. When children's learning occurs in a context that is meaningful to them and that they have discovered for themselves, it will generally be remembered and understood. The following old saying is still relevant:

What I hear, I forget,

What I see, I remember,

What I do, I understand.

8. Early learning experiences are most effective when they take children from simple to more complex levels of knowledge, skill, and understanding, from the concrete to the more abstract, and from the general to the specific.

9. Learning is most effective when play experiences build on what children already know and take them one step further. The new learning task should be just far enough from what the child knows already to be challenging and not so far as to discourage and frustrate. Activities should begin where the child is developmentally and be sequenced step by step in bite-sized chunks.

10. Children have consolidated what they have learned and have built new mental structures when they are able to transfer the learning gained in one context to another context. Piaget claimed that there are two kinds of learning. One kind refers to the acquisition of new responses within specific contexts. This shows that the child has learned the skills appropriate to that context but has not generalized the concept or skill to another context. The second kind of learning occurs when the child has acquired new mental structures that allow the child to transfer the learning gained in one setting to another learning challenge in another setting. Piaget believed that the latter type of learning is the only durable kind (Piaget, 1969).

3. Plan the Use of Resources

The selection of equipment, materials, and supplies (i.e., the resources for play) is another factor that influences the design of the environment. The play equipment, materials, and supplies are both the tools of an early childhood educator's trade and the media that help children learn through their senses. It is easier to select equipment, materials, and supplies when teachers know the developmental objectives their children are ready to address. The choice of resources also influences the organization of the learning environment and determines to a great extent how space will be used. It is important, therefore, to have a thorough knowledge of the various types of play materials and equipment available and to use them effectively within the environment. Chapter 8 describes the various types of equipment, materials, and supplies, and offers criteria for their selection.

Choosing resources involves the following skills:

■ being aware of the varieties of play materials available

■ understanding the range of their play potential

■ being able to link resources to the practice and mastery of specific developmental abilities

■ being aware of the versatility present within flexible learning materials

■ knowing where to locate materials in the play and learning environment in order to maximize their learning potential

■ understanding the material's position in a continuum that ranges from the very simple to the more complex

■ being able to juxtapose play materials and equipment to promote the transfer of skills learned with one material to other similar or complementary materials

These skills involve a unique blend of understanding and professionalism on the part of the well-trained teacher that is generally not possessed by untrained staff.

4. Design and Set up Learning Centres

A rational approach to the design of a learning environment may be based on the relationship between the typical learning centres and the developmental goals and objectives each learning centre intends to address. Principles to assist in the designing and setting up of learning centres are addressed later in this chapter.

5. Evaluate the Learning Environment

Evaluation of the learning environment may be based on children's participation levels and the rate of developmental progress within the classroom. Evaluation data provide the basis upon which environments may be altered and redesigned.

Learning environments are generally evaluated according to a range of criteria such as:

■ Are children able to choose and initiate their own learning?

■ Does the environment provide a variety of developmentally appropriate play opportunities?

■ Does the environment change according to the needs, abilities, and interests of the children?

■ Do teachers function as facilitators of children's learning or do they have to intervene frequently and lead most activities?

All of the above features will influence the use of physical space and the design of the environment. Which learning centres should be represented within available space; how much space should be allocated to each learning centre; the positioning of learning centres; the location of storage units and dividers; the selection of equipment, materials, and supplies for each learning centre; how many children can be accommodated within each learning centre; where pathways and potential space will be created; and many other space-related decisions will be influenced by the planning framework. A Learning Environment Audit (on pages 81–84) addresses several evaluation factors relating to the design of the physical environment. Activities checklists, which are discussed in Chapter 7, focus on evaluating children's levels of participation and mastery of the objectives of self-directed learning experiences.

■ THE FUNCTION OF LEARNING CENTRES

A **learning centre** is *a clearly defined area in the learning environment that houses equipment, materials, and supplies that complement one another and promote children's mastery of related developmental objectives.* Learning centres usually have tangible boundaries, promote a consistent climate, and focus on play and learning that is related to a particular developmental domain.

There are many approaches to organizing space and planning learning centres. A suggested plan for the location and design of learning centres based on a developmental rationale, is outlined below, starting with a description of play zones. It is not the only developmental rationale that may be adopted, but it does represent an attempt to combine developmental theory, principles of learning, practical considerations, and a healthy slice of common sense.

The learning centre approach "provides an intentional strategy for the active involvement of children, experience-based learning and individualization in relation to children's developmental abilities, interests and learning styles" (Myers & Maurer, 1987:21). Well-organized and well-defined learning centres provide messages to children about the kinds of behaviour, activity, and level of involvement expected of them (Houle, 1987; Nash, 1989; Ministry of Education, Ontario, 1991; N.A.E.Y.C, 1991). A well-designed classroom frees the teacher to be a facilitator of play and learning rather than a supervisor and monitor.

A variety of activities are set up in each of the learning centres. Motivation to choose from this variety is enhanced when teachers include children in the planning of activities for learning centres by giving them opportunities to express their interests and make suggestions about what they would like to do and learn.

The successful implementation of the learning centre approach also depends on training children in those behaviours that will promote the profitable and enjoyable

LEARNING CENTRE

use of learning centres (Wortham, 1984). The teacher has to decide how to schedule routines, what rules to establish for appropriate behaviour in learning centres, and how many learning centres to introduce or to change at one time. The behaviour limits then have to be communicated clearly to the children and reminders given frequently thereafter. As with all planning strategies, it is best to keep a list of the training procedures for children that have been completed.

There are many factors to consider when setting up a play and learning environment that follows the learning centre approach, including

- How many learning centres are needed and how much space is available for each centre?
- Should learning centres be a permanent fixture in the learning environment?
- What is the primary rationale to be followed in creating learning centres?
- Are a balance of developmental goals (e.g., cognitive, physical/sensory, social-emotional and creative/expressive goals) addressed by the learning centres?
- How many children can each learning centre accommodate at any given time?
- Do learning centres allow for flexible use of space?

■ PLAY ZONES IN THE LEARNING ENVIRONMENT

Before organizing and locating learning centres, play zones should be established in the learning environment. Each play zone is designed to accommodate particular types and social contexts of play. Organizing the environment according to zones that accommodate complementary learning centres promotes the transfer of learning from one centre to another.

When children are able to transfer the learning gaine
context, teachers can be reasonably sure that real lear
1969). For example, children who explore concepts of m
table may decide to test similar concepts at the sand table.
based on puzzles and stacking toys, that are related to comp.
measurement may also be set up at a table in a quiet play area. In
microcomputers, a software package related to size and measuremen.
to reinforce the concepts practised and learned in the context of play w.
objects. Transfer of the learning gained in one learning centre to another i
the learning gained and gives messages to children that there are usually ma.
ferent ways to know and understand the same concept and solve similar proble.

Zones provide cues to children about the kind of play that is expected in tha
part of the classroom. Zones also help teachers organize equipment, storage units,
and play materials for maximum efficiency close to where they will be used.

There are many ways of organizing a learning environment into play zones.
Zones may be defined according to the major type of play encouraged and the particular domain of development they address. Three potential play zones are: the
role play zone, the concept learning zone, and the creative discovery zone. (See
Figure 6.1).

Figure 6.1   PLAY ZONES IN THE PLAY AND LEARNING ENVIRONMENT

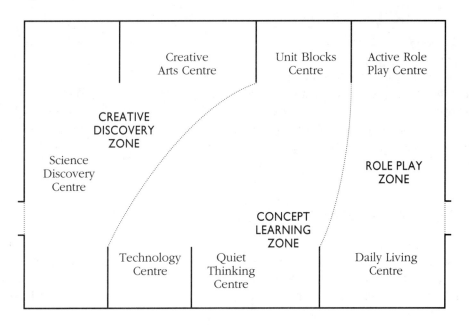

Role Play Zone

ne role play zone may also be called the social or interactive zone, since this is where children are encouraged to engage in symbolic thinking using props for pretend, dramatic, and sociodramatic play. This zone is the most physically active area in the playroom. The two learning centres that make up this zone are the Daily Living Centre and the Active Role Play Centre where social interaction predominates. In these centres, children are often interdependent in their play as they rehearse roles observed in their everyday lives by representing actions and creating a script familiar to them.

ROLE PLAY ZONE

Concept Learning Zone

There are times when young children like to play alone and there are many reasons for encouraging them to do so for part of each day. Although most programs value children's social play and emphasize socialization, children also need to learn to play individually and engage in worthwhile solitary pursuits. It is important that children experience the satisfaction of single-handed achievement that can only be fully realized when they tackle activities and challenges on their own. The play and learning environment should dedicate space where children can play and work individually with specific purpose materials intended to help them learn concepts, symbols, and can practise fine motor, manipulative, and perceptual skills. When a child experiments alone with modular materials, she is challenged to develop her own ideas and to figure out how to realize her own plans.

In the Quiet Thinking Centre, children learn through manipulation of two- and three-dimensional concrete materials. For these materials, the concepts or skills to be learned are embedded in the materials themselves. Formboard puzzles, classification and seriation kits, and a host of modular construction materials, like Lego, are meant for individual table-top play.

A Technology Centre may be located beside the Quiet Thinking Centre in this play zone to promote the transfer of the skills learned and concepts practised with the concrete materials. In the Technology Centre, children are able to transfer the conceptual and perceptual learning gained with concrete materials to the computer screen through the use of a variety of software programs that provide similar challenges.

Although children may go to the concept learning zone to play alone or with others and master objectives individually or together, it is understood that play in this zone should be quiet and that greater attention to the task is required. Children practise and master concepts in all learning centres, but the concept learning zone promotes the development of work-study skills, thinking, problem-solving and attending skills that will last a lifetime.

CONCEPT LEARNING ZONE

Creative Discovery Zone

Children need ample opportunity to express themselves with a variety of open-ended media such as paint, paper, clay, wood, cardboard boxes, and a needle and thread. The creative discovery zone provides these media and is also an area for experimentation and exploration of naturally occurring objects and phenomena. This zone promotes the discovery of concepts related to the natural transformations of materials that are common to our surroundings such as water and sand. Children solve problems in this zone by trying to find a number of alternatives to a problem or by trying a new strategy when the first one has not worked. The play materials and supplies associated with the Creative Arts Centre, which is located in this zone, are largely open-ended and abstract. Children are encouraged to originate their own plan with the media provided, devise a strategy for achieving their plan or idea, follow through and try alternatives when necessary, represent their own ideas, and report on what they have achieved.

The Science Discovery Centre, also located in this zone, is an area where children observe, manipulate, explore, and experience an array of naturally occurring objects that are part of their everyday world. An area dedicated to science reinforces the importance of the natural world and its phenomena. *Young children engage in scientific discovery indoors, outdoors, and in all learning centres, but the dedication of one centre to "sciencing" ensures that planned and spontaneous science learning opportunities are available to children every day.*

The Unit Blocks Centre belongs in this zone also, as unit blocks are open-ended, creative materials that promote children's symbolic thinking and representational skills. Placing the Unit Blocks Centre with the Creative Arts and Science Discovery Centres facilitates transfer of the creative ideas and problem-solving skills used with visual arts media and science discovery to play with blocks.

■ HELPING CHILDREN USE LEARNING CENTRES

The learning centre is the basic unit of classroom organization (Campbell, 1984). Its main purpose is to organize the space, equipment, materials, and supplies so that children receive clear messages about what is available for them and what kinds of play are possible in the learning centre.

Learning and development, however, are never so neatly organized. What children learn and how they develop is not usually determined by boundaries and divisions of space and resources. The clear definition of learning centres does, however, help teachers and children maximize the space available and ensures that the environment provides for a wide spectrum of play and learning opportunities.

Learning centres are not a new idea. Pestalozzi, Dewey, Montessori, Froebel, Patty Smith Hill, Caroline Pratt, and many other early pioneers in this field emphasized the importance of learning through play and hands-on experience with concrete materials. Myers and Mauer (1987:21) call the learning centre approach a "responsive environment" because the activities are planned to meet the individual developmental and experiential needs of the children in the program. Learning centres also build on teachers' previous experiences, training, and educational values.

Teachers influence the types of play that will likely occur by setting up materials, activities, and organizing storage shelves in order to provide messages about what children are to do and learn in that centre. Children should be able to choose the learning centre and play station within it where they want to play. Some teachers conduct a planning circle soon after children have arrived in the morning, at which time they tell them what is available in the learning centres that day and let them select where they want to go. Others prefer to put up planning boards with picture cards for the various play stations, which children can carry with them and deposit in a rack near the play station.

In each learning centre, teachers will set up two or three learning experiences, laying out the materials and/or supplies needed. Children decide which activities they will play with and how they will play. Children determine what the outcomes of their play will be, even when the learning materials are set up for them. The learning centre is an organized and complex juxtaposition of complementary and integrated resources for play designed to move children further in their development.

■ LEARNING CENTRES AND CHILD DEVELOPMENT

Learning centres address a comprehensive range of developmental objectives in all domains—social, emotional, physical, and cognitive. In this way, teachers can be sure that the environment is organized to help children make progress in all domains. In each program, the organization of learning centres will reflect the particular needs of children in the group as determined by the teacher's observations and assessments. Therefore, early childhood classrooms will not all have the same learning centres, nor will the same proportion of total space be allocated to specific learning centres. The configuration and content will vary from program to program, depending on children's identified needs. The identification of developmental objectives for each child in a program through systematic observation, recording, and assessment techniques is not the subject of this textbook, but should be understood well by teachers.

Table 6.1 shows the link between developmental goals and learning centres as well as types of play, social contexts of play, and units of play. Criteria for the selection of appropriate learning materials for each centre are addressed in Chapter 8. Grouping equipment, materials, and activities developmentally promotes the learning potential of each unit of play by locating it near others with related learning objectives. A rational arrangement of this kind helps children see the relationships between ideas and activities, and between materials and learning opportunities (Nash, 1989).

Social-Emotional Development

Between the ages of two and six, certain developmental tasks have to be mastered in order to build a strong foundation for later optimal development and learning. Children are developing a sense of self through many forms of self-expression. They are learning to communicate and acquiring socially desirable ways of interacting and cooperating. They are attempting to gain emotional control and to feel a sense of self-worth that is based on their achievements.

In order to accomplish the wide range of affective tasks that challenge children in the early childhood period, they need opportunities to interact and conform to group requirements that are established by persons or events outside of themselves. Learning experiences that promote social-emotional development encourage children to express themselves using a variety of media and methods, and to interact, communicate, cooperate, care, wonder, and reflect. These abilities are practised in open-ended social and creative play activities related to the visual and manual arts, dramatic and sociodramatic play in indoor learning centres, and outdoors in the context of the natural world.

Physical Development

We know that children are primarily physical beings whose learning occurs largely through the senses and their active interaction with the concrete world. Physical development includes sensory and perceptual experience, motor skills, fitness, body awareness and bodily health, and physical abilities. All learning centres contribute to a range of physical skills. The Creative Arts Centre promotes sensory-perceptual and fine motor abilities; the Active Role Play Centre encourages motor development and physical abilities; the Daily Living Centre facilitates body awareness, spatial awareness, and motor skills. Outdoor play in all areas provides opportunities for freer bodily expression and mastery in all areas—sensory, muscular, coordination, perceptual awareness, and fitness.

Cognitive Development

Cognitive development in early childhood includes perceptual processing abilities, memory, attending abilities, logical reasoning, language, and communication, conceptual understanding, knowledge of everyday living skills, and the ability to problem solve. All learning centres provide opportunities for children to practise and master cognitive skills. The Quiet Thinking, Science Discovery, Unit Blocks, and Technology Centres are primarily dedicated to the development of cognitive skills.

T A B L E   6 . 1

LINKS BETWEEN DEVELOPMENT GOALS, LEARNING CENTRES, TYPES OF PLAY, SOCIAL CONTEXTS OF PLAY, AND PLAY UNITS

Developmental Goals	Learning Centres	Major Types of Play	Social Contexts of Play	Units of Play
SOCIAL-EMOTIONAL: pro-social skills social relations social perceptions expressing oneself early moral understanding	daily living active role play	practice play productive play pretend/dramatic play sociodramatic play	onlooking solitary parallel cooperative associative	housekeeping equipment, doll beds, table and chairs, dressup clothing/ props, musical instruments, hollow blocks, ramps, etc.
PHYSICAL: basic movements physical abilities physical-perceptual skills body awareness skilled movements	active role play outdoor active areas large muscle area vehicle trails open areas	symbolic play dramatic play sociodramatic play creative constructive play	solitary parallel cooperative	hollow blocks/ ramps/boards climber/play-house props musical instruments balance beam trampoline
COGNITIVE: memory basic concepts attending learning-to-learn sensory-perceptual problem-solving language logical thinking	quiet thinking technology science discovery unit blocks	practice play productive play creative-constructive play reproductive play some symbolic play	solitary parallel associative cooperative	books water/sand table activities activities at: discovery table exploring table theme table Workjobs puzzles modular materials other specific purpose materials unit blocks and accessories computer props

■ PRINCIPLES FOR THE LOCATION AND DESIGN OF LEARNING CENTRES

1. Juxtapose centres that address similar developmental goals and types of play

Each learning centre is designed to provide practice for children to master the developmental objectives inherent in learning experiences that lead to longer-term achievement of goals. Juxtaposing centres addressing similar kinds of learning experiences and objectives increases the likelihood that children will rely on the environment to provide messages about what is expected of them in each area of the classroom.

It is wise to place active, noisier centres close together. It also makes sense to place centres that promote social interaction in one area (role play zone), those that promote exploration of things and discovery of concepts in another area (creative discovery zone), and those that promote greater attention to the learning of concepts (concept learning zone) in another part of the playroom.

2. Separate clean and messy learning centres

Wet, messy play materials are best confined to tiled areas near a water source. The Creative Arts and Science Discovery Centres will likely be adjacent to one another for practical purposes as well as to facilitate transfer of learning. Carpeted areas provide warmth, soft surfaces to sit on, and sound absorption. They give messages to children that quieter, cleaner, more individual play will occur in these areas.

3. Dedicate more space to learning centres addressing developmental objectives that have priority

The size of the learning centres varies depending on the priority given to the developmental goals to be addressed there. Physical limitations such as amount of space available, size and amount of equipment and materials needed in the learning centre, location of pathways, and space for storage will also influence the size and configuration of learning centres. Portable storage units help to facilitate flexibility in room arrangement, alteration of the boundaries of a learning centre, or changes in programming priorities.

4. Locate portable storage units close to the learning centres

Enabling children to access their own materials frees teachers to facilitate learning and observe children's play rather than being "go-fors" (Houle, 1987). When children choose materials for themselves they are involved in basic decision making as they try to make viable matches between media and material to be used and the plan they want to pursue in their play. Along with this freedom to access their own materials goes the importance of teaching children how to take proper care of each learning centre and the materials within it. The location of easily accessible storage units in each centre facilitates children's active participation in tidy up, this is a learning activity that promotes cooperation, recall, motor capabilities, and attending skills.

5. Ensure learning centres are clearly visible from major pathways

Teachers should be able to see into the learning centres from most points in the room. Dividers between the centres will be high enough for children to feel "enclosed" in a centre but low enough for teachers to monitor play effectively without interfering or being overly intrusive. Houle (1987) recommends that the free-standing backdrop of a learning centre be four-feet high or less to enable teachers to see into all areas at all times. Free-standing dividers also provide maximum flexibility when teachers want to adjust the size or shape of a learning centre to incorporate new forms of play or more children.

6. Clarify limits and rules for each learning centre

Certain ground rules are necessary for each learning centre and should vary according to the nature of the play anticipated there. These rules can be kept to a minimum when the physical arrangement of the learning centres is consistent with the provision of materials, use of space, and presence of boundaries and other physical cues. Children will participate eagerly in the setting of reasonable ground rules and will help to maintain them when the physical environment, materials, teachers' messages, and activities provide consistent messages (Wortham, 1984).

7. Account for practical details

Certain practical factors should be taken into account. Unchangeable items such as electrical outlets, pathways, doors, windows, noise levels, built-in units, water sources, and cable outlets all influence classroom design. In the interests of conserving space, which is at a premium in most play and learning environments, furniture may be arranged so as to provide clearer pathways or to divide learning centres. Multipurpose furniture such as tables and chests of drawers can be used as play surfaces for children or for storage. An empty table or corner can be designated as potential space, as long as it is bounded by dividers, furniture, or storage units. Walls with bulletin boards at children's eye level may provide posters or photographs offering further clues about the kind of play encouraged in the centre. Messages about the care and maintenance of the learning environment's aesthetic quality are most effective when they come from the learning environment itself.

8. Vary textures and colours

Textures and colours can be used to extend the messages of the centre. A mixture of hard, soft, upholstered, painted, and natural textures in a classroom create a more homelike atmosphere and add variety that allows children to become familiar with the properties of various materials. Variations in texture stimulate the senses, which are an important accompaniment to learning. Hard, smooth surfaces can be easily cleaned and returned to their original state after use. Soft, knubby textures promote relaxation, and require greater care in use. Combining old and new textures integrates the modern, shiny materials of today with the warmth and character of worn products such as weathered wood, sand-blasted brick, and cork.

The selective use of colour can have a direct effect on our moods and feelings. Red, yellow, orange, and brown are generally considered to be warm colours and make a room appear smaller and cozier. Blues are cool and detached, and create feelings of space. They are usually thought to contribute to slow, deliberate behaviours. Greens are generally believed to be calming and easier to tolerate for longer periods of time. Balancing colours skilfully can create a harmonious setting that will suit any time of year and many variations of behaviour and activity.

9. Consider exposure of the learning environment to natural light

The combination of colour and light from both natural and artificial sources is another important factor to consider in the design of a classroom. The exposure of the room to sunlight, maximizing the amount of natural light a room will receive, especially during the dark winter months, is an essential factor in room design in northern climates. Classrooms with eastern exposures will be bright in the mornings but gloomy later in the day. Western exposures work the opposite way. Southern exposures usually retain the largest amount of natural light during the day.

In classrooms where the use of artificial light during the long days of limited natural light in winter is anticipated, choices about the kinds of artificial lighting to use can offset the disadvantages of the absence of natural light. Pod lighting recessed in the ceiling or reflected light in a cove ceiling using incandescent rather than fluorescent light sources are the most natural and easiest to tolerate for long hours.

10. Create a multicultural learning environment in all learning centres

The inclusion of ethnic and cultural artifacts and ornaments in the everyday decor of the classroom are more effective in addressing multicultural goals than any number of special activities honouring specific ethnic customs or occasions (Mock, 1984). Objects from other cultures, such as artwork, tools and utensils, fabric and clothing, lamps and jewellery, add unusual textures and colours that brighten up and add interest to the classroom.

In summary, the arrangement of the learning centres in the classroom will make the child the centre of the environment. It will open up new learning opportunities rather than close options for children. Effective planning of learning centres is the first step towards effective teaching and frees the teacher to be a facilitator of children's play and learning. A beautiful, comfortable setting with a place for everything and space to move freely will more likely be maintained that way. A crowded, haphazard environment offers little incentive and no precedent for children in their daily activities.

▪ DESIGNING THE LEARNING ENVIRONMENT

There are several useful aids to make the tasks involved in locating and designing learning centres easier for teachers.

1. Make templates of equipment furniture

Most equipment, furniture, and storage units for the early learning environment come in relatively standard sizes. A useful tool to facilitate classroom design is to make metric-sized cutouts representing the "footprint" for each major item of equipment, furniture, and storage in the classroom (see Figure 6.2). The scale to be used for these items should correspond with the metric scale used when drawing the classroom to scale. The playroom drawing (see Figure 6.3) indicates doorways, built-in units, windows, location of electrical outlets, water sources, air and heat vents, and any other unchangeable accessories such as telephone cables, intercoms, or television and computer cables.

Once the design plans of the room are known and a simple, to-scale drawing is made of the classroom or classrooms to be used, the next step is to trace the furniture, storage units, and equipment outlining the footprint each unit occupies on the floor. Then convert the size of the footprint for each item of equipment to the same metric scale used for the classroom drawing. Simple cardboard or Bristol board templates can be made and used to experiment with various approaches to the juxtaposed learning centres and the play units within them. They can also be used as templates to trace the location of units and centres on the classroom drawing once final decisions have been made.

Figure 6.2 PAPER TEMPLATES REPRESENTING THE FOOTPRINTS OF MAJOR ITEMS OF FURNITURE/EQUIPMENT IN LEARNING CENTRES

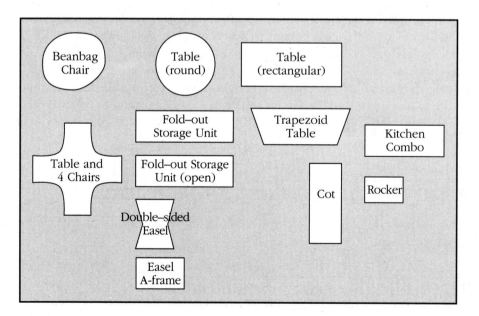

Figure 6.3   A PLAYROOM DIAGRAM

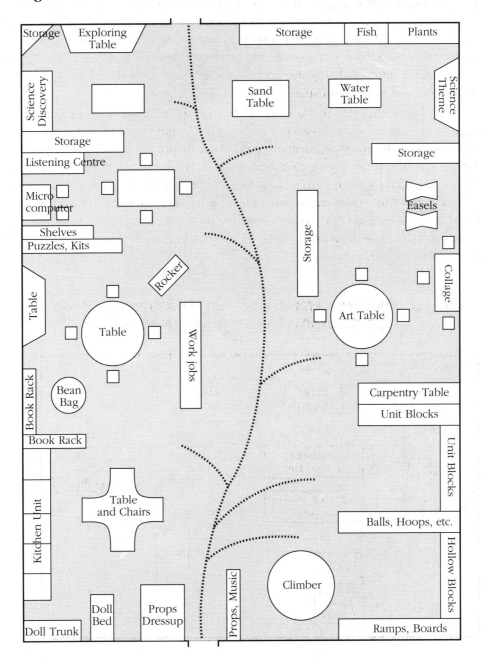

Figure 6.4 LEARNING CENTRES AND PATHWAYS

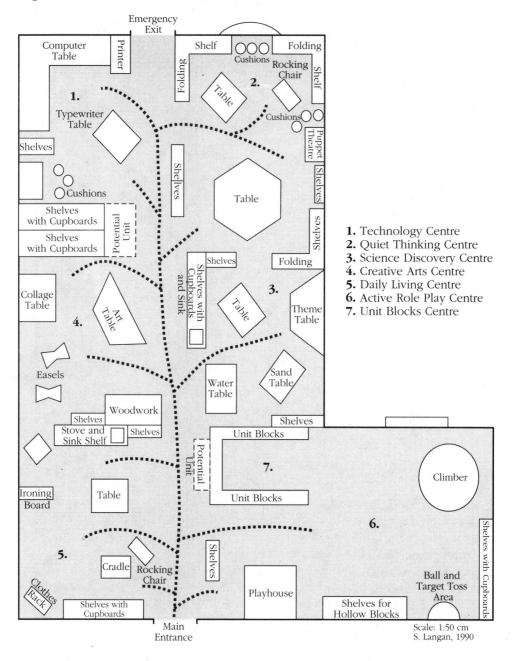

1. Technology Centre
2. Quiet Thinking Centre
3. Science Discovery Centre
4. Creative Arts Centre
5. Daily Living Centre
6. Active Role Play Centre
7. Unit Blocks Centre

Scale: 1:50 cm
S. Langan, 1990

2. Draw a plan—layout diagrams

Once decisions have been made about where to locate learning centres, teachers usually commit their final plans to paper using the templates to experiment with a variety of possible configurations and placements. The next step, once a suitable configuration has been found, is to trace the outlines of the major items of equipment, furniture, and storage units onto the layout diagram. Determining whether the pathways are clear and lead into and out of learning centres and whether there is sufficient play space around play units can be done on paper before physically shifting heavy furniture and equipment.

In programs that have two or more smaller rooms for the setting up of learning centres, rather than one large room for all major learning centres, decisions have to be made about how to group centres. In these cases, it is particularly important to locate complementary centres together in each of the rooms. Supervision of each of them and facilitation of learning are more complicated in these types of environments. When programs have to use more than one room, the active and more social centres are sometimes put in one room (i.e., the Active Role Play and Daily Living Centres together, and the Quiet Thinking, Technology, Science Discovery, and Creative Arts Centres in another room). There is no easy, cut-and-dried solution to this problem. Compromises must always be made and the outcomes are not always as one would wish.

The layout diagrams in Figures 6.3 and 6.4 represent a variety of constraints and configurations that teachers often meet in the real world. Committing one's environmental design decisions to paper provides opportunities for all teachers on a team to make suggestions and see the developmental rationale behind the plan. The clarity of pathways and the amount of empty space can also be examined and calculated to ensure that both comply with agreed-on principles.

■ SUMMARY

Well-planned indoor learning environments for young children provide a window on the world beyond and an invitation to discovery that will help them stretch, imagine, and grow. Children encounter a setting at their eye-level, challenging them to explore, test, and manipulate. Effective learning environments are comfortable, warm, attractive, bright, and full of promise. There is freedom to move, to choose from a wide range of alternatives, to meet and play with others, and to be alone. Teachers are integrated into the setting and cast a reassuring presence over the challenges present in the room. Children recognize many objects. They can see what they are expected to do in each area of the environment. It is easy to figure out how to get from one place to another and there is somewhere to go to at the end of each path. There are interesting smells, familiar and intriguing sounds, pleasing colours and displays, things to touch, and plenty of time to play.

References

Bredekamp, S. (1987). *Developmentally Appropriate Practice in Early Childhood Programs Serving Children From Birth to Age 8*. Washington, D.C.: National Association for the Education of Young Children.

Campbell, S. (1984). *Facilities and Equipment for Day Care*. Ottawa: Health and Welfare Canada.

Gardner, H. (1983) *Frames of Mind*. New York: Basic Books.

Gardner, H. (1989, October). The study of intelligences. Speech delivered to the Annual Conference of the Canadian Association for Young Children. Kingston, Ontario: Queen's University.

Houle, G.B. (1987). *Learning Centres for Young Children*. West Greenwich, RI: Tot-lot Child Care Products.

Ministry of Education, Ontario. (1991). *The Early Years*. A consultation paper. Toronto: Ministry of Education.

Mock, K. (1984). Multicultural education in early childhood: a developmental rationale. In *Multicultural Early Childhood Education*, ed. K. McLeod. Toronto: Guidance Centre, University of Toronto.

Myers, B.K., and Maurer, K. (1987). Teaching with less talking: learning enters in the kindergarten. *Young Children* 42 (4):21.

Nash, C. (1989). *The Learning Environment: A Practical Approach to the Education of the Three-, Four- and Five-Year-Old*. Toronto: Collier-Macmillan.

National Association for the Education of Young Children. (1991). Position Statement: Guidelines for Appropriate Curriculum Content and Assessment in Programs Serving Children Ages 3 Through 8. *Young Children* 46 (3):21–38.

Piaget, J. (1969). *The Psychology of the Child*. New York: Basic Books.

Piaget, J. (1970). *The Science of Education and the Psychology of the Child*. New York: Viking.

Piaget, J. (1972). *To Understand is to Invent*. New York: Grossman.

Wortham, S.C. (1984). *Organizing Instruction in Early Childhood*. Boston: Allyn & Bacon.

S E C T I O N 3

PLANNING LEARNING EXPERIENCES

Planning programs for play and learning should build on a sound understanding of children's development and learning styles. Children in the early years learn best through self-directed, hands-on learning experiences with materials that are developmentally appropriate. The teacher has to know what developmental objectives individual children are ready to practise and master, and plan activities accordingly. The teacher who sets up equipment, materials, and supplies to address specific developmental objectives is planning an activity, even though the activity may involve children's self-directed play and learning. Activities may also be planned to occur in groups with teachers leading the learning experience.

Choosing equipment, materials, and supplies that promote specific development is an important part of activity planning. Chapter 7 addresses activity planning and Chapter 8 deals with the selection of equipment, materials, and supplies.

Section 3 addresses the following topics:

- activity planning according to developmental objectives
- teaching and learning methods
- developmental sequencing
- types of play materials
- criteria for selecting play materials
- equipping learning centres
- using recycled materials
- storage of materials and supplies

C H A P T E R 7

ACTIVITY PLANNING

■ PLAY AND LEARNING ACTIVITIES

An **activity** is an event circumscribed by a time frame, a context, or a specific setting with materials that may be used flexibly (i.e., in self-directed play) or in more structured contexts with teachers directing the activities. Some teachers like to refer to children's play with materials that have been planned and set up by teachers as "learning experiences," rather than activities. The same description might apply to play that is spontaneous, with materials selected by children from shelves and used for their own purposes. It doesn't matter what words are used as long as teachers understand the importance of planning and arranging the learning environment systematically in order to encourage children's play with materials and supplies. Teachers have to set up the learning environment so that children are challenged to interact with the things and events in that environment that will promote knowing and understanding, social awareness, physical well-being, and emotional stability.

Activity planning should be systematic and regular, and follow a curriculum plan that ensures children will make steady developmental progress. Activity planning usually describes the ways in which children will most likely interact with materials and supplies, and practise tasks and skills. Planned activities may define specific, intended learning outcomes as do puzzle solving and matching shapes. Or, planned activities may encourage creative and open-ended play, as in painting a picture, making sandcastles, and creating cardboard sculptures.

Self-directed learning experiences, such as children's playing with scoops and pails in the sand, are planned activities even though they involve self-directed play. Activity planning assumes that teachers carefully select the types of materials they will set up at a play station and for what developmental reasons they will do so. It also implies that teachers are aware, when they set up materials, what their children will be learning from this experience. Teachers have to know that the children are developmentally ready to use the materials, and to practise and master new tasks and skills. Activities planned to promote predetermined objectives and to guide children towards specific learning outcomes permit teachers to observe systematically. They know what to look for and can anticipate what children will do with the materials.

Activities may be planned and led by teachers, and conducted in groups now and then. These learning experiences also involve play and promote developmental progress if they are well matched to the developmental abilities of the children. Unplanned activities describe those times when children select materials from learning centres in order to accomplish their own loosely defined objectives, which evolve as they proceed. Learning environments should allow for both planned and unplanned activities, as there is considerable enjoyment and learning to be derived from both kinds. It is important to add, however, that the early years pass quickly and there is much for children to experience and learn about their environment. *Purposeful planning of environments and activities from which children can choose according to their interests and readiness acknowledges the value of children's time and the importance of ensuring that they will make progress in all domains.*

Gazing at the clouds in the sky while lying on the grass in the playground may not constitute a planned activity if it occurs spontaneously and has no clear objectives. Passing time like this does, however, provide plenty of opportunity for relaxation and learning. Resourceful teachers capitalize on spontaneous events such as this in order to promote incidental learning, and to arouse curiosity and the imagination. They may ask children to follow the movement of clouds with their eyes, find the duck or the elephant shape among the cloud formations, focus on an airplane moving in and out of the clouds, or imagine what it would be like to be a bird flying through the clouds. Even such a simple, quiet activity as this provides practice in ocular-motor skills (pursuit and tracking), shape recognition, discrimination of embedded shapes, and imagining.

Children do not always have to be involved in activities that have clear objectives. Teachers need to respect and support children's wishes at times to just "be." Sensory experiences such as running a stick through a stream to watch the currents and ripples it makes contribute to the richness of childhood and provide precious moments of relaxation and surrender to the senses. There is a wealth of opportunity for development at times like these.

■ PURPOSEFUL PLANNING AND CHILD DEVELOPMENT

The early years lay the foundation for the development of skills, knowledge, and concepts that will be used later in formal learning settings. Days filled with mindless play that is repetitive and redundant, with materials that never change, in an environment that remains the same from fall through spring, waste children's precious time. Children are challenged to grow by a wide range of activities planned to address all domains (Bredekamp, 1987). They also need time for passive play and opportunities to find and follow their own pursuits. Developmentally appropriate programs are flexible and allow children to be uninvolved when they want to be.

PURPOSEFUL PLANNING FOR PLAY

Children need to encounter a wide range of play experiences and learning opportunities that meet their needs in order to develop optimally in all domains. Play that is always left to children's own devices and that uses a random assortment of materials will be too hit-and-miss, and largely physical and exploratory. It is a rare child who will persist in trying to solve a problem without encouragement and support. Children seldom explore and experiment in areas that are unknown, unfamiliar, or uncertain without assurances that they will be supported if they run into difficulties. The influence of home life is so dynamic that when activities are not purposefully planned, children are often content with play that is an extension of their home life in surroundings that are familiar and secure.

Early childhood education programs are obligated to ensure that children encounter a wide range of learning opportunities that will help them stretch and make progress. Children cannot be depended on to carve out an educational agenda for themselves that will take them down roads formerly untravelled or that require them to struggle now and then with alternatives and obstacles in order to solve a new problem or learn a new skill. Educators who are committed to seeing children make developmental progress in all domains do not neglect their activity planning responsibilities. Instead they consciously strive to plan activities that address a comprehensive range of physical, social, emotional, and cognitive objectives that children are ready to work on during the preoperational stage.

Effective planning of learning experiences is based on the following assumptions about the role of play in learning:

■ Play activities should be freely chosen by the child.
■ Flexible use of play materials and accessibility of resources promotes children's self-expression and ability to choose.

■ Children's play is important; therefore schedules and routines should support and extend the day's play and learning times.

■ The development of a "rich inner life" occurs during play in unstructured natural environments, often outdoors, where the child has the privacy and individual freedom to explore both physically and intellectually.

■ Children's learning through play depends largely on the quality and accessibility of a wide range of concrete objects in the environment that respond to the child's actions on them.

■ The dynamic role of play in development and learning means that teachers have to plan activities that address a wide range of developmental abilities in all domains, and encourage and interest children in engaging in as many of these learning opportunities as possible.

■ Children should be free to choose planned activities or not—they may prefer to select materials from shelves or bins that have not been set out and use them for their own purposes.

■ Planning activities to promote children's developmental progress and enjoyment of play and learning is a sophisticated teaching skill that is possessed by the well-trained early childhood educator.

■ DEVELOPMENTAL ACTIVITIES

Each activity should contain elements of skill and knowledge that are familiar to the child, as well as new challenges intended to help the child grow. Some activities address objectives that can be mastered in one sitting. Most allow for periods of practice followed by eventual mastery of the skills, knowledge, or concepts inherent in the activity.

When teachers plan activities that build on children's present strengths and take them one step farther, their programs are dynamic and change with the children. Programs that move with children's developmental progress are different in the spring than they were the previous fall. Planned activities should involve continued challenge and new levels of achievement for children; when they do, children are seldom bored and restless. The stimulation they find day after day absorbs much of their energy and motivates them to learn and grow.

The key to successful developmental activity planning is the careful observation and assessment of children in order to determine their present capabilities, future needs, and interests. Teachers also need to know the developmental sequence in which skills and understanding are acquired by children. They then take all this information and identify the kinds of skills and understanding that children are ready to master next. These "next steps" may be described as developmental objectives. These objectives form the basis for the activities planned for the next period, which may last from two weeks to a month.

> ## THE DEVELOPMENTAL PLANNING PROCESS
>
> - observe and record child's behaviours while playing;
> - assess the learning and development that has occurred;
> - formulate developmental objectives that will take the child to the next step in learning and development from what has already been achieved;
> - create an individual development plan for the child;
> - plan activities that address the developmental objectives identified for each child in the group—in age-graded groups of children, the developmental stages and abilities of the children may be similar for several children, which will simplify the planning task for teachers.

In programs where activities are individualized to meet each child's needs, the terms diagnosis and prescription are sometimes used (Wortham, 1984). **Diagnosis** refers to the teacher's assessment of which objectives children are able to meet successfully and which require more practice. **Prescription** refers to the teacher's analysis of the child's needs. The teacher plans activities that are designed to help the child achieve a new level of understanding or skill. In this sense, *the curriculum emerges as children progress.*

Teachers have the overall blueprint of the curriculum, which provides a guiding framework. The information needed to plan the program comes from the children themselves. Teachers' observations of children help them plan the short-term steps (objectives) that lead to children's mastery of the developmental goals. Developmental goals are listed in Appendix B: Developmental Goals and Objectives for Children Aged Two to Six. Teachers should also solicit children's input into planning through informal discussion with them of what they like to do, listening to their responses and comments when playing, and keeping records of the kinds of activities in which children show interest and participate most often.

■ STATING DEVELOPMENTAL OBJECTIVES

Objectives are short-term steps leading to the attainment of long-term goals. When developmental goals are clearly understood, the objectives relating to them can be sequenced from simple to complex. An important teaching task is the ability to break down into bite-sized chunks the components of practice and learning involved in the mastery of long-term goals. In order to accomplish this task, teachers have to know how concepts are formed and knowledge is acquired. The ability to arrange learning steps in a rational sequence that lead to the attainment of higher levels of learning is a professional skill that differentiates well-trained educators from untrained staff.

TABLE 7.1

EXAMPLES OF THE RELATIONSHIP BETWEEN DEVELOPMENTAL GOALS AND OBJECTIVES

Goals	Objectives
develop pro-social skills (affective domain)	take turns share initiate interactions help others respond to other children
develop visual-perceptual skills (physical domain)	discriminate form perceive depth differentiate figure/ground control eye movements
develop classification skills related to shape (cognitive domain)	recognize basic shapes match basic shapes sort basic shapes

Objectives should be stated as learning outcomes to be achieved such as take turns, share toys, listen, tell a story using props, and make a choice from among alternatives. They relate to one or more long-term developmental goals such as the development of social competence, attending skills, language, and memory, and decision-making abilities.

Objectives should be appropriate to the children whose needs and interests the activities are supposed to address. Objectives should account for the social usefulness and cultural importance of certain kinds of knowledge and learning. For example, in areas with an abundance of lakes and rivers, it is important to include objectives related to safety near water. Appreciating similarities and differences among people and families is also important in multicultural societies. Knowledge-based objectives and social and cultural understanding are suited to early childhood education programs as long as they are developmentally appropriate and relevant to the child's experience and social context.

STATE THE DEVELOPMENTAL OBJECTIVES

Developmental objectives refer to aspects of child development to be addressed by the program and not rigid standards of behaviour which must be achieved by all children under specific conditions. Developmental objectives do not set up rigidly prescribed expectations such as "the child will cut along a straight line marked on construction paper by December" or, "the child will learn to tie his shoe laces without assistance or coaching before the first day of school." Instead, the emphasis is on providing clearly presented, sequenced learning opportunities for children to practise and gain experience from, while receiving help and encouragement for their efforts.

■ THE ACTIVITY CARD SYSTEM

Education in the context of early childhood education refers to:

1. observing and assessing the child's developmental level in each domain
2. stating developmental objectives based on individual needs and capabilities
3. planning activities/learning experiences that address the physical, social, emotional, and cognitive objectives, for example:
   - state the objectives and tasks;
   - name the activity
   - select equipment, materials, and supplies
   - state the previous experience needed in order for children to participate in the activity (sequence activities in a developmental progression)

- describe the learning methods that will maximize children's ability to assume responsibility for their own learning in active ways
- state the teaching methods to be used (for teacher-led activities)
- evaluate the success of the activity in accomplishing what it intends to accomplish

The Activity Card System is an educational tool intended to clarify the links between developmental objectives, activities, materials, and methods to facilitate children's learning. The system outlines the developmental progression of tasks that leads to the achievement of desired learning outcomes. Activity planning is the basis of program planning and the implementation of curriculum. A system for planning activities ensures that a degree of objectivity and structure guides this very important component of the teaching role.

Some teachers view an activity planning system as an attempt to introduce unnecessary structure into the developmental planning process. Such a system has advantages, however, and may accomplish two goals:

1. building a system of activity cards described according to developmental objectives produces an inventory of activity ideas and resources for all learning centres;
2. going through the thought process of finding, planning, and articulating developmentally based activities that address a wide range of objectives, interests, and learning centres reinforces the importance of child-centred programs and activity planning.

Purpose of the System

The Activity Card System is designed to streamline program planning. A-cards outline the information referred to in Figure 7.1 in a clear and abbreviated format. Figure 7.2 shows a format that may be followed. The Activity Card System outlines the steps involved in planning activities based on developmental objectives and provides a permanent record, on cards, of activities that have been carefully planned, implemented, and evaluated. An activity will generally address many objectives, likely from two or more domains, and these should all be stated briefly on the cards.

The Filing System

The activity cards are filed according to the learning centre of the classroom in which they will most frequently be used. The file box for storing cards may contain seven index cards which represent the seven main learning centres in the learning environment, in other words, the Active Role Play, Daily Living, Quiet Thinking, Technology, Unit Blocks, Science Discovery, and Creative Arts Centres. Each of

Figure 7.1   FRAMEWORK FOR A SYSTEM OF ACTIVITY PLANNING

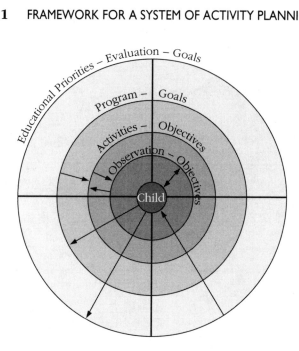

FIGURE 7.2   ACTIVITY CARD FILE SYSTEM

The Card:

NAME OF ACTIVITY:

OBJECTIVES:

PREVIOUS EXPERIENCE NEEDED:

MATERIALS:

METHOD:

these sections will contain cards describing activities that are most likely to be set up in that learning centre, although activities may be presented anywhere in the indoor or outdoor learning environment.

Developmental Sequencing

Children learn most concepts and acquire most skills in a developmental progression. Teachers have to be able to "uncover" the sequential and related tasks involved in learning a specific concept or skill. For example, the skills involved in ordering objects by length, known as **seriation**, can be ranked in order of difficulty using specific-purpose materials designed to take children through the steps involved in learning to seriate. Simple stacking and nesting toys are usually the first seriation materials introduced to children whose play with them is initially sensory and exploratory. After a while, children grasp the notion of sequential stacking or nesting of the various components of the toy. Later, children may be given metric-sized rods (Cuisenaire rods) in ten lengths, with a one-centimetre gradation between each size in the series. For example, being able to order the rods in ascending or descending order consistently and see the relationship of the parts to the whole series are signs that the child is well on the way to mastering the concept of seriation.

Previous Experience Needed

In the A-card system, "previous experience needed" indicates the order in which activities should be sequenced developmentally. This section of the A-card lists the skills, tasks, or concepts children should have mastered before tackling the present activity. Take the example of bead stringing. Initially, children explore large beads and strings in a sensory way, examining their size, shape, and the holes for the string to pass through, and may experiment with trying to insert the string into the hole (sensorimotor play). As they gain experience with these materials, they begin to string beads at random with no particular end in mind other than to practise the skill of inserting the string through the hole and stacking several beads on a knotted string (practice play).

Once they have gained basic proficiency in stringing the beads, the teacher may suggest or the child may herself decide to make a necklace, either with beads of a similar colour, or of a similar size, shape, or texture (productive play). Eventually, the teacher may encourage the child who has strung many necklaces at random to string beads according to a particular repeating pattern arranged according to criteria such as: colour (red, blue, yellow/red, blue yellow; shape (sphere, square/sphere, square); size (small, medium, large/small, medium, large); or property (plastic, wood, glass/plastic, wood, glass).

The stages in the child's development of bead-stringing skills may be identified on the A-card beside "Methods" in order to clarify the usual order in which children progress in their play with these materials. Of course, many skills can be practised at the same time in any activity. Children are practising the hand control and eye-hand coordination needed for pouring while stringing beads and vice versa. The idea here is to be aware of the complementary functions of a variety of activities in promoting the discrete skills that are prerequisites for successful mastery of developmental objectives.

Materials

Equipment, toys, educational materials, and supplies are media that facilitate development. Teachers have to understand the play and learning potential of a wide range of materials and supplies in order to select the right kinds of materials to facilitate children's mastery of developmental objectives. Accurate matching of play materials to developmental objectives is an important teaching task. Chapter 8 discusses the specific features of various kinds of play materials as well as equipment and supplies. A list of the materials and supplies the activity requires in order for children to master the objectives is a vital component of the activity planning process and should be stated on the A-card (see Tables 7.2 and 7.3).

Methods

Methods relate to the learning styles of children involved in the learning process. The emphasis is on how children learn rather than on how teachers teach. Children have their own individual learning styles, which include learning at their own pace. Children move from one level to a higher developmental level when they are ready and as a result of their own learning experiences. "The role of the teacher is to provide opportunities for children to explore, experiment and construct with a variety of materials. The child's experiences with the environment are the powerful factors that promote learning and development" (Wortham, 1984:8).

Children need to explore, ask questions, and find out for themselves. When teachers have time to sit with children playing and observe their strategies and choices, they are in a better position to facilitate learning by making a suggestion or asking a pertinent question. Teacher intervention may be needed when children experience difficulty, lose interest, need redirection, or require specialized assistance with tasks and skills inherent in the activity. There will also be times in the day when teachers will choose to work with children in groups to promote a sense of belonging, a chance to identify with their particular group, share information, learn cooperatively, and practise communicating effectively.

T A B L E   7 . 2

ACTIVITY CARD FOR A FIRST LEVEL BEAD-STRINGING ACTIVITY

NAME OF ACTIVITY:
bead stringing (simple)
OBJECTIVES:
eye-hand coordination, pincer movements, hand control, ocular-motor
skills (tracking, pursuit)
PREVIOUS EXPERIENCE NEEDED:
brush painting, moulding play dough,
formboard puzzles, pouring
MATERIALS:
large wooden beads and laces
METHOD:
place beads with laces on a table; partially string one lace with beads of any
colour or shape; leave model on table;
let children play (child-initiated, self-
directed play)

EVALUATION:
(on reverse side of card)
1. Did the children participate and
string a few laces?
2. Did some children master the
objectives (i.e., was the activity appropriate to the developmental levels of
the children for whom the activity was
planned)?
3. Did children figure out more complex ways of stringing the beads?
4. Next time, I would …

Developmental methods favour learning opportunities in which children are active and self-directed rather than passive. Methods are more active when children are free to choose from a set of alternatives and when exploration, discovery, problem-solving, trial and error, or simple sensory experience are encouraged. Teacher-centred methods are needed when teachers read a story, teach a song or finger play, or lead a physical exercise in the gymnasium, for example. A range of direct and indirect methods are compatible with the developmental approach. The challenge for teachers is to choose a method that will facilitate children's mastery of the developmental objectives of the activity and ensure that the learning process is satisfying enough to motivate them towards further learning. Indirect, child-centred, and self-directed methods encourage children to be investigators, explorers, and originators rather than followers of someone else's ideas and solutions.

Child-Centred Methods

Indirect teaching occurs when teachers rely mostly on skilful and selective planning of the environment to promote child development. It implies a willingness to relinquish to children much of the responsibility for their own learning within the

T A B L E   7 . 3

ACTIVITY CARD FOR A MORE ADVANCED BEAD-STRINGING ACTIVITY

NAME OF ACTIVITY:
bead-stringing according to size and colour

OBJECTIVES:
recognize same-different; match similar beads according to size or colour; classification

PREVIOUS EXPERIENCE NEEDED:
simple bead-stringing activities; simple matching and sorting activities according to colour and size

MATERIALS:
small and large wooden beads of three primary colours, laces

METHOD:
place beads with laces in a basket on a table; partly string one lace with large red beads, another lace with small red beads, another lace with large yellow beads, another with small yellow beads, and so on. Leave on the table for children to play; observe. (child-initiated, self-directed)

EVALUATION:
(on reverse side of card)
1. Did the children participate?
2. Did they understand the task?
3. Did they master the sorting task (i.e., according to size, colour)?
4. Did children invent their own patterns in exploring the materials?
5. Next time, I would …

planned environment. In indirect teaching, the teacher often becomes an observer of children's play in the learning centres. He may also be a **guide** who helps children manipulate a tool or solve a puzzle. As a **resource person**, the teacher responds to children's questions about phenomena or objects, helps them find supplies and materials they need for a project, or joins in their search for a new way of building or making something. The teacher as **facilitator** is always alert to opportunities to enrich and extend children's learning in an activity, find new or alternative solutions to problems, encourage them to ask new questions that will lead to the discovery of new concepts, and help children find new words in order to communicate effectively.

Exploratory and **discovery-oriented** methods are the most common examples of indirect teaching approaches. They refer to the prearrangement of specific materials and equipment for the purpose of stimulating exploratory play and discovery through sensorimotor play and manipulation of the materials provided. Sometimes materials are simply accessible to children to explore rather than being set up as activities. Loose materials such as wood, old bricks, sticks, leaves, branches, and rocks found outdoors, and crayons, paper, blocks, markers, scissors, glue, and fabric pieces indoors can be useful in a variety of projects and smaller tasks that children choose and for which they need a ready supply of tools and materials. Materials may also be carefully selected and set up in learning centres with specific play purposes in mind, for example, in science table exhibits and discovery activities such as examining various kinds of bark with magnifying glasses, pouring and comparing at the water table, workbench carpentry, and collage in the Creative Arts Centre.

Child-initiated activities usually occur spontaneously in the unit block and hollow block areas, at "free" art tables, with construction materials such as Lego, tabletop blocks, modular building materials, and outdoors in natural settings. Environments with an abundance of natural, modular, and open-ended materials arouse children's imaginations and encourage them to use what is around them in new and different ways each day and to set their own goals. In this learning context, children decide which activities they will be involved in, what materials they will use, and how they will use them. Self-correcting activities such as Workjobs (specific activities made from recycled materials outlined in the series of activity books by Baratta-Lorton) and puzzles are considered child-initiated since children are free to choose when and what specific activities they will pursue and are encouraged to pursue them at their own rate following their individual learning styles.

Child-initiated methods may also apply in small group settings when children choose or suggest an activity they wish to pursue. Teachers are particularly useful resource persons for children when the children are involved in "writing" their own stories, planning a field trip, tackling a long-term project, or making an "invention" and need an adult to encourage and support their efforts.

The developmental approach supports initiative and self-motivation in learning. One of the more difficult professional skills for teachers to acquire is the ability to know when to step back and let children be active, self-directed learners. Experience provides ample evidence to teachers that children are capable of learning through their freely chosen, independent involvement with concrete objects in their environment and that the freedom to pursue their own interests motivates children towards further learning.

Teacher-Directed Methods

Direct teaching assumes that the teacher decides, in advance of the learning experience, not only what objectives are to be addressed and how they will be addressed, but also leads the activity, models or demonstrates, and guides the activity to its anticipated learning outcome. The teacher assumes a central role in a directed activity in both a physical and an intellectual sense. She may be at the head of the circle, the front of a line, or physically set apart from the group in order to call instructions and give commands. Direct teaching methods are sometimes referred to as teacher-centred or teacher-as-leader techniques.

One teacher-directed method is **teacher demonstration**, which is often appropriate for gymnasium or playground activities in which the teacher physically demonstrates, with or without the help of the children, how to perform a specific movement or skill. It is often used in the performance of complex group tasks involving the use of electrical appliances. The *teacher as model* method may suit activities such as "follow the leader," "hokey pokey," and finger play. *Teacher introduction* of an activity such as an obstacle course, a cooking experience, or a musical game is often the best way of supporting children's eagerness to be involved, while at the same time ensuring that the experience will be successful and fun for them.

Activity-centred methods such as popping corn, breaking the pinata, making a jack-o-lantern, and cleaning pet cages require direct teaching methods or supervision to ensure children's safety and the success of the activity the first (and perhaps only) time it is undertaken. These methods ensure that certain kinds of experiences will likely occur, since the materials provided suggest the activity to be pursued, the objectives to be addressed, and usually the steps to be followed in order to reach the anticipated outcomes. Even though these kinds of activities are closely supervised and have clearly stated limits, they also contain elements of discovery and active interaction.

Evaluating Activities

Evaluation that is ongoing and dedicated to improving the quality of programs is an important component of the developmental approach to early childhood education. Evaluation practices enable teachers to review and revise activities and other program components. Observation and assessment strategies and reports are relied on to reveal to teachers the developmental progress, interests, and needs of each child. Evaluation involves ongoing activities performed by the teacher who uses a variety of evaluation instruments to acquire information about the activities, program, and curriculum goals.

Worthwhile evaluation requires an efficient system the teacher can use with a minimum of frustration and time. When evaluation is carried out regularly and reveals information that is practical and relevant, the savings of time, energy, and resources for teachers can be significant.

ACTIVITY EVALUATION QUESTIONS/CRITERIA

■ Do children choose this activity? Do they follow through and finish the activity?

■ Does the activity address the developmental objectives stated on the activity card?

■ Do children use the materials for the purposes intended?

■ Are the materials developmentally appropriate?

■ Are the objectives of the activity clear to children when they see the activity set up? Does the setup provide messages or cues to children about what is expected of them?

■ Is there some choice in the way the activity is to be pursued?

■ Is the activity closed- or open-ended? Does the activity focus on process or product?

■ What comments do children make about the activity?

■ Does the activity require children to use new words?

■ Do children return willingly to the activity after an interruption?

■ Do the children appear to relax during the activity?

■ Does the activity have a clear ending? Who decides when the activity is finished?

■ Does the activity provide children with a clear message that they have succeeded (i.e., mastered the objectives)?

■ Does the activity promote positive social behaviour?

■ Are the methods used appropriate to the activity?

■ Is the sequencing of the activity appropriate and effective?

■ Can the activity be used to address developmental objectives not stated on the activity card?

■ Does the activity encourage children to pay attention and develop learning-to-learn skills (e.g., task orientation, blocking out distractions, returning to the activity after an interruption, appropriate attention span)?

Effective evaluation systems do not have to be complicated or sophisticated. Many types can be employed regularly in a minimum of time. An *activity evaluation* may be written on the back of activity cards using a simple question and answer format: Did the activity address the stated objectives? Did the children participate? Were the objectives mastered by all or most of the children? In what ways might the activity be presented or conducted differently next time? Teachers may pick and choose a set of evaluation criteria for an activity from a comprehensive list of questions. Not all questions will apply to all activities.

Figure 7.3 SAMPLE ACTIVITIES CHECKLIST FOR AN INDIVIDUAL CHILD

GOAL	Activity 1			Activity 2			Activity 3			Activity 4			Activity 5			Activity 6			Activity 7			COMMENTS
	P	PM	M	P	PM	M	P	PM	M	P	PM	M	P	PM	M	P	PM	M	P	PM	M	

Child's Name _____ Age _____

Code: P : Participates
PM: Partial Mastery
M : Mastery

Figure 7.4 SAMPLE ACTIVITIES CHECKLIST FOR A GROUP OF CHILDREN

GOAL																																				
ACTIVITY																																				
CHILDREN	P	PM	M	P	PM	M	P	PM	M	P	PM	M	P	PM	M	P	PM	M	P	PM	M	P	PM	M	P	PM	M	P	PM	M	P	PM	M	P	PM	M
LUCY																																				
JOHN																																				
ACTIVITY																																				
CHILDREN																																				

Code: P : Participates
PM: Partial Mastery
M : Mastery

■ ACTIVITIES CHECKLISTS

Activities checklists allow teachers to select specific activities from the curriculum in order to reveal information about which children participated in the activity, and which ones partially or fully mastered the objectives. Information gathered reveals whether the activities are geared to the developmental levels of the children in the group, and how much practice most children require before mastery is achieved. This evaluation instrument shifts the emphasis away from the teacher's performance in the presentation or direction of activities to the teacher's ability to design an environment and plan activities in which children can be self-directed in their learning (see Figures 7.3 and 7.4).

■ IMPORTANCE OF EVALUATION

Systematic evaluation permits teachers to make decisions based on something more precise than guesswork or intuition. As teachers become more sophisticated and comfortable with the use of simple evaluation techniques and learn to evaluate regularly and systematically, they may gradually adopt more comprehensive, standardized tools designed by evaluation experts. To date, few evaluation tools exist for early childhood educators. Often the most effective evaluation instruments are those designed by the teachers themselves, to be used in their own contexts and to reveal the data and information they know they require.

Once teachers have experienced the benefits of systematic evaluation of programs, they often become more open to formal appraisals of their own teaching. Meaningful performance appraisal provides insight to teachers about their own teaching styles, needs for professional development, and special areas of interest and expertise that emerge as the teacher gains experience.

References

Bredekamp, S. (1987). *Developmentally Appropriate Practice in Early Childhood Programs Serving Children from Birth to Age 8*. Washington, D.C.: National Association for the Education of Young children.

Elkind, D. (1989). Developmentally-appropriate practice: philosophical and practical implications. *Phi Delta Kappan* 71 (2):113–17.

Fowler, W. (1971). On the value of both play and structure in early education. *Young Children* 27 (1):24–36.

Gardner, H. (1989). *To Open Minds*. New York: Basic.

Katz, L.G., and Chard, S.C. (1989). *Engaging Children's Minds: the Project Approach*. Norwood, NJ: Ablex.

Wortham, S.C. (1984). *Organizing Instruction in Early Childhood*. Boston: Allyn & Bacon.

PLAY EQUIPMENT, MATERIALS, AND SUPPLIES

Since children learn primarily through their interactions with concrete objects and experiences in the environment, choosing concrete objects for the learning environment is an important teaching task which affects the nature and quality of children's learning. The best concrete objects invite exploration and manipulation by children, respond to their actions on them, provide sensory stimulation and challenge and promote independent and creative pursuits.

■ EQUIPMENT

Equipment refers to the furniture, storage containers, and large items of play equipment that are often used to define the boundaries of a learning centre and the type of play that is encouraged there. Equipment makes a stable "footprint" on the floor; that is, it covers floor space on a more or less permanent basis. Tables, children's chairs, water and sand tables, free-standing easels, climbers, and playhouses are examples of equipment. The choice of equipment and its location influences the quality and type of play and learning that occur. Important criteria for choosing equipment are appearance, practicality, durability, portability, texture, contour, size and shape, and overall aesthetic quality.

As most children's furniture comes in standard sizes, the criteria for choice are often limited to quality of construction, building materials used, and whether accessories are included. All equipment should be joined with screws rather than simply nails and glue. Solid wood or plywood is stronger than particle board and resists splintering. Surfaces should be easy to clean and covered with non-toxic paints or stain. Equipment forms the backbone of the environment and provides the framework into which materials are placed.

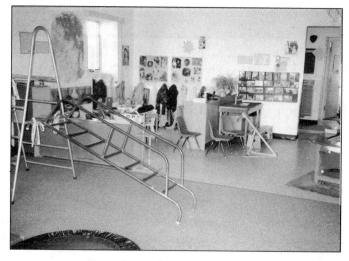

EQUIPMENT

■ MATERIALS

Materials are the toys and smaller concrete objects that appear in the foreground of the learning environment and are for children to play with, manipulate, test, and transform. Materials should be consistent with the stated goals of the program for it is through their play with materials that children achieve these goals. Durability, variety, safety, cleanliness, attractiveness, responsiveness, and versatility are other important criteria for the selection of materials.

The most cost-effective and valuable materials in a learning environment are those that are extendable, may be used for more than one purpose, address a wide range of objectives, and invite open-ended play by children. Materials such as unit blocks, Lego, and modular materials fit this description. When sturdy and relevant play materials cannot be found commercially, or when costs are prohibitive, home-made materials such as those found in Workjobs (Baratta-Lorton, 1972) or others made from recycled materials extend the range of developmentally appropriate resources available for children's play.

■ SUPPLIES

Supplies are the consumable items in the learning environment that should be replenished periodically. They include papers of various kinds, crayons, paints, paste, wood, chalk, playdough, brushes, sand, markers, and cardboard boxes. In

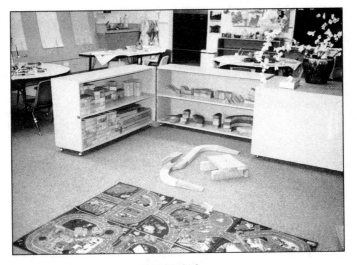

MATERIALS

North America's product-rich, consumer-oriented society, the choice of supplies and materials is seemingly limitless. Teachers generally choose supplies that are easy to manipulate, durable, colourful, attractive, clean, and easy to store. Storage is an important factor in the choice of supplies. Plastic bins, paper containers reinforced with adhesive covering, and fitted shelves may be purchased along with supplies to ensure adequate capacity and neat fit on shelves or in cupboards. When choosing equipment for storage, teachers should take into account the specifications necessary in order for all supplies to be accommodated neatly, accessibly, and attractively.

Children are interested in the variety and appearance of supplies. Shiny paper, unusual colour in crayons and paints, stamp pads, or erasers in different shapes will often determine whether a child will choose a particular activity over others that are available. The creation of a multicultural environment depends on the inclusion of some supplies that have a cultural bias such as paper for origami, rice paper, natural sponge, candles, rope for weaving, grasscloth, twine, silk, bamboo, and skin-toned crayons.

■ TYPES OF PLAY MATERIALS

Play materials are of two main types: open-ended and structured, specific-purpose materials. Within these two broad categories are subclasses of materials. Generally, the two types are defined by the number and nature of the tasks for which children use them.

Open-Ended Materials

Materials are **open-ended** if they have an indefinite number of outcomes and a maximum amount of flexibility in the ways the materials may be used by children (Fowler, 1980). The outcomes may be planned or spontaneous, and there are usually no rules or very simple ones outlining steps to be followed in using the materials to achieve some outcome. Open-ended materials may be modular or free-form. Modular materials usually lead to construction play. Materials such as Lego, unit blocks, hollow blocks, Tinkertoy, parquetry, and tabletop blocks are modular. They have many pieces (multiple units), usually of uniform shapes and sizes, which are made to fit together in specific ways. These materials are composed of discrete, rigid forms (modules) that are designed using fixed units of measurement, such as inches or centimetres, which are important attributes of the material, and can be arranged into a variety of structures. In materials such as unit blocks, the units come in various shapes and sizes, but the units are usually exact multiples of one basic unit. Structures children build using modular materials are often formed using add-on processes, since the units cannot be altered in either shape or form. Modular materials are sometimes referred to as noncontinuous materials.

Free-form materials are more concerned with how things flow (rather than fit) together to make the whole (Fowler, 1980). These open-ended materials are what Fowler calls *surface diffusable, free-form materials*, and these are generally those used for painting and drawing such as paint, markers, brushes, sponges, chalk, crayons and used with various kinds of papers, slate, woods, clays, or plastics. These media allow free-form shaping only within the limitations of the surface area being used (i.e., the size and shape of the paper or slate). With free-form materials like paint and clay, the parts often lose their discrete identity as they become merged into the whole.

Free-form substances like earth, sand, and water, which are sometimes called *continuous materials*, are often used for construction purposes as in building sandcastles, making canals, and building mud huts. These substances are much harder to control and manipulate towards specified outcomes than rigid, modular materials, as it is difficult to maintain their consistency and shape when working with them. Free-form substances like clay, plasticene, and playdough have more predictable properties and are therefore referred to as *malleable materials*. They are the materials children choose in order to build more lifelike representations.

Specific-Purpose Materials

Specific purpose materials have an internal structure that guides the outcome of play with the materials as well as providing the steps to be followed in reaching the outcome. There are specific ways in which the materials should be used. Sometimes called "means-ends" materials (Fowler, 1980), they include Workjobs, pegboards, formboard and jigsaw puzzles, dominoes, lotto games, and a variety of other materials, for all of which the results are somewhat predictable. Some specific-purpose materials can be used for purposes other than the obvious and anticipated ways. For example, dominoes can double as building blocks, and formboard puzzle pieces, beads and Lego blocks can be used as objects to be classified. For the most part, however, specific-purpose materials are kept together as sets to be used in standard, often rule-bound ways towards a precise, predictable end product and learning outcome.

Specific-purpose materials promote design concepts and/or content concepts (Fowler, 1980). Design concepts are addressed by formboard puzzles that deal with shape learning, configurations of shapes, and interlocking and inlaid shapes to form patterns and abstract representations. Some structured materials are designed to help children practise and learn concepts such as seriation, classification, number, size, part-whole, and functional relationships. Many so-called educational materials fall into this category and include sets of objects for children to classify, Cuisenaire rods for seriation, interlocking blocks for identifying part-whole relationships, and stacking cups for ordering by size.

Two-Dimensional and Three-Dimensional Materials

Materials may also be differentiated according to whether they are two- or three-dimensional. **Two-dimensional materials** are those with flat surface areas such as drawings on paper, collages on paper or cardboard, computer monitor screens, and formboard puzzles. They are often representations of whole objects that have only length and width but little depth. Three-dimensional materials have length, width, and depth. A two-dimensional material would be a wooden puzzle piece the colour and shape of an apple, or a picture of an apple flashed on a computer monitor. A **three-dimensional material** would be a real apple or a lifelike representation of the real thing having length, width, and depth. A small artifact of a cow, a car, or a sailboat is three-dimensional; pictures of the same things in a book are two-dimensional.

Many play materials, especially open-ended ones, are found in both three-dimensional and two-dimensional form. Many specific-purpose, three-dimensional materials such as block puzzles are represented in two-dimensional form on the computer screen. The introduction of microcomputers and educational software into the preschool classroom has made it possible to transfer manipulations of construction materials from the three-dimensional world to the two-dimensional monitor.

Children benefit from experience with both three- and two-dimensional versions of concrete objects in the environment in their learning to fully understand them. The use of props or child-sized artifacts representing the real thing in the adult world, such as toy cups and saucers, which are used at child-sized tables and chairs, are examples of three-dimensional materials which facilitate symbolic play.

Developmentally Appropriate Play Materials

Materials are the vehicles for learning in early childhood. Teachers facilitate the link between the concrete world and children's learning of the physical properties of things by providing concrete materials for the child to manipulate physically.

The ability to match play materials to children's developmental levels, skills, and interests both individually and in small groups is a higher-order teaching skill that is acquired through training and experience. The teacher needs to have a thorough working knowledge of the "tools of the trade"; these are the equipment, materials, and supplies that compose the foreground of the learning environment.

How do play materials support and encourage development? Piaget's research and developmental theory confirmed that children learn largely through the senses. When they are actively involved with concrete materials in the environment, children learn first about the physical properties of objects and later form concepts based on the relationships they see and experience among objects. They relate textures they have touched and link sounds to direction, specific persons, and messages. They feel the shape of a letter or number by tracing these symbols in sand or salt trays, or by shaping their own bodies in the same configuration as the magnetic number or letter on the magnetic board.

The developmental appropriateness of any play material depends on the match the teacher is able to make between the material itself and the developmental level of the child who will be playing with it. The often wide range of developmental levels and abilities represented in the typical early childhood classroom should be accompanied by the presence of materials that address a similarly wide range of developmental skills and concepts. Usually, an early learning environment will provide play materials that move children from sensorimotor, physical exploration of the materials to an understanding of the many relationships that exist between materials and the total environment.

The presentation of play materials will also change as the children make developmental progress. The classroom will not look the same in June as it did in Sep-

Figure 8.1   MAJOR TYPES OF PLAY AND LEARNING MATERIALS

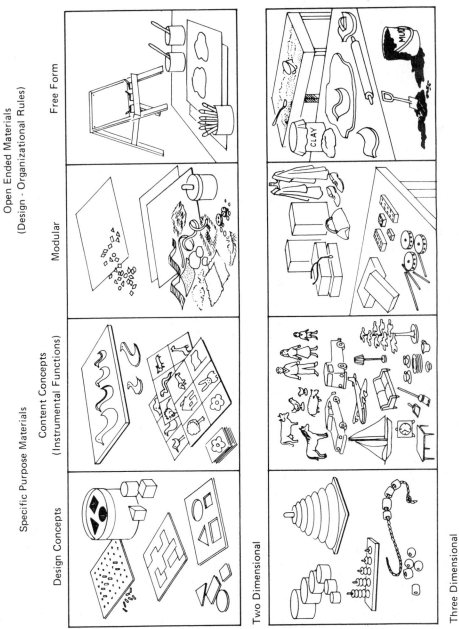

From W. Fowler, *Infant and Child Care: A Guide to Education in Group Settings.* (Toronto: Allyn & Bacon, 1980). Used with permission of the author.

tember. It will instead reflect the developmental progress children have made in all domains in the intervening ten months. More complex, creative materials will have replaced the many single-purpose simple units. Children will be observed using multipurpose materials in a variety of ways. Specific-purpose tools and materials will be used to stimulate more complex, conceptual learning instead of simple sensory exploration of the materials.

■ PLAY MATERIALS AS RESPONSIVE MEDIA FOR LEARNING

The most effective materials for development can be manipulated and changed by children's actions on them. Creative materials usually found in the Creative Arts Centre fall into this category, along with blocks, and other construction materials like Lego, Tinkertoy, cardboard or box construction, and those used in woodworking and sewing. Paints, paste, papers, collage, clay, and plasticene similarly respond according to the child's actions on them. Initially, they are used in sensory ways; at later stages children play with them in more purposeful ways and they take the shape that the child intends as a result of her creative plan and greater skill in using tools and materials. The responsive play environment includes a wide range of flexible, open-ended materials that respond to the child's actions on them.

Effective learning in early childhood is a two-way street. The child's action on things in the environment and the ways in which the materials respond to the child's actions on them create a dynamic interaction between the child and the learning environment that moves from physical exploration and experimentation to an understanding of many of the interrelationships that exist in the physical world. Play materials vary greatly in the potential they offer for meaningful learning and understanding.

Consider the difference in play and learning potential, for instance, between a windup mechanical train engine and a set of tabletop blocks. Once children wind up the train and observe its movements a few times, their interest in it wanes. The train responds to the child's winding of the mechanical key by moving along the track or floor and perhaps making train sounds. It does not change its shape, alter its play potential, or provide variety and flexibility in the ways it can be used by the child. The play potential of the windup train is passive more than active, and the child's role is largely that of observer.

Tabletop blocks, on the other hand, take the shape that the child creates as he plays. They respond to the child's actions, and the new configuration in turn invites another response by the child who continues to shape the blocks into a planned or purely exploratory structure. The flexibility and inherent potential of the blocks to inspire a child's creativity depend on the child's action on them. A variety of responses by the child and the blocks themselves is possible. The play which occurs is a two-way interactional exchange between the child and the play materials. As the child explores the blocks and uses them for his own purposes, he learns about the properties of the blocks and eventually uses them to represent a plan. The blocks respond more flexibly and creatively as the child's ability to manipulate and use them expands.

Experiencing the physical properties of the blocks leads to an understanding of the various ways in which they may interrelate in order to create a variety of structures. In these ways, blocks are a truly constructivist toy. Children's growing understanding of blocks as play materials leads to their more sophisticated use of them for building and creating.

Specific-purpose play materials also respond to children's actions on them, although their responses bring about specialized kinds of learning, usually the development of a discrete skill or the understanding of a concept. For example, dominoes promote visual discrimination of the similar configurations of dots on a tile. They also promote understanding of quantity to the extent that the child will recognize that the tile with five dots should be placed next to another tile with five dots. The child must also understand the concept of matching likenesses, which, in this case, usually involves the recognition of similar configurations of dots. Sometimes tactile or colour and shape clues are added to provide additional sensory information for the child to make appropriate juxtapositions.

When play and learning environments provide diverse materials to promote a comprehensive range of developmentally appropriate sensory, conceptual, and social learning for children, the likelihood that children will attempt to use materials for unintended purposes is reduced. Nonetheless, one of the characteristics of many specific-purpose materials is that they also contain possibilities for more flexible use.

■ CRITERIA FOR SELECTING PLAY MATERIALS

The selection of play materials for the learning environment depends on practical, economic, aesthetic, and developmental educational criteria.

Practical Criteria

Practical criteria for selecting play materials include safety, adaptability, cleanliness, ease of storage, and functional quality.

Safety

The safety of play materials is the paramount consideration in selection. Government-sponsored organizations such as the Canadian Toy Testing Council exist to monitor the safety of commercially produced toys for children. Toy manufacturers must comply with government standards that exist to meet basic safety concerns. However, the careful selection and monitoring of the safety of materials for young children should not rely exclusively on either government standards or systematic testing of a limited range of toys on the market. Non-commercially produced materials made by private manufacturing companies and local craftspeople should be carefully screened by teachers to ensure their compliance with safety standards.

Safety features that should be examined carefully include the durability of the toy, kind of paint used, size of detachable parts, presence of sharp edges, and ease of cleaning and disinfecting. Toys that break easily may leave rough edges that can cut the skin and sharp pieces that can be swallowed. Toxic paint can be chewed and absorbed by small children. Wood preservatives containing insecticidal agents can be absorbed through contact with uncovered skin even without being chewed or coming in contact with the mouth in any way. Materials with joints or ridges that cannot be disassembled to allow for cleaning and disinfecting in the cracks may harbour bacteria, which can lead to infections.

Safety is also influenced by the developmental appropriateness of a material or piece of equipment. A wooden rocking horse may be safe for one two-year-old and not for another who cannot yet balance and hold on.

Adaptability

Adaptability is a practical consideration that recognizes that programs generally have to stretch budgets. The selection of play materials that are adaptable to a variety of purposes also stretches children's imaginations as they invent a number of ways of integrating a piece of equipment or play material into their play. Open-ended materials are generally more adaptable than specific-purpose materials. The adaptability of materials in the environment also depends on the teacher's ability to see the play potential inherent in toys. Teachers should know how to place materials in learning centres in ways that will lead to more flexible use of the materials.

Cleanliness

Cleanliness is determined largely by the toy's capacity to be cleaned by washing, dry cleaning, painting, and disinfecting. Often play materials made of artificial products such as plastics are easier to clean than products made of wood, sponge, or cloth. The need to keep play materials clean has to be balanced with a consideration for the aesthetic quality of the learning environment.

The importance of natural materials like wood and fabric that add interest, tactile variation, and beauty should not be overlooked. In today's world, many wooden products are easily washed and fabrics sustain frequent washing. The frequency of cleaning and disinfecting toys also depends on the ages and vulnerability of the children. In programs where children still explore by putting most materials into their mouths, or in centres and schools where the incidence of illness is high, the need to choose materials that are easily washed and disinfected is a particularly important consideration.

Ease of Storage

Play materials usually spend some time on shelves, in cupboards or in storage rooms outside of learning centres. The issue of where and how to store play materials not in use is especially important in programs where space is limited. For example, jungle gyms may be fun and effective in promoting physical development, but the recognition that they can create a storage problem when they are not in use may mean their purchase will assume lower priority than the purchase of materials like balance beams, skipping ropes, skateboards, and tumbling mats, which are more easily stored and address many of the same developmental skills.

Functional Quality

Children are easily discouraged by materials that do not perform the function for which they appear to have been designed. Many teachers may recall their frustration as children when the child-sized sewing machine or toy stove they received as a gift would not work. Play materials for groups of children should function well and with a minimum of intervention by adults. The toy should be built to sustain a range of exploration and testing by children who may handle and manipulate the material in a variety of different ways. The toy cash register that opens only when the knobs are pushed aggressively will discourage the timid child who expects it to respond to a single stroke.

Generally, the simpler the structure of the toy and the greater its freedom from unnecessary detail, the more functional it will be. The ease with which children are able to manipulate the materials in the environment will determine the extent to which the teacher will be free to facilitate learning and observe children's play rather than stopping to repair a toy or help a child make it work.

Economic Criteria

Economic criteria for the selection of play materials are cost, quantity needed, and sturdiness and durability.

Cost

The actual cost of a toy is based on the number of times it will be used in a day or week and the length of time it will serve without repair or replacement. Higher cost does not necessarily mean higher quality or greater usefulness and effectiveness. It is usually more economical in the long run, however, to pay more for play materials that must endure manipulation by many children who use the materials in many different ways. Inexpensive materials that last only one season are not economical. Exploratory and sensory play materials must also be of high quality. The purchase of high quality unit blocks and sturdy tricycles is usually rewarded by the greater longevity and aesthetic appeal of the toy for its entire lifetime. It may be wiser to economize instead on supplies such as paper, paste, paint, and sand as long as they meet safety and health standards.

Quantity Needed

The quantity of any given play material that must be purchased is another economic factor which may help teachers decide whether or not to introduce it. Sometimes more is better. For example, the presence of one or two tricycles in a playground may cause more problems because of long waits by children wanting to use them than they are worth in terms of play and learning value. Often clear limits and rules need to be established when there is not enough of an item to accommodate a number of children in a group. Half a set of unit blocks is virtually useless for a group of children and limits play opportunities rather than expanding them. Two sets are much more viable in order to promote the social and cooperative play and creativity that these materials are designed to encourage. When budgets are not flexible enough to purchase a sufficient number of an item to make its presence worthwhile, it is often best to delay the purchase until sufficient quantities can be provided.

Sturdiness and Durability

Children do not like materials that break down easily or that they have to handle carefully in order not to break delicate mechanisms. Toys need to be sturdy enough to allow children to play freely without fear of breaking the toy. Sometimes broken toys leave splinters or sharp edges that pose a safety hazard. *Sturdiness* and *durability* are important criteria in selection. When toys do break down through extensive use, they need to be repairable, preferably by a teacher or parent, to avoid unanticipated expense for repair. The choice of materials that are sturdy and can be repaired easily when broken also provides important messages to children about how to look after things, and how to mend them when they break down.

Environmental awareness and the encouragement of values that stress conservation, valuing, and recycling of materials can be modelled most effectively by programs that consciously choose well-made, durable products, maintain them carefully, and repair and refurbish them when they break down. Using toys that can be passed on from one child to a younger child, and from one group to the next group, also teaches children to respect their playthings in order to preserve them for continued use by others who will follow.

Aesthetic Criteria

Beautiful toys are often more interesting and attractive to children. Colour, shape, size, proportion, design, and construction qualities affect the appeal of toys and contribute to the aesthetic quality of the environment. Form, colour, and proportion influence children's choice of materials and the development of aesthetic values.

Dolls and stuffed animals with stylized or exaggerated features are often not as appealing, even to children, as lifelike representations that more closely represent the real world. Cartoon creatures hung on the walls have less aesthetic appeal than beautiful photographs or paintings of real animals or people. Cartoons represent a Walt Disney and Hollywood view of the world that early childhood education programs should not feel obligated to reinforce. The presence of objects in the environment that represent reality, rather than distort it, help children see beauty and harmony in the everyday, real world around them. They learn through the choice of well-designed materials to appreciate line, form, composition and structure that is relevant to the function and context in which the material will be used.

Learning to appreciate beautiful things in a meaningful context and to care for them appropriately helps children become sensitive to aesthetic values and principles. This learning is usually conveyed by the quality of the environment and by the way in which adults model behaviours that treat the environment and the things in it with respect and appreciation.

Developmental/Educational Criteria

Interest for young children and relevance of the materials to the child's everyday experience are two criteria that determine the developmental and educational value of the materials in programs.

Interest is a criterion that will influence the extent to which children are motivated to play with materials. Usually, the most interesting are the simple materials that can be used in a variety of ways by children of different developmental levels. Toys should be fun, but not just for the first few minutes. Effective toys will provide children with hours of pleasure over a period of months or even years. The most interesting toys are often those that require the child to use her own energy and capabilities in order to play with them. A toy telephone will encourage a child to speak and manipulate the dial; a sturdy plastic rattle can be chewed, rattled, and manipulated. Children learn to perform more interesting and challenging tasks with these toys as they mature. Play materials that respond to children's hands-on actions on them are more interesting than passive toys such as a jack-in-the-box and a windup car.

Relevance is a measure of the extent to which a toy belongs in the cultural context in which it will be used by a child and to his life experiences. For example, a toy tractor will mean less to a city child than a red fire engine. Classrooms for the early years should be a microcosm of the child's world and work best when the equipment and materials are familiar and represent everyday reality. Play opportunities that reflect experiences that are close to the child are easier to comprehend and relate to than those that are outside the child's experience. Learning about family and the neighbourhood are much more meaningful than learning about times, places, people, and things that lie beyond children's comprehension.

Relevant toys form a bridge between the world of play and the real world children inhabit. They help children understand everyday living concepts such as family relationships, community roles, culture, festivals, and traditions. Artifact toys such as those found in the housekeeping area, including the child-sized refrigerator, stove, cupboards, and doll furniture, and models of villages, schools, airports, and garages all represent things children see in the real world. They foster role play of adult roles that children associate with these props. Materials that encourage children to rehearse real-life events such as hospital visits, an airplane trip, or a farm visit help children adapt more readily to unfamiliar and potentially frightening experiences.

Play materials promote development in specific domains. Materials like blocks, housekeeping artifacts, climbing apparatus, dressup clothes, and supermarket props encourage children to play together cooperatively. In the process, they learn to cooperate, communicate, experiment with perspectives other than their own and consider the needs and interests of others. Social skills are practised and mastered within the context of sociodramatic play. Large and small muscles of the body as well as manipulative and perceptual abilities are developed when children play with hoops, bean bags, racquets, ropes, balls, and climbing apparatus. They develop physical abilities such as cardio-vascular stamina, muscular endurance, agility, flexibility, and speed, as well as body awareness and kinesthetic discrimination when playing games with targets, balls, flags, and bats. Cognitive development occurs when children play with modular and specific-purpose materials that lead to concept formation as in colour, time, space, and size concepts.

T A B L E   8 . 1

CRITERIA FOR SELECTING PLAY MATERIALS

Practical Criteria	Economic Criteria	Aesthetic Criteria	Developmental/ Educational Criteria
safety	cost	form/line	interest
adaptability	quantity needed	colour	relevance/applicability
cleanliness	sturdiness/durability	proportion	to real life
storage/size		design/structure	cultural compatibility
functionality		properties	familiarity to child
simplicity			expandability

■ RECYCLING VALUABLE JUNK

No discussion about play and learning materials in the 1990s is complete without an examination of the usefulness and role of recycled products. Recycling is one environmental issue among many that should assume a high priority in early childhood education.

Children are the inheritors of our world and its resources; they are also most vulnerable to environmental imbalances and among the first to feel deficiencies in resources. The toxins that accumulate in food, soil, and human bodies have more devastating potential long-term effects on young children than on adults. Green earth policies, resource management efforts, and conservationist practices can be interpreted simply in order that children can understand them.

Generally, children are eager learners and sensitive to the characteristics of their environments. They demonstrate the earnest attempts to protect and save and respect nature that would challenge and embarrass most adults. The transmission to children of cultural values that portray respect for the environment and the protection and conservation of natural resources is most effective when environmentally conscious practices are modelled by the adults in their lives. One way of modelling sincere concern for the environment is for teachers to make use of recycled materials in the classroom.

More attention is being given these days to the use of recycled products for making children's play materials. Many activity books explain in detail the steps to follow in making specific-purpose play and learning materials from recycled products. Items normally discarded such as packaging, cardboard boxes, wood pieces, cans, jars, magazines and other printed materials, plastic products, polyethylene products, fabrics, sponge, and a variety of other human-made and naturally occurring substances, may become resources for making play materials.

Resource books show teachers how to use household products, by-products, and waste items for play purposes. Worn-out clothing can be cut into rags to be used instead of paper towels for mopping up and cleaning; egg cartons and other packaging make sturdy storage containers for small items in the Creative Arts Centre. Practices like these model creative uses of recycled materials in the early learning environment.

Programs that use recycled materials in learning centres and for storage purposes should provide areas and bins for the collection of recyclable materials. Parents can usually be relied on to get involved in program-based recycling efforts aimed at collecting and saving recycled materials. These joint efforts by parents and teachers provide powerful messages to children about the importance of working together to save our earth.

■ STORING PLAY MATERIALS

Materials for play and learning should be stored as closely as possible to the learning centre where they will most likely be used. Materials need to be accessed easily by children or teachers, and be neatly arranged and protected. Specially designed shelving for materials and supplies in the Creative Arts Centre, for example, will maximize the use of storage space and provide easy accessibility by children. The neat display of carefully arranged materials in custom-crafted shelving will also enhance the aesthetic quality of the space.

When children have access to materials and supplies within each learning centre, the teacher is freed and, therefore, can facilitate children's learning, observe their skills in the use of the materials, and assist them when they need help. The strategic placement of storage racks, shelves, and compartments for bins containing supplies and materials makes it easier for children to choose, be independent, and think for themselves without relying on teachers to provide what they believe children need.

■ SUMMARY

Equipment, materials, and supplies are the tools of the trade in early childhood education, given that children learn through their interaction with concrete objects in the environment. Effective early childhood education depends on the teacher's ability to match materials and supplies to the developmental levels and needs of the individual children being taught. Well-designed learning environments will ensure that there is a balance of specific-purpose and open-ended materials to promote a wide range of developmental abilities. Teachers need to select and purchase materials according to specific criteria to ensure that a wide variety and a range of play materials can address the many aspects of child development. The use of materials made from recycled products is especially relevant in today's world and conveys important messages about careful use of environmental resources. Storing play materials close to the centres where they will be used most frequently encourages children's independence in learning and frees teachers to facilitate learning.

References

Baratta-Lorton, M. (1972). *Workjobs*. Menlo Park, CA: Addison-Wesley.

Canadian Toy Testing Council. (1990). *1990 Toy Report*. Ottawa: Canadian Toy Testing Council.

Fowler, W. (1980). *Infant and Child Care: A Guide to Education in Group Settings*. Toronto: Allyn & Bacon.

Javna, J. (1990). *50 Simple Things Kids Can Do To Save The Earth*. Kansas, MO: The EarthWorks Group, Andrews and McMeel, A Universal Press Syndicate Company.

National Association for the Education of Young Children. (1985). *Toys: Tools for Learning*. Washington, D.C.: National Association for the Education of Young Children.

Plummer, B. (1974). *Earth Presents*. Washington, D.C.: A & W Visual Library.

S E C T I O N 4

FACILITATING SYMBOLIC PLAY

Section 4 emphasizes the important role of symbolic play in the development and learning of young children. Chapter 9 defines various types of symbolic play and outlines its relationship to child development. Chapter 10 describes the components and role of the Daily Living Centre in facilitating symbolic play through careful planning of the props and activities needed to stimulate and enhance role play. Chapter 11 outlines the symbolic play potential of the Active Role Play Centre through the use of larger, more expansive props, constructive materials, and planned activities.

Section 4 addresses the following topics:
- definition and types of symbolic play
- facilitating dramatic and sociodramatic play
- planning the Daily Living Centre
- planning the Active Role Play Centre
- facilitating the development of physical skills
- adapting the environment for the child who is disabled
- integrating the child who is disabled in active play
- planning play stations within learning centres
- activities to promote symbolic play
- activities to promote active play

C H A P T E R 9

SYMBOLIC PLAY

■ INTRODUCTION TO SYMBOLIC PLAY

Symbolic play involves the child's growing ability to represent using drama. Other types of play (outlined in Chapter 2) focus mainly on sensory and physical activity and the exploration and use of materials. *Symbolic play* begins when children are able to use actions to convey meanings, usually at the end of their first year. Later, during the second year, they are able to use words and objects to stand for other objects or to represent meaning, for example, when a child raises a cup and says "doos," or picks up his blanket and puts his thumb in his mouth as it gets close to naptime. The dramatic development of symbolic thought is a major developmental task of the two- to four-year-old child.

During the sensorimotor stage of development, usually sometime in the second year, *pretend play* emerges. This early type of symbolic play involves momentary, short-lived imitation of remembered action. A child closing her eyes while sitting on the rocking chair, pretending to sleep, or picking up the baby bottle and pretending to drink from it and then putting it aside, is engaging in the kind of pretend play that continues throughout the early years. The ability to represent remembered action reflects increasing cognitive maturity. These abilities gradually become longer, more deliberate, abstract, and comprehensive.

■ Dramatic and Sociodramatic Play

More mature forms of symbolic play are dramatic and sociodramatic play. The focus on social roles and interaction is what distinguishes dramatic and sociodramatic from other types of play (Smilansky & Sheftaya, 1990).

ASSUMING ROLES

Dramatic Play

Dramatic play is sustained pretend play in which one child persists in acting out a role using gestures, sometimes using props, and by imitating movements (Butler, Gotts, & Quisenberry, 1978). It occurs when a child imitates remembered events or sustained actions such as bathing dolls, taking the dolls in a carriage for a walk, and dressing up in a hat, briefcase, dress, and grown-up shoes to go to work. In dramatic play, children identify with events they remember and imitate each single remembered act as closely as possible to the way in which they observed it. This type of play is common in children under three or four.

From about two to four years of age, children often engage in dramatic play alone (solitary play) or beside other children (parallel play). They may play jointly with another child or a teacher, or they may involve the other player in a passive, objective role while retaining control of the pretend roles. For example, a child may say to the stuffed animals or to a child nearby, "watch out, here comes Batman," as he floats by his passive audience fully immersed in his own pretending, but he will not necessarily rely on other children to participate in his fantasy. In order to pretend in a reciprocal dramatic play situation with others, the child must have acquired knowledge of social roles and relationships and be able to communicate and negotiate effectively with other players (Garvey, 1977).

Sociodramatic Play

Sociodramatic play is dramatic play involving two or more children who assume related roles and follow each other's cues in acting out an event or social context from the adult world. It occurs when children are able to cooperate and respond to other children. To engage in this type of play successfully, children need to be able to assign roles, carry them out over a period of time and agree upon a "script" related to the event or relationship they are representing. They also have to be able to continually revise or renegotiate the implicit "contract." Sociodramatic play occurs when children begin to observe that social communication is more than a series of isolated behaviours and is instead composed of a complex network of mutually interdependent behaviours and responses.

For example, children playing in a super unit such as a supermarket will generally assume recognizable roles as the cashier, a shopper or customer, or the grocery packer. From three-and-a-half to five years of age, they exhibit awareness of the interdependence of the roles, the conventions or customs that govern the roles, and the kind of verbal banter that often accompanies shopping and checking out groceries at the counter. Their dialogue is often very familiar: "Yes, Jane, the prices are getting higher every week"; "nice day today"; "would you like to have a cart to carry these bags to your car?"

The aim of children's sociodramatic play is much more than simply imitating observed behaviours. It is to act out as closely as possible the actions and reactions they have observed as a way of understanding their meanings. In order to dramatize complex interactions they have observed, children often have to rely on other children to participate in the attempt to recreate an event or social exchange. This desire to represent reality in sociodramatic play as exactly as possible is consistent with the child's increasing interest in depicting "real life" in all creative endeavours—an interest that continues into the early primary years. Sociodramatic play opportunities are powerful agents in the development of all aspects of social cognition.

Sociodrama

Sociodramatic play is different from **sociodrama** which is the enactment through pretend play of a story or some other dramatic form. Sociodrama is externally motivated and limitations are imposed upon the roles and behaviours by the events, actions, and script present in a story or another drama (Smilansky & Sheftaya, 1990). An example of sociodrama would be children's attempts to recreate a favourite television program by assuming the roles of the characters and remaining as close as possible to the television script. Another example might be one resulting from a teacher's suggestion to children that they try to act out the story she has just read to them.

∎ SOCIODRAMATIC PLAY AND CHILD DEVELOPMENT

Sociodramatic play promotes three areas of development in children: creativity, cognitive growth, and social abilities (Smilansky, 1971). The dynamic quality of this type of play comes from children's portrayal of real-life situations and actions by adults that children have witnessed and experienced, and that they still remember. The motivation and script for representing these remembered experiences come from within the child.

Language, perception, and memory play important roles in sociodramatic play. Pelligrini (1980) demonstrated that sociodramatic play is important to the development of many intellectual and social capacities in young children. For example, children's ability to *decentre* (i.e., become less egocentric) and become more *sociocentric* (i.e., more focused on the group than the self) seems to be determined by the ease and frequency with which children engage in sociodramatic play (Rubin, 1980). In the interests of sustaining a play episode with their peers, it is necessary for children to be able to take a perspective other than their own and be willing to do so. Children who are able to decentre develop the ability to explain information in words more easily, rather than assuming that their peers understand what they are trying to do or say (Pelligrini, 1984). Their play is punctuated with brief explanations such as "OK, I'll pretend now to be afraid and run away and you can coax me back." This ability to use explicit language is essential to children's progress in symbolic play, and to their ability both to evolve more complex and abstract themes and roles and to sustain a sociodramatic play episode. Children who engage successfully in dramatic and sociodramatic play appear to be better readers and writers than children who engage primarily in functional and constructive play (Pelligrini, 1984).

BENEFITS OF SOCIODRAMATIC PLAY

Sociodramatic play facilitates the following abilities and is, in turn, enhanced by children's progress in these abilities:
- ability to decentre and be more sociocentric
- use of explicit language—better at explaining
- increased ability to engage in symbolic play and evolve more complex and abstract roles and ideas
- better reading and writing

Sociodramatic play seems to occur at more complex levels in children from upper- and middle-class socioeconomic backgrounds. Children who are disadvantaged seem less inclined to engage in sociodramatic play and when they do it is often of short duration and not as complex (Smilansky, 1968). This evidence implies that teachers have to know when intervention is important (Garvey, 1977; Pelligrini, 1984; Rubin, Fein & Vandenberg, 1983). They also have to know how to facilitate sociodramatic play so that all children can benefit from this important type of play.

In dramatic and sociodramatic play, concrete objects and play materials are less important than what children do and say, and the ways in which they interact with each other. Divergent and convergent thinking skills, problem-solving abilities, and the ability to take a perspective other than one's own are more important to successful sociodramatic play experiences. Social skills such as the ability to initiate interaction, accept other children's ideas, and observe and follow the interpretations of others are also involved. Memory skills, including the ability to remember many past experiences and the behavioural subtleties that accompany them, are important to the child's desire to represent real life. More research on the relationship between sociodramatic play and child development is needed.

SOCIODRAMATIC PLAY

■ TEACHERS' ROLES IN FACILITATING SOCIODRAMATIC PLAY

A major component of teachers' roles in facilitating sociodramatic play involves establishing a play and learning environment that will support and encourage this type of play. This strategy includes planning the schedule to allow for long, unhurried play periods and arranging space so as to maximize children's freedom to play without interference or interruption. Meaningful opportunities for children to engage in dramatic and sociodramatic play require space that is dedicated to encouraging and supporting these types of play.

Sociodramatic play, in particular, relies on the interdependence of two or more children who take cues from each other and engage in the joint creation of a script that is familiar and meaningful to all of the children involved. Such creative play requires time and freedom from interruption. Teachers have to provide a supportive environment, props, and the relative seclusion required for sociodramatic play to begin and flourish. Learning centres rich in props, with sufficient space for movement, and some protection from the heavy traffic areas and noise from other centres enhance and support the special nature of symbolic play. By adding more varied and realistic props for play, teachers can facilitate symbolic processes.

Children's ability to use symbols generally moves from the simple to the more complex. That is, they need more realistic props initially (e.g., a toy telephone will prompt a child to dial and put the receiver to her ear); then more abstract props (e.g., a block for a car, a rolled blanket for a baby); and finally, the use of verbal representation without a concrete prop (e.g., "let's say that I'm holding a sign that says 'STOP'") (Pelligrini, 1984).

Sometimes teachers feel uncomfortable when children are engaged in dramatic play because they cannot find a role for themselves. Dramatic and sociodramatic play offer children the chance to reconstruct their own experiences and to pursue their own agendas. Teachers should not impose on them their own vision of how children should play and what they should pretend, symbolize, or dramatize. Children will be able to recreate experiences according to their own understanding of them.

Teachers contribute positively to children's sociodramatic play when they take children on field trips to interesting places and read them stories that relate to real-life events. It is from the well of their own experience that children draw the ideas and motivation for dramatizing and trying to understand the world around them. The importance of enriching experiences in the outside world of the neighbourhood and broader community is all the more crucial for children whose everyday experiences are limited.

Once sociodramatic play has begun, it is often best for teachers to become observers rather than intervene unnecessarily in play that is sustained. This means that unless their play poses some risk to themselves or others, children should be permitted to play out even negative episodes (Sawyers & Rogers, 1988). Pretend violence, for example, is not at all uncommon in preoperational children and allowing them to indulge their violent fantasies will not cause them to grow up to become violent adults (Bettelheim, 1976; 1987). It is best for teachers to observe carefully and try to determine the purpose and meaning behind the negative feelings demonstrated than to risk stopping the play prematurely. The same thinking applies to permitting children to use props in a variety of different and unusual ways that often stretch the imagination and to letting them act out bizarre roles that seem to have no bearing on real life (Sawyers & Rogers, 1988).

The only times when intervention by teachers in sociodramatic play is justified occurs when children need help in order to hold onto an idea or a script, or when they are having difficulty choosing a new direction for their role play. The teacher may at such times intervene with a question or comment, or even assume a role briefly herself without interrupting or changing the nature of the episode being dramatized; for example, she may say, "I'll be the grandmother and take the baby for a walk so that the mummy can take the bus to see her friend in the hospital."

Teachers respect the integrity of sociodramatic play when they protect children from interference in it, provide appropriate props, and let children choose and decide how long they will play (Sawyers & Rogers, 1988). They observe children's behaviours and respond to their questions when they arise, but do so without causing children to lose track of their own script. Learning centres that promote dramatic and sociodramatic play foster an emergent curriculum that children build for themselves as they interact and cue in to each other. The Daily Living Centre and the Active Role Play Centre are dedicated to supporting dramatic and sociodramatic play.

References

Bettelheim, B. (1976). *The Uses of Enchantment*. New York: Vintage.

Bettelheim, B. (1987). The importance of play. *The Atlantic* 262 (3):35–46.

Butler, A., Gotts, E.E., and Quisenberry, N. (1978). *Play as Development*. Columbus, OH: Merrill.

Christie, J.F., and Wardle, F. (1992). How much time is needed for play? *Young Children* 47 (3):28–32.

Garvey, C. (1977). *Play*. Cambridge, MA: Harvard University Press.

Pelligrini, A.D. (1980). The relationships between kindergartners' play and reading, writing and language achievement. *Psychology in the School* 17:530–35.

Pelligrini, A.D. (1984). Children's play and language: infancy through early childhood. In *Child's Play and Play Therapy*, ed.T.D.

Yawkey and A.D. Pelligrini, pp. 45–58. Lancaster, PA: Technomic Publishing Co. Inc.

Rubin, K.H. (1980). Fantasy play: its role in the development of social skills and social cognition. In *New Directions in Child Development: Children's Play*, ed. K.H. Rubin, pp. 69–84. San Francisco: Jossey-Bass.

Rubin, K., Fein, G., and Vandenberg, B. (1983). Play. In *Handbook of Child Psychology: Vol. 4. Socialization, Personality and Social Development*, ed. P.H. Mussen and E.M. Hetherington, pp. 693–774. New York: Wiley.

Sawyers, J.K., and Rogers, C.S. (1988). *Young Children Develop Through Play*. Washington, D.C.: National Association for the Education of Young Children.

Smilansky, S. (1968). *The Effects of Sociodramatic Play on Disadvantaged Preschool Children*. New York: Wiley.

Smilansky, S. (1971). Can adults facilitate play in children? In *Play: The Child Strives Toward Self-Realization*, ed. S. Arnaud and N. Curry. Washington, D.C.: National Association for the Education of Young Children.

Smilansky, S., and Sheftaya, L. (1990). *Facilitating Play: A Medium for Promoting Cognitive, Socio-Emotional and Academic Development in Young Children*. Gaithersburg, MD: Psychosocial & Educational Publications.

C H A P T E R 10

THE DAILY LIVING CENTRE

■ PURPOSE OF THE DAILY LIVING CENTRE

In the Daily Living Centre, children are able to relate to the props that represent things typically found at home and in the child's surrounding neighbourhood. They use props such as adult clothing and accessories for family life and work, miniature household appliances and furniture, telephones, radios, and gear associated with various occupational groups. Children go to this centre to enjoy a homelike setting and practise roles from the family and community which are familiar and meaningful to them.

The Daily Living Centre reinforces the importance of family and community living and the similarities that exist among families however they are constituted. This learning centre should impose no constraints on how families can be defined. The range of equipment, materials, and supplies found here should reflect the cultural diversity of the child and family population in the community.

As children become increasingly capable in their use of symbols and are able to represent concrete and imagined experiences, fantasy, and events from real life, they engage more frequently in pretend play. Their play alone or in groups is increasingly reproductive of the world as they experience it. Props that can be used to symbolize whatever the child has in mind are important components of the learning environment.

The physical setting and climate of this learning centre provides messages to children that they may assume roles of the adult world and pretend to be someone or something else. Here, they cooperate with other children in recreating scenes or events from real life and allow their imaginations and each other to dictate the flow of their play together or alone.

■ THE DAILY LIVING CENTRE AND CHILD DEVELOPMENT

Nash (1989) sees two related types of learning occurring in this centre: factual concepts and feelings concepts. *Factual concepts* relate to everyday life. They are the answers to questions like What is a restaurant? a briefcase? a condominium? Can boys be nurses? How does a beauty salon work? What is it like where my mummy works? *Feelings concepts* are explored through play that allows children to project themselves into highly emotional situations that are often more complex than they can describe in words. What is it like to have a baby sister? Can I look after a baby too? What does it mean to be unemployed? Why are my daddy and mummy angry? Such questions arouse intense feelings in children, which they are often at a loss to understand without "trying on" the roles involved. Role play is an important teaching strategy that allows adults to gain a more complete perspective on the situations with which children must learn to deal effectively. Children, too, find some answers to calm their fears and cast some light on the complexities of everyday life by assuming certain roles for themselves.

The child who pretends to care for a baby sister and who stuffs the large purse to represent a briefcase and pretends to be mummy leaving for work in the morning comes closer to an understanding of what life will be like with a new baby in the house and what her mother's life is like when she is away from her. Children also express feelings about their own life experiences while they are engaged in dramatic and sociodramatic play. They may express anger that mummy is always too tired to play with them and anguish at the fear of being displaced by a new baby. One child was overheard to express his fear of being a "trade-in" before his new sibling was born. By replaying a scene in which he had accompanied his parents to trade in the old car for a new one in recent weeks, an observant teacher concluded that he was afraid that his father and expectant mother would trade him in for a new baby brother or sister.

Sociodramatic play encourages a level of intimacy among children who agree implicitly to pursue common aims in their pretending. It teaches children that families are similar and different, people behave in predictable and unpredictable ways, there are happy feelings and sad feelings, and events and contexts are continually changing.

Language development, concept learning, emotional expression, and social interaction emerge from role play and props, which contribute to the rich learning potential of the Daily Living Centre. Cooperative play with props also promotes manipulative abilities (e.g., doing up zippers, tying bows, rolling dough, and stacking dishes) and teaches factual information such as "this is a garlic press," "my daddy wears overalls to fix cars," and "Angie's family eats with chopsticks like these." Factual knowledge, emotional expression, language, logical concepts, and social understanding are enhanced by children's reproductive play with props and artifacts.

■ ORGANIZATION AND DESIGN OF THE DAILY LIVING CENTRE

Specialized Play Areas

The Daily Living Centre includes a housekeeping area, doll play area, and clothing and props area. Props such as a puppet theatre and doll house may be located close to the housekeeping area but should not be allowed to interfere with family-dynamic play. Puppet theatres may also be used for other purposes like a store counter or post office, and the doll house may be moved to a more prominent position in the learning centre or removed temporarily. Specialized play areas may be clearly defined or open to each other without any visible boundaries. When space allows, the inclusion of a potential unit where special or theme-based play activities may be set up, adds richness and variety to the types of play activities normally found in this learning centre.

A table with four chairs where children can use playdough as a prop for moulding and cutting playdough cookies or rolling out the dough is an important specialized play area in the Daily Living Centre. It is usually located in the housekeeping area. In this context, dough is regarded as a prop to enhance symbolic play rather than as a creative substance. The texture and consistency of the dough and the use of specialized implements such as rolling pins, cookie cutters, and cutlery also provide important opportunities for children to practise fine motor skills, eye-hand coordination, hand control, and a wide range of other manipulative and perceptual abilities.

Equipment, Materials, and Supplies

Equipment—kitchen set, including refrigerator, stove, dish cupboard and sink, small table with chairs; cradle, storage shelves for equipment, rack for dressup clothing; child-sized bed, child-sized rocking chair, dresser for doll clothes.

Materials—house play: baking utensil set, dish set, pots and pans set, laundry and cleaning equipment, iron and ironing board, tea towels, sponges, dish rack, mirror, laundry basket, broom and mop, dustpan.

role play: male and female small-sized adult clothing; mirror; occupational clothing, including helmets, hats, shoes, lunch bucket, briefcase, masks, wigs; prop kits containing props for store, hospital, restaurant, beauty salon, barber shop, mechanic

Figure 10.1   THE DAILY LIVING CENTRE

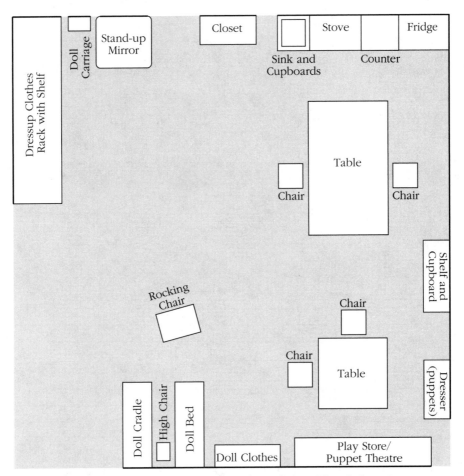

Social contexts of play emphasized in the Daily Living Centre

solitary
parallel (pretend and dramatic play)
cooperative (sociodramatic play)

Categories of play emphasized in the Daily Living Centre

functional: practice play
productive play
symbolic: pretend
dramatic
sociodramatic play

shop, farms, and for specific cultural, historical, and mythical themes. Prop kits should be set up one or two at a time; too many prop kits available at one time could lead to confusion and overstimulation.

doll play: assorted dolls, ethnic doll accessories, bedding, baby bottles, doll clothing, doll strollers, doll bathtub, doll high chair.

miscellaneous: telephone, cuddly stuffed toys, puppets–hand/finger puppets, people puppets, puppet theatre.

Supplies—play dough, paper towels, liquid soap, Kleenex, Q-tips, bandages, J-cloths.

RATINGS OF THE CHARACTERISTICS OF PLAY

THE DAILY LIVING CENTRE

noisy	——————————	quiet
teacher-centred	——————————	child-centred
structured	——————————	open
concrete	——————————	abstract
clean	——————————	messy
specific-purpose materials	——————————	open-ended materials
group	——————————	individual

(Adapted with permission of the Board of Education, City of Hamilton. *Getting It All Together* (1981).)

■ PLAY STATIONS IN THE DAILY LIVING CENTRE

Housekeeping Area

At a glance, the housekeeping area in most classrooms resembles a basic house or apartment. It should contain a child-sized fridge, stove, cupboards for dishes and pans, a small table and chairs, an iron and ironing board, a child-sized bed, rocking chair, or sofa. A miniature window with curtains may be built onto the wall or divider, pretty placemats and cushions may decorate the tables and chairs, and a non-toxic plant or two may be added to enhance the domesticity and coziness of the setting. Posters on the walls or small, framed prints add homelike qualities.

A miniature house or apartment setting provides clear cues to children that role play of family and household events and roles are possible and encouraged in this

HOUSEKEEPING AREA

part of the classroom. Miniature appliances and furniture are props that support family life role play. Children are able to explore the complex relationships and responsibilities of life in a typical household and become aware of the similarities between their lives at home and those of their peers. Props and artifacts of home life are usually instantly recognizable to children whose pretend play with them often leads to sociodramatic play.

Where space permits, the housekeeping centre with table and chairs and relevant props becomes an interesting setting in which teachers, visiting parents, or other guests may conduct individual cooking activities with small groups of children. These activities may also be an opportunity to demonstrate the ethnic mix of children in the group. Individual portion cookery is most appropriate for young children and reduces possible hazards associated with infection (Veitch & Harms, 1981). In some jurisdictions, local health authorities have established guidelines for the conduct of cooking activities, which must be observed.

Multiculturalism in the Housekeeping Area

The housekeeping area should integrate multicultural artifacts, implements, everyday clothing, clothing for celebration, and festival ornaments. These props often contain several recognizable elements for all children in the group and reinforce the similarities that exist among all cultures. For example, children recognize chopsticks as eating implements like knives and forks and the wok as another kind of cooking pan. All families have both particular and universal rituals associated with mealtimes. All cultural groups spend time in food preparation and rely on specific tools to facilitate meal planning and cooking. The housekeeping area is a powerful learning environment for reinforcing the similarities that exist across cultures.

Activities in the Housekeeping Area

(for younger children, ages two to four)

1. Sort the pots, pans, trays, dishes in order to tidy up the cupboards. Let children decide on the categories for sorting or help them by setting out some possible groups.

2. Use the cookie cutters to cut out shapes from rolled-out playdough and pretend to bake them in the oven. Move from three basic shapes to more complex ones and then go to other configurations that children will recognize (e.g., Christmas trees, teddy bears, gingerbread children, hearts, wreaths, stars, flowers.

3. Wash the dishes using real water and suds in the sink. Encourage cooperative play by suggesting that another child help to dry the dishes.

4. Wash the doll clothes in the sink. Children may work together and learn to care for the clothes by following steps such as using suds, rinsing well, blotting dry with a towel, and hanging on the clothesline.

5. Practise using chopsticks to pick up small pieces of pea-sized playdough that the children have made.

6. Polish the shoes from the dressup area. This is a cooperative task that also involves waiting for the polish to dry.

7. Brush the teeth of a plaster cast (from the local dentist or orthodontist) with tooth brushes and tooth powder at the table and chairs (using individual bowls of water).

8. Match pairs of smelly jars, each jar to its mate, which has the same smell (children cannot identify the substance through the jar).

9. Use tweezers to put navy beans or kidney beans in small cups.

10. Use a gravy strainer to syringe coloured water from bowls on a tray and squirt into containers with small openings (at the table and chairs).

11. Sift and measure, using sifters and measuring cups, a cornmeal or flour mixture.

12. Sort bowls of unshelled mixed nuts into categories according to criteria chosen by the children.

13. Sort substances according to taste with separate tasting bowls for each child and individual popsicle sticks to use for each substance they taste.

14. Match lids to pots, pans, jars, other storage items. Practise putting the lids on the containers—a range of difficulty from very easy lids to screw on to plastic lids which have to be moulded, using the hand and fingers to seal the lid.

15. Compare raw and cooked foods according to taste, touch, smell, and temperature. Eat the foods for a snack.

16. Fold the laundry (e.g., tea towels, napkins, placemats, diapers for dolls, baby clothes, blankets and bedding, and cushion covers).

(for older children, ages four to six)

17. Stack measuring cups, measuring spoons, and scoops in seriated order. Include multicultural implements in items to be stacked and seriated.
18. Plan a tea party with invited guests. Children will draw up the menu, plan the "food," assemble the dishes, and make invitations for the guests (likely in the Creative Arts Centre).
19. Make some celery stalks stuffed with cream cheese and raisins for a snack. Children should remember the steps to follow, beginning with washing their hands as they work with individual portions to be consumed by themselves.
20. Make, decorate, and bake individual portion cookies for special occasions such as Valentine's Day and Halloween.
21. Have children peel and section tangerines and mandarin oranges for their own snacks, placing wafers at the side of their own napkin or plate.
22. Suggest that children go and play "house." Ensure that props are accessible to them as they become useful to the evolving script of the children. Step into their "drama" as a character who may fit in with the dramatic context in order to give a message or attempt to help them extend an idea. For example, there are two knocks at the door. The teacher enters the "house" and says, "good morning; here is your newspaper which says that a snack will be available today at the table in the Quiet Thinking Centre"; or, "Mrs. Jones just called to say that it's a beautiful day to take the baby for a walk..."
23. Polish the silver and brass ornaments (wear plastic gloves) and shine them well. Children should be encouraged to cooperate with this task, which involves learning to care for property and take pride in the quality of one's work.
24. Clean dirty golf balls with a tooth brush and liquid soap at the sink.
25. Sort miscellaneous materials according to texture (e.g., pieces of fur, plastic, sticks, sandpaper, rocks, foam rubber, styrofoam, fabrics of different textures (at table and chairs).

Doll Play Area in the Daily Living Centre

Main items of equipment include doll cribs, trunk or drawers for doll clothes, doll high chair, and doll stroller or carriage. The explicit purpose of the doll area is to promote children's role play of family and caregiving roles such as mother, father, teacher, babysitter, doctor, and nurse. The ability to care for and nurture others is an important social-emotional objective for early childhood.

ROLE PLAY

Children's mental health is affected by how they feel about other people and whether they are able to extend themselves in caring for others (Yardley, 1988). Practising the gestures, behaviours, and language associated with caregiving, gentleness, dependence, and nurturing helps children internalize and understand feelings associated with close, dependent relationships. Ability to care and look after others are powerful emotional capacities which promote self-expression, empathy, sympathy, and compassion. These affective characteristics are closely related to developing a spiritual life in which children learn respect and reverence for life, express feelings of wonder, and act out attitudes of consideration and concern for others.

Play with dolls may take many forms. A very young child cradling a doll tenderly and cooing softly while curled up on a cushion in a corner, begins to feel and integrate a sense of what it is like to extend oneself in the care of another human being. Besides imitating the actions of a mother or father rocking the baby, the child is rehearsing a familiar family caregiving role and feeling what it must be like to be a parent.

The doll play area provides opportunities for associative play in which children play with dolls individually, but beside others, rehearsing their own mental scripts without interacting. Social interaction occurs when children combine their dramatic play scripts to take specific roles and follow a jointly conceived plan that unfolds as play continues. One child may appoint herself the mummy, another child the daddy, and another the baby, and then announces to her playmates the script to be followed as the other two children happily comply with the plan. Sometimes considerable negotiation occurs with all children participating in the allocation of roles. Many social contexts and types of play are possible in the doll play area.

DOLL PLAY AREA

In today's world, it is an unfortunate fact of life for many children that their parents are busy, often preoccupied, and have little time for traditional and special family events, which used to be taken for granted. Some families have the amenities and resources to continue to build rituals and regular family-centred experiences in their children's lives. But the reality these days is that the family sometimes fails to teach children "family skills" and delegates this responsibility to child care programs, schools, and teachers (Smilansky, 1990). The doll play and housekeeping areas may become important settings in which teachers provide an environment and materials with which children may help each other dramatize and practise familiar rituals from their own families.

The doll play area is an important place in the playroom to encourage non-stereotypic play and tolerance for others. Role play by boys as well as girls in the doll play area should be encouraged and supported. Dolls representing many cultural and racial groups help to break down stereotyped views, which prevent the development of enlightened attitudes and positive relationships among ethnic groups. The doll play area should be arranged and set up to provide cues to boys that they are welcome and that this is an area in which they can express themselves emotionally, develop nurturing skills, and practise caregiving roles with babies.

Activities in the Doll Play Area

(for younger children, ages two to four)

1. Dress dolls in a variety of clothes with different types of closures such as snaps, buttons, velcro, ties, buckles, and hooks and eyes.

2. Iron doll clothes using toy iron and ironing board.

3. Tidy up and sort doll clothes in drawers or trunk.

4. Fold towels, blankets, sheets for cribs; make up doll cribs with bedding and tuck dolls in.

5. Provide special dolls (e.g., Dapper Dan and Dressy Bessy) for children to practise dressing skills that they can transfer to dressing and undressing more lifelike dolls and themselves.

6. Set up a baby nursery with props such as bottles and bibs for feeding, baby food jars and small spoons, baby bath for bathing babies, baby clothes, and receiving blankets.

7. Provide infant toys for children to use to play with the "babies." (Children will enjoy using rattles, teething rings, baby bottles, squeezy toys, foam animals and balls, and other infant toys from their own experience while caring for the dolls.)

8. Play lullabies on the tape or record player and encourage children to sing along to their "babies."

(for older children, ages four to six)

9. Set up a hospital setting in the doll play area by adding hospital/doctor/nurse play materials to promote role play with typical hospital artifacts. Provide syringes, stethoscopes, tongue depressors, bandages, prescription pads, hospital gowns, nurse caps, blood pressure kits, etc.

10. Read stories that children may dramatize in the doll play area in which males and females share caregiving and nurturing roles. Provide props needed for children to dramatize male/female roles, for example, male nurses, female doctors, and mothering and fathering roles.

11. Classify the doll clothes in the trunk or drawers when tidying up; sort the blankets, sheets, nighties, dresses, overalls, hats, socks, etc.

12. Identify the body parts of dolls.

13. Label and name the dolls and the clothing.

14. Provide dolls from other cultures and read stories in which the culture is represented by a doll who is dressed like a character in the story.

15. Suggest a project to children in which they will measure, compare, and fit the dolls for new clothes. Use measuring tape, trace dolls onto paper to provide a model, plan materials to use, etc.

Dressup/Props Area in the Daily Living Centre

Dressup clothing and props should be stored in mobile wooden cabinets on wheels that open to define a boundary for play space and are closed when not in use. Hooks may be used to hang clothing. Sometimes shelves for storing hats, belts, shoes, purses, and the like are built into the cabinet. A wide selection of adult clothing for both genders, in good repair, preferably washable and in small sizes, which may include dresses, overalls, pants, uniforms, gowns, aprons, blazers, coats, blouses and skirts, shirts, and a variety of men's and women's shoes both low-heeled and some with slightly high heels, for sports as well as day and evening wear, are typical for this play area. Multicultural clothing for everyday and ceremonial occasions enrich play and expose children to clothing typical of other lifestyles and customs within North America and in other countries.

DRESSUP/PROPS AREA

It is important that all clothing be easy for children to put on and take off. Sometimes difficult zippers or fasteners need to be replaced with velcro strips, especially in integrated programs where children with special needs may have difficulty pulling clothing over limbs or trying to move freely.

Dramatic and sociodramatic play are facilitated by the provision of adult-style clothing and props that add a real-life quality to children's pretend play. The child trotting around in a pair of high-heeled shoes, carrying a purse, and wearing a hat feels all the more the mummy she is pretending to be on her way to a garden party. Capes, briefcases, canes, dresses, overalls, hats representing occupational groups, lunch buckets, shopping bags, and numerous other familiar everyday living objects add to the duration, depth, and realism of symbolic play.

When children assume roles familiar to them in their lives, they gain a better understanding of what it must be like to be an adult in that role. Role play facilitates children's growing cognitive ability to take a perspective other than their own and to put themselves in another's shoes. By simply putting on clothing that represents a role that is strange yet interesting to them, children achieve a clearer sense of their own self-concept and secretly wonder "should I aspire to become a police officer?

farmer? television personality? nurse?" Roles never before imagined for themselves or for others come into clearer focus by virtue of adding the concrete symbols of the role to their small bodies.

Clothing and props in the Daily Living Centre also communicate messages to children that enhance and extend sociodramatic play. The presence of dressup clothing and props representative of the roles they are playing provide the necessary cues to the group that will help prolong the script and the roles being assumed. Clothing and props are visual cues that allow the teacher to assess quickly the roles and life experiences being dramatized. Teachers may gain further insight into the aspirations, motivations, and interests of children by tuning in to their conversations and assumptions as they follow a plan or evolve a script.

Activities in the Dressup/Props Area

(for younger children, ages two to four)

1. Set up a pet hospital using medical kits, ironing board, hospital gowns, masks, gloves, and stuffed animals.
2. Distribute clothing and jewellery with unusual fasteners for children to practise fastening and unfastening on each other as well as themselves (also clips, snaps, buckles, small and large buttons, clasps, spring fasteners, etc.).
3. Provide clothing that enhances certain body parts such as chaps for the legs, tall riding boots, belts for the waist, gloves, knee supports, hats, and shoulder pads.

(for older children, ages four to six)

4. Add office equipment and supplies to the dressup/prop area to facilitate children's dramatic or sociodramatic play involving the roles of mothers and fathers at work.
5. Suggest a familiar role to a group of children who are already dressed up in clothing reminiscent of an event or experience that you know they have recently had.
6. Ask children from other cultures to bring discarded clothing from home to show, demonstrate how to wear it, and explain what it is called and when it is worn.
7. Encourage children to act out an event about which they show evidence of fear and concern. For example, during the Gulf War, children were demonstrating fearful reactions to media reports of events of the war and were unable to understand their meaning, proximity to themselves, or whether they themselves would be personally affected. Engaging in sociodramatic play at times like these helps children unravel some of the complexities of the events and confront and maybe verbalize their deepest fears.

8. Encourage play using prop boxes. Prop boxes are addressed in Chapter 17, which looks at the Science Discovery Centre. Teachers may provide props associated with various themes in separate boxes for each type of theme-related play. For example, in the Dressup/Props Area, there may be prop boxes containing props for hospital/medical play, beauty salon play, auto repair shop play, deep sea diver play, and so on.

Puppets/Doll House Area

Most early childhood classrooms provide a puppet theatre, puppets of various kinds, and a doll house with miniature furniture. These play materials are usually mobile and may be located in the Quiet Thinking Centre or in or near the Daily Living Centre. In the Daily Living Centre they are primarily intended to encourage dramatic play with the puppets or miniature dolls in the doll house. Children's identification with a puppet or miniature doll in a doll house is not as complete or active as when they assume the role themselves. They may, however, feel less inhibited about expressing anger, sadness, hurt, confusion, or aggressive feelings through an "arm's length" drama, using puppets or miniature dolls as props.

In the Quiet Thinking Centre, teachers frequently use puppets during group time to talk to the children or enhance the telling or reading of a story. When teachers engage in dialogue with a puppet, they model conversation that facilitates language development as well as children's understanding of the rules for engaging in polite conversation.

Activities in the Puppets/Doll House Area

(for younger children, ages two to four)

1. Provide hand puppets in the Quiet Thinking Centre for children to use while looking at books and reading stories.

2. Encourage children to play with puppets when they appear distressed or angry as a way to unleash negative emotions or to help them unravel complex feelings or events.

3. Provide a puppet for a child who appears troubled and is unable to tell the teacher what is troubling him. Ask him to let the puppet explain how he feels.

4. Use finger puppets with finger plays.

5. Provide hand puppets for children to manipulate during storytime or while singing.

(for older children, ages four to six)

6. Take children to see a puppet theatre production. Encourage them to put on a puppet show for themselves.

7. Read a story and suggest that children act out a scene from the story using the clothing and props.

8. Encourage children to make their own hand or finger puppets in the Creative Arts Centre and to then tell a story using their puppets.

References

Conlon, A. (1992). Giving Mrs. Jones a hand; making group storytime more pleasurable and meaningful for young children. *Young Children* 47(3): 14–18.

Nash, C. (1989). *The Learning Environment: a Practical Approach to the Education of the Three-, Four- and Five-Year-Old*. Toronto: Collier-Macmillan.

Smilansky, S. (1990). A new model for home/school relationships and the development of responsibility in children. A pre-conference presentation sponsored by Nova University at the Annual Conference of the National Association for the Education of Young Children. Washington, D.C.: November 14, 1990.

Veitch, B., and Harms, T. (1981). *Cook and Learn: Pictorial Single Portion Recipes*. Menlo Park, CA: Addison-Wesley.

Yardley, A. (1988). *Senses and Sensitivity*. Young Children Learning series. Oakville, Ontario: Rubicon.

THE ACTIVE ROLE PLAY CENTRE

■ PURPOSE OF THE ACTIVE ROLE PLAY CENTRE

The Active Role Play Centre is dedicated to large muscle, gross motor play, including active sociodramatic play, with large equipment and props. This learning centre provides opportunities for children to develop physically while engaging in role play. When children assume roles in a cooperative play context, they practise expressing themselves verbally and physically, use divergent thinking skills, increase their language competence, develop their bodies, and enhance their images of themselves.

Children's self-concept is closely related to their perceptions of the competence of their own bodies in physical activities. The muscles, skeleton, and proportions of the body are for the most part genetically determined and are well developed by the later stages of early childhood. Practice and plenty of physical activity promote the child's motor coordination and physical abilities.

The climber, hollow blocks, planks and ramps, vehicles and props such as blankets, firefighters' hats and hoses, big cardboard boxes, and a playhouse, give children messages that active, social play is encouraged in this area. Larger open space in which to move encourages more expansive role play than the closer quarters of the Daily Living Centre. Children should have room to use hollow blocks to build large structures onto which they can climb or to make intricate road networks for cars and trucks. Ramps and planks allow children to cordon off a large play structure or to close in a playhouse made of blocks. Children may be encouraged to develop their own super units in the Active Role Play Centre such as a space station, an undersea exploration site, or a fire station. Relevant props to extend and enhance role play may be added to support the setting children have tried to create.

Active problem solving, representation, spatial concepts, the development of teamwork, cooperation, and language are important developmental goals in this

PURPOSE OF THE ACTIVE ROLE PLAY AREA

learning centre. To maximize the range of role play opportunities available, the Active Role Play Centre should be situated close to the Daily Living Centre. This juxtaposition allows props to be shared between the two centres, role play to be extended from one centre to the other, and larger groups of children to be accommodated.

When space in a classroom is limited, the Active Role Play Centre is often separated from the other centres, and may even be located in another part of the school or child care centre. However, there are some disadvantages when this learning centre is isolated from the others. One is that opportunities for transfer of play and learning from one centre to another are decreased; another may be that of missed opportunities to combine the use of props, materials, and accessories from one role play area to another.

On the other hand, separation from the other learning centres may also mean that a greater amount of space is available to the Active Role Play Centre, especially if it is located in a basement or a specially designed psychomotor room. A bigger space may also mean that large, stationary equipment such as tunnels, ramps, spheres, climbing apparatus, and even vehicles and vehicle pathways may be more or less permanently installed, still leaving open space for sociodramatic play.

The Active Role Play Centre often provides interesting space for a *potential unit.* An empty corner with boundaries may become a place for children to create a super unit such as a courier depot for trucks and cars, an auto repair shop, or a fire department with hoses, ramps, trucks, helmets, and rubber boots.

The Active Role Play Centre may also serve as an indoor active play substitute for the playground on days when it is too cold, wet, or hot for children to play outdoors. When children cannot play outdoors, the Active Role Play Centre may become the principal area where children can stretch their limbs, be active and noisy, and release energy. On these occasions, teachers will have to put away some props, accessories, and play materials temporarily in order to provide more room for large muscle play, organized physical activities, and group games.

Organized physical programs may be conducted daily or several times a week in this psychomotor learning centre. Children require many free play opportunities every day for vigorous physical play that is self-directed, self-initiated, and free of constraints. They also need regular, planned programs of physical activity that make it more likely that all developmental goals of the physical domain will be addressed systematically and mastered by children. One way to be sure that children have opportunities to develop optimally in all areas of physical development is to plan organized activities which address specific skills. These specialized programs may or may not take place in the Active Role Play Centre, depending on the space available and the season of the year. The Canadian Institute of Child Health has recommended that pre-service and in-service training in physical education for young children be offered nationwide in order to upgrade the skills of teachers in facilitating children's physical development (Nault & Hanvey, 1991).

■ FACILITATING THE DEVELOPMENT OF PHYSICAL SKILLS

The young child's relationship with the concrete world is intimate and compelling. The responsive environment gives back messages as the child acts upon it. Physically challenging environments are like cognitively stimulating environments; they are rich in concrete objects, media to explore, sensory experiences, problems to solve, and opportunities for risk taking. New opportunities are provided when former challenges have been mastered.

Physical development is linked to cognitive, emotional, and social development. In the cognitive domain, concept learning such as the understanding of space, direction, time-space orientation, position, distance, and body awareness may be achieved through physical activity. Think of the learning that takes place when children try running an obstacle course. They bend, climb, stretch, jump, hop, and roll while passing the stations in the obstacle course, and build muscles and motor skills in the process. They are simultaneously learning directional prepositions such as *around, over, through*, and *between*. In order to negotiate the obstacles correctly, children have to attend to the teacher's verbal instructions or pictorial signs at each station and then be able to execute those instructions successfully. When trying to squeeze through a tunnel, they have to figure out how small to make their bodies so as to fit and pass through. Spatial awareness, which is also a cognitive skill, is developed along with muscular and motor competence.

Although children also develop physically through spontaneous play in unplanned environments, their physical development is enhanced through play in a planned environment that promotes regular, active involvement in activities that address a comprehensive range of physical skills. (See Appendix B).

Children gain knowledge and understanding through physical games that incorporate the learning of colours, time, size, numbers, social behaviour, language, cultural awareness, and other everyday living concepts. Children find it easier to communicate and use language fluently while performing physical tasks. Words learned in the context of a physical experience are usually understood and seldom forgotten. For example, a teacher may respond to block play in the Active Role Play Centre by saying, "it looks a little like a condominium to me," to a child who doesn't know what to call the multi-level structure she has constructed with hollow blocks. The teacher's suggestion of a word at that moment is likely to make a more lasting impression than a group activity on words that describe types of houses.

Children's self-concept is related to their perceptions of their own physical characteristics and abilities. They are particularly vulnerable to criticism or mockery of their physical abilities or appearance. We know that positive self-concept is, in the early years, linked to children's abilities to use their bodies effectively and to be admired and accepted by their peers (Whitehurst, 1971; Gallahue, 1982). Physical activity, whether always competently executed or not, has the side effect of permitting a release and a channelling of emotion and pent-up energy. Creative physical programming facilitates children's social adaptation, emotional well-being, spiritual growth, creativity, and intellectual growth.

Physical development occurs indoors and outdoors; the classroom and the playground complement one another. The world beyond the physical boundaries of the school is also a learning environment. The sensory experience the child gains outdoors making mud pies or listening to the rustle of the leaves on a tree is extended to indoor play, when making pies with playdough or singing a song about leaves swishing in the breeze. The teacher who puts child development into compartments and believes that physical competence is acquired only on the jungle gym, or only outdoors playing active games has forgotten about the interdependence of children's learning in all domains.

The indoor environment is rich in opportunities to perceive using all the senses. The creative tables are a physical learning environment where children touch, smell, develop pincer movements, learn to grasp or crush, mould, manipulate, bend, fold, and guide. Eye-hand coordination, sensory acuity, and fine motor skills are developed at the collage table just as surely as the large muscles are exercised on the climber. All classroom learning centres promote progress in several domains and not just the most obvious one.

Creativity, language, representation, and self-expression are fostered by children's assumptions of roles such as those of a firefighter, police officer, deep-sea diver, or astronaut. In this centre children also solve problems such as "how many hollow blocks do I need to stand on in order to be as high as the top of the climber?" Communication, representation, and social skills are practised as children collaborate in the building of a space station with blocks, blankets, and the climber. Logical thinking skills are challenged by estimating how many giant steps will bring them to the end of the room. The Active Role Play Centre promotes the development of the whole child.

■ ORGANIZATION AND DESIGN OF THE ACTIVE ROLE PLAY CENTRE

The Active Role Play Centre should include a large muscle play area (physical activities), a playhouse area, a hollow block area with various props, and a music and movement area.

RATINGS OF THE CHARACTERISTICS OF PLAY

THE ACTIVE ROLE PLAY CENTRE

noisy	quiet
teacher-centred	child-centred
structured	open
concrete	abstract
clean	messy
specific-purpose materials	open-ended materials
group	individual

(Adapted with permission of the Board of Education, City of Hamilton. *Getting It All Together.* (1981).)

Equipment and Materials

Equipment—climbing apparatus, shelves for materials, shelves for hollow blocks, boards, ramps, prop rack, wall pegboard for hanging props and materials.

Figure 11.1   THE ACTIVE ROLE PLAY CENTRE

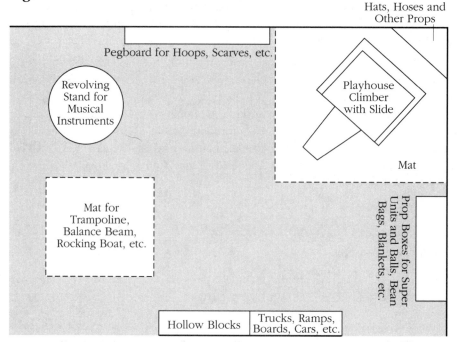

Social contexts of play emphasized in the Active Role Play Centre

parallel
associative
cooperative play

Categories of play emphasized in the Active Role Play Centre

functional: practice play
productive play
creative-constructive play
symbolic: pretend play
dramatic play
sociodramatic play

Materials—dressup hats and helmets; hoses, blankets, hollow blocks, artifact sets (such as Fisher-Price village, airport, farm school, hospital, garage, castle, and zoo), large trucks, wagons, cars, kiddie cars, large boxes, tunnels, skipping ropes, hoops, balls of all sizes, cylinders, punching bag, balance beam, large ropes, bean bags, rocking boat, springboard, box horse, trampoline with tumbling mats for soft landing, props for role play such as wooden chairs, and blankets to make a space station.

■ PLAY STATIONS IN THE ACTIVE ROLE PLAY CENTRE

Large Muscle Play Area

Large muscle play requires materials and equipment that allow children to move freely, impose some stress on their muscles for short periods of time as in climbing, pushing, and pulling, and coordinate large muscle movements in performing specific tasks such as running, jumping, hopping, leaping, galloping, marching, and skipping. In larger Active Role Play Centres, tunnels, spheres, and climbers, may be left out for children to play freely and explore. Big building equipment, large blocks, tumble boards, trampolines, rocking boats, and mats encourage children to lift, press, push, bounce, sway, tumble, and perform other movements designed to develop muscles of the legs, arms, and torso. Balance beams, balance boards, punching bags, skipping ropes, parachutes, hula hoops and vehicles promote gross motor movements requiring greater precision and control of the muscles.

Cooperative Games

Cooperative games are rich in potential for development in all domains and may be accommodated indoors in the Active Role Play Centre during times when they cannot be played outdoors. In addition to promoting prosocial and cognitive skills, cooperative games also provide practice in many fundamental movement patterns and large muscle development. Among the props stored in this centre will likely be a parachute, hoops and ropes, and other materials commonly used in cooperative games.

Activities in the Large Muscle Area

(for younger children, ages two to four)

1. Helicopter run. Children run in a small circle with arms swinging in a circular motion.
2. Children jump over lines on the floor using both feet.

3. Dramatic jumping. Children pretend to be rabbits, kangaroos, grasshoppers, frogs, popcorn, etc.

4. Hoop hopping. Children hop in and out, around, inside, and over hoops spread out on the floor.

5. Leap movements. Have "puddles" cut out of paper and fastened down with tape on the floor and encourage children to run and leap over them.

6. Children pretend to be galloping horses in a paddock.

7. Have children pretend to be caterpillars by lying on the floor, and creeping and crawling along the floor. Show pictures to illustrate how a caterpillar moves.

8. Pattern walking—walk in circles, figure eights, triangles, squares, etc.

9. Dramatic hopping—children imitate bouncing ball movements.

10. Object leaping—children leap over beanbags, hoops, blocks, rope, carpet squares, etc.

11. Galloping train—children line up and hold onto the child in front of them, then gallop in a straight or curved line. This can be done to music with train sounds.

12. Galloping horses—children pretend that they are in stables and come galloping out of their stalls and return to the stalls on the cues of the music.

(for older children, ages four to six)

13. Blanket toss. Have several children hold onto the sides of a blanket, bounce a soccer ball in the air, and try to prevent it from falling onto the floor.

14. Jumping jacks. During physical program time have children jump on the spot in a bilateral movement with arms swinging together above the head and legs in and apart in a smooth motion.

15. Prepare baskets filled with objects like balls of wool, rolled up mittens and socks, bean bags, and so on, and have children imitate pictures of people carrying heavy baskets on their heads.

16. Pathways—create pathways using masking tape or rope with obstacles such as cones and chairs that the child can follow by walking, running, or steering a riding toy. Pathways may be curved, straight, angular, and so on.

17. Giant steps—have the children ask the giant if they can take two giant steps sideways or three baby steps backwards.

18. Tambourine game. The teacher uses a code of signals on the tambourine, each code standing for a basic movement; children have to remember when to walk, jump, hop, crawl, slide, or gallop, depending on the code. Simplify using three movements and codes at first, then gradually increase complexity.

19. Animal tag—divide the children into two groups. One group imitates an animal; if group two guesses correctly which animal group one is imitating, they chase group one and tag as many children as possible. The children who are tagged go onto the group two side. (*Note:* This activity will suit five- and six-year-olds best.)

20. Big turtle—divide a group of children into two groups. Group one, made up of three or more children, gets on their hands and knees, and are covered by a large blanket or parachute. Group two yells commands to the turtle such as "big turtle, go over to the tree," "big turtle move to your left to the wall." The children in group one try to follow the commands staying under the parachute. Group two then becomes the big turtle, and the roles are reversed.

21. Carpet activities—have each child stand on a carpet square. To move, the child must twist by rotating his hips. Once the basic movement is mastered, children can play tag or have relay races while remaining on the carpet.

22. Dramatic walking—children pretend to walk through honey, oil, glue, potato chips, smarties, and so on.

23. Weather walks—walk as if you are in a tornado, walking on leaves, walking in deep snow, ice, and mud.

24. Walk as if in a special place—a haunted house, a toy shop, busy traffic, a jungle, or a swamp.

25. Directional gallop—children gallop and change direction on cue, using taped music or a tambourine.

The Hollow Blocks Area

Hollow blocks have a place in the Active Role Play Centre because their size and weight promote large muscle development and because they may be used as highly adaptable props to promote symbolic play. As they are **creative-constructive play** material, hollow blocks also provide problem-solving opportunities and challenge children to construct representations of structures observed in real life from these relatively crude materials. When children want to extend their sociodramatic play beyond the constraints of the climber and ramps to make a super unit such as a space station or an airport, the hollow blocks are very useful. Sometimes hollow blocks are stored in the same area as the large dump trucks, machinery such as steam shovels and tractors, and with accessories like wooden tree stands, large wooden houses and buildings, and a wooden train set.

The hollow block area may also become the site for many physical science discovery activities. This area can be converted into a place for the investigation of planes and inclines; relationships among motion, speed, and distance; the motion and use of pulleys; the balance of weights and counterweights; the swinging of a pendulum hung from the ceiling to a table holding a fulcrum; the use of levers and wedges for lifting; and many other physical science experiences that require space for children to experiment with large materials. The typical Science Discovery Cen-

HOLLOW BLOCKS

tre may not be large enough for experiments requiring the setting up of large equipment and materials for testing and exploring the many mechanical and physical phenomena that interest children.

Children may also interact with hollow blocks in purely sensorimotor ways, especially when they are very young and enjoy lifting, pulling, pushing, and tugging large objects as a way of developing the large muscles and gross motor skills. Stacks of hollow blocks may become an ideal support for a blanket being used for a tent or fort. Laid out in a grid along the floor, they become clear boundaries for a village or roads for a network of highways. As crude, abstract symbols that can easily assume any role that children assign to them, this area provides great potential for stimulating representational thinking and imagination. Hollow blocks are excellent materials for extending and enriching sociodramatic play in the Active Role Play Centre. Their bulk and weight also add to their usefulness by promoting physical development.

Activities in the Hollow Blocks Area

(for younger children, ages two to four)

1. Practise "bricklaying" after visiting a construction site and watching the bricklayers form a regular pattern with the bricks. Encourage children to build a wall or "foundation" using the blocks. Children may build a wall around the playhouse or around a fort they have constructed from the blocks.

2. Using wagons, have children load and stack and unload the hollow blocks as they deliver them from the Active Role Play Centre to the unit blocks area where they are needed to create a large structure to add to a city, to an apartment complex, or to an amusement park.

(for older children, ages four to six)

3. Take children to visit a local construction site. Back at the centre, suggest that children set up a construction site using the hollow blocks, ramps, trucks, and whatever else they find necessary.

4. Read a story about children sitting around a campfire at night. Provide blankets, parachutes, or large sheets and suggest that children make a tent using the hollow blocks and chairs as props to hold the blanket and pretend to have a campfire. Conduct a circle pretending that the group is sitting around the campfire outside the tent at night.

5. Have children create an obstacle course using the hollow blocks; encourage them to make a variety of obstacles of different configurations. Let the children choose how they will stack the blocks to make each obstacle. Help the children decide on the directions and movements needed to execute the obstacle course.

6. Create a steeplechase track using hollow blocks for children to step over as part of the daily exercise program. Show children pictures of the fences, hedges, and water traps which make up a typical steeplechase track.

7. Help children organize a small play or pageant. Encourage them to build a small platform stage for the performers.

The Accessories and Props Area

An area should be designated for the storage of accessories and props that fill a multitude of purposes determined by the children in their sociodramatic play. This learning centre allows children to role play using larger materials and props that require space. Hanging them from pegboards with hooks, or storing them on open shelves or in large wooden toy boxes with lift-up lids make these materials easily accessible to children at a moment's notice. Ideally, children should be able to reach them for themselves when the mood strikes or when they have a sudden flash of an idea that requires a prop.

The accessories and props area should be located close to the hollow blocks and out of the way of the climber, tricycles, tunnels, large cylinders, and spheres. A pathway to the accessories and props should be kept clear in order that children may easily and safely pull hoops or hats off wall hooks, or lift the drums out of the toy box. The accessories and props area is a useful place to store the musical instru-

ACCESSORIES AND PROPS IN ACTIVE ROLE PLAY

ments that may be kept in a cupboard with doors to ensure that they remain out of the line of fire when they are not in use.

Space to house a table or create a boundary, partially sealing off the accessories and props area from the rest of the centre, may become useful *potential space*. It may be set up as a super unit or specialized play activity using the accessories and props. Given the materials that are available in the props area to serve the entire centre, the potential space could become a sports shop, a repair station, or a music store. Prop boxes, each one containing items addressing a specific theme, may also be made available in the accessories and props area to facilitate children's creation of a particular super unit for sociodramatic play. Prop boxes are addressed in more detail in Chapter 17.

Playhouse Area

An Active Role Play Centre may be large enough to hold a stand-alone playhouse or a combination playhouse and climber that children can enter and use as the focal point for their role play. It is helpful if the playhouse comes equipped with climbing accessories such as a slide, a ramp, and steps, especially if the centre is not large enough to house a full-size climber. The more basic, solid, and unadorned the playhouse is, the better. The absence of accessories makes it easier for children to imagine that the playhouse is any type of structure they want it to become in their play.

Playhouses that are roughly hewn—with four walls, a roof, a window, a door, and some built-in climbing potential—encourage children to decorate the house themselves by adding cushions and curtains to create a domestic atmosphere, or they may add a sign and counter with telephone and cash register if it is to represent a business. The presence of a roof allows the playhouse to become a private place sometimes, where children may find some refuge from the mainstream and find some quiet. Houses with removable roofs provide added flexibility for the teacher who may at times feel a need to monitor or observe children's play in this area. Situating a playhouse in an area where there is some space around it to add wagons, blocks, and ramps permits children to use the playhouse as the centrepiece for a super unit they may wish to create.

SUPERHERO PLAY

■ SUPERHERO PLAY

Some discussion of children's superhero play is relevant to the subject of the Active Role Play Centre, since it is where much of this type of play occurs. Children have had superheroes for as long as children's play has been observed and documented. In the Middle Ages, children played at being knights and infidels just as our own children play cowboys, Batman, Superman, and Ninja turtles (Bettelheim, 1987). The popularity of superheroes escalates and declines with the times, like the fashions and fads that come and go. It is mainly through the media, especially television and film, as well as through comic books, cartoons, software programs, and toys that children are introduced from a very young age to contemporary childhood heroes and heroines.

Teachers' problems with superhero play seem to focus on the level of aggression and violence that often accompanies role playing of various heroes. The fear seems to be that playing with guns and engaging in rough-and-tumble play behaviour will somehow increase the chances that children will become aggressive and violent adults. That fear, as well as a sense of moral indignation at the prevalence of violence in society today, often leads teachers to outlaw guns and superhero play in the learning environment. The tendency is to project their own feelings about aggression and violence onto children's superhero play instead of trying to understand and use it constructively.

Superhero play is closely associated with rough-and-tumble play, which often includes play fighting (Pelligrini, 1991). Vigorous kinds of superhero play are for many children a useful outlet for basic human urges that contain violence and aggression (Kostelnik, Whiren & Stein, 1986). Used positively, superhero play, even pretend violence, can help children gain some control over their aggressive feelings (Bettelheim, 1987).

Superheroes play an important role in the lives of children. Assuming the superhero role themselves provides children with opportunities to feel physically and understand more vividly the confusing forces of good and evil, which superheroes or antiheroes often represent. Passive watching of superheroes on television does not permit children to experience the mysterious forces the hero represents as readily as trying on the role for themselves. In children's minds, superheroes take on the superhuman characteristics they are meant to depict. They are usually good in an absolute sense with extraordinary qualities of wisdom, bravery, strength, and power. They demonstrate skills and mystical powers, which children often wish they had. In addition, they usually overcome or defeat any counterforce that attempts to thwart them, seem to have all the answers and be in control, and are usually popular and admired members of their own social group (Kostelnik, Whiren & Stein, 1986).

Sometimes children want to assume the roles of antiheroes whose characteristics are all bad. This moving back and forth between superhero and antihero roles puts children in touch with the opposing forces of good and evil and helps them feel these forces physically and emotionally. Their play heroes avoid the ambiguities and conflicting behaviours and values children so often see in the adults around them and which are often confusing and disturbing to them. Just as children's assumption of the roles of caregiver, parent, and teacher provide an opportunity for children to experience the feelings of nurturing and power associated with these roles, so superhero play allows children to unravel some of the mysteries surrounding good and evil. Superhero play that is well supervised, understood, and appreciated by teachers for its humanizing potential, as well as its universal appeal to the animal instincts deep within each of us, can become a powerful agent in the young child's moral development.

Kostelnik, Whiren, and Stein provide some useful suggestions to help teachers capitalize on the positive and growth-enhancing characteristics embedded in superhero play:

- help children recognize humane characteristics of superheroes
- discuss real heroes and heroines
- talk about the pretend world of acting
- limit the time and place for superhero play
- explore related concepts
- help children develop goals for superheroes
- help children de-escalate rough-and-tumble play
- make it clear that aggression is unacceptable
- give children control over their lives
- praise children's attempts at mastery. (1986:7)

Once teachers have decided that the benefits of superhero play outweigh the potential hazards, the next step is to ensure that this type of play is well managed and guided. Teachers should set limits that will help children differentiate between fantasy and reality so that they recognize that hitting is not allowed even in the context of pretend play (Austin, 1986). Effective supervision of superhero play includes recognizing the danger signs and anticipating when play is likely to turn to aggression and violence. When children's voices and faces become angry, threats are uttered, and laughing stops, teachers need to redirect the play and offer suggestions for more productive activity (Kostelnik, Whiren & Stein, 1986).

■ INTEGRATING CHILDREN WITH DISABILITIES IN THE ACTIVE ROLE PLAY CENTRE

The development of a healthy personality is closely associated with the child's confidence and trust in her own body (Erikson, 1963). It is, therefore, important to help the child who has a physical disability minimize its impact. We should also help these children maximize their sense of achievement in overcoming physical obstacles to the limits that their bodies will allow.

The prime time for developing many motor skills is during the early childhood period, particularly before the age of six (Cook, Tessier & Armbruster, 1987). For children with physical disabilities, the importance of implementing physical programs adapted to their individual needs and abilities during the early years cannot be overemphasized. Integrated programs should ensure that intervention in the physical development of the physically disabled child minimizes the delaying effects of inactivity and motor disabilities on the development of the body as a whole. Therefore, it is important that the Active Role Play Centre, as well as the outdoor play areas, be adapted to accommodate and challenge the child with physical disabilities to practise motor play and activity that will maximize his capabilities.

In planning the environment and play activities, teachers should provide physical activities that take the child with disabilities through the normal progressions in development as much as possible. Part of the process of integrating children with physical disabilities involves creating an affective climate in which they feel psychologically safe and willing to take risks. Full integration of children with physical disabilities will occur when all children in the group share responsibility for helping the child with a physical disability deal with the challenges of the large muscle play area. Non-disabled children should be encouraged to appreciate their shared responsibility in helping the challenged child participate in their games and activities (Paasche, Gorrill & Strom, 1990). These opportunities help children become both aware of the needs of others and more sensitive to the appropriate times to offer help (Ramsey, 1982).

The social-emotional climate of the program is helpful in this regard. Role play often provides the inspiration for active play in this centre. Children can often agree on a suitable role for the child with disabilities to play, in which the effects of the handicap will be minimized, while enabling some physical involvement in the play.

■ ADAPTING THE ENVIRONMENT FOR THE CHILD WITH DISABILITIES

Teachers have to adapt the learning environment to provide equipment and materials suited to the capabilities of the child with a physical disability. The teacher often has to intervene to help the child with a disability accomplish a physical goal. For example, even obstacle courses can be adapted to give the child with cerebral palsy an opportunity to surmount those obstacles closest to the ground, over which she can crawl and pull herself using the upper part of her body.

Integration of children with physical disabilities into regular early childhood education environments should take into account the nature of the child's disabilities. The learning environment should then be adapted accordingly. Many of the obstacles to the child's freedom of movement and interaction with other children can be removed by thoughtful teachers who have made careful observations.

Rogers-Warren (1982) provides guidelines, set out in the form of questions, for teachers who want to adapt the environment to accommodate the child with physical disabilities in the regular classroom.

- How does the setting appear at a child's level? Are there interesting things to see and touch such as windows, mirrors, mobiles, aquariums, and toys?

- Is there room for a wheelchair-bound or awkwardly mobile child to negotiate in and out of spaces and turn around?

- Are shelves and tables at a comfortable level for a child's height? Is there a place (preferably more than one) that can accommodate a child in each activity area?

- Are shelves, tables, sinks, and other fixtures sturdy enough to hold the weight of a minimally mobile child who may need support?

- Are prosthetic devices (such as a standing cuff) easily accessible in the areas where children might gain practice standing or sitting without an adult's assistance while engaged in an activity?

- Are some of the materials and toys accessible to a child without assistance even if he is minimally mobile?

- Is the sound level and acoustic arrangement of the room satisfactory for a child with a hearing impairment? Are there some special quiet areas for children to work with minimal noise distraction?

- Does the environment contain sufficient contrasts to attract the notice of a visually impaired child? Do colour and light contrasts complement texture and height contrasts?

- Are the cues (use of colour, change of levels, dividers) that designate different areas clear and consistent?

- How much of the environment is designed for self-management or self-engagement? How frequently do children use these opportunities? Does a child need training to use these opportunities?

- Does the arrangement of the room allow for quiet and social places to meet children's changing needs?

(From A.K. Rogers–Warren, "Behavioral ecology in classrooms for young handicapped children." *Topics in Early Childhood Special Education* 2 (1) (1982): 21–32. Adapted with permission of PRO-ED, Inc., Publishers.)

References

Austin, E.M. (1986). Beyond superheroes: constructive power play in the preschool. Presentation at the Annual Conference of the National Association for the Education of Young Children.

Bettelheim, B. (1987). The importance of play. *The Atlantic* 262 (3): 35–46.

Cooke, R., Tessier, A., and Armbruster, V. (1987). *Adapting Early Childhood Curricula for Children with Special Needs.* 2d ed. Columbus, OH: Merrill.

Erikson, E. (1963). *Childhood and Society.* New York: Norton.

Gallahue, D. (1982). *Understanding Motor Development in Children.* New York: Wiley.

Kostelnik, M.J., Whiren, A.P., and Stein, L.C. (1986). Living with he-man: managing superhero fantasy play. *Young Children* 41(3):3–9.

Nault, M., and Hanvey, L. (1991). *The Canadian Child Care Physical Activity Survey Report.* Ottawa: Canadian Institute of Child Health/Fitness and Amateur Sport Canada.

Paasche, C., Gorrill, L., and Strom, B. (1990). *Children with Special Needs in Early Childhood Settings: Identification, Intervention, Mainstreaming.* Toronto: Addison-Wesley.

Pelligrini, A.D. (1991). A longitudinal study of popular and rejected children's rough-and-tumble play. *Early Education and Development* 2 (3): 205–13.

Ramsey, P. (1982). Multicultural education in early childhood. In *Curriculum Planning for Young Children,* ed. J. Brown. Washington, D.C.: National Association for the Education of Young Children.

Rogers-Warren, A.K. (1982). Behavioral ecology in classrooms for young handicapped children. *Topics in Early Childhood Special Education* 2 (1):21–32.

Whitehurst, K.E. (1971). The young child; what movement means to him. In *The Significance of the Young Child's Motor Development.* Proceedings of a conference sponsored by the American Association for Health, Physical Education and Recreation and the National Association for the Education of Young Children.

MUSIC AND MOVEMENT IN THE ACTIVE ROLE PLAY CENTRE

Music is important to child development, and it provides an avenue for creative expression. Barbara Cass-Beggs (1974:5) states, "Perhaps the most important thing about music is the child's ability to enjoy both making and listening to it, and this ability needs to be 'caught.'" The allocation of space for music making and movement activities and an accessible place for storing musical instruments will go a long way towards ensuring that music becomes an important part of the early childhood program.

Too often, music as a medium for self-expression, creativity, social experience, and physical and perceptual development is neglected. The music area should be dedicated to children's active involvement in making their own music and moving to music. A music learning centre "should function as a support to the singing, listening and playing that goes on among children and adults" (Watts, 1991:75).

Locating the music area in the Active Role Play Centre ensures that there is space for musical instruments and for movement, which is an important aspect of a music program. It also underlines the importance of music and movement by assigning it a permanent and obvious place in the play and learning environment.

■ MUSIC AND CHILD DEVELOPMENT

Clear relationships exist between music and physical development, music and social-emotional development, and music and cognitive development. Musical accompaniment to physical activities and exercises enhances the physical experience and often motivates children to try harder and become more involved in the experience. Sensory-perceptual skills such as listening, auditory discrimination (recognition of various tones, rhythms, and sounds), and auditory-motor integration (ability to coordinate one's body movements to the command of musical sounds) are also promoted.

T A B L E   1 2 . 1

CHILD'S DEVELOPMENT OF MUSIC PERCEPTIONS AND BEHAVIOURS

Age in months	Developmental Characteristics	Musical Development
1	trusts/mistrusts environment responds to stimuli by moving the body	quiet singing and rocking soothe the baby sound stimuli are important—child reacts by moving entire body
1–4	differentiates sounds changes from hearing to listening turns head to stimulus follows moving objects with eyes	turns head in direction of sound follows sound of moving object if visible
4–8	interested in cause/effect relationships engages in purposeful activity reproduces interesting events develops eye-hand coordination	hits suspended bells repeatedly to reproduce sound
8–12	coordinates two schema anticipates events, exhibits intention knows that objects have stable functions imitates actions	hits drum or xylophone with stick claps hands to music hits instrument to produce a sound understands purpose of instrument
12–18	invents new actions uses trial and error to solve problems	experiments by hitting instrument in different ways with different objects
18–24	creates new actions through prior thought imitates actions after person leaves	continues music activity after adult stops
24	steps in place pats/runs increases language has short attention span attends to a few spoken words independent, curious	enjoys action songs and moving to music learns short, simple songs activities with short, simple directions experiments with instruments and sound

36	jumps, runs, walks to music	special music for special movements
	controls self	
	attends for longer period	waits for a turn
	uses more words	longer songs or activities
	compares two objects	compares sounds
	able to plan	suggests words for songs and added activities
	shows some initiative	
		likes to choose and try out ideas
48	improved motor control	may begin skipping
	interested in rules	rule songs and games
	plans ahead with adults	makes suggestions for music activities
	likes to imagine	
		adds words to songs, creates songs on instruments, makes dramatic movements to music or song
60	has motor control	can sit longer
	likes to have rules	enjoys songs and games with rules, likes specific rhythm patterns

Adapted from S. Moomaw, *Discovering Music in Early Childhood* (Boston, MA: Allyn & Bacon, 1984). Used with permission of the author and publisher.

Music helps children develop cognitive skills, such as memory, and classification skills, such as the ability to recognize groups of sounds and rhythms, and to replicate patterns of musical sounds. Language is enhanced by singing songs that help teach language appreciation, vocabulary, and rhyme.

Music may also play an important role in the spiritual development of human beings. When music is associated with special events and times of the year, it often becomes a significant reference point in our lives from childhood on. Music is a powerful vehicle for self-expression and an antidote to anxiety and anger. Affective well-being, which is influenced by self-esteem and by the ability to use acceptable emotional outlets, may be enhanced through musical self-expression. Music can also "break down barriers of race and language, for in a variety of forms, music is common to all races and is enjoyed by all races, and the enjoyment can transcend the cultural differences of race and language" (Cass-Beggs, 1974:3).

Children feel a sense of harmony when their bodies, souls, minds, and emotions are integrated in the execution of a march, dance, or interpretive movement activity. Perceptual skills are heightened by active listening and imitation of a musical beat.

Rhythm and melody are enhanced by clapping, swaying, swinging, dancing, and marching to music. Whole bodies move more responsively when music guides the tempo and direction of the movement. Coordinated movement to music and responsiveness to the commands of sound, tempo, and rhythm promote cognitive abilities. Children will often be inclined to risk and abandon themselves more completely in movement activities to the accompaniment of music.

■ MUSIC AND SELF-EXPRESSION

Creative self-expression, which is being developed in the early years, can be supported through access to musical instruments to represent and interpret what words or actions alone will not convey. Music gives colour and meaning to life and is for many of us the accompaniment to our daily tasks (Houle, 1987). Live music from instruments has a calming effect on children even when the beat is lively and they move their bodies in time with the rhythm of the musical instruments.

Music may induce a shy, introverted child to attempt movements to rhythm and sound that they would not risk without the stimulation that music provides. Musical experiences and exposure to opportunities to make music is important in early childhood education programs in order to detect children with unusual talent or musical intelligence (Gardner, 1982; 1989). The accessibility of musical instruments allows children to explore the construction and sounds of the instruments themselves. Encouraging children to make their own music with musical instruments, rather than always resorting to technology, is consistent with the value that children learn best when they are actively involved. Children learn about sound by creating it as well as by listening to it; instruments provide an opportunity for children to experience the creation of sound, rhythm, and harmony.

■ MUSIC FOR MENTAL HEALTH

There are few human beings who do not respond emotionally to music. For most of us music tends to reach into our deepest feelings and sensibilities. The importance of music to disturbed or anxious children is seen in its capacity to release pent-up feelings, calm a troubled spirit, divert an anxious child, and provide some moments of peace and relief from emotional preoccupations.

The effect of music on the group is also obvious to teachers who regularly pick up an autoharp and play to children while they await the arrival of their parents after a long day, or organize an impromptu singsong to calm a restless group. Live music with instruments, whether played by the teacher or by children or both, has effective and positive mood-altering capacities that may be relied upon daily.

■ LEARNING THROUGH MUSIC

For generations, music educators have demonstrated their interest in advancing musical literacy in young children. Kodaly created a music program based on folk songs for children in Hungary after the communist takeover in 1945; his program focused on singing and the playing of simple percussion instruments. He stressed the importance of sight reading and believed that musical training would promote the development of the whole personality of the child. Carl Orff in Germany in the late nineteenth and early twentieth centuries saw movement as the heart of music education and developed a teaching approach that encouraged children to integrate language, music, and movement. Dalcroze in Switzerland in the early years of this century also believed that the body was the vehicle for music expression and, therefore, focused on the teaching of eurythmics to integrate body, sound, and interpretation of music. All three music educators believed in the power of music to affect the cognitive, physical, and affective growth of young children.

MUSIC HELPS CHILDREN DEVELOP COGNITIVE SKILLS

Gardner (1989:298) makes a strong case for providing young children with a music program by showing that their keen sensory capacities and fluent use of symbols and metaphors make the early years a period of heightened "creative orientation." This creative period should, of course, be accounted for in early education. Planned music programs offer teachers the opportunity to observe and predict exceptional talent and intervene accordingly. Musical intelligence has been identified by Gardner (1983) as one of seven types of intelligence, and, according to him, it involves heightened perceptual discrimination abilities, body awareness, rhythm, and sensitivity to pitch and melody. Gardner links music concepts to an understanding of concepts found in physics, sound, and mathematics.

Young children are also ready to learn some music concepts: rhythm, tempo, pitch, timbre, dynamics (loud/soft), and melody. These may be practised and developed through singing, chanting, movement activities, playing instruments, listening to music, and making up tunes and songs (Schwartz & Robison, 1982). Concepts and specific musical skills may be learned through direct instruction in planned group experiences led by teachers and through spontaneous, child-initiated, and self-directed experiences with musical instruments, songs, and movement.

Children need many musical opportunities to develop and grow through their self-directed play as well as in the context of planned group times. Musical instruments that have been introduced to children through demonstration and practice times in group learning periods should be accessible to children throughout the day. The presence of musical instruments in the Active Role Play Centre reminds children of the importance of music in every aspect of our lives and facilitates active movement that always seems smoother and more enjoyable when set to music. Music, drama, and movement have always been compatible partners. Musical instruments and physical activities are therefore consistent with many of the materials and activities in the Active Role Play Centre.

■ MUSIC AS A WAY OF LIFE

Early childhood is an excellent time to introduce children to the world of music, and to the relaxation, internal harmony, and sense of well-being that music can contribute to daily living. "Canned" music on tapes, compact discs, and records, however, should never replace the experience of making one's own music by playing the instruments themselves. Instruments are the tools of music, children must be taught to care for and respect them (Houle, 1987). When children are able to select and use musical instruments spontaneously and are taught at the same time how to care for them, they develop an ear for the kinds of sounds specific instruments make and a respect for the care and protection of the instrument. Leaving instruments available makes it more likely that children will add music to sociodramatic play. They may also follow the beat of a drum when marching or skipping or performing some other gross motor skill. Musical accompaniment to a physical program, which challenges children's abilities to move, exercise, and extend themselves to the limits of their endurance and strength, enhances their self-concept, body awareness, and body image.

■ STORING MUSICAL INSTRUMENTS

Musical instruments should be stored close to the space where music and movement activities will most likely occur. They should be distanced from the large muscle or construction activities to avoid adding to the noise level that is usually high in these play areas. Some teachers like to make musical instruments available to children in a separate hallway or alcove, but doing so limits the integration of instruments into active and sociodramatic play in the Active Role Play Centre. Having musical instruments available for a wide range of play activities "makes them a more natural, accessible and integrated part of your curriculum much like books and pencils for language arts" (Watts, 1991:78). They should be located away from the *listening centre,* which is a place where children listen relatively passively to audiocassette tapes, records, and the radio. The music-making area is much more active than the listening centre and accommodates musical instruments and accessories that may be used to enhance movement to music.

As some musical instruments should be available to children at all times, space should be provided for the accessible storage of simple, sturdy instruments that children may select themselves and play spontaneously. A combination of cupboards with doors and some open shelves allows precious and fragile instruments to be kept behind closed doors for use by the teacher with the children, while the simpler, more durable instruments may be left out. Rhythm sticks, drums, maracas, and triangles, for example, may be simple musical accompaniments for an impromptu parade or a "rock concert" presented by the children. Watts (1991:79) recommends that instruments available in the music-making area be changed at least once a week and that the changes be "from hand drums to tamborines or tamborines to cymbals, rather than from one kind of sticks to another."

■ MUSICAL ACTIVITIES

Music and Movement Activities

1. Children sing action songs involving movements: bend and stretch, reach the sky, sway like a tree, sway like a sailboat in the wind.
2. Children sing a song and clap the rhythm of the song simultaneously.
3. Children pretend they are a boat on the sea swaying in the waves to the sound of the sea (use a tape of sounds of the sea).
4. Children sway with a partner to music, holding hands.
5. Children perform simple dance steps to music swinging arms as they move their feet and bodies, and sway to the rhythm.
6. Children sing "Row, row, row your boat" sitting with partners each holding a hoop between them with their hands.
7. Children swing and swish a parachute to the sound of music that replicates the sound of waves in the sea.

Musical Activities with Instruments

1. Each child takes a musical instrument to play as they march around the centre wearing costumes or hats.

2. Children may play musical instruments as they rock in the rocking boat and try to coordinate the rhythm of their instrument with the rocking motion of the boat.

3. Some children play music using the instruments, while others form a team to put away the hollow blocks.

4. Children skip, sway, and jump with a partner to drum beats while holding hands.

5. Children dress up and pretend to be a band marching in a parade.

6. Children use hollow blocks, ramps, and boards to make a platform or stage for a musical production using instruments.

7. Children simulate the rhythm using instruments as the teacher plays some music that goes well with movement on the tape or record players such as a rousing march, the "William Tell Overture," *The Sorcerer's Apprentice*, or something by Scott Joplin.

References

Cass-Beggs, B. (1974). *To Listen, To Like, To Learn*. Toronto: Peter Martin Associates Ltd.

Gardner. H. (1982). *Art, Mind and Brain*. New York: Basic Books.

Gardner, H. (1983). *Frames of Mind*. New York: Basic Books.

Gardner, H. (1989). *To Open Minds*. New York: Basic Books.

Houle, G.B. (1987). *Learning Centres for Young Children*. West Greenwich, RI: Tot-lot Child Care Products.

Moomaw, S. (1984). *Discovering Music in Early Childhood*. Boston, MA: Allyn & Bacon.

Schwartz, S.L., and Robison, H.F. (1982). *Designing Curriculum for Early Childhood*. Boston, MA: Allyn & Bacon.

Watts, D.W. (1991). *Exploring the Joy of Music*. Richmond Hill, Ontario: Scholastic Canada Ltd.

S E C T I O N 5

PLAY AND LEARNING
TO LEARN

Section 5 addresses children's acquisition of concepts and knowledge that help provide a foundation for academic learning later on. The learning centres and play stations discussed in Section 5 are dedicated largely to motivating children to become interested, self-directed, self-initiating, curious learners. Chapter 13 addresses constructivist, hands-on learning with specific-purpose materials in the Quiet Thinking Centre. Language learning and early literacy are addressed in Chapter 14. Chapter 15 emphasizes the learning of logical concepts. The role of technology, particularly the microcomputer, in play and learning is discussed in Chapter 16.

Section 5 addresses the following topics:

- learning-to-learn skills
- constructivist early childhood education
- Piaget's types of knowledge
- planning a Quiet Thinking Centre
- language learning and literacy skills
- logical concepts—seriation, classification, number
- planning a Technology Centre
- issues related to computers in early childhood education
- integrating computers in early childhood classrooms
- computers as learning tools for children with disabilities

C H A P T E R 13

THE QUIET THINKING CENTRE— LEARNING TO LEARN

Early childhood education involves helping children derive more value from their play. Designing and organizing an effective learning environment and planning activities that promote development guide children's learning and development in specific directions. An effective learning climate stimulates curiosity, motivation, initiative, and independence in learning. But what about helping children become more effective learners, that is, learners who know how to plan, attend to a task, resist distractions, persevere in the face of obstacles, and use time well? It is the role of early childhood educators to provide opportunities to practise these learning-to-learn skills.

The Quiet Thinking Centre is dedicated to helping children master some basic skills involved in being a purposeful, organized, enthusiastic learner. The content for learning in this centre primarily addresses language, literacy, and logical concepts. The central goals, which are often more implicit than explicit, relate to many of the basic work-study skills that are so important to success in school and adult life. In order to promote effective learning, teachers must first have a clear understanding of how children learn.

■ CONSTRUCTIVIST EARLY CHILDHOOD EDUCATION

This textbook has already addressed the fact that children are physical beings who come to know and understand largely through their hands-on, physical interaction with things and events in the play and learning environment. The source of understanding or concept formation basically lies within the child, since she constructs an understanding of the concepts in her own way.

DeVries and Kohlberg (1987) describe the ways in which children construct their own knowledge and understanding of concepts in *Constructivist Early Education: Overview and Comparison with Other Programs*. Children's interest, play, experimentation, and cooperation in learning are essential to their being self-directed learners who construct their own intelligence. The role of the play and learning environment is to respond to the child's interest, action, experience, and level of development. This means that children need opportunities to play with materials that change according to the child's actions on them, and materials in which the internal structure of the concept to be learned is embedded in the material itself. Modular and specific-purpose materials fit these criteria best.

Piaget explained that when children engage in self-directed learning through play during the preoperational years, they are actually building mental structures, which are the intellectual foundation for formal learning later on (Piaget, 1969). Structure building occurs when each component of the concept to be learned is understood by and meaningful to the child. For example, it is not appropriate to expect that when they reach grade one, children will accept on faith alone that 2 + 2 = 4; they will need to understand concepts of quantity, equality, and number constancy in order to "know" the meaning of mathematical equations.

The child's construction of knowledge depends on opportunities to play with responsive materials that encourage spontaneous, self-directed exploration, and provide time and space for the child to discover and understand when he is ready (Forman & Kuschner, 1988). Play materials involving parts that fit together in specific ways are important to the child's ability to construct relationships and acquire an understanding of spatial concepts. Constructive play also helps children gain hands-on understanding of seriation, classification, number, and order.

These important basic concepts may be acquired through social and cooperative learning experiences. It is important, however, that there also be time and opportunity for young children to play and work alone with concrete materials in order to understand basic concepts in their own ways. The Quiet Thinking Centre is dedicated to this purpose. Social and cooperative play experiences reinforce the understanding children have acquired through solitary play. Playing alone with materials also prompts children to try out for themselves ideas they have observed in groups.

■ PIAGET'S THREE TYPES OF KNOWLEDGE

Piaget identified three types of knowledge: physical, social-conventional, and logical-mathematical (Piaget, 1969). These three types of knowledge were described in Chapter 4. All types of knowledge are important to the formation of concepts, but the way in which children acquire physical and social-conventional knowledge is very different from the way they acquire logical-mathematical knowledge. This difference has to be recognized by teachers of young children.

When exposed to new learning situations involving unfamiliar play materials, children first explore the physical properties of things through their senses; in other words, they suck, chew, touch, manipulate, bounce, snap together, stack, bang, put together, and take apart. Physical knowledge is acquired through children's sensory exploration of nearly everything that they can reach.

Social-conventional knowledge involves the learning of social and cultural conventions. In early childhood, it is acquired largely through informal social and cultural transmission. Children learn from adults who pass on to them social norms, expectations, and factual data. They learn from children's books and other print material, from television programs and videocassettes, from educational software, and through observation of social life and human interactions in the home, child care centre, kindergarten, neighbourhood, and community.

Much of social-conventional knowledge acquisition is language-based; that is, children learn by listening to others speak, watching television, and hearing stories and poetry read to them. The sources of physical and social-conventional knowledge lie largely outside the child: there is a body of factual data, information, and knowledge about physical reality, which is mostly concrete, that the child accumulates through physical experience and social transmission.

Logical-mathematical knowledge is acquired from the time children become capable of rudimentary thought. This type of abstract understanding depends on the child's discovery of relationships among things and phenomena. Logical-mathematical thinking progresses from relatively simple understanding of concepts of same-different and part-whole, to the more complex concepts of cause and effect and ordering. Piaget demonstrated that the source of logical-mathematical knowledge lies within the child; in other words, it is intrinsic. Children's active manipulation of play materials contributes to their ability to uncover, discover, "construct," and eventually understand relationships. When children play with modular materials such as beads and strings, pegs and pegboards, bingo chips, Cuisenaire rods, Lego, and tabletop blocks, they compare, contrast, arrange, sort, measure, count, quantify, and relate things in many different ways, eventually discovering or "constructing" relationships for themselves.

■ CONCEPT FORMATION

A **concept** is an idea of a general class that implies an understanding of relationships that exist between objects, people, or events. Hiebert and Lefevre (1986) describe conceptual knowledge as a web of knowledge or a network in which the linking relationships are as important as the discrete pieces of information. Concept formation is achieved by constructing relationships between separate pieces of information. The ability to make these connections is described by Bruner (1960) as the essence of discovery learning. In Piagetian terms, concept formation occurs through the equilibration process, which takes place when new or previously unrelated pieces of information are assimilated into already existing mental structures that alter themselves to accommodate the new level of understanding. In this way, new information becomes part of an existing network or concept (Hiebert & Lefevre, 1986).

Concept formation is fundamental to the development of both logical thinking skills and the ability to reason. As children gain understanding of concepts, their ability to organize their experiences and perceive a natural order in the world contributes to rational thinking. Children acquire information largely from experience in the concrete world. Their ability to classify and order their experiences increases as they build on the framework of knowledge and understanding they have already acquired.

Developmental readiness to build concepts is an essential prerequisite to concept formation. When adults try to impose concept learning on children before they are ready, or when they try to "teach" concepts as if they were the same as physical or social knowledge, children often memorize facts instead of understanding concepts. Teaching arithmetic by rote is an example. When children learn to perform arithmetical operations by memorizing rules and tables and following formulas without understanding the concepts behind them, the operation becomes mainly verbal rather than logical. When this happens, children's mathematical progress in school stops. When reliance on the rules and verbal explanations that have been memorized fails them and they have to rely instead on logic and understanding, they find that they are unable to solve abstract mathematical problems.

Children are helped to form concepts by playing with a variety of objects that are similar to one another in one or more ways. The ways in which the objects are similar represent the concept or criterion that integrates the objects. Concept formation has been achieved when children are able to classify other objects correctly as members or non-members of the set. For example, a red chip and a yellow chip are different, at least according to the criterion of colour. When we recognize that they are different, we create a relationship between the two chips by saying that they are different because they are of different colours. It is in placing the

HANDS-ON LEARNING

two objects in relationship to one another and comparing them on the basis of the criterion of colour that the concept of "same" or "different" becomes apparent. The difference between the two chips is understood cognitively by the child who determines the criterion that will define their relationship.

■ HANDS-ON PLAY

Hands-on learning through play is a learning style that reflects young children's strong sensory orientation. It refers to children's physical manipulation and sensory exploration of concrete objects, which are essential to concept formation. The pre-operational child's ability to think is perceptually bound, meaning that what a child sees, hears, tastes, touches, and smells is what *is*. For example, young children will generally perceive taller people as being older than short people. In relation to other things in their environment, children's position in space is integrated through real experiences such as feeling the distance between themselves and others at a table and learning about the size and shape of a Lego piece that will fit into an open notch in order to complete the bridge. Later, when they are school age, children will be able to understand concepts in the absence of the sensory stimulus. Since their learning is largely sensory bound until they achieve concrete-operational thought at around the age of seven, hands-on play experiences are essential to development and learning.

THE IMPORTANCE OF
CONCRETE MATERIALS

■ THE IMPORTANCE OF CONCRETE MATERIALS

One of Montessori's major contributions to early childhood education was to bring children into direct physical contact with play materials. She was primarily concerned with children's motor, sensory, and language or intellectual education. Her method was to rely on the presentation of materials to promote development in the three areas she identified as most important: practical, daily life materials; sensory materials; and conceptual or academic materials. Montessori believed that language, literacy skills, and mathematical understanding evolved from repetitive manipulation of specialized materials and built on the earlier understanding of more basic skills (Lindauer, 1987). Early childhood education practice in the 1990s owes much to Montessori's pioneering work.

■ CREATING A CLIMATE FOR LEARNING IN THE QUIET THINKING CENTRE

All learning centres promote language and concept development. The designation of the Quiet Thinking Centre as one play and learning centre in the playroom where children are expected to play quietly and become involved in activities individually, at least for part of each day, respects the importance of work-study skills to effective learning throughout life.

■ THE IMPORTANCE OF SOLITARY PLAY

Children need opportunities to tackle activities on their own, to plan purposefully, to learn to solve problems by relying on their own resources, at least for a short period of time, and to experience the satisfaction that comes from individual achievement. MacKinnon (1962) studied 600 highly creative people and found strong links between high levels of creative and imaginative behaviour and a preference for solitary activities. These people were also able to concentrate for extended periods of time and were unusually persistent. Strom (1981) claims that the consequences of failing to encourage periods of solitary play in early childhood are an increased incidence of hyperactivity, disruptive behaviour, impulsiveness, and inattentiveness.

Early childhood education typically emphasizes the importance of social interaction and cooperation in learning. It is just as important, however, for young children to learn that there is also a time and place for independent play and solitary endeavour. One learning centre should be dedicated to individual play and to learning that provides relative freedom from the demands of socialization and group activities.

The Quiet Thinking Centre emphasizes individual, hands-on, self-directed learning at planned activities with specific-purpose materials. Teachers set up the activities and children determine their own learning outcomes by choosing their activity and how they will use the materials that go with it. All play and learning environments rely on some structure. In the Quiet Thinking Centre, structure refers to the teacher's careful planning of materials and activities at play stations that address the observed developmental levels and interests of individual children.

■ LEARNING-TO-LEARN SKILLS

Children in their early years are forming an elementary understanding of their role as learners. Like so many other dispositions, positive work-study habits begin very early (Stipek, 1982). The dedication of the Quiet Thinking Centre to the development of learning-to-learn skills recognizes their importance to children's later successful school experiences.

Young children are ready to practise attending, organization, planning, and problem-solving skills. Casey (1990) demonstrated that children who participated in a preschool program designed to develop planning and problem-solving abilities showed the improved thinking abilities associated with successful learners. Attending skills include attention span, being able to focus one's attention, and task orientation, which includes making choices and persistence.

LEARNING TO LEARN

Attention span is the amount of time a child can remain at an endeavour, assuming that it is appropriate and interesting (Nash, 1979, 1989). For young children, the length of the period of attention is less important than the quality of the time spent. Attention span and task orientation are demonstrated when children look at a book from beginning to end, and start and finish activities that are interesting and appropriate for them. In assessing these abilities, teachers should look for signs that children are actively involved and interested in what they are doing, rather than simply conforming to the expectation that they should be quiet and busy.

The ability to be purposeful in one's activity and plan systematically is a learning-to-learn skill that many adults have assumed children would learn on their own.

The fact is that, although they are able to do so, most children do not develop these skills while they are young. However bright children may be, without the ability to organize and plan, their cognitive potential is wasted. Casey and Lippmann (1991) have reported that the ability to plan systematically is related to higher achievement scores in elementary and secondary school. As with so many other aptitudes for learning, the development of effective planning and organization skills can be assisted and enhanced by knowledgeable teachers.

■ THE TEACHER AS FACILITATOR OF LEARNING-TO-LEARN SKILLS

Several strategies for facilitating the development of learning-to-learn skills have already been addressed in this textbook. The planning and organization of the learning environment, the effective use of space, the design of learning centres that will provide clear messages and realistic and interesting challenges, and a schedule that allows sufficient time for children to tackle and complete worthwhile projects and activities are all techniques that foster effective work-study skills.

Children are helped to develop good attention spans and task orientation when teachers acknowledge their interest and involvement (process of learning), as well as their completion of challenging tasks. When children are able to choose activities suited to their own abilities, they also acquire a sense of the amount of time needed to begin and finish an activity. Some children need help understanding the nature of the task involved in a chosen activity. The teacher's help sends the message that it is important for children to try to understand a task before beginning and to plan how they will proceed.

The development of attending skills depends on a schedule that provides sufficient time for children to pursue meaningful activities, in which some can be completed in one sitting and some will take longer because they are more complex. Programs should provide a balance of short one-step activities and longer two- and three-step activities that may require children to return to them after an interruption.

Many teachers encourage learning-to-learn skills by using a planning board that presents pictures or symbols of activities available in each learning centre on a given day and by asking children to select which activities they will pursue (Hohmann, Banet & Weikart, 1979; Nash, 1989; Casey & Lippmann, 1991). Encouraging children to engage in longer-term projects is a particularly effective way to teach planning skills to children (Katz & Chard, 1989). Longer-term projects require that children define the project, know the steps involved in it, formulate and implement plans, and communicate what they have accomplished (Casey & Lippmann, 1991).

Activities to Promote Learning-to-Learn Skills

(for children, ages three to six)

1. Formboard and jigsaw puzzles have both clear beginnings and endings, as well as an internal structure that dictates the steps to be followed in order to complete the activity successfully. The completed puzzle provides a message that the child has finished and has succeeded in mastering the task involved in the activity.

2. Workjobs (Baratta-Lorton, 1972) have a definite beginning and ending, as well as a clear set of steps to follow and are, therefore, well suited to helping children develop task-orientation skills. These kits provide clear messages about the tasks to be performed and make it easy for teachers to observe and record children's levels of mastery of the developmental objectives inherent in the activity.

3. Play with Lego, tinker toy, and other modular construction materials promotes children's visual discrimination abilities, spatial concepts, directionality, problem-solving abilities, manipulative and fine motor skills, and eye-hand coordination. They are also materials that challenge children to formulate a plan, to follow it through, and to decide when they have finished. Play with these materials demands a high level of concentration and an ability to block out distractions.

4. Reading stories to children in small groups provides practice for the children at focusing on the activity when requested to do so by the teacher. Children have to attend in order to be active participants in the story-reading session by looking at illustrations, by using felts at the flannelboard to enhance the story, and by asking and responding to questions.

5. Play with specific-purpose materials such as attribute blocks, classification kits of various kinds, seriation materials, and one-to-one correspondence kits gives children practice in defining the task, beginning, following through, and finishing.

(for older children, ages four to six)

6. Encourage children to undertake a project such as: putting on a puppet show or pantomime for parents or another group of children in the child care centre or school, making a snow sculpture for winter carnival, creating a restaurant, making baskets to take on a nature study walk, and building a hill in the playground out of snow for easy sliding on magic carpets. Projects usually involve two or three stages, and may take one or two weeks to complete for four- and five-year olds, and even longer for older children.

References

Baratta-Lorton, M. (1972). *Workjobs*. Menlo Park, CA: Addison-Wesley.

Bruner, J. (1960). *The Process of Education*. Cambridge, MA: Harvard University Press.

Casey, B. (1990). A planning and problem-solving preschool model: the methodology of being a good learner. *Early Childhood Research Quarterly* 5 (1):53–68.

Casey, B., and Lippmann, M. (1991). Learning to plan through play. *Young Children* 46 (4): 52–58.

DeVries, R., and Kohlberg, L. (1987). *Constructivist Early Education: Overview and Comparison with Other Programs*. Washington, D.C.: National Association for the Education of Young Children.

Forman, G.E., and Kuschner, D.S. (1988). *The Child's Construction of Knowledge: Piaget for Teaching Children*. Washington, D.C.: National Association for the Education of Young Children.

Hiebert, J., and Lefevre, P. (1986). Conceptual and procedural knowledge in mathematics: an introductory analysis. In *Conceptual and Procedural Knowledge:The Case of Mathematics*, ed. J. Hiebert, pp. 1–27. Hillsdale, NJ: Lawrence Erlbaum Associates.

Hohmann, M., Banet, B., and Weikart, D. (1979). *Young Children in Action*. Ypsilanti, MI. High/Scope.

Katz, L., and Chard, S. (1989). *Engaging Children's Minds: The Project Approach*. Norwood, NJ: Ablex.

Lindauer, S.K. (1987). Montessori education for young children. In *Approaches to Early Childhood Education*, ed. J.L. Roopnarine and J.E. Johnson, pp. 109–26. Columbus, OH: Merrill.

MacKinnon, D.W. (1962). The nature and nurture of creative talent. *American Psychologist* 17 (7):484–95.

Nash, C. (1979, 1989). *The Learning Environment: A Practical Approach to the Education of the Three-, Four- and Five-Year-Old*. Toronto: Collier-Macmillan.

Orem, R.C., ed. (1966). *A Montessori Handbook*. New York: Capricorn Books.

Piaget, J. (1969). *The Psychology of the Child*. New York: Basic Books.

Stipek, D.J. (1982). Work habits begin in preschool. In *Curriculum Planning for Young Children*, ed. J.F. Brown. Washington, D.C.: National Association for the Education of Young Children.

Strom, R.D.(1981). The merits of solitary play. In *Growing Through Play*, ed. R.D. Strom. Monterey, CA: Brooks/Cole.

THE QUIET THINKING CENTRE— LEARNING LANGUAGE

■ THEORETICAL VIEWPOINTS

Children construct their own understanding of language as early as the first few months of life, long before they actually use formal language. Culture and social context shape the characteristics of each person's developing language systems, lending unique qualities called dialect to language as it is spoken in different geographical areas (Wortham, 1984). For the most part, however, language learning is unique: people pass through similar stages in their language development but ultimately develop their own particular language styles.

Imitation of the language of adults by children plays a relatively minor role in the development of grammatical structures or syntax (Cazden, 1981). It is important, however, that adults model the correct syntax and pronunciation of words so that children hear language correctly. Adults sometimes make the mistake of imitating the child's incorrect words or pronunciation, or present unclear or distorted models and speech that may impede the child's progress in language learning. Children learn the particular language heard at home, and the rhythm, accent, and pace of their speech are influenced by models close to them.

Children do not learn language by being corrected by adults. Their ability to understand the construction and rules of language develops over time and through a series of stages. Even though they hear and understand the language used by teachers and parents, they continue to use their own constructions. Most of us recall times when we have tried to correct children's language by repeating a sentence using proper syntax:

Child: I don't gots my mittens.
Teacher: You don't have your mittens.
Child: Yes, Jamie have gots my mittens.

Children acquire the grammatical structure of their language in a predictable developmental order that some theorists believe is closely related to the child's level of cognitive development (Gleason, 1989:29). Piaget (1926) believed that children always have the language they need to express what they are capable of thinking at any stage. Kamii (1972) emphasized the importance of stimulating thinking and general cognitive growth in order to promote language development. Bruner (1973, 1983) stressed that language development depends on rich learning environments and plenty of opportunities for children to develop cognitive abilities.

Theorists disagree about how and whether language should be taught to young children (Wortham, 1984). This textbook emphasizes the role of both developmental and environmental factors in language learning. Active, experiential learning in a well-planned environment facilitates language development and literacy, and should be emphasized. The two learning centres that primarily address the development of cognitive abilities, including language, are the Quiet Thinking Centre and the Technology Centre.

■ THE ROLE OF PERCEPTION IN LANGUAGE LEARNING

Most developmental skills related to language learning involve sensory perception. Visual perceptual and auditory perceptual skills, in particular, are vital to the learning of both verbal and written language. In order to use language fluently, children have to acquire perceptual processing abilities, especially sight and hearing. Language learning is somewhat influenced by hearing the language of others, and by imitating and practising it, but it is mostly a concrete learning task in which words, both printed and verbal, are accessible through the senses. Language is usually received by the eyes and ears, and may be tactilely received as in the case of Braille for persons who are blind. Later, the ability to read also depends on a complex network of physical perceptual and cognitive perceptual skills that are practised as children acquire basic language abilities.

■ THE NATURE OF LANGUAGE LEARNING

Section 4 focused on symbolic play, a particular play form in which children engage in increasingly complex representational behaviours using drama. The earliest type of symbolic play begins with simple imitation of remembered events at about the time that children begin to acquire language, which is near the end of the second year. This dramatic play becomes increasingly complex throughout the preoperational period. Language and dramatic play develop simultaneously as they both involve symbolic thinking. As children progress from simple imitations of single events to complex dramatizations of familiar episodes from everyday life, often involving several roles, they are also developing the ability to use more elaborate language and to communicate effectively.

Children's ability to use one object to stand for another develops very early. As soon as children acquire an understanding that objects have an existence beyond their own capacity to see and touch them, they begin to acquire the ability to use objects as symbols. The child's early play with blocks to create a tower, running a block along the carpet pretending that it is a vehicle, and drawing a square with a triangle on top to represent a house are early examples of the ability to use symbols. As children become verbal, around the age of two, they learn to use letters for sounds and words to represent things. At this stage, language systems become important and interesting to them.

Learning to understand and use symbol systems like language is a fairly concrete, knowledge-based task. It is usually simpler for the young child to learn language than it is to acquire more abstract logical concepts. In language, the learning process involves the symbolic task of associating letters with sounds and words with meanings. It is different from learning abstract concepts which involves the capacity to understand relationships that often cannot be seen. Both types of learning, however, require individual, active involvement, attention, and concentration. Therefore, the requirements with respect to the play and learning environment are similar.

Children benefit from access to concrete symbols such as letters, pictures, and three-dimensional objects. They need time to explore books and the wealth of experience that pictures and stories open up to them. They need opportunities to experience letter and word symbols through their senses, as in tracing or printing letter symbols on salt or sand trays. The ability to absorb the full impact of books and other literacy materials requires some individual effort, concentration, and a relatively quiet environment. Providing a learning centre in the classroom for children's individual exploration of literacy materials is therefore important. Modular and open-ended materials, as well as specific-purpose learning kits and play materials such as lotto games, puzzles, Workjobs, and tabletop construction materials facilitate language learning. A language arts area in the Quiet Thinking Centre promotes recognition and interpretation of sounds and letter symbols, linking language symbols to pictures, and enjoyment of books and literature.

T A B L E   1 4 . 1

SENSORY-PERCEPTUAL SKILLS RELATED TO LANGUAGE AND READING

VISUAL SKILLS—PHYSICAL

- form discrimination
  recognize basic form and shape
  recognize similarities and differences in simple one- and two-dimensional forms and shapes
  recognize shape symbols embedded in the environment
- depth perception
  accurately judge distance and height
- figure-ground perception
  select a figure from a detailed picture or poster
  find small objects or creatures in illustrated books
  look at only one part of a picture at a time and ignore other areas
  shift attention from one part of a picture to another or from one detail to another
- ocular-motor skills
  accommodation or near-far focusing adjustment
  fixation or ability of eyes to look simultaneously and accurately from one target to another
  pursuit or ability of the eyes to follow a moving target without moving the head
  tracking or ability of the eyes to make a series of saccades or long sweeps smoothly across a page, board, or screen

VISUAL SKILLS—COGNITIVE

- identify and label objects seen
- identify similarities and differences
- match similar objects
- identify an object when only part is revealed
- identify familiar objects from pictures
- pick out small details in a visual field

AUDITORY SKILLS—PHYSICAL

- recognize sound sources
- listen to auditory clues
- hear differences and similarities in sounds and tones
- detect one tonal quality from an auditory field
- hear repeated patterns of sound and silence
- execute well-timed responses to auditory cues

AUDITORY SKILLS—COGNITIVE

- identify and label sounds
- focus on a sound and attend to it
- link what is heard to its source
- interpret sounds
- match sounds according to similarities
- differentiate musical notes: high/low; sharp/soft
- identify where a sound is coming from (direction)
- follow the sound
- follow verbal instructions

■ ORGANIZATION AND DESIGN OF THE QUIET THINKING CENTRE

The Quiet Thinking Centre usually contains a reading area, tabletop play area, a sensory exploration/display table, and an area for play with specific-purpose materials such as Workjobs (see Figure 14.1). All play areas in this learning centre encourage primarily individual involvement and quiet behaviours. However, the play activity and the interests of the children require that flexibility be practised here too, as there may be times when children will choose to play together in this learning centre and times when teachers plan and set up a cooperative activity. Sometimes, too, children simply enjoy looking at the same book together or collaborating in using the flannelboard and felts while telling or reading a story.

Equipment, Materials, and Supplies

Equipment—book shelves consisting of a regular book shelf and a display rack for books; carpet; large cushions/beanbag chair, adult rocking chair or armchair, and child-sized rocking chair; storage shelves and rack for puzzles; modular materials; specific-purpose materials and kits; chairs and two tables; and chalkboard.

Literacy materials—early reading materials, including picture books, storybooks, child-made books, activity books, visual discrimination books with detailed illustrations (e.g., *Where's Waldo?*, and Richard Scarry books); picture files; photo albums; felt books; flannelboard and felts; posters; letter and number sets; magnetic board and magnetic letters; small flipchart stand; formboard puzzles; jigsaw puzzles;

Figure 14.1   THE QUIET THINKING CENTRE

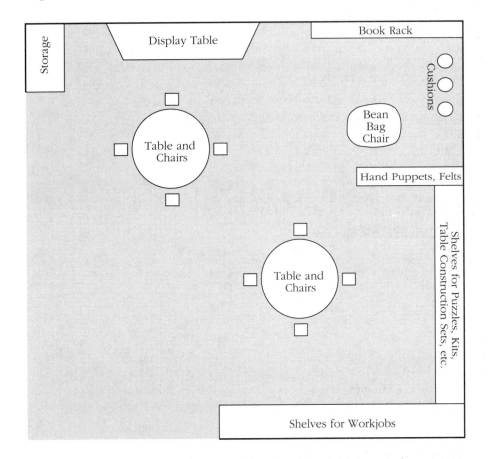

Social contexts of play emphasized in the Quiet Thinking Centre

solitary
parallel

Categories of play emphasized in the Quiet Thinking Centre

functional: practice play
                    productive play
creative-constructive play
games-with-rules play

textured fabric kits; lotto games; card games; board games; picture blocks; and language Workjobs.

Thinking materials—sets of modular materials for classification, seriation, number, and conservation; part-whole kits; dominoes; pegboards and pegs; beads and strings; sequence sets; mathematics Workjobs; parquetry tiles; Unifix materials; pattern blocks; people pieces; attribute blocks; centimetre cubes; colour cubes; counting chips; Cuisenaire rods; Tinkertoy; Lego sets; abacus; tabletop blocks; nesting blocks; beakers/cups/dolls/rings; and sorting sets.

Supplies—crayons, pencils, felt-tipped markers (non-toxic), paper, chalk, string or cord, brads (for making children's books), cardboard, and Bristol board.

RATINGS OF THE CHARACTERISTICS OF PLAY

The Quiet Thinking Centre

noisy	_____	quiet
teacher-centred	_____	child-centred
structured	_____	open
concrete	_____	abstract
clean	_____	messy
specific-purpose materials	_____	open-ended materials
group	_____	individual

(Adapted with permission of the Board of Education, City of Hamilton. *Getting It All Together* (1981).)

■ PLAY STATIONS IN THE QUIET THINKING CENTRE
The Book Nook

Children need to experience books in order to develop an interest in and an appreciation for reading. Beautiful books transport children to another world, even when they are simply looking at pictures, feeling the shiny paper of the pages, tracing little fingers around shapes, and softly caressing a book's cover. For many of us our most treasured possessions from childhood are our favourite, well-worn books. They provide a sensory, intellectual, and affective experience for children. Through books children learn about experiences, events, and places remote from themselves. Sitting snuggled up on a chair or cushion looking at a book and letting one's mind drift provides relief from the daily routine, solace from an anxious day, respite from the demands of the group, and an opportunity to escape emotionally and intellectually into a world created by someone else. Children who learn to love books and the freedom of spirit they provide receive a precious boost for mental health that may last a lifetime.

The book nook is best located in a comfortable corner created by two adjoining dividers to provide some privacy and seclusion from the tabletop play areas of the Quiet Thinking Centre. If the area is large enough, an upholstered chair, a rocking chair with cushions, or a beanbag allow children to curl up with the books. The use of pretty, bright fabric to cover cushions and blankets, and perhaps a washable quilt or knitted blanket add colour and coziness to this corner.

BOOK NOOK

Two kinds of bookshelves may be provided in the library area. One set of shelves may house the program's "collection" of books with spines facing outward. A book rack, displaying up to thirty attractive books, should be located at eye level for the children. Torn, dirty books with pages missing and damaged illustrations should be replaced. Books that have been well cared for encourage respect for the books and their careful handling. Framed prints, posters, or paintings on the wall in the book nook stretch the mind and spirit and are visual reminders that this is a place for dreaming, imagining, and thinking.

Books should be shelved by category. The variety and type of books will depend on the ages of the children. For younger children, picture books with large illustrations and print featuring human and animal families, colours, shapes, pop-up pictures, number and letter symbols, familiar nursery rhymes and popular characters, and familiar landscapes such as those of farms, countrysides, and cities, are most appropriate. Older children have their favourite storybooks, which should always be on the shelves, as well as a weekly selection of new or theme-oriented books to spark children's interest. Arguments may be made for including literacy-related play materials such as Speak and Spell, Etch-a-Sketch, and other soft technology games that children can play with quietly.

Certain rules should be clarified at the outset and modelled by teachers when children are introduced to the book nook—rules such as washing sticky or paint-covered hands before looking at books, turning the pages carefully, replacing the book on the rack when finished, and holding them so as not to bend the cover or break the binding. Teachers should always introduce books to children by showing them how books should be held, pointing out the often fragile binding that holds the pages together, and encouraging children to feel the pages in order to understand that they may tear easily unless handled gently.

The careful selection of books to support special themes or occasions and developmental objectives helps to integrate the book nook into the total learning environment. For example, when children are learning about road safety, it is useful to have books on that topic available for children in the book nook. Flannelboards and felt characters representing familiar characters from children's favourite books encourage children to tell stories based on those they have heard and the books they have "read" on the racks. Children should always have access to the flannelboard and felts in this area once they have been properly introduced to their care and handling.

Activities in the Book Nook

(for younger children, ages two to four)

1. Provide props such as teddy bears, stuffed animals, dolls, hats, jewellery, and scarves that relate to a new book on the shelves. Children may use the props, or wear the hats and jewellery while reading the new book.

2. Provide a flannelboard with felt characters representing the characters of favourite books or a new book. Encourage children to tell the story using the felt characters after having read or while looking at the storybook.

3. Ask children to make a book in the Creative Arts Centre that they can add to the shelves in the book nook. Provide a permanent place on the book rack for the storage of books that children and teachers have created together. Ensure that at least one book is a photo album containing photographs taken of the children playing and during special events, which will enhance memory skills and conversation about the event.

(for older children, ages four to six)

4. Set up a lending library in the book nook. Provide a small table, pencils, some library cards, and a stamp pad. Gather a selection of books from ones that have been on the rack for a while and that the program is prepared to "lend" to children to take home either for their parents to read to them or to look at by themselves. Appoint one child as the librarian or ask for a volunteer. Children may come to the library desk during the morning to borrow a book to take home, which the librarian will stamp. Each child will print her name or draw her symbol on the borrowing card.

5. Set up a book repair shop in the Creative Arts Centre or in the book nook. Remove all damaged books from the shelves and racks. Show children how to wipe finger marks off pages with a damp cloth or repair torn pages and binding with glue. Reinforce the importance of caring for books and repairing those that still have potential. Support the idea that books are usually precious possessions that we never want to throw away.

6. Provide a range of picture books that address visual and perceptual skills associated with reading such as ocular-motor skills and visual discrimination abilities. *Where's Waldo?* books, for example, require children to look for and focus on a specific character on busy pages. Inexpensive activity books for the early years challenge children with dot-to-dot activities, matching and same-different activities, picture outlines embedded within detailed line illustrations, and simple-to-complex mazes for children to follow with a pencil or crayon.

7. Provide an informal storytime for children who wish to hear a story every day in the book nook. Later on, choosing a story that is serialized (i.e., read over three or four storyreading sessions) promotes attending skills and enjoyment of more complex literature, builds anticipation, and encourages recall and development of memory.

8. Include children's magazines, which change with each new edition, on the book racks. *Owl, Chickadee, Turtle,* and *Children's Digest* are examples. Introduce children to the concept of magazine subscriptions by which new issues arrive each month and address new topics.

The Language Arts Area

Literacy learning begins long before children go to school. Interest in reading and writing starts as soon as children are introduced to the world of print, literature, and graphic activity. Literacy skills need to be supported by the environment (Schickedanz, 1986). When literature, print, graphic activity, and all forms of communication are valued, children will be interested in trying to read and write long before they are exposed to formal instruction. What matters is that the learning environment promote a culture of respect and enjoyment of literacy. Children's early efforts to read and print should be encouraged and valued on their own merit; these early attempts do not have to match adult models in order to be noteworthy.

Children learn to read and write in much the same way that they learn oral language, that is, through constructing their own understanding of structure, relationships, and protocol (Fields & Lee, 1987). The concept of emergent literacy implies that skills involved in reading and writing begin early in life, are an integral part of daily living, develop concurrently in young children, and involve active play and learning with materials (Teale & Sulzby, 1989). The importance of providing a literate environment for young children at home and at school cannot be overestimated (Essa, 1992).

LANGUAGE ARTS AREA

The language arts area should provide two tables with chairs, storage shelves for puzzles, specific-purpose materials, modular materials, small construction materials, a theme table, possibly a chalkboard and chalk, a magnetic board on a stand, and a puppet theatre. A wide range of emergent reading skills should be addressed in this area and should emphasize the development of visual-perceptual abilities that are fundamental to reading and writing. Near one of the tables, graphic tools such as felt-tipped markers, crayons, pencils, and chalk and a chalkboard should be provided, along with a supply of paper of various sizes and types. Index cards and file boxes, writing folders for each child, and materials for making books would be of interest in the language arts area.

Sometimes referred to as the tabletop area, the language arts area provides materials that introduce children to letters and words, as well as to a wide range of activities that promote visual-perceptual abilities. Tabletop construction toys such as Lego, Tinkertoy, pegboards, and table blocks foster development of spatial concepts, figure-ground perception, depth perception, left-to-right progression, scanning, visual tracking, and other visual skills.

The many kits, baskets, and bins containing modular, specific-purpose, and construction materials found in this area require efficient, easily accessed storage space.

Storage units with compartments for holding boxed materials, baskets, and plastic bins are very useful. Movable storage shelves and cupboards may also serve as boundaries for the language arts area.

Activities in the Language Arts Area

(for younger children, ages two to four)

1. Provide formboard and jigsaw puzzles for children in their appropriate developmental sequence moving from simple formboard puzzles, in which children replace a single shape in a similar slot, to complex jigsaw puzzles. These two-dimensional puzzles promote visual discrimination, shape and colour recognition, eye-hand coordination, fine-motor skills, figure-ground perception, directional positioning, spatial relationships, and ocular-motor skills, all of which are related to emergent reading abilities. Puzzles also promote problem-solving and task-orientation abilities.

2. Set up magnetic letters and numbers, and magnet boards to promote directional positioning of letter and number symbols.

3. Provide salt trays and sand trays to encourage children to experience in a sensorimotor way the shape and formation of letter symbols, and to practise directional positioning.

4. Set up picture and letter blocks to encourage children to form pictures and words.

5. Alphabet sets with wooden or plastic letters promote children's sensorimotor exploration of the shapes of letters.

6. Provide chalkboard and chalk with which children may try to print or draw pictures representing a picture book they have looked at or a story they have heard.

7. Hang a large poster on the wall close to the language arts area that leads children progressively from the left to the right side of the poster.

(for older children, ages four to six)

8. Provide bins with Lego and encourage children to build creatively with these construction materials after they have spent time exploring them physically. It is useful, on occasion, for children to try to replicate a model using a diagram of a truck, a helicopter, or some other vehicle or structure as a way of practising visual discrimination abilities, spatial concept, directional positioning, figure-ground abilities, and problem-solving skills.

9. Tabletop blocks and Tinkertoys promote visual-perceptual abilities, attending, problem solving, creativity, fine-motor skills, manipulative abilities, and ocular-motor skills. Any experiences that children have manipulating small construc-

tion materials and working to make intricate structures with specific space constraints promote spatial concepts and physical abilities such as the fine-motor skills and eye-hand coordination required for printing and writing. Provide tabletop construction sets for children to create their own structures, and provide diagrams and models for children to replicate using the materials.

10. Set up an office at a table with a typewriter, office supplies, paper, envelopes, stamps, stamp pad, briefcase, and other office accessories children enjoy. Encourage sociodramatic play.

11. Provide a Viewmaster and slides, kaleidoscopes, and a slide projector to promote visual-perceptual abilities.

12. Set up Ready to Read sets with a letter symbol and object together on each card (e.g., an A and a picture of an Apple, a B and a picture of a Book, and so on).

The Display Table

A display table may be thought of as a potential space in the Quiet Thinking Centre that may be set up to address a special theme or introduce a new topic for exploration. This display table may also be used to introduce new books and address emergent reading, problem-solving, perceptual, and fine-motor skills.

A cutting activity may be set up at this table if it cannot be accommodated in the Creative Arts Centre. Cutting activities often involve tracing, drawing, and cutting for the purpose of staying within boundaries or on lines. Cutting skills are an essential prerequisite to printing and writing, and are therefore closely related to language arts. Cutting activities help children acquire laterality skills, left-right progression, figure-ground perception, manipulative abilities, fine-motor skills, eye-hand coordination, and many other perceptual-motor and physical abilities related to reading and writing.

The display table should be changed every couple of weeks so that children become accustomed to checking to see what is there for them to explore. Interesting display tables stimulate language, add new vocabulary, and encourage conversation. A small picture file may also be placed on the display table for children to explore. Children enjoy small picture files on cards stored in 10- by 15-cm file card boxes as much as larger pictures mounted on construction paper, and they are just as effective in stimulating language.

Ideas for the Display Table in the Quiet Thinking Centre

People pictures; travel photographs; special occasion displays of winter carnival time, festivals, and holidays; multicultural displays; calendars; books, famous paintings and portraits; photography books; albums; and catalogues.

Workjobs

Mary Baratta-Lorton's series of books, *Workjobs* (1972), has gained renewed popularity because of concern about the environment and attention to recycling and protecting natural resources. Since the early 1970s, several approaches to creating play and learning materials from recycled products or beautiful junk have emerged. The Baratta-Lorton approach has widespread appeal in early childhood education because the activity ideas are developmentally appropriate and emphasize learning-to-learn skills.

Workjobs kits should occupy a special place on low shelves that are accessible to children. All Workjobs are stored in individual kits with word and picture labels in order that children can recognize which Workjob is contained in each box or sack before removing it from the shelf. The Workjobs shelves may be located close to an open carpeted area in the Quiet Thinking Centre where children can place their kit on the floor, play with it, finish, and replace it on the shelf.

Some teachers specify a time of day for all children to play with the Workjobs kits. This regularity frees teachers to observe and assess children's mastery of the developmental skills addressed by each kit, and to work with a child individually on a difficult or unfamiliar task. The designation of a Workjobs time of day depends on the availability of a sufficiently large inventory of kits to permit plenty of choice for children.

Workjobs challenge children to develop a wide range of work-study skills important for effective learning through the following tasks:

- put away the Workjob in the box as it was found
- find the Workjob's proper place on the shelf
- find alternative solutions to the "problem" presented by the Workjob
- practise and repeat an action
- plan ahead, anticipate a result, form a hypothesis
- test the solution
- communicate what has been done or completed
- transfer the learning gained by doing the Workjob to other activities

References

Baratta-Lorton, M. (1972). *Workjobs*. Menlo Park, CA: Addison-Wesley.

Bohannon, J.N., III, and Warren-Leubecker, A. (1989). Theoretical approaches to language acquisition. In *The Development of Language*. 2d ed. Ed. J. Berko Gleason, pp. 167–223. Columbus, OH: Merrill.

Bruner, J., and Anglin, J. (1973). *Beyond the Information Given: Studies in the Psychology of Knowing*. New York: W.W. Norton.

Bruner, J. (1983). *Child's Talk: Learning to Use Language.* New York: W.W. Norton.

Cazden, C. (1981). Language development and the preschool environment. In *Language in Early Childhood Education,* ed. C. Cazden, pp. 3–16. Washington, D.C.: National Association for the Education of Young Children.

Essa, E. (1992). *Introduction to Early Childhood Education.* Albany, NY: Delmar.

Fields, M., and Lee, D. (1987). *Let's Begin Reading Right: A Developmental Approach to Beginning Literacy.* Columbus, OH: Merrill.

Gleason, J. Berko. (1989). Studying language development. In *The Development of Language.* 2d ed. Ed. J. Berko Gleason, pp. 1–34. Columbus, OH: Merrill.

Kamii, C. (1972). An application of Piaget's theory to the conceptualization of a preschool curriculum. In *The Preschool in Action,* ed. R. Parker. Boston: Allyn & Bacon.

Morrow, L.M. (1989). Designing the classroom to promote literacy development. In *Emerging Literacy: Young Children Learn to Read and Write,* ed. D.S. Strickland and L.M. Morrow. Newark, DE: International Reading Association.

Pflaum, S.W. (1974). *The Development of Language and Reading in the Young Child.* Columbus, OH: Merrill.

Piaget, J. (1926, 1955). *The Language and Thought of the Child.* New York: Meridian Books.

Schickedanz, J.A. (1986). *More Than the ABC's: The Early Stages of Reading and Writing.* Washington, D.C.: National Association for the Education of Young Children.

Teale, W.H., and Sulzby, E. (1989). Emerging literacy: new perspectives. In *Emerging Literacy: Young Children Learn to Read and Write,* ed. D.S. Strickland and L.M. Morrow, pp. 1–15. Newark, DE: International Reading Association.

Wood, D. (1988). *How Children Think and Learn.* Oxford, England: Basil Blackwell Ltd.

Wortham, S.C. (1984). *Organizing Instruction in Early Childhood: A Handbook of Assessment and Activities.* Boston, MA: Allyn & Bacon.

C H A P T E R 15

THE QUIET THINKING CENTRE— LOGICAL CONCEPTS

■ LOGICAL-MATHEMATICAL UNDERSTANDING

Piaget defined physical, social-conventional, and logical-mathematical understanding largely according to the source of learning. Physical and social-conventional knowledge are mainly external to the individual, in other words, they are something that can be acquired through sensory exploration or social transmission. Logical-mathematical knowledge originates within the individual and involves the child's construction of relationships among objects that have no existence in external reality (Kamii, 1985:9).

Logical-mathematical understanding consists of the coordination of concepts or relationships such as same-different, more-less, part-whole, cause-effect, and number operations such as two plus two is four. It is the kind of knowledge or conceptual understanding that defines a relationship that is not directly observable. The source of logical-mathematical understanding is inherent in the relationship itself, which exists in the mind. For example, a red button and a blue button placed side by side constitute two buttons. This understanding is different from knowing their observable characteristics and properties such as colour, shape, and the substance of which they are made (i.e., plastic or wood). Logical-mathematical concepts are universal in that they are the same in all cultures.

Arriving at an understanding of an underlying, unifying concept among objects or events involves making a mental leap from the simple recognition of things/objects in their external, physical, observable reality and the knowledge of their social-conventional meaning to the realm of concept formation. Understanding the concept involves knowing that a relationship exists in an abstract sense. Piaget claimed that the construction of logical-mathematical understanding is essential to the development of intelligence and cognition (Piaget, 1969).

■ LEARNING LOGICAL CONCEPTS IN THE QUIET THINKING CENTRE

The Quiet Thinking Centre provides planned learning opportunities that address logical-mathematical understanding. Children can engage in similar learning using different materials in the Science Discovery Centre. They require opportunities in many learning contexts to form relationships among objects in many ways such as manipulating, combining, separating, and classifying objects through their active, physical play with modular materials, specialized kits, and puzzles.

Children's learning of logical concepts—seriation, classification, and number—is a function of their gradual understanding of the concrete and abstract relationships that exist among items in a set. Children develop these concepts by moving from the simple to the complex through a sequence of play activities in which the relationships among objects are perceptually apparent to the child. Numerous sensorimotor experiences lead to the child's later understanding of relationships without having to refer to the concrete materials. This kind of learning cannot be rushed and is dependent on the individual learning style and experience of the learner. Children need encouragement to choose play materials freely and manipulate them physically. In this way, they integrate the concepts first through their sensorimotor play.

PROBLEM SOLVING

The extent to which children develop an understanding of logical concepts in early childhood depends on the nature and kind of play experiences they have in the early years. The mastery of logical concepts and the ability to reason and think in the abstract, without relying on the physical presence of concrete objects, is important to later school success. Kamii (1982) reminds us, however, that knowing that a child has to construct her own knowledge does not mean that the teacher has to leave the child alone. Children have individual needs for assistance, clarification, and encouragement when they approach challenging learning tasks. Teachers create an environment that promotes self-directed learning, but they may still remain close by to ask questions and guide children in ways that will help to motivate them and respond to their needs.

The rate and efficiency with which their understanding of concepts develops depends on the sensitivity of teachers to the children's individual needs. When children experience success in meeting challenges and learning abstract concepts, more advanced learning tasks are entered into with greater enthusiasm, positive feelings, and confidence in their ability to succeed. Children's play with specific-purpose and modular materials in the Quiet Thinking Centre contributes to their understanding of logical concepts, including seriation, classification, and number concepts.

■ STEPS IN LEARNING CONCEPT OF NUMBER

Children have to acquire the concept of number before they are able to understand the meaning of arithmetical operations such as addition, subtraction, multiplication, and division. Mathematical problem solving using numbers and other symbols also depends on a solid foundation in number concept. Number is a form of logical-mathematical knowledge that depends on an understanding of relationships, classes or sets, order, quantity, equality, and constancy. Learning concepts of classification (sorting, set/groups) and order (temporal order, spatial order, and seriation, which is order by length) are closely related to the learning of number concept.

As with all types of concept learning, it is easiest for children to experience number first in a physical-sensory way. Later, children acquire social-conventional knowledge about number. Much of children's earliest experience with number involves becoming socialized to a world that includes understanding the diverse roles that number plays in our daily lives. Before children begin to learn about the logical nature of number, which leads to number concept, they learn to recognize numbers, sing and chant numbers, feel the shape of number symbols, and experience many daily contexts in which using number is both necessary and helpful. Understanding the social meaning of number and recognizing the sight and sound of number are important sensory and social learning experiences that precede the logical-mathematical steps involved in learning number concept.

Physical Knowledge about Number

Physical knowledge about number involves children's early experiences with the sight and sound of number symbols. They see number pasted up on the display board, they feel the number symbols hanging from the number tree, they sing songs about number during group time—"one little two little three little chickadees"—and they recite finger plays and rhymes using number—"one, two, buckle my shoe."

Social-Conventional Knowledge of Number

When teachers draw attention to the presence of numbers in cooking recipes, ages, addresses, sizes, weights, distances, speeds, telephone numbers, prices, money, and a host of other contexts, they are sensitizing children to the presence and meaning of number in all aspects of our daily lives. Social-conventional knowledge of number involves learning that numbers are used to represent birthdays, that certain numbers such as 18 or 21 have social importance, and that other special numbers (dates) are associated with festive occasions and traditional holidays. Conventional knowledge about number makes children aware that number has social and cultural meaning.

■ LEARNING CONCEPT OF NUMBER—LOGICAL-MATHEMATICAL UNDERSTANDING

Eventually children are ready to move from a physical and social-conventional knowledge of number to an understanding of number as a symbol, a system for describing relationships, and a tool for solving problems. Kamii (1982:27) has identified three types of learning activities that help children move towards gradual understanding of number concept: the creation of all kinds of relationships; the quantification of objects; and social interaction with peers and teachers to reinforce concepts and demonstrate level of conceptual understanding.

The Creation of All Kinds of Relationships

Early number concept involves many open-ended play experiences that are not directly related to number but that stimulate their learning of concepts and ability to create relationships among things mentally. For example, when children sort objects into groups or collections of things with common properties, they begin to understand the notion of **set.** Set is a fundamental idea in mathematics, and understanding it usually precedes the ability to quantify. As children notice relationships between objects they are comparing, matching, joining, and dividing, they develop their earliest understandings of mathematical operations (Donaldson, 1978). As they create relationships between objects on the basis of order, for example, in order of size from biggest to smallest, or in order of colour or shape, they learn about the many kinds of relationships that exist among things in our environment. From early experiences of sorting, making sets, and ordering objects, children begin to integrate the notions of pattern and structure that are essential to an understanding of mathematics.

Number concept depends on the child's ability to form relationships among things on the basis of order and classification criteria. It is only when children are able to understand relationships like same/different, more/less, first/last, big/bigger/biggest, that they are able to understand the logical significance of number. Children need plenty of opportunities to match objects according to a variety of criteria in order to understand the diverse variables upon which things or ideas may be grouped.

Ordering

Ordering is a more complicated form of comparing that is based on a particular relationship between two objects. To order a set of objects involves creating a relationship between an object and the set of objects to which it is being related (Cruikshank, Fitzgerald & Jensen, 1980). Ordering begins to develop during the sensorimotor period when children play with nesting and stacking toys (Charlesworth & Radeloff, 1991). Children need to experience ordering by size (seriation), pattern (spatial order), time (temporal order), numerical order (order of number symbols 1, 2, 3 ...), and ordinal numbers (first, second, third).

Play materials such as stacking and nesting sets, Cuisenaire rods, and sequencing and seriation kits may be used by children to practise making a set in a given order. Children may order following a model, extending a pattern or order, filling in gaps in an ordered set, and creating an order for a set of objects with ordinal properties such as length, time, and size. Children should be able to order objects successfully before they are asked to order numbers (Cruikshank, Fitzgerald & Jensen, 1980).

Seriation

Seriation is an arrangement of objects based on graduated order. Ordered sets of objects are sets in which the gradations or differences in size between each object in the series and the ones next to it are equal: all the objects in the set are needed in order to help children grasp this logical concept. Cuisenaire rods, measuring cups, nested blocks, dolls, eggs, or barrels are usually based on multiples of one basic unit of measurement and can be used to help children learn to seriate if they are placed in a graduated order from smallest to largest or vice versa. The essential problem for children to solve when seriating is "what comes next in the series?"

When children are learning to seriate a set of objects, they usually experiment using trial and error, and may start by placing objects at each end and moving towards the middle, fitting the middle two in last. As children progress in their understanding of seriation concept, they will be able to order by moving in one direction and planning ahead. Frequently, children understand the concept of building steps and stairs but fail to account for the common base line that will ensure that each object in the ordered series is one graduated size larger or smaller than the previous one. Eventually, children should be encouraged to evolve a plan for their ordering and proceed systematically without having to make any alterations in the order as they proceed. When children have learned to seriate one whole set of objects by moving in one direction only and without hesitation, they are ready to double seriate. This final step involves the child's ability to place two sets of objects in ordered sets using one-to-one correspondence and following a systematic plan (see Figure 15.1).

Spatial Order/Topology

Ordering according to spatial characteristics refers to placing objects in a certain order by shape, usually by making or following patterns and creating equal sets using one-to-one correspondence. (One-to-one correspondence will be addressed later in this chapter.) Young children are interested in the topological properties of shapes in space and should be encouraged to draw and arrange them in diverse ways (Sime, 1973). Topology is the study of space in the context of position or location in which shape and length may be altered without affecting the figure's properties of being open or closed (Cruikshank, Fitzgerald, & Jensen, 1980). (See Figure 15.2.) Preoperational children are more interested in the topological properties of space than they are in the Euclidean properties that define specific geometric shapes in standard ways and are learned later (Laurendeau & Pinard, 1968). Forming relationships based on the spatial configuration and order of objects helps children develop an understanding of distance (near/far), part-whole (part of/not part of), position (before/after), and boundary (inside/outside).

Temporal Order

Temporal order refers to the order in which events have taken place. Sequencing activities often address temporal ordering concepts when they provide a set of cards containing a series of pictures related to an ongoing event or process that occurs over time. Sequenced cards may represent a series of events, which may consist of getting up in the morning, having breakfast, going to school, coming home, having dinner, and going to bed, or planting a seed, seeing the plant grow, picking the vegetable, and cooking it.

Numerical Order

Children learn to recognize the sight and sound of number symbols very early. Their recognition of the order in which number symbols appear when they are in numerical order, 1–2–3–4–5, is largely socially transmitted through songs, finger

Figure 15.1   EARLY STAGES OF SERIATION

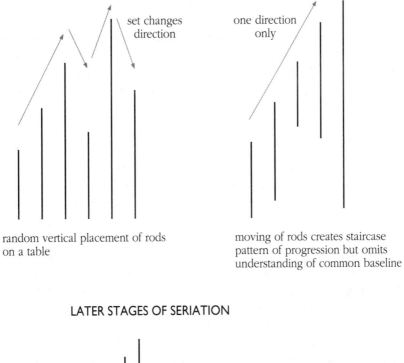

set changes
direction

one direction
only

random vertical placement of rods
on a table

moving of rods creates staircase
pattern of progression but omits
understanding of common baseline

LATER STAGES OF SERIATION

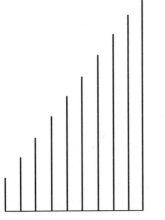

ordering by length in one direction only,
respects the equal gradations that should
be between each successive item in a series
with a common baseline

double seriation

Figure 15.2   TOPOLOGY

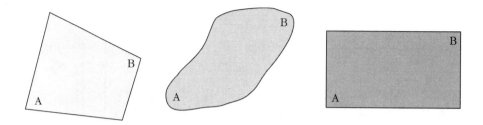

Altering shapes without affecting the figure's properties of being open or closed (Cruikshank, Fitzgerald, & Jensen, 1980).

plays, rhymes, and activities. Children usually acquire an understanding of the numerical order of number symbols well before they are able to understand what each number represents in terms of quantity.

Ordinal Number

Children's understanding of ordinal number is often acquired through physical experiences such as lining up and taking turns in organized physical activities and board games. The ability to form relationships based on which comes first, second, third, fourth, and so on in a series is generally acquired through active involvement in real-life situations from an early age. The ability to relate the physical knowledge of ordinal number to an understanding of the concept of order by number develops at the same time that children are learning to count, understand notions of quantity, and appreciate concepts of greater than and less than.

Classification

Classification is the putting of objects into groups according to similar attributes. These attributes may be decided on by the teacher or by the children. Classification is a form of sorting and involves creating a set based on a criterion common to all the objects in the set. The common criterion may be concrete and observable, such as colour, shape, or size; or it may be knowledge-based, such as nocturnal versus diurnal animals; or it may be abstract, such as things I like/don't like, beautiful/ugly, or safe/dangerous.

Children's ability to classify progresses from simple sorting activities, such as sorting according to one attribute (grouping the large teddy bears and the small teddy bears) to sorting according to two and even three attributes (separating the small, grey teddy bears from the large, brown teddy bears). Objects with concrete, observable characteristics that distinguish one set from another are easiest to sort, followed by those that can be distinguished on the basis of knowledge, such as the bedroom furniture versus the living room furniture. Forming sets based on abstract criteria, (i.e., happy/funny/silly), and forming subsets (i.e., creating hierarchies of classes such as food/fruit/melons/berries) are the most challenging classification tasks for children.

ORDERING

When children are learning to classify, it is important for them to follow some key principles. Often the teacher has to point these out after the children have had opportunities to play and practise sorting using their own methods. In addition to understanding that all objects in a set must have at least one common, unifying characteristic, they must learn that the same characteristic must apply to all objects put into that set and that unrelated characteristics are ignored. As they become more experienced, children learn that all available objects to be sorted must be included in one of the groups being made and that no object can remain unclassified. Eventually children understand that the classes in the classification system should not overlap; that is, no member of the set to be sorted should fit into more than one of the classes (see Figure 15.3).

Number Concept

Once children have had experience ordering and classifying sets of objects, they are more likely to understand concepts related to the logical nature of number. Learning number concept is a very different enterprise from acquiring social knowledge about number, even though children will have been exposed to activities and everyday living experiences that introduce them to the world of number (Kamii,

Figure 15.3   CLASSIFICATION

FORMING SETS

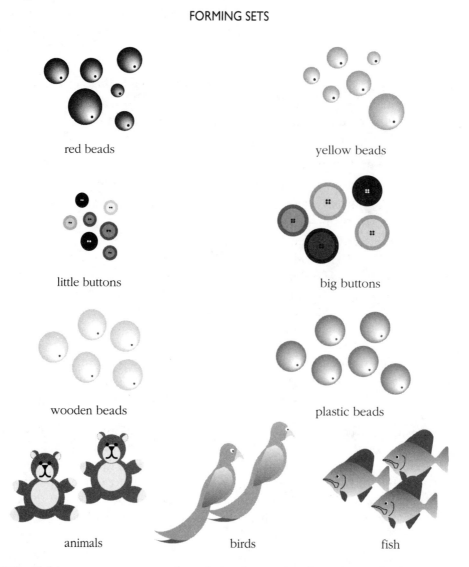

red beads

yellow beads

little buttons

big buttons

wooden beads

plastic beads

animals

birds

fish

1982). Children must construct the relationships related to understanding number concept for themselves. As in learning other concepts, children acquire number concept through social play and active interaction with concrete objects.

An early understanding of number starts with the child's attempts to put objects in order using size or temporal order as the criterion for ordering and to create groupings or sets of objects according to specific criteria (i.e., classification). Concepts of order and set are related to number concept and are achieved through children's self-directed explorations of specific-purpose materials such as graduated cylinders, rods, or stacking toys and sorting activities with buttons, bingo chips, miniature animals, foods, and sets of vehicles. The ability to sort objects begins with both recognizing similarities and differences and matching one object to another on the basis of some observable criterion. This step is usually followed by sorting according to a knowledge-based criterion such as all the spoons together and all the cutting instruments together. About the same time, children learn to match one cup to one saucer, one knife to one fork, one egg to one egg cup, and one hat to each doll. At this stage, they are ready for one-to-one correspondence activities.

One-to-One Correspondence

One-to-one correspondence is the ability to match each object in set B to an object in set A when the numbers of objects in each set are the same. When children place an egg in each slot of the egg carton, give a spoon to each doll, and a cup to each child in the circle, they are learning the pairing of one member of set A with one member of set B. After considerable practice with this kind of simple matching of an object in one set to an object in another set, children begin to grasp the idea that the number of objects in set A is the same as the number in set B simply by looking at the configuration of the sets. Similarly, they begin to learn that there is an absence of one-to-one correspondence if they have some objects left over in set A after they have finished putting one object from set A with one object in set B. Having some objects left over in set A is visual proof that set A must be larger than set B (see Figure 15.4). After many play opportunities with one-to-one correspondence materials, children acquire an understanding of what makes sets equal in size.

These understandings are acquired by children through their self-directed play with materials that have been carefully selected and set up in the environment by

Figure 15.4   ONE-TO-ONE CORRESPONDENCE

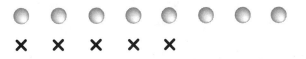

creating two equal sets—equal number of balls and jacks

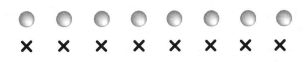

unequal sets—more jacks than balls

the teacher. At this stage, it is still too early to begin counting with children, as they are simply gaining the notion of the creation of sets through one-to-one correspondence (Donaldson, 1978). Similarly, when children play with groups of objects by sorting them into sets having a common property like colour, size, shape, or social meaning, they are adding to their understanding of a set as a group of objects, each of which has a common attribute. One-to-one correspondence, seriation, and classification activities are essential to the development of number concept before children are able to count and quantify.

Counting Objects in a Set

Once children form sets using one-to-one correspondence without hesitation, they can begin counting the number of objects in each set, usually by pointing with their index fingers to each object in turn in the set. This action is in itself a form of one-to-one correspondence as the task children have to practise is that of pointing the index finger once and only once to each object in turn in the series. The idea is that each object, as one progresses in the series, is one more than the previous one. At this stage, one-to-one correspondence moves from the realm of a simple matching activity to an early understanding of quantity. At the same time, counting as rhyme and song, or the simple recitation of number, changes to counting with some understanding of the mathematical significance of number. The child at this stage is beginning to attach number symbols used in counting to objects in a set, and to compare the number of objects in one set to the number of objects in the second set. When children begin to match and compare equal sets of objects arranged in one-to-one correspondence, they are beginning to acquire an understanding of the mathematical value of number.

Children may be encouraged to count objects in a series when they are at the stage of learning about the equality of sets and the concept of quantity. It is always easier for children to count objects when they are physically ordered—children will not readily order the objects mentally in their heads. Sometimes, even the physical ordering of objects in a row will not prevent skip counting (see Figure 15.5). Frequently, children will double count objects in a group unless they are physically ordered in a row (see Figure 15.6).

Figure 15.5   SKIP COUNTING

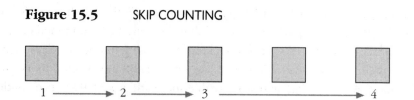

Figure 15.6   DOUBLE COUNTING

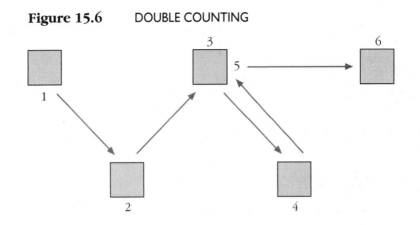

Figure 15.7   UNDERSTANDING QUANTITY (when objects in two sets are perceptually different from each other)

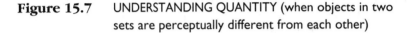

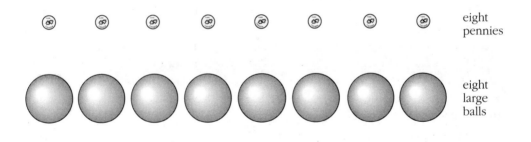

Children may count the number of objects in each set correctly. When asked whether there are more pennies or more balls, if they are focusing only on the perceptual characteristics (i.e., size of objects in each set), they will say that there are more balls than pennies).

When children are learning concept of quantity, they frequently assume that the quantity of objects in a set changes when the objects in the set change. That is, children will count a set of pennies and find that there are eight, and then count a corresponding set of eight balls placed next to them in one-to-one correspondence and find that there are eight (see Figure 15.7). When asked, however, if there are more balls or more pennies, the child will say that there are more balls. Since children are perceptually bound in the preoperational stage, they make this error because they are focusing on the size of the balls, which is so much bigger than that of the pennies. At this stage, children still believe that number depends on size because size is perceptually apparent.

Number Constancy

It is only when they understand that number does not change according to the properties of the objects counted and that the quality of fiveness or eightness remains the same whatever is being counted that children begin to understand the constancy of number. Number constancy means that the quality of eightness, oneness, or fiveness does not change in spite of the properties (e.g., size, shape, texture, medium) of the objects being counted. In order to ensure that children understand the constancy of number, at least eight objects should be included in a set to prevent visual estimation of the number of objects to be counted (Kamii, 1982). (See Figure 15.8.)

Figure 15.8   NUMBER CONSTANCY

 = 8 pennies

 = 8 kittens

The child says that there are the same number of kittens as there are pennies.

Conservation of Number

Children's ability to conserve number involves understanding that the quantity or number of objects in a set remains the same in spite of transformations or changes in the configuration of the set (Piaget, 1969). Preoperational children are unable to conserve largely because their ability to think and "know" depends on their senses, as in "what I see is what I believe."

Children are often confused by differences in the configuration of sets of objects they are counting. For example, when a young child counts, in turn, a long row of eight pennies and a small vertical stack of eight pennies, he will arrive at the answer that there are eight pennies in each set. When asked, however, whether the number of pennies in the row or in the stack are the same or whether there are more in one set, he will reply that there are more pennies in the row. This child is focusing on the visual dimensions of the long row and relies on his perception of physical boundaries of the set to make his judgement rather than on what he knows. It is only when they are certain that quantity is independent of the configuration of objects in a set being counted that children are able to conserve numbers. When they are able to retain in their heads the understanding that the number of pennies in both the row and the stack are the same in spite of differences in the configuration of each set, we can safely say that they have achieved number concept (see Figure 15.9).

Figure 15.9   CONSERVATION OF NUMBER

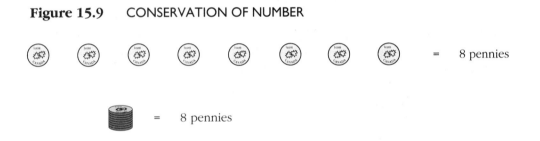

The child says that there are the same number of pennies in each set.

■ PLAY MATERIALS TO PROMOTE NUMBER CONCEPT

Children develop number concept through their freely chosen play with things, usually modular materials that they can order, sort, arrange, count, and quantify. The Quiet Thinking Centre should provide a wide variety of modular materials that promote the development of number concept, such as pegs and pegboards, bingo chips, Cuisenaire rods, attribute blocks, stacking and nesting blocks, Unifix (interlocking sets), pattern blocks, people pieces, centimetre cubes, colour cubes, counting chips, and parquetry. The key to helping children learn number concept using these materials lies in teachers' skilled observations of their levels of understanding of number. Teachers then carefully select and set up materials to promote children's progress to the next stage. Observing children as they play provides insight as to when encouragement, support, and coaching are needed in order to facilitate the acquisition of a more mature understanding of number that builds on what they already know.

■ ACTIVITIES TO PROMOTE LOGICAL CONCEPTS

The activities listed below may be presented to children from the age of two, and the complexity of the tasks may be increased as children make progress.

Order

1. Use sets of seriated objects such as stacking cups, cylinders, barrels, and dolls; sets of cardboard graduated cutouts of bears, dolls, elephants; Cuisenaire rods; graduated blocks for tabletop play; and unit blocks. Set up the sets on a table for children to play with individually. Teachers may start the stacking or arranging of the sets (i.e., provide a model to follow), or simply leave the objects in a set on the table and observe children's play. Children will initially explore the materials before they begin to seriate the objects. When teachers observe that children need help moving to the next stage in the learning process, they may make a suggestion, demonstrate the seriating properties of the objects, or coach the child. When children are able to seriate a set of objects moving from the smallest to the largest, or vice versa, but moving in one direction only, without hesitation and without making errors, children have mastered the concept of single set seriation.

2. Once children have had numerous play opportunities with single seriated sets of objects, teachers may introduce them to the task of double seriation. They will place two sets of seriated objects on the table and may encourage children to make two sets of seriated objects, first by seriating one set and then creating a second set using one-to-one correspondence and estimating the order in which objects will be placed to create two seriated sets.

3. Provide a set of ordered objects for a child to seriate at a table and then add additional objects and encourage the child to extend the order. If a pattern is discernible in the ordered set—for example, a colour or shape pattern—encourage children to extend the order of the set by repeating the pattern.

4. Set up a set of ordered materials with some gaps in the order and encourage children to fill in the gaps.

5. Play "closest to" and "farthest from." Position each child in the group in a different location in the playroom. Have them sit down. Teacher asks, "Who is closest to the blocks?" "Who is farthest from the computer?" "Who is closest to the sink?" Each child stands when his or her position is called. All children in the group participate in deciding which child is the one in the position called by the teacher.

6. Play "Fit into" with a group of children. The object is for the children to decide which objects fit into various containers that have been selected for each of the

objects. The children are asked, "Would a cat fit into a cup?" "Would a crayon fit into a jar?" "Would a piano fit into a toy box?" "Would a tricycle fit into a bucket?"

Classification

7. Sort two sets of buttons of the same size and shape but of two different colours—for instance, red and yellow—for children to classify. Mix up the red and yellow buttons on the table and begin to sort two sets according to colour—e.g., two red buttons in one group and two yellow buttons in a second group). The same activity may be repeated several times using two sets that are different on the basis of shape (circles and squares) and size (big and little beads of the same colour and shape). Always ensure at the early stages that the two sets can be sorted on the basis of one distinct criterion only.

8. Set up sets of bingo chips or buttons for children to classify on the basis of two observable criteria—say, colour and shape. All the red round objects and all the square yellow objects are, therefore, separated. Ensure that all objects to be sorted fit both criteria for one or the other set.

9. Encourage children to sort the cups and the saucers, and forks and spoons, that have been borrowed from the Daily Living Centre (or set up the same activity in that centre).

10. Sort a miscellany of objects with some recognizable similarities and let children choose the criteria that define the groups they make. Children will have fun grouping all the "pointy" objects, all the objects with holes, all the soft objects, and so forth. When they have sorted all the objects into one of their categories, encourage them to define new categories or "teams" according to other similarities that they can find. Ensure that children respect the rule that all objects must fit into one of the groups they have identified and that no object is a member of more than one group at the same time.

11. Set up objects at a table that can be sorted according to identifiable, "knowledge-based" criteria such as: kitchen furniture, bedroom furniture, appliances, patio furniture; vehicles that travel on ground, water, or in the air; tools for the kitchen, workshop, garden, office; and nocturnal and diurnal animals.

12. Encourage children to sort hierarchies of classes such as domestic animals, farm animals, zoo animals; then farm animals with wool, and whose hair is long or short; carnivorous animals and plant-eating animals; rodents and canine, feline, and bovine animals. Choose similar hierarchical classes using various food groups and then dividing foods into subcategories within food groups. For example, classify subclasses of fruits into citrus, melons, berries, et cetera; and fruits that grow on trees, bushes, vines, and so on.

13. Provide objects for which the sorting criteria may be more abstract or subjective, such as: beautiful/ugly things; useful/not useful things; safe/dangerous things; happy and sad things; things you do when you're playing/working.

14. Encourage children to classify objects that are alike in more than one way according to two knowledge-based or abstract criteria. Examples include: all the land vehicles with motors; land vehicles that must be hauled; and pictures that are beautiful/sad, ugly/funny, and happy/loving.

Number (Physical and Social Knowledge)

15. Sing number songs and recite number rhymes.

16. Look at a Richard Scarry book with children and have them search with you for all the numbers they can find in the pictures.

17. Play "Number—I Spy" in the classroom, requiring children to spy a number symbol somewhere in the learning environment.

18. Make a number tree and have children hang textured number symbols on the branches. Numbers can be cut out of sandpaper, felt, smooth paper, cardboard, various fabrics, and so on.

19. Set out measuring instruments such as a scale, tape measure, ruler, thermometer, measuring cups; a calculator and other numbered instruments; assorted clocks and an old radio on the theme table.

20. Set up puzzles with number symbols.

21. Set up a salt or sand tray with number symbols pasted at the top of the tray and let children practise making the number symbols in the salt or sand.

22. Set up a magnetic board and magnetic number symbols for children to play with.

Number Concept

23. Set up specific-purpose activities designed to promote one-to-one correspondence, such as sets of eggs and egg cups, dolls and hats, cups and saucers, cars and garages, stamps and envelopes, and encourage children to make two equal sets.

24. Use the Baratta-Lorton Workjobs to promote quantification skills such as the Apples and Trees kit, the number bracelets, the tongue depressors, and number cans.

25. Practise counting with small groups of children the two equal sets of objects that children have created using one-to-one correspondence.

26. Using the flannelboard and felt number symbols and felt objects, work with a small group of children at creating sets of objects representing the number symbol for each set.

27. Set up modular units such as buttons, bingo chips, pegs, and pegboards of different sizes and encourage children to count sets of different objects—some big, some little—in order that they can explore the constancy of number irrespective of the properties of the objects.

References

Charlesworth, R., and Radeloff, D. (1991). *Experiences in Math for Young Children*. 2d ed. Albany NY: Delmar.

Cruikshank, D.E., Fitzgerald, D.L., and Jensen, L.R. (1980). *Young Children Learning Mathematics*. Boston: Allyn & Bacon.

Donaldson, M. (1978). *Children's Minds*. London: Fontana.

Kamii, C. (1982). *Number in the Preschool*. Washington, D.C.: National Association for the Education of Young Children.

Kamii, C., and DeClark, G. (1985). *Young Children Reinvent Arithmetic: Implications of Piaget's Theory*. New York: Teachers College Press, Columbia University.

Laurendeau, M., and Pinard, A. (1968). *Les Premières Notions Spatiales de l'Enfant*. Montreal: Delachaux & Niestle.

Lovell, K. (1971). *The Growth of Basic Mathematical and Scientific Concepts in Children*. London: University of London Press.

Nash, C. (1989). *The Learning Environment: A Practical Approach to the Education of the Three-, Four- and Five-Year-Old*. Toronto: Collier-Macmillan.

Piaget, J. (1969). *The Psychology of the Child*. New York: Basic Books.

Sauvy, J., and Sauvy, S. (1974). *The Child's Discovery of Space: From Hopscotch to Mazes: An Introduction to Intuitive Topology*. London: Penguin.

Sime, M. (1973). *A Child's Eye View: Piaget for Parents and Teachers*. London: Thames & Hudson.

C H A P T E R 16

THE TECHNOLOGY CENTRE

The place of technology in the early learning environment is not new. Teachers have for many years relied on tape players, television, videocassette players, record players, typewriters, and film projectors to bring more of the outside world into the classroom. The microcomputer, however, has caused much heated debate among early childhood professionals.

Educators are increasingly seeing the classroom microcomputer as a useful tool to enhance skills and consolidate learning already achieved through the child's active exploration of the concrete environment. Technological devices should not be considered a substitute, however, for children's active experience with concrete, malleable, responsive, three-dimensional materials.

■ WHAT THE LITERATURE SAYS ABOUT COMPUTERS IN EARLY CHILDHOOD EDUCATION

Ever since Seymour Papert's *Mindstorms* in 1980, debate about the viability of computers in early childhood education has focused on whether computers serve children any better than can the experiences they gain in their interactions with the concrete world. Turkle (1984) claimed that computers open and extend children's thinking just as different kinds of play with concrete materials produce different modes of thinking. Other educators advised against jumping on the computer bandwagon, saying that doing so might be detrimental to children and recommending a critical examination of their potential and hazards before they were introduced into early childhood classrooms (Sullivan, 1985; Hunka, 1987; Ragsdale, 1987).

Computers as Educational Tools

Some educators fear that computers may have a limiting rather than a liberating influence on the development of children's thinking abilities. They believe that computers are biased against discovery learning and that they rush children much too soon into academic, repetitive, knowledge-based tasks that ultimately turn children off school and computers (Streibel, 1984, Elkind, 1987). Burg (1984:30) suggested that computers, like all educational tools, "are value-neutral ... they can be used to promote divergent thinking or conformity, freedom or restriction, self-confidence or fear." What remains critical is the knowledge, creativity, and thoughtfulness of the early childhood educator who has an obligation to learn how to use computers to benefit children.

Demands on children and adults to develop higher-level intellectual skills are increasing. There is evidence that computers enhance cognitive development. Computers address visual, auditory, and kinetic abilities; promote awareness of cause and effect; and encourage children to explore relationships and associations between objects and events (Shade, 1985). Beaty and Tucker (1987) argue that the computer also equalizes learning opportunities for all children by encouraging the shy child who does not respond well to group activities and by drawing out the quiet, passive child who may emerge as a leader in the Technology Centre.

One of the most convincing areas of investigation comes from cognitive psychologists who suggest that computers may be able to prolong the period of right-brain creativity through spatial imagery, visual media, and graphic representation. The left hemisphere is primarily dedicated to language and intuitive functioning; it translates images and concepts into language-defined categories. The right hemisphere is more important in the processing of visual and spatial cues.

One theory suggests that children's greater attention in middle childhood to producing realistic drawings that obey rules and conventions may be related to the increasing dominance of the left hemisphere of the brain during the school years (Gardner, 1982:283). This increasing left-brain dominance is attributed to the preoccupation during the early primary years with mastering the rules of language and reading.

In primary school, the increased emphasis on literacy skills and the extensive use of language for problem solving tends to dominate cognitive activity and undermines the child's natural tendency to communicate through visual images. It is possible that the use of computers, which promotes graphic activity as a means of communication, may extend the period of children's reliance on spatial and visual skills, that is, right-brain activities, as an important medium for communication.

The Relationship Between Computers and Child Development

Computers and developmentally appropriate software may enhance and extend children's learning with concrete materials and promote certain kinds of learning and development more efficiently than the two- and three-dimensional materials with which children typically play. Some studies show that the computer can provide children with developmentally appropriate experiences that stimulate divergent thinking and lead to creativity as well as improved language, problem solving, early mathematics, and reading skills (Burg, 1984). Educational software that requires perceptual skills such as visual discrimination; ocular-motor skills such as visual closure, tracking, pursuit, scanning and fixation; spatial concepts; part-whole and figure-ground relationships; auditory skills; memory and decision-making skills and logical thinking skills provides focused practice of these skills that are addressed in more indirect ways in free play situations (Anselmo & Zinck, 1987). Imagine the range of books, materials, games, and toys teachers would have to provide to cover this wide a range and diversity of perceptual skills that may be presented to children in one such software package.

Fine-motor skills are practised when children colour, draw, or play games using a joystick or a mouse. Many software packages also promote autonomy and decision-making skills by encouraging children to choose from a variety of alternatives and make clear choices of one path or one item on a menu. On-screen encouragement of their mastery of tasks that is part of the software motivates them to proceed to the next level. Children are encouraged to cooperate by sharing information and ideas, discussing alternative decisions, taking turns, and helping one another. The computer is most effective in facilitating development when teachers know the developmental needs and capabilities of their children and also possess the knowledge and experience needed to tailor computer activities and software challenges to individual needs (Burg, 1984).

Piel and Baller (1986) studied forty-four preschoolers, aged two to four, to determine whether computer-assisted learning could enhance performance on Piagetian classification and conservation tasks. They found that using a computer facilitated the transfer of concepts from the computer to the clinical testing situation, even for the two-year-olds. Several other studies have shown that computers can promote the acquisition of school readiness skills and improve cooperation and social interaction skills, reading and writing skills, and attending and task-orientation skills (McGarvey, 1986; Riel, 1985; Hungate, 1982; Piel & Baller, 1986).

Computers and Special Education

Teachers have observed high motivation in the exceptional child as well as improved integration of children with disabilities in regular programs that have computers (Malka & Schulman, 1986). Burg (1984) found that children with language delays, fine-motor skills immaturity, and social problems made significant gains because of their play at a computer. In some instances, computers and carefully selected software have reduced the effects of disabilities by accommodating the disability and permitting children to perform certain tasks and operations independently. Opportunities for language and communication are greatly enhanced by voice synthesizers and word processors. The child with physical disabilities may use a computer to turn on the television, answer the telephone, or perform other tasks that were previously impossible to do.

Computers are able to provide immediate feedback to children and are always patient. The responsiveness of the computer to children's actions on it gives them a sense of control and mastery as well as boosting their emotional security, which is necessary when facing the new learning tasks presented by the computer. Educators of exceptional children have observed first hand that the introduction of the computer into special education may be the most important improvement in special needs education since laws integrating exceptional children into community-based programs came into effect in many North American jurisdictions (Behrmann & Levy, 1986).

■ PRINCIPLES TO GUIDE TEACHER TRAINING

1. Effective use of computers with young children depends on the careful training of teachers to use computers in their classrooms in developmentally appropriate ways (Ragsdale, 1985; Coburn et al., 1985; Burg, 1984).

2. The use of computers as programmed learning instruments seems to lead to predefined structures of thought rather than problem-solving and logical thinking skills. Therefore, their use as teaching machines should be avoided (Elkind, 1987; Sullivan, 1985; Streibel, 1984).

3. Computers are useful instruments in classrooms for equalizing and democratizing learning opportunities for boys and girls, for children of all cultural groups, and for exceptional children. Teacher training should address the ways in which computers can be used to meet children's individual approaches to computers. (Beaty & Tucker, 1987; Turkle, 1984; Malka & Schulman, 1986; Behrmann & Levy, 1986; Lipinski et al., 1984; Siann & Macleod, 1986; Olson & Sullivan, 1987).

4. The selection of software is crucial to the effectiveness of computers in the development of cognitive styles and skills. Teachers should be trained both to

evaluate software and to select the software for children that is developmentally appropriate and growth enhancing (Turkle, 1984; Papert, 1980; Piel & Baller, 1986; McGarvey, 1986; Burg, 1984; Anselmo & Zinck, 1987; Shade, 1985; Riel, 1985; Hungate, 1982).

5. Children aged three or less do not show much interest in computers (Anselmo & Zinck, 1987; Klein, 1988). Four-year-olds demonstrate moderate interest, while five- and six-year-olds are enthusiastic about them. Teachers should be trained to use computers with children who are between the ages of four and six, and to integrate computer software with the regular curriculum in order to facilitate the transfer of learning from other media to the computer and vice versa (Johnson, 1985; Barnes & Hill, 1983; Klein, 1988.).

6. Computers promote learning in social contexts. Therefore, teachers should learn where to locate computers in classrooms in order to maximize both their use and the social learning and cooperation that may result (Brady & Hill, 1984; Dickson & Vereen, 1983; Slavin, 1980; Beaty & Tucker, 1987).

7. Computers have the potential to promote creativity. Teachers need training in using them creatively with children and in maximizing their usefulness as instruments for promoting divergent thinking skills, problem solving, spatial reasoning skills, and representational abilities (Tisone & Wismar, 1985; Steffin, 1986; Anselmo & Zinck, 1987; Burg, 1984; Alexander, 1983; Beaty & Tucker, 1987).

8. Children's interaction with computers meets most of the criteria that define the nature of play when computers are used developmentally. Teachers should be trained to promote their use with children in ways that are fun, social, and discovery-oriented (Kimmel, 1981).

■ CHOOSING A COMPUTER

The range of computer systems hardware on the market and the rapid development in technology make it difficult to recommend one brand over another, or even to suggest a standard in terms of hardware capacities and components. It is economical for early childhood programs to consider purchasing the less expensive, second-hand models that computer users sell as they upgrade to faster, more powerful models. A few important requirements, however, are dictated by recent developments in software technology.

Some of the developmentally appropriate software requires a minimum capacity of 640K and built-in (internal) graphics capacity, preferably with VGA graphics cards. Colour monitors are essential to software evaluation, as monochrome monitors provide limited opportunity to examine the aesthetic features of programs. Care should be taken to purchase colour monitors that have built-in protection to reduce the low-level of radiation that colour screens produce in greater intensity than do the monochrome monitors.

Including a printer is advantageous because it will encourage creative production at the computer that involves using graphics features of word processors, as well as drawing or painting software programs. Younger children usually work more easily at the computer if it has special keyboards with electronic keypads, and larger letter and number symbols. Drawing pads are an interesting peripheral device to complement drawing on the screen. A mouse or a joystick promotes eye-hand coordination, manipulative abilities, and fine-motor skills. A mouse is a hand-held control device that simulates a drawing tool and can be used to produce graphics on the monitor screen. It usually sits on a "mouse pad," which is designed to protect the mouse.

■ INTEGRATING THE COMPUTER INTO THE PROGRAM

The integration of the computer into the classroom is preferable to the provision of a separate computer lab for children (Davidson, 1989). The computer should be available for children's spontaneous play and exploration, and as an alternative medium to help them transfer the learning gained through concrete materials. If children are removed from the classroom to the computer lab two or three times a week or even daily, computer learning often tends to become isolated from other play and learning. The likelihood of computers being used inappropriately, that is, as teaching machines, is greater in laboratories than in the regular learning environment.

■ CHOOSING DEVELOPMENTALLY APPROPRIATE SOFTWARE

Teachers have to see computers as versatile tools for enhancing development rather than for structuring learning (Neilsen, 1986). The key to the use of computers in developmentally appropriate ways lies in the teacher's ability to choose software that will promote the transfer of learning to and from other learning centres. Good software allows children to manage their own learning and to reflect on the results of their actions; it also permits them to revise their plans and actions (Kuschner, 1986). Some software does not allow children to execute their own conceptual plan and, therefore, creates conflict and disappointment, which detract from successful and positive experiences at the computer (Burns, Goin, & Donlon, 1990). Teachers have to understand the principles of learning and decide which developmental objectives they are trying to achieve with their children before selecting software.

COMPUTERS AND DEVELOPMENTALLY APPROPRIATE
SOFTWARE MAY ENHANCE CHILDREN'S LEARNING

The most effective software to promote cognitive development does not use voice synthesizers (Grover, 1986). Software design is also an important determinant of success with children; the graphics displays, cueing, feedback, and reinforcers provided should all be designed according to cognitive developmental principles (Hofmann, 1986). The software should assume the role of the teacher and therefore be flexible enough to accommodate incorrect responses. Feedback should vary according to children's responses and include encouragements to children to revise or correct their responses. Software content should be sequenced from simple to more complex concepts and build on previous learning. Software programs should permit choice, active problem solving by children, and discovery of concepts through manipulation of pictures on the screen. It should allow the child to change the configuration of screen images in order to explore relationships. Above all, software should be easy to use, "bug-free," colourful, and clear and should promote positive values (Lewin, 1981).

The same selection criteria should be applied to software as is used for television programs for children: namely, violent and mindless content should be avoided. Aesthetic quality also greatly affects the overall appeal of software for children and should be an important criterion in its selection just as it is for children's books.

Several guides to the selection of developmentally appropriate software are available to help teachers make wise decisions (Shade & Haugland, 1990; Buckleitner, 1987; EPIE Institute, 1986–87).

■ ORGANIZATION AND DESIGN OF THE TECHNOLOGY CENTRE

The Technology Centre usually contains a computer area with one or two micro-computers and two chairs at each computer, a listening centre, a viewing area, and an office/desk area (see Figure 16.1).

RATINGS OF THE CHARACTERISTICS OF PLAY

The Technology Centre

noisy	quiet
teacher-centred	child-centred
structured	open
concrete	abstract
clean	messy
specific-purpose materials	open-ended materials
group	individual

(Adapted with permission of the Board of Education, City of Hamilton. *Getting It All Together* (1981).)

Equipment, Materials, and Supplies

Equipment—computer table, desk, chairs and table, listening centre table, VCR/television trolley or shelf, storage shelves.

Materials—microcomputer, printer, mouse, other peripherals, developmental software, typewriter, office supplies, audiocassette player, headphones, record player, slide projector, slides in slide holders, Viewmaster, movie projector, filmstrip projector, telephone.

Supplies—computer paper, stationery/envelopes, pencils, paper clips, stapler, scissors, tape, diskettes, erasers, gluestick, handi-note pads.

■ LOCATING THE TECHNOLOGY CENTRE

The Technology Centre is usually located near a quiet area, well away from messy play, and with sufficient space for children to work individually or in small groups. It is best located adjacently to the Quiet Thinking Centre, well out of the way of the

Figure 16.1   THE TECHNOLOGY CENTRE

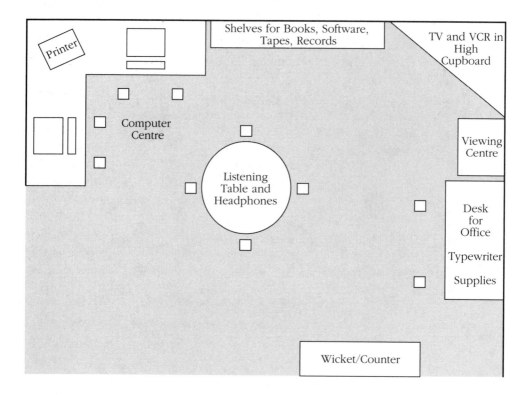

Social contexts of play emphasized in the Technology Centre

solitary
parallel
cooperative
associative

Categories of play emphasized in the Technology Centre

functional: practice play
             constructive play
             productive play
symbolic: dramatic
             sociodramatic
             games-with-rules play

main traffic areas. The computer and peripherals such as a special keyboard for children, a printer, mouse, and drawing pad should be placed on a computer table for easy access from the two chairs placed in front of the computer monitor and keyboard. The microcomputer should be placed on an interior wall, close to an outlet, and on a table with chairs for two children. As computers are sensitive to heat and dust they should not be placed near heat sources, chalkboards, or dusty carpets. Dust covers should be used to cover the components when the computer area is not in use.

Placing the Technology Centre close to the Quiet Thinking Centre means that the computer and other devices complement the perceptual and conceptual learning that is occurring as children play nearby with specific-purpose and modular materials. Here, the Technology Centre provides opportunities for children to move from play with modular and specific-purpose kits to the computer monitor where they can try out the same strategies using the computer as they explore the three-dimensional materials. Many computer software programs replicate similar images on the screen in a two-dimensional context that children have experienced in the three-dimensional context. Some software programs, for example, make use of movable building blocks on the screen; others make extensive use of shape configurations in puzzles or let children manipulate shapes and symbols.

The Technology Centre also provides opportunities for children to transfer drawing, painting, and design problems they have solved using graphic materials in the Creative Arts Centre to software drawing and painting programs on the computer. Developmentally appropriate software promotes specific developmental objectives and enhances the complementarity of the Technology Centre with the developmental objectives, and play and learning potential of the Quiet Thinking, Science Discovery, and Creative Arts Centres in particular.

■ PLAY STATIONS IN THE TECHNOLOGY CENTRE

Computer Area

Beaty and Tucker (1987) recommend that the computer be placed in a sectioned-off area where distractions can be minimized, against a wall and away from direct sunlight to prevent glare. An electrical outlet and preferably a power surge suppressor bar should be close by to handle the computer, printer, and auxiliary lighting, which may be necessary. Computer monitors with built-in ultraviolet protection and glare reduction should be used—not television screens, which cause eyestrain.

Children should be permitted to operate and control both the hardware and software, but a few rules for their use must be clarified and consistently reinforced.

Three rules are essential in the Technology Centre: no liquids or food in the computer area; use fingers only; and come to the computer with clean hands.

The computer table holding a computer, monitor, keyboard, peripherals such as a child's keyboard, drawing pad, mouse, and printer dominates the Technology Centre. Two chairs should be placed in front of the computer. Software packages, manuals, and booklets of printed activities that support the software should be stored on shelves close to the computer table. When the Technology Centre is large enough to house two computers, they should be placed at right angles to each other in one of the corners of the Centre in order to encourage cooperative play and peer helping as well as discussion about the software among the four children playing in the area. Placing two computers and four chairs together gives children the message that computer play is a social experience as well as a learning time (Davidson, 1989).

Several studies have shown that encouraging two children to play together at a computer promotes problem solving, cooperation, language, and turn taking (Dickson & Vereen, 1983; Davidson, 1989). When pairs of children work at a computer, turn taking and games for two players become the normal practice. With three or more children, turn taking is less successful, but some accommodations can be made to optimize the learning for small groups of children. Certain software encourages children in groups to cooperate in solving puzzles and to reach a consensus, perhaps by voting, before the next key is pressed. Another strategy for groups of three is to have one child assume responsibility for operating the keyboard or joystick while the remaining pair cooperate in solving the puzzle or playing the game (Dickson & Vereen, 1983).

In multicultural classrooms, there are many advantages to having pairs and triads composed of both minority-group and non-minority-group children and to assigning cross-sex pairs to work together to foster cooperation and understanding. Slavin (1980) reported that children frequently identified friends of other races when they were involved in cooperative learning activities.

The computer area should provide shelves for computer books, computer magazines, and some general reference items for children and adults. Installing a bulletin board on the wall of the Technology Centre near the computer allows teachers to display instructions for the use of the computer as well as graphics productions made by children using the computer. A cupboard is essential for storing used and unused diskettes, dust-free cloths for dusting furniture and equipment surfaces, extra printer ribbons, paper, and diskette-filing accessories such as stickers, file cases, and diskette envelopes (Houle, 1987).

The Listening Table

A listening table in the Technology Centre adds to children's understanding of the various uses we make of technological instruments to facilitate and enhance communications, convey information, practise specific skills, and add to our enjoyment of life. The listening table should be located in a quiet section of the learning environment where children can avoid distracting influences.

The number of chairs for children to sit down on at the table should correspond to the number of headsets available for the tape recorder or record player. As the rate at which children retreat to the listening table to escape from the sounds and activity of the rest of the learning environment is not great, two or three headsets at the table at a time are usually sufficient. Storage for records, tapes, and combination story and record or tape books should be located beside the listening table for easy access by children.

The listening table promotes auditory discrimination abilities, auditory integration skills, receptive and expressive language, and enjoyment of taped and recorded music. It also provides respite from the auditory stimuli in the learning environment as the headsets separate the child from the playroom temporarily. At the listening table, children learn how to operate electronic equipment such as radios, record players, audiocassette recorders and players, and head sets. The ability to use technological devices enhances children's feelings of mastery and control over their environment.

Some teachers prefer to locate the listening table close to the musical instruments, since both are closely associated with music and listening. A listening table in the Technology Centre emphasizes the development of perceptual, manipulative, and cognitive abilities. When it is placed with musical instruments, there is bound to be some conflict between children who are there to listen and those who are there to move to the sounds of the music.

Recorded stories on tapes with verbal instructions to children about when to turn the page, when to sing along, and what to say in response to recorded questions are a central feature of the listening table. It is also stocked with records and tapes that are as much dedicated to stories, rhymes, and promotion of language skills as to the development of music appreciation and listening abilities. It is better to locate musical instruments in an area with space for children to move to the music and the listening table in an area which is primarily dedicated to individual or small group activity that is less active, quieter, and more task-oriented. There is also nothing to prevent a teacher from moving the record player or tape player from the Technology Centre to the Active Role Play Centre when recorded music is needed for movement activities.

Selection of records and tapes for the listening table should be based on developmental principles in the same way that software selection adheres to a developmental rationale. Many records and tapes for children are clearly designed to promote specific auditory discrimination abilities, as does the old favourite "Peter and the Wolf," which teaches children about the sounds of instruments in the orchestra, and as do animal stories that have recorded animal and nature sounds.

The Viewing Area

Children who live most of their childhood years without access to television programs that are positive and enriching may be considered culturally deprived (Nash, 1975). The problem with television, in child care programs in particular, is that some children spend far too many hours watching mindless television programs without adult supervision. If television is to be permitted in the play and learning environment, discretion must be exercised by teachers in determining the amount and type of television or videotape watching children will do within the context of the early childhood education program. Arguments may be made for permitting children to watch educational programs of high quality at times of the day when their energies and interest in active play have waned. Sometimes a well-selected videotape or television program can be relaxing and enjoyable, quite apart from whatever educational value it may have, as children are waiting for a parent to come and take them home. Late afternoons, after a day of active play indoors and outdoors and many social demands, are times when a more passive activity may be helpful and positive.

A viewing area may be arranged around a raised cupboard with doors holding a television and videocassette player combination which, when opened, is visible to a group of children seated on the floor below. Children should not control the television, and keeping it out of reach solves a multitude of problems.

A table or wide shelf may be placed under the TV/VCR cupboard for handheld viewing materials such as a Viewmaster and a transparency viewer. With so many sophisticated technological devices on the market, we sometimes forget the simple pleasures children derive from a Viewmaster, which can transport them to faraway places. Although the simple Viewmaster hardly qualifies as technology, it is a useful addition to the viewing area, in part because it offers a contrast to the more complex electronic toys such as Nintendo systems, which some children have at home. A filmstrip projector and small screen serve a similar purpose and can be easily operated by children after giving them some instruction and demonstration. When children have access to a range of mechanical, electrical, and technological devices that they can be taught to operate, they feel an enhanced sense of control over their environment.

The viewing area may also include a range of kaleidoscopes and drawing devices like Etch-a-Sketch. All of these materials complement the three-dimensional materials in other learning centres.

The Office Area

The Technology Centre may also contain a desk with a typewriter and office supplies that are developmentally appropriate. Children have fun with office supplies such as paper clips, used envelopes and notepads, stamps, stamp pads, and other gadgets for desks.

OFFICE AREA

A desk with a typewriter and age-appropriate office supplies in the Technology Centre provides an environment for sociodramatic play and an opportunity for children to develop a range of manipulative, fine-motor, perceptual, expressive language, and coordination skills. The office area also promotes dramatic and sociodramatic play that addresses literacy skills, particularly the use of letter symbols, the "writing" of messages and memos, and the production of letters and stories.

Space is needed in the Technology Centre for a chair and table large enough to accommodate a manual typewriter, typewriter paper, notepads, message pads, envelopes, large and small paper clips, brads, folders, pencils, elastic bands, and other small gadgets that may provide hours of enjoyment for children. A bulletin board for children to tack messages, mount posters, and display children's productions on the typewriter and word processor adds to the literacy emphasis of the office area.

Keyboard skills may be transferred from the computer keyboard to the typewriter and vice versa. When children use word processors and typewriters, they necessarily learn letter and number symbols while producing letters, memoranda, notes, and stories in their dramatic and sociodramatic play. The introduction of an office area into the Technology Centre contributes to the "production" orientation of this part of the learning environment. In our society, which emphasizes literacy and verbal and written communication using a variety of production instruments, children readily identify with the learning opportunities in the office area.

Activities for the Office Area

(for older children, ages four to six)

1. Set up an office in the Technology Centre with a telephone, typewriter, office supplies, computer and word processing software, a counter, note and memo pads, and a "reception" desk.

2. Set up a "publishing" company using a desk with paper, binders, brads, crayons and pencils, and encourage children to make books out of their productions at the computer and typewriter. Art productions from the Creative Arts Centre may be added to their books.

3. Encourage children to produce their own messages by imitating a poster hung on the wall or by replicating a set of symbols on the computer screen using a graphics program. Help them print out their own productions.

4. Set up a post office with stamps, envelopes, mail slots, a postal worker's uniform, mailbags, and address, postal code, and telephone directories. Create a counter in the post office for selling stamps and sorting and dispatching letters and parcels. At a small table provide sheets of brown paper wrapping, small boxes, and masking tape to encourage children to wrap and address parcels for mailing. This makes an interesting activity for the day or two leading up to St. Valentine's Day. Children may be asked to draw their own stamps in the Creative Arts Centre and to use a glue stick in the post office to stick their stamps to envelopes.

5. Using a child's desktop publishing software package, a graphics program, and a simple word processor, encourage children to create a page or two for a newsletter for parents.

6. Younger children will enjoy play with large plastic paper clips, hole punchers, brads, and binders, which provide opportunities to practise eye-hand coordination, manipulative and fine-motor skills, hand control, pincer grasp, and other skills. Provide plenty of scrap paper, used envelopes, glue sticks, used stamps, and file holders.

7. Set up a picture framing workshop for children to frame the drawings and paintings created in the Creative Arts Centre. Using pieces of construction paper and cardboard pieces, glue sticks, paste, scissors, and masking tape, encourage children to choose the appropriate colour, paper, and other materials to frame their own productions.

References

Alexander, D. (1983). Children's Computer Drawings. ERIC Document, ED238562.

Anselmo, S., and Zinck, R.A. (1987). Computers for Young Children? Perhaps. *Young Children*. March, 1987: 22–27.

Barnes, B.J., and Hill, S. (1983). Should Young Children Use Microcomputers: LOGO before LEGO? *The Computing Teacher* 10 (9):11–14.

Beaty, J.J., and Tucker, W.H. (1987). *The Computer as a Paintbrush: Creative Uses for the Personal Computer in the Preschool Classroom*. Columbus OH: Merrill.

Behrmann, M.M., and Levy, S.A. (1986). Computers and Special Education. In *Computers in Early Childhood Education*, ed. J. Hoot, pp. 104–27. Englewood Cliffs, NJ: Prentice-Hall.

Brady, E.H., and Hill, S. (1984). Young children and microcomputers: research issues and directions. *Young Children* 39 (3):49–59.

Buckleitner, W. (1987). *Survey of Early Educational Software*. Ypsilanti, MI: High/Scope.

Burg, K. (1984). The microcomputer in the kindergarten: a magical, useful, expensive toy. *Young Children* 39 (3):28–33.

Burns, M.S., Goin, L., and Donlon, J.T. (1990). A computer in my room. *Young Children* 45 (1):62–67.

Clements, D.H. (1986). Logo programming in the early grades: research and implications. In *Computers in Early Childhood Education: Issues and Practices,* ed. J. Hoot, pp. 174–97. Englewood Cliffs: Prentice-Hall.

Coburn, P., Kilman, P., Roberts, N., Snyder, F.F., Watt, D., and Weiner, C. (1985). *Practical Guide to Computers in Education*. 2d ed. Reading: Addison-Wesley.

Davidson, J.I. (1989). *Children and Computers: Together in the Early Childhood Classroom*. Albany, NY: Delmar.

Dickson, W.P., and Vereen, M. (1983). Two students at one microcomputer. *Theory into Practice* 22 (4):296–300.

Educational Products Information Exchange Institute (EPIE) (1986–87). *T.E.S.S. Educational Software Selector*. New York: New York College Press.

Elkind, D. (1987). The child yesterday, today and tomorrow. *Young Children* 42 (3):5–11.

Gardner, H. (1980). *Artful Scribbles: The Significance of Children's Drawings*. New York: Basic Books.

Gardner, H. (1982). *Art, Mind and Brain*. New York: Basic Books.

Grover, S. (1986). A field study of the use of cognitive-developmental principles in microcomputer design for young children. *Journal of Educational Research* 79 (4): 325–32.

Hofmann, R. (1986). Piaget and microcomputer learning environments. *Journal of Learning Disabilities* 19 (3):181–84.

Houle, G. (1987). *Learning Centres for Young Children*. 3d ed. West Greenwich, RI: Tot-lot Child Care Products.

Howell, R.D., Scott, P.B., and Diamond, J. (1987). The effects of "instant" LOGO computing language on the cognitive development of very young children. *Journal of Educational Computing Research* 3 (2):449–60.

Hungate, H. (1982). Computers in the kindergarten. *The Computing Teacher* 9 (5):15–18.

Hunka, S. (1987). The role of computers in Canadian education. In *Contemporary Educational Issues: The Canadian Mosaic*, ed. L.L. Stewin and S.J.H. McCann, pp. 69–81. Toronto: Copp Clark Pitman.

Johnson, J.E. (1985). Characteristics of preschoolers interested in microcomputers. *Journal of Educational Research* 78 (5):299–305.

Kimmel, S. (1981). Programs for preschoolers: starting out young. *Creative Computing* 7 (10):50–53.

Klein, P.S. (1988). Children's feelings toward

computers: a phenomenological view of some developmental aspects. *International Journal of Early Childhood* (OMEP) 20 (1):52–60.

Kuschner, D. (1986). This computer gives you a hard bargain. Is it conflict or frustration when software won't let you change your mind? ERIC document ED 279311.

Lewin, A.W. (1981). Down with green lambs: creating quality software for children. *Theory into Practice* 24 (4):277–80.

Lipinski, J.M., Nida, R.E, Shade, D.D., and Watson, J.A. (1984). Competence, gender and preschoolers' freeplay choices when a microcomputer is present in the classroom. ERIC Document, ED243609.

Malka, M., and Schulman, S. (1986). Microcomputers in special education: renewed expectations for solutions to chronic difficulties. *The Exceptional Child* 33 (3):199–205.

McGarvey, L. (1986). Microcomputer use in kindergarten and at home: design of the study and effects of computer use on school readiness. ERIC Document, ED272275.

Nash, C. (1975). *The Learning Environment: A Practical Approach to the Education of the Three-, Four- and Five*-Year-Old. Toronto: Collier-Macmillan.

Neilsen, J. (1986). Not the computer but human interaction is the basis for cognitive development and education. *Education and Computing* 2 (1–2):53–61.

Olson, C.P., and Sullivan, E.V. (1987). Beyond the mania: critical approaches to computers in education. In *Contemporary Educational Issues: The Canadian Mosaic*, ed. L.L. Stewin and S.J.H. McCann, pp. 95–106. Toronto: Copp Clark Pitman.

Papert, S. (1980). *Mindstorms: Children, Computers and Powerful Ideas*. New York: Basic Books.

Piel, J.A., and Baller, W.A. (1986). Effects of computer assistance on acquisition of Piagetian conceptualization among children of ages two to four. *AEDS Journal* 19 (2-3):210–15.

Ragsdale, R.G. (1985). Response to Sullivan on Papert's "Mindstorms." *Interchange* 16 (3):19–36.

Ragsdale, R.G. (1987). Computers in Canada: communications and curriculum. In *Contemporary Educational Issues: The Canadian Mosaic,* ed. L.L. Stewin and S.J.H. McCann, pp. 82–94. Toronto: Copp Clark Pitman.

Riel, M. (1985). The computer chronicles newswire: a functional learning environment for acquiring literary skills. *Educational Computing Research* 1(3):317–37.

Shade, D.D. (1985). Will a microcomputer really benefit preschool children? A theoretical examination of computer applications in ECE. ERIC Document, ED264951.

Shade, D.D., and Haugland, S.W. (1990). *Developmental Evaluations of Software for Young Children.* Albany, NY: Delmar.

Siann, G., and Macleod, H. (1986). Computers and children of primary school age: issues and questions. *British Journal of Educational Technology* 17 (2):133–44.

Simon, T. (1985). Play and learning with computers. *Early Childhood Development and Care* 19 (1–2):69–78.

Slavin, R. (1980). Cooperative learning. *Review of Educational Research* 50:315–42.

Steffin, S.A. (1986). Using the micro as a weapon: fighting against convergent thinking. *Childhood Education* 59 (2):251–58.

Streibel, M.J. (1984). An analysis of the theoretical foundations for the use of microcomputers in ECE. ERIC Document, ED248971.

Sullivan, E.V. (1985). Computers, culture and educational futures—a meditation on "Mindstorms." *Interchange* 16 (3):1–18.

Tisone, M., and Wismar, B.L. (1985). Microcomputers: how can they be used to enhance creative development? *Journal of Creative Behavior* 19 (2):97–103.

Turkle, S. (1984). The intimate machine: eavesdropping on the secret lives of computers and kids. *Science* (April):41–46.

DISCOVERY AND CREATIVE PLAY

One of the joys of being a child is that there are so many new things in the world to explore, discover, create, and figure out. Children are naturally curious and need time and support for their explorations with a wide variety of objects and phenomena. Early childhood education should expose children to a rich and diverse range of materials and media, let children explore in their own ways, and support the development of a "creative orientation" (Gardner, 1989:298). Section 6 highlights the importance of exploration, discovery, creativity, and problem solving in early childhood education. The three learning centres dedicated to these pursuits are the Science Discovery Centre, the Creative Arts Centre, and the Unit Blocks Centre.

Section 6 addresses the following topics:

- "sciencing" with young children
- developing dispositions to explore, discover, create, and solve problems
- Science Discovery Centre
- development of a "creative orientation"
- developmental stages in children's art and block play
- Creative Arts Centre
- Unit Blocks Centre
- facilitating creative-constructive play with graphic materials, textiles, wood, cardboard, and blocks

C H A P T E R   17

THE SCIENCE DISCOVERY CENTRE—EXPLORING AND PROBLEM SOLVING

"Young children are scientists more than they are anything else." This quotation from Zimiles highlights the wonderful curiosity and eagerness to explore that characterizes the behaviour of young children as soon as they can crawl.

Exploring

Exploring is largely an open-ended, sensory activity in which any outcome, if there is one, is unpredictable. It usually implies physical action of some kind, freedom to move wherever and however one wants (within safe limits), and an absence of specific objectives or tasks. Children need plenty of time and opportunity to explore.

Discovery

Sometimes when children explore, a realization of something new emerges, which may be concrete, like a fact, or intangible, like a sensation or an idea. It is through discovery that children usually acquire physical knowledge and logical understanding (Bruner, 1960; DeVries & Kohlberg, 1987). Exploring does not always lead to discovery but when it does the child is all the more motivated to keep exploring. Some learning centres should be set up so that the likelihood that exploring will lead to meaningful discovery is increased by that setup.

Creative Play

Creative play often happens when children feel psychologically safe, free to experiment, and permitted to express themselves. In a supportive, affective environment children will explore and make discoveries that permit them to see everyday phenomena and events in new contexts and from unique perspectives. Using their explorations and discoveries as a starting point, they may pursue their own plans or goals. Creative play usually involves the ability to plan and think creatively. Thinking creatively is a state of mind or an approach that characterizes persons who pursue creative goals.

Torrance (1966:6) defines creative thinking as "the process of becoming sensitive to problems, deficiencies, gaps in knowledge, missing elements, disharmonies and so on; identifying the difficulty, searching for solutions, making guesses, or formulating hypotheses about the deficiencies; testing and retesting these hypotheses, and possibly modifying and retesting them; and finally, communicating the results." The Torrance definition of creative thinking bears some resemblance to the scientific method, which provides a disciplined approach to defining and solving novel problems that results in new insights and knowledge.

Problem Solving

Newell, Shaw, and Simon (1962:65–66) suggest that problem solving may be called creative when one or more of the following conditions are satisfied: the outcome of the thinking has novelty and value for the creator or her culture; the thinking is unconventional and departs from traditional beliefs or paradigms; the creative product or representation requires time, motivation, and persistence; and the process of posing and defining the question or problem is an important component of the creative endeavour. Creativity and problem-solving abilities have much in common.

Problem solving uses critical thinking skills, which leads to further questioning and hypothesis setting rather than representation of an original idea or insight. More cognitive in nature than creativity, problem solving often involves all three developmental domains acting together (Gardner, 1982).

Creative thinking, inquiry, and problem solving can be fostered in all learning centres. Creativity is not confined to the art area or to the unit blocks. Original thinking, self-expression, flexibility, the ability to ask interesting questions, and the resourcefulness to answer them are important developmental abilities that are beginning to develop during the early years in a wide range of contexts.

Exploring and creative play are encouraged in all learning centres but they are particularly fostered and supported in the Science Discovery Centre, the Creative Arts Centre, and the Unit Blocks Centre. In these three learning centres, the process of learning is emphasized over the product or outcome.

■ SCIENCING WITH YOUNG CHILDREN

The word science comes from the Latin "scire," which means "to know," and "scientia," which means a state of knowing usually acquired from systematic observation, study, and experimentation. Although the word "science" is a noun, not an action word or verb, the verbal noun "sciencing" captures the idea that in science education the child is in active pursuit of coming to know through hands-on exploration of objects and phenomena in the environment. Science in early childhood education helps children "know" through their physical and sensory interaction with concrete objects.

A process approach to learning connects the processes of scientific investigation (sciencing) to creative endeavour. That is, children explore, formulate plans, ask questions, consider possibilities, evolve and follow strategies, and communicate results. Children engage in endeavours with similar steps in the Science Discovery Centre, the Creative Arts Centre, and the Unit Blocks Centre. In science, art, and block-building activities, children are exploring materials, making discoveries, and planning ways of using or trying out their new discoveries.

Science for young children fosters the learning of science in a context that fits with children's cognitive development (Althouse, 1988). With young children, science is not so much a matter of teaching children what happens, when it happens, and why it happens with respect to specific phenomena as it is a matter of encouraging them to ask questions and solve problems. It is through their play with substances, objects, and elements that respond to their actions on them that children discover and experience the relationships that exist in the natural and physical world, such as categories of animals and plants, understanding of part-whole, cause and effect, and action and reaction phenomena.

In this sense, science education is constructivist education. Children develop their abilities to take perspectives, consider variables, organize their actions, and observe results that contribute to their cognitive development. The idea is for children to explore objects in an atmosphere of experimentation and to define problems, ask questions, and pursue answers as they encounter them in their play (DeVries and Kohlberg, 1987).

There are so many aspects of the physical and natural world to be explored with young children. Science education that is knowledge-oriented is more meaningful for older children who are capable of concrete operational thought. Spending precious time performing experiments that produce mysterious chemical reactions, or trying to convey the principles of electricity to young children, for example, do not lead to meaningful learning in children who are in the preoperational period. Teachers waste their energies when they try to impose knowledge and concepts on children who have not yet acquired the physical and conceptual frameworks they need in order to understand scientific concepts. For this reason, subjects that address abstract concepts, such as magnetism, matter and energy, planets, weather cycles, day and night, and electricity, are inappropriate topics for early childhood science education (Kamii & DeVries, 1978; Smith, 1987).

Sciencing with young children should involve exploring, discovering, problem solving, creating, and communicating. The best science activities are those that appeal directly to and involve the senses. Children need to be active participants in sciencing as a process of discovery. DeVries and Kohlberg (1987) suggest two criteria for good physical knowledge activities: the activity should allow children to: (1) act on objects and observe their reactions and, (2) act on objects to produce a desired result. The best activities are those in which the physical transformations that occur in nature are observable to the child. There are so many learning opportunities that meet these criteria that young children could spend all their time on sciencing activities alone. "Science is observing, questioning, wondering, testing, guesses, recording findings—it is *not* being told facts about science-related subjects" (Perry and Rivkin, 1992:11).

■ SPIRITUAL DEVELOPMENT IN THE SCIENCE DISCOVERY CENTRE

An important educational goal of early childhood science education is to help children "begin to understand life, growth, death and generation" (Furman, 1990). This textbook has already claimed that one of the most important tasks of early childhood is the building of a "rich inner life," which is acquired for the most part through spontaneous experiences with nature and with naturally occurring objects in the environment (Bettelheim, 1987). The development of a sense of the interconnectedness and mutual interdependence of all living things is a noble goal of science programming for young children. It is also one that provides guidance for teachers in choosing topics and activities.

Much of Piaget's work describes the inherent limitations of children's abstract thinking ability. These descriptions support our knowledge that children learn best in the presence of immediate, concrete, observable experiences. We also know, however, that children have the capacity to wonder, feel a sense of awe, and be moved by mysterious and spiritual events. New evidence demonstrates that children think about abstract questions of a spiritual nature (Coles, 1990). Not only do they ponder questions of life and death, but children also appear to possess astounding insight about natural phenomena. The child whose pet has just died and who can say, "He was a happy dog when he lived with us and I'll always remember him," demonstrates some understanding of the mortality of all living things as well as a sense of what matters in life.

Science curriculum that focuses on the whole life cycle and its generational sequence helps children begin to understand life, death, and the connection between them. "[C]oping with death depends on first knowing what dead means. A basic concept of death is best grasped, not when a loved one dies, but in situations of minimal emotional significance, such as with dead insects or worms ... Plants provide the most prevalent, accessible, and emotionally neutral opportunities to learn about life and death" (Furman, 1990:16–17).

Children need opportunities to explore natural phenomena in order to further their curiosity; whet their appetites for problem solving; kindle a sense of awe and wonder at the mysteries, beauty, and surprises of nature; and fuel their confidence and self-worth. These capacities and feelings arise from a sense of connectedness with nature. A deep-seated sense that "the world is a wonderful place" is surely one of the most abiding gifts that a well-conceived science program can offer to young children.

Science in this sense has very little to do with the complex, abstract mathematical formulas and problems many of us associate with science, but everything to do with fostering a sense of self-worth, respect for life, and love of nature. It is in this kind of psychological environment that a fundamental concern for the health of the environment and the protection and replenishment of natural resources can be instilled into the present generation of children. A science centre that is designed to promote children's spiritual connectedness with the world of nature and all living things will help them acquire feelings of mastery and self-worth through reduced fear of the unknown and a sense of the basic harmony that exists in the physical and natural world (Holt, 1989).

■ CHOOSING TOPICS FOR SCIENCING WITH YOUNG CHILDREN

Natural science (earth and plant science), ecology and the study of the ecosystems that support life, environmental science, physical science, and life science all contain topics that make interesting and appropriate sciencing in early childhood education. The Science Discovery Centre should encourage investigation of the environment from the child's unique vantage point, and explore subjects that are close to the child. Science exploration begins with the child's own body, family, home, neighbourhood, and community, and gradually extends to the outer reaches of his daily life experience. Holt (1989:118) uses the term "personal ecology" to describe this approach to science with young children. Her "distance-from-self criterion" implies that the science experiences should begin close to children's daily reality and should move farther from the child as development proceeds. Developmentally appropriate science for young children places the child at the heart of any topic under investigation. This means that children will learn about themselves, their pets, domestic animals and plants, and naturally occurring elements in their own environments before they learn about camels, deserts, elephants or jungles. An argument can therefore be made for omitting dinosaur activities in the context of science curriculum since they are far too remote for the child to understand their scientific relevance. Dinosaur activities are best reserved for other learning centres and should not be used in the Science Discovery Centre.

Our knowledge of how children think and view reality is the framework from which a science curriculum for young children should emerge (Smith, 1989). Planning appropriate science experiences for young children requires knowledge of children's cognitive thinking styles. Young children find it difficult to take a perspective other than their own, learn best through the senses and in active, hands-on learning situations, and are unable to focus on more than one attribute of an object or transformation simultaneously. They depend on "seeing is believing" and are unable to think abstractly. Their qualitatively different thinking styles have to be accounted for in sciencing activities. They need hands-on, experiential, sensory-based learning opportunities in which all transformations that occur are visible to the child. For this reason, natural science explorations are the best activities because children can touch, see, hear, feel, taste, and smell the conditions, states, transformations, and outcomes they are investigating. Children also tend to believe that phenomena they cannot observe directly must be magic. It is not the purpose of early science experiences to contribute to magical thinking in young children.

A science program for young children that focuses on natural science activities alone will still be rich, stimulating, and full of new learning. The greatest obstacle to effective sciencing with young children is often the teacher's own childhood learning experience with science. In most cases, it was presented as remote and mysterious. As teachers learn to tackle science from a child's perspective, a rich new world of challenge and discovery opens up for them and the children.

A few simple guidelines may help. Science is not a subject to be explored piecemeal, with a volcano experiment here, a seed planting activity there, a shell sorting activity somewhere else, and a water pressure experiment at another time and place. To have meaning for children, sciencing activities should be planned, coherent, and integrated. The program should be satisfying for teachers, who can see their own and the children's progress, and it should promote curiosity, inquiry, exploration, discovery, and positive attitudes. Teachers may choose an area to investigate over a period of time and develop that topic with several exploratory activities sequenced from the simple to the complex. Even if only two or three topics are addressed in a school year, children will gain more meaningful learning from integrated, longer-term investigations.

A series of activities that focuses on physical learning about a particular element like water, the gathering of knowledge about animal classes, or learning about the human body through body awareness activities is richer for children than activities that address a long list of unrelated topics. Children need time to acquire physical knowledge, link causes and effects through hands-on experience, chart progress and change, observe transformations and outcomes, and report on what they have observed.

■ LOCATING THE SCIENCE DISCOVERY CENTRE

The Science Discovery Centre is generally located in an area of the classroom near natural light, close to a water source, and on tiled floors, which, when spills occur, can easily be mopped up. It should be close to the Creative Arts Centre and the Unit Blocks Centre to complement the exploration, discovery, problem solving, and creative play that occur in all three centres.

Practical considerations provide many reasons for juxtaposing these centres. The Creative Arts Centre encourages exploration of a wide variety of artistic media and materials. The Science Discovery Centre provides water, sand, and other naturally occurring substances at the science tables, as well as tools for measuring, sifting, pouring, observing, investigating, and inventing.

Children often like to borrow naturally occurring substances and items in science collections for their collages or posters. Experimentation with clay in the Creative Arts Centre and wet sand in the Science Discovery Centre addresses similar understandings about texture, the effects of adding water to a substance, compacting, moulding, and drying. Children explore concepts of size, shape, texture, consistency, mass, and space in the context of their drawings, paintings, carvings, box construction, and sewing, just as they do with water, sand, leaves, bark, shells, nuts, and soils at the science tables. Both areas promote the development of sensorimotor, fine-motor, and perceptual motor abilities. Transfer of learning becomes a reality when adjacent learning centres complement each other.

■ ORGANIZATION AND DESIGN OF THE SCIENCE DISCOVERY CENTRE

The Science Discovery Centre may accommodate an exploring table, water and sand area, nature corner, and a resource table (see Figure 17.1).

Figure 17.1   THE SCIENCE DISCOVERY CENTRE

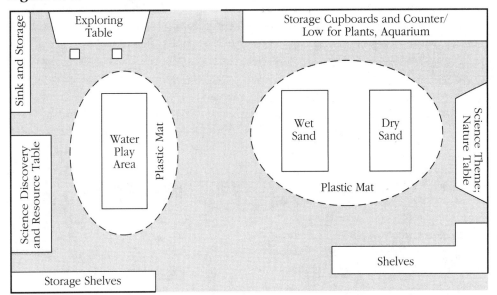

Social contexts of play emphasized in the Science Discovery Centre

solitary
parallel
associative
cooperative

Categories of play emphasized in the Science Discovery Centre

functional: practice play
              productive play
creative-constructive play
symbolic: dramatic play
              sociodramatic play (sand, water tables)

Equipment, Materials, and Supplies

Equipment—sand tables (dry sand, wet sand), water table, shelf for materials, theme table and chairs, exploring table and chairs, table or shelves for pet cages, plants.

Materials—plastic beakers, measuring cups, pails, shovels, sifters, funnels, small vehicles, miniature people, animal sets, rakes and hoes, moulds and cookie cutters, sprinkler can, pet cages, plants, aquarium, beam balance, magnifying glasses, prisms, thermometer, microscope, flashlight, magnets, watering can, terrarium, potting materials, cooking utensils, aprons, egg beater, sieve, sponges and mop, bowls of assorted sizes, siphons, plastic tubing, floating and sinking kits, bubble kits, water pump, water wheel, cables, pulleys, ropes, shell collections, rock collections, sand and soil collections, leaf collections, bark collections, science resource books, science picture file, posters, baskets, rags, rulers, measuring tapes.

Supplies—liquid soap, food colouring, paper towel, cloth towels, straws, sand, pet food, fish food, potting soil, baggies, twist ties, tongue depressors, popsicle sticks, J-cloths

RATINGS OF THE CHARACTERISTICS OF PLAY

The Science Discovery Centre

noisy	——————————	quiet
teacher-centred	——————————	child-centred
structured	——————————	open
concrete	——————————	abstract
clean	——————————	messy
specific-purpose		
materials	——————————	open-ended materials
group	——————————	individual

(Adapted with permission of the Board of Education, City of Hamilton. *Getting It All Together* (1981).)

■ PLAY STATIONS IN THE SCIENCE DISCOVERY CENTRE

The Exploring Table

The exploring table provides an opportunity for children to transfer the learning they are acquiring about number to activities involving measurement, volume, weight, and space. The formation of mathematical and logical concepts depends on children's experience with specific-purpose materials. The exploring table addresses logical skills and concepts by encouraging children to feel, transform, act on, examine, observe, describe, and record using non-numeric forms of measurement. Tools that enhance observation and examination may be provided, such as magnifying glasses, string, and balances.

EXPLORING TABLE

Children like to touch and inspect interesting objects, especially the natural kind found outdoors. The more specimens, artifacts, naturally occurring objects, and collections children and teachers can find and bring into the indoor learning environment, the more the playroom becomes a microcosm of the world outside. Locating the exploring table close to storage shelves and cupboards allows easy access to many items that will be useful for displays, activities, and projects.

Stored items should include implements for exploring—balance and weights, a small cooking scale, a timer, magnifying glasses, a small microscope, tweezers, tongue depressors, prisms, bowls and sponges, J-cloths, baskets for collections, compass, binoculars, transparent plastic jars and small glass containers, tape measure, baggies for carrying and storing treasures, flashlight, string, tape, cotton and soft cloths, paper, pencil, notepad, and mirror.

Measuring and Comparing

Measurement involves comparing properties of objects and finding relationships between them on the basis of their physical properties, using number to describe how they can be compared on the basis of the same characteristics. Discovering the physical properties of objects is closely related to an understanding of concepts related to number such as order, quantity, and constancy. In an exploring curriculum, young children profit from learning opportunities related to length, area, volume, and weight. Understanding of properties such as mass and temperature usually develops later, during the concrete operational period, along with concepts of time, speed, pressure, and distance, which involve combinations of basic measurements.

During the preoperational period, children's ability to know depends on their senses. What they experience through physical manipulation of things, they understand. Measurement begins with physical experience long before children are able to understand and use standardized units. Comparing the properties of objects in order to discover relationships among them helps children develop concepts related to basic measurement.

Children pass through stages in developing an understanding of measurement. The first stage begins during the sensorimotor stage. This stage involves exploring things and substances physically, such as pouring, stacking, and combining. In the second stage, children compare objects and discover concepts of bigger-smaller, greater than and less than, longer-shorter, and heavier-lighter using direct comparisons. Placing objects close to one another in order to compare specific properties such as longer than, smaller than, and so on makes direct comparisons easier (Cruikshank, Fitzgerald & Jensen, 1980). The sand and water tables as well as the exploring table facilitate development at these two stages.

Towards the end of the preoperational period, children use arbitrary units such as a pencil, an eraser, a piece of string, a length of cardboard, a cup, or a pot as a unit of measurement. This type of measurement involves indirect comparison using the selected arbitrary unit as the standard against which all objects are compared (Cruikshank, Fitzgerald & Jensen, 1980). Children seek to determine how many string lengths or how many potfuls there are in whatever is being measured. The ability to use standard units of measurement such as centimetres and grams meaningfully does not occur until the child has acquired the ability to conserve number, length, and volume, which is a characteristic of concrete operational thought (Charlesworth & Radeloff, 1991).

Planning Activities for the Exploring Table

The exploring table promotes acquisition of physical knowledge through play. Physical knowledge activities are mainly those that involve the movement of objects and changes in objects. Children act on these objects and observe the responsiveness and reaction of the objects to their actions. Physical activities should allow children to cause a specific response or action by their own actions and then change their actions in order to monitor the changes in response. It is necessary that children see the reaction and that it occur immediately after the child's action (DeVries and Kohlberg, 1987:92–93).

Longer-term investigations that lead to in-depth exploration and acquisition of physical knowledge are best. Short-term, isolated activities that address measuring one day, sinking and floating the next day, and colour mixing on the following day do little to further children's understanding of scientific phenomena. Simple, sequenced, observable activities related to a single area of investigation give children a chance to discover properties, reactions, and transformations using a variety of materials and methods. Children learn the causes of specific observable events and transformations by observing the consistency of reactions and responses of materials under certain conditions.

Developmentally appropriate sciencing activities should do more than simply lead children to discover the immediate effects of their actions on objects or substances (Forman and Kuschner, 1983). Units of activities that focus on various aspects of physical knowledge encourage children's awareness of the organization of their actions and their ability to consciously bring about change or transformation.

Activities at the Exploring Table

1. For younger children choose an arbitrary unit such as a piece of string or a crayon and provide linear objects for children to measure using the arbitrary unit. For example, measure the table in number of lengths of the string, sticks collected from outdoors, or strips of paper. Older children may record the number of lengths on a chart.

2. Tack a 1.5-metre strip of Bristol board vertically on the wall near the exploring table. Encourage children to measure each other on this growth chart. The teacher will print each child's name next to the mark designating her height on the growth chart.

3. For younger children provide objects of geometric shapes for children to measure and compare, for instance, a ball, an orange, a book, a triangle, a stop sign, and a clockface. Provide lengths of string for children to measure various dimensions at various points on the object.

4. Provide a balance and encourage children to weigh and measure many of the objects previously measured. Ask them to predict which of the measured objects will be heaviest. Encourage older children to chart their findings.

5. Place carrot tops in plastic cups with a little water in the bottom of the cups and encourage children to chart the growth of the carrot tops by measuring them each day with a length of string.

6. Set up the balance and provide objects that are small and heavy and ones that are large and light. Encourage children to weigh all objects and make predictions about which ones will be heavy and which will be light. Promote handling and estimating before actually putting objects on the balance.

7. Provide substances that are dry and substances that are wet (e.g., dry sand and wet sand, dry cloths and wet cloths, dry sponges and wet sponges) and encourage children to predict which ones will be heavier/lighter. Then have children test their hypotheses by weighing each object.

8. Provide containers and encourage children to predict differences in the weight of various substances. Use similar amounts of different substances (e.g., sand, water, earth, pebbles, wood chips, styrofoam pieces) before children weigh them on the balance.

9. Set up small cars of different sizes and weights on an incline made out of planks. Let children play with the cars and compare the distance they will achieve as they roll down the incline. Encourage children to compare and chart the distances achieved by each car. Ask children what they think will happen if they change the incline and make a steeper or a shallower incline. Let them experiment and compare differences in distance travelled. Provide a balance and suggest that children weigh the cars to see which ones are heavier and which are lighter. Let children play and discover the relationships between weight, speed, incline, and distance travelled down the incline.

10. Explore a variety of objects that move in different ways—on wheels, with or without motors, through water, on sand or earth, and in the air.

11. Observe the movement of a pendulum with children. Set up a second pendulum with a heavier object and a string the same length and encourage children to compare the movement of the second pendulum with the first. Suggest that children change the lengths of the strings supporting the pendulum and observe what happens.

12. Provide a sheet of plexiglass, some ball bearings, and a magnet. Show children how to control the movement of the ball bearings on top of the plexiglass by moving the magnet underneath the plexiglass.

13. Provide materials for children to make their own target games in order to see what happens when they attempt to direct movement. They may use egg cartons and cardboard cylinders, and try to knock the cartons off the top of the cylinders where they are resting.

14. Place straws and feathers, cotton balls, and small cubes of foam rubber on the table. Encourage children to move the objects along the table by blowing through the straws. Encourage children to vary the strength of their blowing and note the reactions of the objects to the changes.

15. Children may make their own mazes by cutting small round holes in a shallow cardboard box and with their super balls try to direct the box to make the super balls fall through the hole.

16. At the sand table, encourage children to make pathways in the sand to create a maze for their cars or marbles to travel. Encourage children to note the direction of movement imposed by the sunken pathways.

Water and Sand Area

The water and sand tables are together the centrepiece of the Science Discovery Centre. They are often located in the middle of the learning centre on a sheet of plastic that catches spilled sand and water. Placing them close together facilitates transfer of learning gained in one medium to the other medium (Nash, 1989). Water and sand hold special attraction for young children because they are highly sensory media, offering endless elements of surprise and delight in which every child has an opportunity to feel successful (Hill, 1977). In sand and water, children observe reactions to their actions and transformations that occur in the substances under specific observable conditions. Sand and water tables are dynamic contexts for learning through play.

The Water Play Table

Water has always been a therapeutic element in which children tend to lose themselves to the pleasures of sensory exploration. It is an element of infinite delight because of its powers of transformation and responsiveness to a range of stimuli. A clear plastic table on four legs with rolling casters makes the water and objects in it visible from all sides and from above and below. The table should be placed close enough to a cupboard or shelves for teachers and children to fetch various implements, play materials, and measuring devices that contribute to children's experimentation with the properties of water.

Water is close to the child's daily life experience. It has infinite potential for transformation under various circumstances: for example, splashing produces bubbles; adding food colouring changes the colour of the water; certain substances dissolve in water; when mixed with water some substances take on new properties such as wetness, smoothness, different texture, and a thinness in consistency; water takes the shape of the container into which it is poured; and water can remove all traces of some

WATER PLAY

substances from objects. These reactions and transformations are just a few examples of the amazing, observable properties of water that children are able to investigate through their play. Water offers children the opportunity to ask their own questions, ponder a multitude of "what if ... " questions, experiment and find observable answers through their own investigations, and alter their thinking about concepts such as conservation of volume, mass, and weight.

Some teachers argue that because water is a sensory medium that has recognized therapeutic value for its soothing, calming influence on children, it should be located close to other learning centres that address emotional objectives such as the Daily Living Centre or the Creative Arts Centre. The sensory pleasure of splashing, bubbles, pouring, and making currents can transport an anxious child into a more serene world. Children will generally remain with water play for significant periods of time and leave feeling more relaxed (Hendrick, 1988). It is also a medium in which children develop eye-hand coordination abilities, fine-motor and manipulative skills, and heightened perceptual awareness.

The child's fascination with water may be partly explained by the responsiveness of the element to the child's actions on it and its capacity to change under certain observable conditions. Children feel an increased sense of effectiveness and ability to make things happen. Water play is most compatible with the exploratory, experimental atmosphere of the Science Discovery Centre in which children ask their own questions, find answers through their own investigations, and learn to predict outcomes and monitor causes and effects.

The key to effective water play is careful selection by teachers of water play materials that promote specific kinds of learning. Teachers also have a facilitative role to play in thinking through the nature of children's learning at the water table. They have to know when children are ready for different props that will contribute to discovery and expand their learning. Providing a random assortment of plastic toys such as balls, dolls, pails,

POURING

metal cars, wood chunks, pitchers and, plastic tubing in the water table at one time defeats the purpose of water play as a medium for investigation of specific properties. In the presence of randomly selected play materials, children's play becomes random and undirected as well. Consciously setting out materials that lead children to ask questions and explore promotes physical knowledge of the properties of water. Guiding discovery learning for children facilitates their learning of concepts.

For example, when children investigate in a variety of ways the notion of sinking and floating using coordinated materials such as large and small objects that sink and float, they begin to derive an experientially-based understanding of the relationship between volume and weight in the context of objects that sink or float.

Water tables should be equipped with a wide range of play materials children can use to investigate the properties of water, such as: jugs; pails; pitchers; scoops; beakers; measuring cups; plastic tubing; handheld water pump; funnels; siphons; squeeze bottles; watering cans; spray containers; plastic syringes; eyedroppers; sponges; corks; styrofoam; light pieces of wood; and an assortment of large and small objects that will sink such as ball bearings, marbles, buttons, kitchen utensils, and plastic containers of the same volume but different shapes (such as honey containers, plastic ketchup bottles, peanut butter jars, yogurt containers, paint brushes, paint rollers, cloths, and paint trays).

Encouraging children to wear plastic aprons at the water table provides cues about the number of children able to play at the table at one time, protects clothing, and adds to the child's sense of freedom and ability to explore. Providing sponges for children to mop up their own spills gives them a sense of both independence and responsibility for their own actions, which children generally accept and respect. Children should also be expected to wash their hands before and after leaving the water table.

WATER PLAY TABLE

Activities at the Water Play Table

(for younger children, ages two to four)

1. Practise pouring, emptying, filling, comparing, making currents in the water, and directing water into small openings. Add pitchers, measuring cups, pails, and measured plastic containers initially; as children develop pouring skills, add jars with small openings, funnels, watering cans, siphons, syringes, and droppers for them to investigate various ways of transferring water from one container to another.

2. Experiment with the sinking and floating properties of objects in water. Choose objects initially in which it is obvious which ones will sink and which will float, and then add objects that create a conflict between their visible characteristics (size) and their sinking properties, such as small marbles and large inflatable or sponge balls.

3. Dissolve food colouring or bubbling liquid into the water table for children to explore what happens when various liquids are dissolved in water. Provide smaller bottles and eyedroppers for children to experiment with this phenomenon themselves.

4. Wash objects (e.g., plastic toys that need to be cleaned) in sudsy water in order for children to observe the cleansing properties of water and soap. Provide a pail of water with a siphon beside the water table for children to rinse the toys, and a tea towel or dusters for children to cooperate in drying the toys and putting them away.

5. Set up sponges of various colours, densities, and textures. Provide both natural and artificial sponges. Let children experience the absorptive qualities of the sponges and see what happens when the water is squeezed out of them.

6. Make water pressure cans by punching three holes one above the other, about 5 cm apart, in a tall coffee can. Ensure that all sharp edges are covered with sturdy tape. Let children fill the cans and observe what happens as the water spurts out of all three holes in the can.

7. Provide a strong solution of water and liquid soap along with small and large wands for children to make bubbles.

8. Add rocks and other naturally occurring objects such as seaweed, shells, sand, and sea salt to the water table for children to explore what happens to things when they are immersed in water. Objects change colour, change texture, disperse, dissolve, and so on.

The Sand Play Table

For children older than three-and-a-half the juxtaposition of sand and water tables will facilitate the transfer of learning from one table to the other. It will also allow

SAND PLAY

children to observe the transformation of the sand when it is wet. Children should be discouraged from adding sand to the water table, however. The sand simply sinks to the bottom and the water has to be carefully strained from the water tub in order to prevent it from going down the sink. Children also have to learn to keep the play accessories for sand and water quite separate. Similar water play protocol also applies to the sand table: children should wear aprons and wash their hands before and after leaving the sand table.

Play and learning with sand are enhanced when there is sufficient space in the Science Discovery Centre to accommodate a wet sand and a dry sand table. The different properties of wet sand and dry sand promote greater understanding of the substance and encourage a broader range of play. Wet sand is ideal for promoting dramatic play and testing play that promotes physical knowledge. An argument can be made for introducing small figures of people, trucks, cars, and other props that encourage children to cooperate in creating a sand replica of a road system, fort, or castle. The malleable properties of wet sand make representations of buildings, road systems, dams, and bridges feasible. Digging, piling, moulding, and compacting are much easier with wet sand.

Dry sand pours more easily than wet sand and is, therefore, more suitable for play with materials that promote pouring, measuring, comparing, sifting, and stirring. Colanders, sifters, sieves, plastic shaker bottles or cans, and a variety of baking pans, scoops, spoons, shovels, pails, sand moulds, cookie cutters, measured containers, handheld garden tools, and plant pots provide the flexibility children need to explore the various properties of wet and dry sand.

Activities at the Wet and Dry Sand Tables

(for younger children, two to four years)

1. Set up measured containers of different shapes and sizes in the dry sand table and encourage children to fill, compare, weigh, pour, and sift the sand.

2. Add a pail of water with a siphon beside the sand table and let children experiment by pumping water into the sand table. Encourage them to build streams and dams so as to shore up the water. When the sand is wet, provide moulding instruments such as empty flower pots for children to compact the sand and create castles or other representations.

3. Add plastic cars, trucks, steam shovels, and miniature people to the dry sand.

4. Add plastic farm animals, a barn, miniature farm machinery, and fences to the dry sand and let children create a farm scene.

5. Provide articulated construction toys such as steam shovels, Tonka dumptrucks, and backhoes in the dry sand table.

The Nature Corner

Sciencing with young children implies that teachers should model and teach attitudes and values that promote respect for the environment, appreciation of nature and naturally occurring objects, a sense of the mutual interdependence of all living things, and a conservationist attitude towards optimizing the use and replenishment of natural resources. The nature corner is an area replete with specimens from the outdoors, including plants and pets, and facilities and implements for recreating outdoor life indoors, such as terrariums and aquariums, plant-and-grow kits; hand-held planting tools; and materials for making and maintaining collections of naturally occurring objects. In addition, the nature corner has supplies for planting, for cleaning and feeding pets, and for making nature trips (baskets, baggies, small bottles and plastic containers to hold specimens, plastic gloves, etc.); microscope; magnifying glasses; binoculars; and brushes of various sizes.

The nature corner should be located close to the resource table, where resource books, albums, picture files, posters, and science-related magazines for children are kept.

Ecology

Ecology is the study of the interrelationships of living things with the environments in which they exist. The nature corner should include activities related to the study of ecosystems so that children can observe the interactions between living things and the settings in which they are sustained. Children need to develop a lifestyle that is compatible with nature and understand the impact nature has on our daily lives.

Young children benefit from activities in which they can observe living things in their natural habitat; for example, watching plants in a terrarium, fish in an aquarium, ants in earth, and so on. Ecological experiences help children understand the interdependence of all living things. It is important when planning these learning opportunities to understand how children perceive the ecosystem, what features interest them, and what relationships they understand. When a child observes a frog in a pond, the frog is the focus of her attention, and what the frog eats and how the frog responds to external sounds and sensations is of particular interest to her. These are the first steps towards understanding the frog's ecosystem. Children relate the frog's habitat to what they know already about the frog's needs for nourishment and how it protects itself, as well as to what they know about other ecosystems. Ecological understanding is promoted when new experiences are related and added to what is already known and familiar to the child.

Conservation

A natural science curriculum for the 1990s has to help children develop conservationist attitudes in order to respect, preserve, and maximize the use of precious natural resources. It should promote awareness of the importance of natural resources, how to use them properly, and how to replace what we take away from our environment. When children develop conservationist values early in life, there is a greater likelihood that these values will influence their everyday habits and continue throughout life.

Conservation activities should focus on concrete knowledge and social conventions that children can relate to, such as recognition of natural resources, knowing what we need to live and using only what we need, and knowing what kinds of polluting conditions endanger our natural resources. Many programs have adopted recycling programs as one way of sensitizing children to the importance of preserving natural resources and preventing waste and pollution. A conservationist curriculum encourages children to respect and value the products of nature and appreciate all living things.

Organization of the Nature Corner

There should be space in the storage cupboard for storing collections of rock specimens, different sands from many locations, shells, bottles of different types of soil, leaf collections, and other specimen collections that children may have gathered and assembled themselves. Specimens borrowed from local museums may also be displayed at the exploring table, in keeping with the style in this area of promoting hands-on active involvement with things rather than observing.

The nature corner should consist of a table with three or four chairs, some shelves, and a cupboard for storing a vast array of materials and supplies. This area is dedicated to the development of conservationist skills and provides close contact with living things and earth. Maintenance and repair materials such as sponges, soft cloths, soap, vinegar, and other safe cleaning agents; tape; paste or wood glue; and brushes for cleaning and shining all foster values related to the preservation of resources, tools, materials, and supplies.

Children should be able to explore the interrelationships of living things by creating ecosystems in jars, a terrarium, and a fish tank. Awareness of the interdependence of living things for survival instills an understanding of the need to protect resources that preserve the balance necessary to sustain existing plant and animal species.

Activities in the Nature Corner

(for children ages three to six)

1. Set up a planting activity with small pots, potting soil, vermiculite, hand tools, bulbs, and seeds. Encourage each child to plant a bulb and some grass seed in two separate pots. Place the planted pots on a window ledge.

2. In clear plastic cups set on wet paper towels have children "plant" a mung bean or alfalfa seeds and cover it or them with a moistened paper towel. Children enjoy watching the sprouting take place and won't have to wait long for results.

3. Start seeds in flats with prepared potting soil for children to grow small vegetable and flower plants that will be ready for planting in the garden patch outdoors in the spring. Try surefire "crops" such as radishes, marigolds, snapdragons, and lettuce initially, and then move on to more demanding planting projects using tomato, bean, and pepper seeds.

4. Let children sort collections of naturally occurring objects such as shells, nuts in shells, pretty stones and rocks, and samples of various kinds of bark according to criteria they will identify.

5. Provide small containers of various textures and colours of sand collected by teachers, parents, or children from various parts of the country or world. Let children feel and test the sands for differences in texture, colour, smell, and weight.

6. Make birdhouses, from directions in a resource book, to feed the birds in winter.

(for children four to six years)

7. Create an ecosystem in a jar.

8. Build a terrarium by collecting various species of compatible plants following directions in a resource book.

9. Create an earthworm farm in a large glass jar.

10. Set up an aquarium with the children, using stones, gravel, plant life, and the food necessary to sustain fish life. Show children how to care for the fish by keeping the aquarium clean and inducing air into the water.

11. Make an ant farm with the children.

12. Encourage children to investigate the growing conditions necessary to sustain plants and animals that are part of their everyday environment. They can do so by investigating the conditions outdoors in which the plants and animals live and by using resource books and pictures. Older children may make a growth chart on which they will record nourishment needs, sources of nourishment, needs for shelter, habitat, sleeping-waking patterns (animals), sun and shade exposure (plants), physical characteristics, and any other details relevant to the plants, animals, or birds being investigated.

13. Make birds' nests using pieces of string, ribbon, thread, baskets of straw, twigs, earth, and water. Set a real nest on the table for children to examine as they are building their nests.

14. Make scavenger baskets with each child's name printed on his or her own basket. Encourage children to collect special objects from nature in their scavenger baskets when they go out on teacher-accompanied walks. Have them talk about the ways they can use their treasures for making things in the nature corner or in the Creative Arts Centre.

15. Mix cleaning solutions of vinegar and water in small pails or dishpans and let children clean and wipe the utensils, materials, storage shelves, and surface areas in the Science Discovery Centre.

16. Store objects such as silverware on trays with silver cleaning polish, damp sponges, and soft cloths, and let children clean and polish the silver. Provide cloth gloves to protect hands.

17. Make paper with children.

18. Shine shoes with neutral polish and soft rags.

19. Have children identify classes and subclasses of foods using pictures to promote understanding of the importance of a variety of foods to maintain health and vigour.

20. Using plastic containers, coffee filters, and snow from outdoors, have children investigate and observe the presence of dirt particles in the apparently clean snow.

21. Provide various leaves from trees and have children clean them with cotton balls, using a water and soda solution in bowls. Children observe the scum and dirt that gather on leaves and they relate it to the dirt that collects on their cotton balls and in the water solution. Teachers may provide leaves from trees in the country as well as the city in order for children to investigate and observe, using magnifying glasses, the differences in the amount of pollution that collects on the leaves.

The Resource Table

The Science Discovery Centre needs a place where resource materials such as science books, field guides, picture files, nature and science posters, and specimens and collections borrowed from museums can be stored for children's activities and projects. It is helpful to have shelves close to the resource table to store books, files, and specimens, since only a few of each may be displayed on the table at a time. Children like space at this table to pore over books and picture files when they are seeking information and ideas or are merely browsing.

Science picture files are an endless source of delight to children when they have been carefully selected, mounted, and filed by teachers. Beautiful pictures of a range of scientific phenomena and resources introduce children to a world beyond their immediate environment. They also provide new and interesting perspectives from which they, too, can view the everyday things in the natural world around them. Children enjoy small picture files on file cards stored in shoebox files or metal recipe boxes that they can hold easily and spread out before them. Large pictures mounted on construction paper may be hung in the Science Discovery Centre from time to time as children embark on specific projects and activities. Prop boxes containing materials for specific science-related projects may also be available for children to use at the resource table.

Field guides, especially books of pictures identifying birds, plants, trees, rocks, and shells are particularly useful for children to consult when they want to see a picture of the specimen or collection of naturally occurring objects they just sorted or mounted on cardboard. Teachers should be familiar with local museums and arrange borrowings of specimens from them that would be of interest to children in the classroom. Butterfly and insect collections, various birds, and stuffed animals mounted in glass cases are always interesting to children. Specimens such as bird nests, bee hives, wasp nests, and snake skins make fascinating objects for children to handle gently in order to investigate their composition, texture, and design.

Activities at the Resource Table

(for children ages four to six)

1. Ask children what project they would like to undertake. Suggest some possibilities like making feeders for birds, making birds' nests, creating a poster of pretty leaves, learning about animal habitats, or making paper. Encourage children to search the resource books and picture files for some ideas of what they would like to do. Discuss with them what they will need in order to undertake the project.

2. Set out selected pictures from the picture files that are related to a project or activities going on elsewhere in the learning environment and let children peruse them.

3. Leave the field guides to birds out on the table for children to look up species that come to the feeders.

4. Set out glue sticks, paste, construction paper, markers, and nature magazines or old scenic calendars and let children create their own picture file or add to the one already there.

5. Set out pine cones, acorns, and ground nuts in bowls and let children identify them by finding pictures of these specimens in the picture files or resource books.

Prop Boxes

The Science Discovery Centre is a good location for prop boxes that hold collections of objects children can explore, use for projects, or use as props for play. Prop boxes are sometimes called activity boxes and are wonderful resources for transition periods, or times when a child wants to find a quiet corner to pursue an activity alone. As previously mentioned, prop boxes may also be located in the Daily Living Centre and the Active Role Play Centre.

A prop box might contain concept-related objects, theme- or project-related objects, collections of things like jewellery, bells of different sizes, old music boxes, old clocks, a flashlight, sets of keys, old catalogues, tools, a camera, old radios, or other small appliances for children to take apart and put together. Children are fascinated by old objects, especially old toys, which resemble those that they may have inherited from their parents' collections of childhood toys.

Prop boxes may be "project" or theme boxes, especially when each box contains a number of toys, props, and accessories that will enable children to undertake a specific kind of project or play particular roles. Some teachers provide a prop box for car and truck repair, a camper box, an astronaut's box, a book repair box, and many other kinds (Bender, 1971).

Prop boxes place objects related according to function, role, or project into a container, which is labelled so that children can identify the theme of the box. Sturdy cardboard boxes or large plastic containers without lids, like laundry baskets or even dishpans, can be used for storing items for a particular theme or project (Suskind & Kittel, 1989). Not all prop boxes need to be accessible at all times. As they take valuable storage space, only four or five prop boxes are made available at any one time, with the rest in a storage room, waiting to be brought out to replace those that have lost their appeal. Many teachers find that prop boxes with multicultural themes are a good way to introduce anti-bias activities and cultural awareness, and to ensure that multiculturalism is an integral part of a program.

Another activity box that has a place in the Science Discovery Centre is the "junk box," which contains objects that teachers, parents, and children gather from a variety of sources (Lind, 1991). These boxes may be categorized to ensure that the "junk" is sorted as it is deposited in the various boxes, which may include a hardware box, boxes for plastic containers, tins, and film containers, and so on. Children are very creative in determining a number of uses for the contents of junk boxes for their projects, water and sand play, and discovery play in the Science Discovery Centre and other areas of the classroom.

References

Althouse, R. (1988). *Investigating Science with Young Children*. New York: Teachers College Press, Columbia University.

Bender, J. (1971). Have you ever thought of a prop box? *Young Children* 27 (1):164–69.

Bettelheim, B. (1987). The importance of play. *The Atlantic* 262 (3):35–43 (262/3):35–43.

Bruner, J. (1960). *The Process of Education*. Cambridge, MA: Harvard University Press.

Charlesworth, R., and Radeloff, D.J. (1991). *Experiences in Math for Young Children*. 2d ed. Albany, NY: Delmar.

Coles, R. (1990). *The Spiritual Life of Children*. Boston: Houghton-Mifflin.

Communications Directorate, Environment Canada. (1990). *What We Can Do For Our Environment?: Hundreds of Things To Do Now*. Ottawa: Minister of Supply and Services.

Cruikshank, D.E., Fitzgerald, D.L., and Jensen, L.R. (1980). *Young Children Learning Mathematics*. Boston: Allyn & Bacon.

DeVries, R., and Kohlberg, L. (1987). *Constructivist Early Education: Overview and Comparison with Other Programs*. Washington, D.C.: National Association for the Education of Young Children.

Forman, G., and Kuschner, D.S. (1983). *The Child's Construction of Knowledge: Piaget for Teaching Children*. Washington, D.C.: National Association for the Education of Young Children.

Furman, E. (1990). Plant a potato—learn about life (and death). *Young Children* 45 (6):15–20.

Gardner, H. (1982). *Art, Mind and Brain*. New York: Basic Books.

Gardner, H. (1989). *To Open Minds*. New York: Basic Books.

Hendrick, J. (1988). *The Whole Child*. Columbus, OH: Merrill.

Holt, B. (1989). *Science with Young Children*. Rev. ed. Washington, D.C.: National Association for the Education of Young Children.

Hill, D.M. (1977). *Mud, Sand, and Water*. Washington, D.C.: National Association for the Education of Young Children.

Javna, J. (1990). *50 Simple Things Kids Can Do To Save the Earth*. Kansas City, MO: The EarthWorks Group.

Kamii, C., and DeVries, R. (1978). *Physical Knowledge in Preschool Education: Implications of Piaget's Theory*. Englewood Cliffs, NJ: Prentice-Hall.

Lind, K.K. (1991). *Exploring Science in Early Childhood: A Developmental Approach*. Albany, NY: Delmar.

Nash, C. (1989). *The Learning Environment: A Practical Approach to the Education of the*

Three-, Four- and Five-year-old. Toronto: Collier-Macmillan.

Newell, A., Shaw, J.C., and Simon, H.A. (1962). In *Contemporary Approaches to Creative Thinking*, ed. H.E. Gruber, G. Terrell, and M. Wertheimer, pp. 65–66. New York: Atherton.

Nichols, W., and Nichols, D. (1990). *Wonderscience: a developmentally appropriate guide to hands-on science for young children*. Palo Alto, CA: Learning Expo Publishing.

Perry, G., and Rivkin, M. (1992). Teachers and science. *Young Children* 47 (4): 9–16.

Smith, R.F. (1982). Early childhood science education: a Piagetian perspective. In *Cur-riculum Planning for Young Children*, ed. J.F. Brown, pp. 143–50. Washington, D.C.: National Association for the Education of Young Children.

Smith, R.F. (1987). Theoretical framework for preschool science experiences. *Young Children* 42 (1): 34–40.

Suskind, D., and Kittel, J. (1989). Clocks, cameras, and chatter, chatter, chatter: activity boxes as curriculum. *Young Children* 44 (1):46–50.

Torrance, P. (1966). Torrance Tests of Creative Thinking. Norms Technical Manual Research Edition. Princeton, NJ: Personnel Press.

THE CREATIVE ARTS CENTRE

■ WHAT IS CREATIVITY?

Creativity involves the ability to perceive things in new ways, think unconventionally, form unique combinations, and represent an original idea or insight (Schirrmacher, 1988). Not everything that occurs in the Creative Arts Centre is creative. This is, however, the area in the classroom where children are encouraged to express themselves, using a range of art materials, and to develop a "creative orientation" (Gardner, 1980, 1982, 1989).

Young children need abundant opportunity for sensory exploration of creative materials and media. Creative activity in the early years is largely a matter of children experiencing the properties of materials and media, and learning to use them to represent their world as they see it. Young children do not yet have the artistic skills, discipline, ability to plan and follow through, and the perspective required to fashion an artistic product that will make a significant impact. They are at a stage, however, when they are able to express themselves freely, acquire knowledge of materials and techniques, and develop their sensory abilities for later creative achievement. In the early years, creativity is largely a process of planning, experiencing, and using materials in order to represent something that the child understands (Anderson, 1975).

Creative exploration and experimentation occur whenever children are able to explore and experiment with materials, media, and their own bodies in order to represent something they know or feel. It occurs outdoors when children are building forts or playing in wet sand; it occurs in the Active Role Play Centre when they are marching to their own music or planning a space station they will make out of hollow blocks. Planning the learning environment is largely a matter of designing learning centres that emphasize and support play that encourages children to practise specific developmental abilities. A well-planned Creative Arts Centre ensures that creative explorations and abilities using graphic materials of many kinds, malleable substances such as clay, plasticene, papier-mâché; and other media such as collage, paste, fabric, wood, and cardboard, will be both possible and encouraged.

Creative behaviour involves having original or unusual ideas that bear some relationship to real problems, situations, or goals, and that are planned, thought through, and sustained until some realization or outcome occurs (MacKinnon, 1971). That is, creativity is not a flash in the pan that emerges from mindless experimentation or dabbling, but deliberate, purposeful activity directed towards the representation of an idea or insight, using a creative medium. Children's experimentation with art materials such as dipping their brushes and putting endless blobs of paint on the paper usually constitutes exploration of the properties of the brushes, paint, and paper, and does not represent creativity. This type of exploration is an essential stage in learning how to use materials creatively and testing their potential in a variety of artistic contexts.

Are children's delightful innovations in art and language just "happy accidents" as Gardner has speculated? He suggests that young children have a "first draft" sense of what it means to draw a picture, tell a story, or invent a song that should be encouraged. The years from five to seven are a "golden period" of early creative behaviour, when the child should be enriched and supported in creative exploration and experimentation (Gardner, 1982, 1989).

The vibrant burst of artistry in children who are between five and seven coincides with their developmental abilities. Children at this stage possess keen, expressive urges, the willingness to take risks, sharp and harmonious perceptions, and sufficient graphic capability to organize drawings, paintings, and other artistic executions (Gardner, 1980:94). They usually demonstrate tremendous enthusiasm and drive in expressing themselves, and produce freely and unaffectedly the images that represent what is meaningful and understandable to them through artistic media. Their sensory perceptual skills are sharp, and their imaginations are vivid. Visual imagination, inquisitiveness, and willingness are also important parts of the creative process that children possess. As children have limited life experience, and immature cognitive abilities and graphic skills, it is too much to expect from them original insights and novel solutions to problems, but preschool and kindergarten children are able to produce products or representations without reference to a model.

Few adults retain more than a fraction of the creative impulses, perceptual sensitivities, and unique ways of viewing the world that are common in childhood. What happens to these creative behaviours in the growing years? Chapter 16 has already referred to the decline in right-brain activity when children enter the school years. Artistic endeavours in the visual arts are largely right-brain activities that capitalize on visualization abilities, spatial awareness and spatial reasoning skills, and the retention of visual patterns such as geometric designs, graphs, and diagrams

(Rubenzer, 1984). Many thinking abilities traditionally considered to be hallmarks of creative thinking are also dominated by right-brain activities. These include the ability to respond to data intuitively, create and use imagery and symbols, handle information spontaneously, deal with events, actions, group information, and objects randomly, and process ideas and theories in divergent ways (Cherry, Godwin & Staples, 1989).

As discussed in Chapter 16, one argument for the introduction of computer technology into the early childhood education environment is the capacity of computer software to promote and sustain right-brain cognitive processes in children well into middle childhood. Beaty and Tucker (1987:9) state that creativity seems to be connected to the ability to "create images in the mind's eye," or think visually, which is a right-brain activity. Young children think more easily with images than words during the years before their verbal skills are highly developed.

By the age of seven or eight, much of the creativity that arises from children's visual thinking has decreased along with the increased definition of the right and left hemispheres of the brain. As the functioning of the left brain, which controls verbal and abstract thought, increases in importance during the school years, the visual thinking of the right hemisphere becomes less useful and loses its impact. At this stage, researchers in creativity in young children have seen a corresponding dramatic decrease in the child's creative abilities (Gardner, 1980). It is at this point in the child's development and schooling that computers may be a useful instrument for extending and enhancing visual thinking, creative impulses, and the visual imagination well into middle childhood.

■ DEVELOPMENTAL STAGES OF CHILDREN'S ART

Many theorists have noted that children's artistic development passes through distinct stages that have particular characteristics. Montessori described the years from two to four as a "sensitive period" for painting, drawing, and other artistic activity that could be integrated with the motor, sensory, and intellectual components of a curriculum. She believed that self-expression could be more easily achieved by young children through mastery of the tools and skills involved in art rather than through writing or movement. The key to using art as a medium for child development, according to Montessori, lay in providing the materials children need to express their individuality and abstract understanding or perspective within a concrete, observable form.

Kellogg (1967,1969) saw children's art as proof of the human being's quest for order and balance. She proposed a stage theory in which the units and arrangements of figures and patterns at any stage reflect what children have understood during an earlier stage. Children respond at each stage to the order they see in the shapes they depict. Successive shapes and patterns, called *combines* or *aggregates*, contain elements of earlier ones they have created. Although Kellogg proposed that the shapes created by children at each stage are universal and occur in every culture, more recent research has shown significant cultural differences in the characteristics of children's artistic and graphic development at similar ages and stages (Gardner, 1982, 1989).

The stages of children's graphic development correspond with Piaget's cognitive developmental stages. Lowenfeld and Brittain (1987) have carefully documented the stages of children's graphic development from eighteen months to nine years of age. During the first two years of life, when children play with graphic materials, they are engaged in sensorimotor exploration of the crayon or marker they are holding. Their awkward and random movement of the crayon over a page, usually with the crayon held in a tight fist, is called *disordered scribbling*. The intention at this stage is to explore the properties of both the crayon and the paper, along with the movements of the arm and hand. Children generally delight in the marks made on the page and do not lift the crayon from the paper. In fact, given the opportunity, they will draw incessantly whenever they are presented with simple graphic materials. Often they do not even require paper—a fresh wall or floor will do! These zig-zag motions across the page signal the beginning of the *scribbling stage*, which lasts until about the age of four.

Controlled scribbling appears after about six months of sensorimotor play with graphic materials. At this stage, children have gained greater control over their hand and eye movements, and employ a lighter grasp of the crayon or marker. The former random and unrestrained movement of the arms gives way to more purposeful behaviour at this stage, and children generally respect the boundaries of the chalkboard, paper, or easel on which they are working. At this stage, children are much more aware of the marks they are making, although the play remains largely exploratory and repetitive. Children lift the brush or crayon from the page frequently, often to switch colours or vary the intensity or direction of the brush stroke or crayon lines.

As children begin to name their scribbles, at about three-and-a-half years of age, they also start using their graphic play as a symbolic medium. This stage corresponds with the intuitive phase of preoperational thought, a period when children are able to use mental symbols to represent absent events and objects. As their memory increases and their skill in manipulating graphic materials improves, along with fine-motor skills and visual perceptual abilities, children are increasingly able to make their brush strokes and crayon lines do what they want them to do. They also become able to maintain an idea in their heads of the image they are trying to capture on the page. In other words, children's drawings on paper take on meaning for them. They are able to use graphic activity as another vehicle for self-expression in the same way that language and role-playing abilities allow them to express themselves verbally and represent reality through drama.

This stage is called the *preschematic stage.* Although many of the drawn figures at this stage are crude versions of the real world, they are very real for the child, who has no difficulty assigning a name, a purpose, and a context to her graphic production. At this stage, "graphic work is truly visible thinking" (Goodnow, 1982:145). As children are still egocentric at this stage and see the world from a unique perspective, their own representations of the real world are satisfying to them, and they do not demand that adults find their drawings immediately recognizable.

The final stage of graphic development in early childhood occurs from about the ages of seven to nine and is called the *schematic stage.* As this stage corresponds with children's intense preoccupation with learning to read, performing operations with numbers using rules, and acquiring factual information through rote learning, much of the earlier exuberance and freedom evident in children's graphic work begins to fade. Graphic work becomes increasingly a matter of the faithful reproduction of forms—a concern with realistically depicting what is seen (Gardner, 1982). Children tend to produce fewer drawings and three-dimensional creations with clay and blocks at this stage and are dissatisfied when their productions do not sufficiently represent real life as they see it.

Just as children are entering the concrete-operational period of greater objectivity and increased capacity to think and solve problems in the absence of concrete objects, their drawings become more objective and literal, and less impressionistic. In fact, at this stage children express disdain for their own creations and those of others when they are not sufficiently lifelike.

■ THE ROLE OF ART IN EARLY CHILDHOOD EDUCATION

"Art has the role in education of helping children become more themselves instead of more like everyone else" (Clemens, 1991:4). Exploration of and representation using a range of artistic media offer important vehicles for self-expression. Therefore, planning for play in the art area is a matter of providing children with an abundance of reliable, high-quality, beautiful and divergent materials, and supplies with which they can express their individuality. The same rule of thumb that applies to other types of materials also applies to art materials and supplies: the simple, the basic, and the easy-to-use are best.

Teachers assume responsibility for selecting and setting up materials, ensuring that they are in good condition, clean, and functional, and encouraging children to appreciate the process in which they are involved as well as the results of their own efforts and those of others. The art area is a busy place in which a teacher is needed to manage the materials and display children's artistic creations, treating them with the respect they deserve rather than piling them hurriedly on a shelf.

Evaluative comments about the quality of a particular work of art send messages to children about what the teacher thinks about their artwork and suggests it is important to produce what will please the teacher. That, however, is *not* the function of art in early childhood education. "Nothing is more important about art than that it reflects our feelings about ourselves and the people in our lives" (Clemens, 1991:6). A far more effective teaching strategy is to express interest in what the child is doing, perhaps by commenting on something factual about the artwork (e.g., "the black shows up nicely against the white background," or, "I see you've used three colours this time") rather than expressing an opinion. Most of all, *teachers should avoid setting a standard* for children to emulate or encouraging them to produce something that will be teacher-pleasing.

The issue of copying models and patterns provided by teachers has been debated frequently (Goodnow, 1977; Gardner, 1980; Clemens, 1991). Copying is an unacceptable practice in early childhood education because it does not promote creativity and discourages those children who perceive that they can never live up to the standard the teacher has set. Many children stop drawing for this reason. Copying substitutes someone else's representation of an idea or an image for the child's internal image and undermines her capacity to express what she feels or sees in her own way. "It is in the activity of the young child—his preconscious sense of form, his willingness to explore and to solve problems that arise, his capacity to take risks, his affective needs which must be worked out in a symbolic realm—that we find the crucial seeds of the greatest artistic achievements" (Gardner, 1980:269).

■ LOCATING THE CREATIVE ARTS CENTRE

Placing the Creative Arts Centre close to the Science Discovery Centre makes sense in that many of the play and learning experiences available in each centre are complementary. As discussed in Chapter 17, there are times when children may wish to borrow the naturally occurring substances and items in science collections for their collages or posters. Experimentation with clay in the Creative Arts Centre and wet sand in the Science Discovery Centre, for example, addresses similar understandings about texture, the effects of adding water, compacting, moulding, and leaving the clay or sand to dry. Both of these centres are also compatible with the creative thrust of the Unit Blocks Centre, which may be located nearby.

■ ORGANIZATION AND DESIGN OF THE CREATIVE ARTS CENTRE

The Creative Arts Centre includes areas that support and encourage children's exploration, representation, and production using a variety of visual arts media such as paint, paper, cardboard, glue, paste, wood, fabric, and clay. These areas are the art area, the wood construction table, and the sewing table (see Figure 18.1). Although supplies and materials should be arranged neatly and be accessible to children, tidiness is not an important priority in this learning centre because of the nature of the play behaviours, which encourage physical, sensory, emotional, and cognitive experiences. Like the Science Discovery centre, this centre functions better with easy access to a water source and on tile floors that are easy to mop up.

Equipment, Materials, and Supplies

Equipment—easels, storage shelves, drying rack, paper storage rack, two art tables and four to six chairs per table, woodwork bench and stools, sewing table, and chairs.

Materials—hammer, saw, vise grips, clamps, soft wood scraps, nails with large heads, screwdriver, screws, brace and bit, pliers, spools, brushes, scissors, paste paddles, sewing kit, needles, thimbles, embroidery and crewel hoops, knitting basket, and sewing cards.

Supplies—sandpaper, paints, glue, paste, tape, collage supplies, aluminum foil, paper towels, paper plates, paper cups, wooden stirring sticks, powdered alum, glycerine, wool, thread, rubber bands, masking tape, egg cartons, soap, brads, paper clips, clothes pegs, thumbtacks, cardboard boxes, straight pins, wax paper, straws, tongue depressors, pipe cleaners, fingerpaints, plasticene, clay, glitter, burlap, fabric pieces, cotton puffs, Q-tips, sponges, assorted papers (crêpe, cellophane, tissue, Bristol board, cardboard, corrugated cardboard, construction paper, newsprint, computer paper, shiny paper, poster paper, gummed stars and stickers, tracing paper, onion skin), paint cans, soap flakes, cornstarch, liquid soap, tempera paints, heavy-gauge plastic, wallpaper and paste, MacTac, crayons, markers, chalk, pencils, erasers, rulers, oil pastels, fabric crayons, pencil crayons, paste containers, rubber cement, and fabric and wood glue.

Figure 18.1   THE CREATIVE ARTS CENTRE

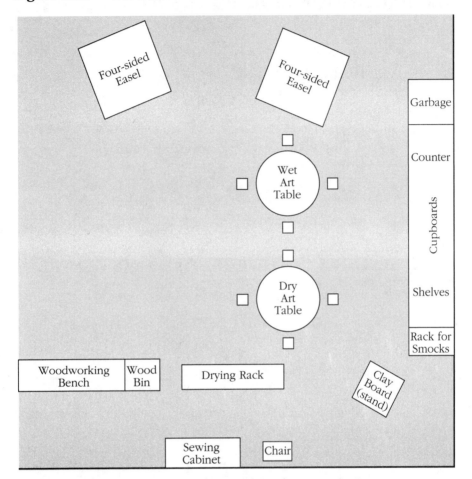

Social contexts of play emphasized in the Creative Arts Centre

solitary
parallel
associative
cooperative (cardboard carpentry, woodworking projects)

Categories of play emphasized in the Creative Arts Centre

functional play: practice play
                            productive play
symbolic play (reproductive play)
creative-constructive play

RATINGS OF THE CHARACTERISTICS OF PLAY

The Creative Arts Centre

noisy	_____	quiet
teacher-centred	_____	child-centred
structured	_____	open
clean	_____	messy
specific-purpose materials	_____	open-ended materials
group	_____	individual

(Adapted with permission of the Board of Education, City of Hamilton. *Getting It All Together* (1981).)

■ PLAY STATIONS IN THE CREATIVE ARTS CENTRE

Art Area

The art area is the most important part of the Creative Arts Centre and will occupy the lion's share of the space. The art area appeals to children's interest in graphic activity that uses a wide range of media. They see it as a place where the processes involved in scribbling, drawing, painting, cutting, and pasting are much more important than the products of their endeavours. They enjoy having their artwork displayed and are often eager to make something for mother to hang on the refrigerator at home. However, *the process is much more interesting and developmentally appropriate than is the product* for children. One wonders if taking something home to show each day is not done more to please the teacher and the parent than because of the child's enthusiasm for the outcome of her artistic play.

The importance of process in the artistic endeavours of children in this area is obvious when one observes the absorption and determination children exhibit as they practise making brush strokes of just the right width and height, choosing just the right colour to represent their images, and dedicating considerable time to filling a special spot on the page with a particular configuration of strokes. Artistic creation is for children an extension of their innermost feelings, perceptions, and thought processes. It is in this highly expressive mode that they experience emotional release, mastery of tools in the immediate environment, physical control, and management of symbols as they perceive them.

The Art Area promotes physical development, particularly fine-motor skills, perceptual acuity, eye-hand coordination, manipulative abilities, and body awareness.

Non-locomotor abilities and laterality skills are practised as children struggle to hold the paper steady with one hand while attempting to cut deliberately and evenly with the other. At the easel children often sway to the movement of the brush and reach on tiptoe to paint sky and clouds at the top of the easel.

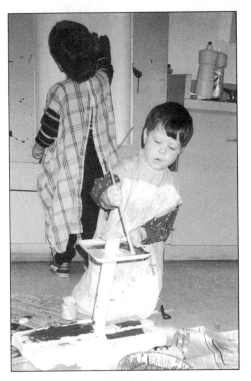

ART AREA

The watchword of the art area is simplicity. It is an area for children to make their own choices of basic art materials and to execute their own plans. *Precut materials rob children of opportunities to represent things and experiences as they see them, and diminish the importance of individual self-expression through art.* "Precut or patterned activities teach children that their own work is not valuable because it's never as tidy or realistic as the patterns" (Clemens, 1991:9). Children tend to represent what they know much more than what they see. This understanding makes the presentation of models for children to follow or precut art materials for them to assemble a futile and potentially soul-destroying enterprise for children.

"Cute" models of popular artifacts such as Easter bunnies with bows, decorated turkeys, and cartoons of Garfield and other characters from television are out of place and inappropriate for the art area. Teachers' versions of how an art activity should be executed and what the final product should look like also defeat the purpose of the art area. Children should have the opportunity here to use open-ended materials to express feelings, perceptions, and individuality. The art area is similar to the exploring table in the Science Discovery Centre in that they both encourage children to explore basic materials and observe the responsiveness of the materials to their actions on them.

Art Appreciation

As with music and literature, young children need adult guidance in developing a taste for quality and an appreciation of beauty and harmony. Artistic appreciation develops best in an atmosphere that is beautiful. Aesthetics are important throughout the whole learning environment but especially in the art area. This is *not* a place to hang posters of characters from Disneyland or popular TV programs. Nor is it appropriate to hang teachers' versions of what jack-o'-lanterns and Valentine's Day cards should look like. Only the artistic creations of children should decorate the bulletin boards on the walls of the playroom. An "art gallery" of children's art situated somewhere else in the building, perhaps at the entrance to the child care centre or school, or in a wide hallway, allows parents and visitors to stop to admire children's beautiful productions.

✳The careful arrangement of artwork, the storage of supplies and materials in neat cubicles, and the maintenance of instruments, paper, paste, wood, fabric, and other supplies in clean, neat condition are important priorities. Old supplies such as stubby crayons, frayed brushes, and paint-caked paint pots should be discarded or cleaned carefully. Furniture should be in neutral colours, preferably wooden, sturdy, and easy to clean.✳

Children have a natural, almost insatiable desire to explore and create with basic art materials in a variety of ways. Understanding this need is the key to providing for effective play and learning in the art area.✳The sensory and affective pleasures derived from paint, clay, paper, paste, cardboard, chalk, and crayons do not vanish just because the child uses them every day. The simplicity and responsiveness of the materials facilitate children's continuing abilities to express themselves as they find newer and more effective ways of using them to produce what they want and not what the teacher wants.

Teachers could save themselves a lot of needless work and worry if they would set aside their beliefs that children need cute, new, and different ideas in order to "have fun" in the art area. For children, self-expression through art is a serious business, not a superficial, casual enterprise designed to entertain and keep them occupied for a while. Seldom will children tire of having unrestricted access to basic art materials and supplies that leave them *in charge of planning and executing what they themselves feel, perceive, and imagine in their own minds.* A story of two children at an art table, both busily pasting precut bows on precut bunnies, reinforces this point. One child asks the other, "Why are we doing this?" The other child replies, "I don't know, but my mother sure is going to like it."

✳ Clay

Clay is an underestimated art material that promotes children's self-expression using a plastic medium. It is relaxing and sensuous for children, as it responds to their kneading and moulding. In this way, clay is a truly responsive medium that reacts immediately to children's actions on it.

Teachers sometimes make excuses for not providing clay because of their own intolerance of its messiness, because it demands careful preparation before it can be used by children, and because the cleanup tasks involved are time-consuming. Some children react negatively to getting their hands so "dirty" and having to spend time washing them carefully, sometimes all the way up to their shoulders! Some teachers like to take children on excursions to dig their own clay, but in today's environmentally conscious world there is a need to be very sure that natural clay has been extracted from areas where there is no risk of toxic contamination from agricultural pesticides used in the soil.

Most natural clay is sold in large, semi-moist lumps and has to be prepared using the printed instructions that usually accompany it. There is virtually no substitute for the sensory qualities, transformational potential, and responsiveness of natural clay. Playdough does not have the same creative potential, and plasticene is a very poor second (Clemens, 1991). The inherent stiffness and tendency of plasticene to harden quickly and break apart can frustrate children.

Although children love the texture of playdough and sometimes use it for artistic representation, it is largely a sensory material that also serves as a prop for symbolic play (see Chapter 10, pages 162–63). For creative purposes, neither playdough nor plasticene should be used as a substitute for clay although they may be used in the art area in an introduction to the use of malleable materials.

Like unit blocks, clay grows along with the child whose skills in using it will develop with time and practice. Children use the material first to explore in a sensorimotor fashion: pounding, kneading, and pinching. They may then gain some mastery over the substance by making balls, clay "worms," and coils, followed by two-dimensional figures pounded and laid out flat on the board or table. Later, they may move on to three-dimensional representation with clay.

The responsive qualities of clay surpass those of paints and brushes. The form of the clay responds immediately to the actions of the child's hands, often erasing completely any segment of what was formerly there. In painting, which is also a responsive medium, children make frequent modifications to their work but what is there can never be completely erased. Often, instead of continuing with a work they have started, they will simply discard their first attempt at a painting and start afresh in order to explore some new idea or image in their heads. With clay, children always have the option of returning to the lump of clay with which they began in order to make a new attempt at transforming the lump to their own representation of form or image. In this way, clay is a more flexible medium than paint and encourages children to entertain new ideas sparked by the responsiveness of the medium to their own actions.

Children may work with clay alone or with other children at a table or a clay board. It is helpful to set clay on a cool surface in order to preserve as long as possible its texture and consistency. A ball of clay about grapefruit size is recommended for each child. Children should always wear vinyl or plastic aprons or smocks that are easily wiped clean, and should have access to a deep sink in order to clean their hands and arms independently.

The usefulness of clay as a responsive, creative substance reinforces the importance of process in the artistic endeavours of children. The clay productions of children are much less important than the child's physical, cognitive, and affective involvement in the act of transforming the clay. For this reason, it is not essential for the productions of children to be fired or preserved in any way, certainly not at the stage when children are using clay mostly as a medium for exploration and simple transformation (Clemens, 1991). As children become more skilled in using clay to represent their view of reality in some three-dimensional structure, there may be some value in preserving the product, especially if that will make the child happy. Until that stage is reached, however, the clay with which children have been working should be returned to its airtight container and treated with water to restore and retain its malleable qualities until the next use.

Messy Art and Dry Art Tables

Teachers frequently think in terms of two kinds of artistic endeavours at each of the two tables commonly found in the art area; one table is for the messy art activities, and the other is for the dry art. This arrangement will work providing that the activities planned for each table reflect a developmental approach based on the physical experiences, concepts, thinking styles, and emotional outlets that art activities have a marvellous potential to address. A more educationally sound approach to arranging the art area may be to regard the two art tables as *potential space* that serves children's developmental readiness for specific, expressive materials. It makes sense to allocate one table for messy and the other for dry art when both messy and dry art activities address children's developmental abilities.

Dry art activities may include collage; drawing with markers, crayons, or chalk; and activities in which children use scissors to draw and cut their own patterns and outlines. Messy art activities include pasting, fingerpainting, cornstarch and water play (goop), and papier-mâché creations.

Drawing and Painting

Most children enjoy endless opportunities to express themselves with brushes, paint, and paper at tables and at the easels. The pleasure and opportunities for self-expression afforded by painting make it important that the easels always be available with paint, clean brushes, and fresh paper. Drawing and painting at tables with tools other than brushes adds to the range of graphic experiences available to children. Felt-tipped markers, crayons, straws, chalk, charcoal, and other instruments are interesting for children to explore with papers of different textures and weight.

⚹Drawing with crayons on sandpaper and using felt-tipped markers on blotting paper, coloured chalk on construction paper, and thick paint and paste paddles on cardboard further promote exploration of the sensory and graphic qualities of a range of materials, textures, and consistencies⚹Even natural products such as flowers, leaves, soft rocks, and natural clay can be used as implements to make an imprint on cardboard (McArdle & Barker, 1990).

Children's artwork varies depending on whether it is executed while sitting at a table or standing at an easel. The angle and height of the easel will influence the nature of their work. For this reason, different types of easels in the art area add variety to the type of exploration and production in which children can engage. Conventional double-sided easels allow freedom of movement and privacy for children to execute their own painting without interruption from someone painting beside them. Sometimes the angle of these easels places constraints on the perspective children can gain of their creation. Wall easels are stable and, when placed side by side on a wall, allow for social interaction between children as they paint. Makeshift easels, in which a triangular-shaped tunnel sits on the floor providing surface area for two children to paint opposite one another, allow children a broader perspective on their painting than do conventional easels or those that are built into the wall (Lasky & Mukerji, 1980). (See Figure 18.2.)

Children also enjoy painting on large sheets of paper tacked to a movable frame on the floor or taped directly onto the floor. Painting on paper on the floor facilitates cooperative creative endeavours.

Activities for the Art Area

1. Provide paper, brushes, and paints at the easels every day. Painting is an activity that will always appeal to children and does not need any interference from the teacher. Let the children play and explore the materials, plan and execute their own creations, and decide for themselves when they are ready to stop. Encourage children to remove and hang their own paintings when finished. Instead of preoccupying a teacher with writing names on products, encourage children to print the first letter of their names on the page or paint a small symbol on the bottom of the page to identify it as theirs. Or, post small cards or stickers containing children's names on them in the art area and encourage the children to take a card or sticker with their name on it and clip, staple, or stick it wherever they choose on their artwork. There is no need, however, to be overzealous and identify the production of each child all the time. Keep in mind that it is the process that is most important for the child.

2. Drawing using markers, crayons, and sometimes pastels or chalk on heavy paper at an art table.

Figure 18.2   FOUR TYPES OF EASELS

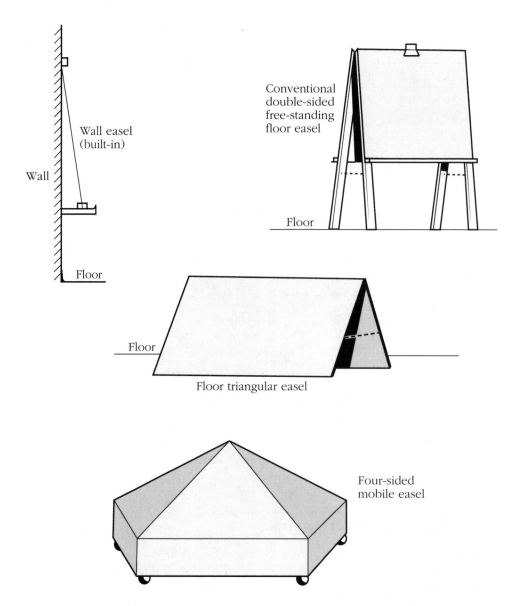

Wall easel
(built-in)

Wall

Floor

Conventional
double-sided
free-standing
floor easel

Floor

Floor

Floor triangular easel

Four-sided
mobile easel

3. Collage using cardboard and stiff novelty papers, paper plates, or construction paper and paste with paste paddles. Let children play and then have them set their own creations on a counter to dry.

4. Clay at the clay board set on an art table or at its own small table if space allows. The clay must be carefully prepared and at the right level of moisture and temperature. Provide smocks for the children and place the clay board or table close to a sink for easy cleanup.

5. Fingerpainting using commercial fingerpaint or homemade fingerpaint made of a cornstarch pudding base for younger children. Place fingerpaint on a tray to contain the paint if that is preferred; otherwise let children play with the fingerpaint right on the table surface, especially if it is melamine, which wipes off easily.

6. For older preschoolers and kindergarten children, provide cardboard, scissors, markers, crayons, and paste, and let children make their own greeting cards for special occasions, or decorations for festival times. A ball of clay or plasticene may be used as a base for a table centre made out of naturally occurring objects such as pine cones, twigs, shells, leaves, and dried flowers. These items can be pressed into the clay or plasticene directly or mounted on pipe cleaners and stuck into the clay or plasticene.

7. Wet chalk drawing and felt pen wash (McArdle & Barker, 1990). Use white paper, coloured chalk, brushes, and a water jar. The child wets the paper using the brush and water, then draws on the paper using the chalk, creating an effect similar to watercolour painting. More water can be added when the paper dries and different coloured chalks can be overlapped to produce new colours. Provide felt-tipped pens and smooth white paper for children to draw on. Then provide brushes and a water jar, which children will use to brush over the drawing, letting the felt-marker drawing smudge and run so that a muted effect is created.

Wood Construction Area

The sensory pleasures of working with wood, combined with the opportunities for emotional expression, creative endeavour, and physical development, make wood a highly satisfying and growth-enhancing medium for young children. The best woods to work with are the soft woods such as pine, cedar, and balsa, which are sufficiently porous for children to be able to hammer nails into them and light enough to hold together when glued. High-quality tools and supplies like wood glue, sandpaper, nails, and screws are needed for wood construction. The woodworking area is also used for box construction, sometimes called cardboard carpentry.

Preschool and kindergarten children are able to use well-made adult tools, as long as they are carefully supervised. Electrically powered tools are inappropriate, but children can be shown how to use lightweight claw hammers with large-head nails, manual drills, back saws, clamps, and a screwdriver. Teachers will have to demonstrate the handling and use of hammers and saws, and watch children carefully at the beginning to ensure that they have mastered the basics. Children should hold hammers about eight centimetres from the end of the hammer and keep their eyes on the top of the tee or nail being hammered. They should be encouraged to tap lightly and slowly at first until the nail has been started, then remove the hand that has been holding the nail steady and tap with greater force. Sometimes teachers may start the nail for them, letting the child take over once it no longer has to be steadied with the hand. Using a wrist movement rather than the whole arm will facilitate greater accuracy and more control over the hammer.

WOODWORKING

A mitre box should be used when sawing to steady the wood board while children saw. Clamps to hold the wood pieces firmly to the workbench may also be used. Children also enjoy using hand drills, to make holes in wood pieces that are soft enough, before hammering in nails or inserting screws.

An interesting introduction to the use of hammers, saws, and drills can be provided in outdoor play by giving children practice hammering and sawing in a large tree stump in the playground. Generally, the fact that they are hammering or sawing

WOODWORKING AREA

into the endgrain will make their first use of hammers and saws easier for children. By the time they have had practice outdoors, they are usually ready for more intricate work at the workbench indoors.

Some teachers introduce valuable junk into the wood construction area to stimulate creativity and promote recycling practices. Frozen orange juice can tops and metal screw tops from jam jars and juice bottles make marvellous wheels for wooden vehicles and are easily hammered. Small scraps of wood, wood shavings, and even strips of bark can also be added to decorate wood creations.

The main reason for setting the workbench, wood, boxes, cardboard, recycled materials, styrofoam, and glue apart from the art area in the Creative Arts Centre is to differentiate wood and cardboard from other art media. The play in this area also involves constructing, fitting, and assembling more than free expression with continuous and surface-diffusable materials such as paint, crayon, chalk, and markers. The wood and box construction area is also dedicated primarily to the creation of three-dimensional productions in contrast to the two-dimensional paintings, collage, and drawings of the art area. Important supplies for this area include a range of sizes of wood pieces, preferably soft wood, chunks and strips of styrofoam, wood scraps, recycled materials, paste and wood glue, and cardboard boxes and pieces. For four-to-six-year-olds, woodworking tools, hammers, nails with large heads, screws, and screwdrivers may be added.

Wood is a marvellous material with its soft texture, beautiful lustre, unique smell, and the interesting sound it makes when knocked or when pieces are ham-

BOX CONSTRUCTION

mered together. The early years are a good time to become acquainted with the many attractions and beauties of wood, and working with it is an appropriate way to introduce children to the value and fragility of our trees and forests. Children who learn to enjoy wood when they are young will relate more readily to the urgency of both protecting our forests and reforesting wood-cutting areas. Woodworking introduces children to an important resource in our society; it is a part of the North American heritage national fabric with which we want children to identify from an early age.

Box Construction

Box construction or cardboard carpentry is, in some programs, an underestimated play and learning activity that not only addresses a multitude of perceptual and physical skills but also promotes spatial reasoning abilities. It is an area of the learning environment in which children can experience first-hand the usefulness of recycling, since discarded packaging, boxes, and cartons are the principal supplies required. Although the workbench with a drawer and shelf for tools and supplies is the centre of the wood and box construction area, space around the workbench and preferably a low counter or another table make useful work surfaces when children are engaging in box construction. When large packing boxes are used, children can just as easily work on the floor. Placing a plastic sheet on the floor to hold the box structure prevents glue from sticking to the floor tiles.

Activities for the Wood Construction Area

(for children ages three to five)

1. Glue pieces and strips of balsa wood and let children make their own creations. (Styrofoam chunks may sometimes be used as long as it is clean styrofoam previously used for packing fragile or bulky items for shipment. Some health authorities are ordering child care program administrators to discontinue the use of styrofoam meat trays because they have been found to harbour residues of meat and other spoilable foods, allowing bacteria to form.)

2. Using mallets or light hammers, golf tees, and chunks of styrofoam, let children practise hammering golf tees into the styrofoam.

3. Make boats to sail in the water table with small pieces of balsa wood, wood-carving tools, string, and fabric pieces.

4. Set up pinewood chunks of two-by-fours and one-inch particle board, along with the hammers and nails, and let children explore the materials and tools by hammering and joining pieces of wood together.

5. Set up pieces of hardwoods such as cherry, oak, walnut (if you can find some), and birch, and let children sand and polish the wood to a rich lustre. A non-toxic paste wax is best. Soft cloths for polishing will also be needed.

6. Set up wooden packing crates and paste and let children make their own three-dimensional creations. Once their products have dried they may want to take them to the art area to paint and decorate them.

7. Set up large packing boxes for children to explore. They may come up with the idea of making a clubhouse out of them and will need heavy scissors, wood glue, and masking tape to cut, fit, join, and fuse the various boxes to make a large structure. If the product is too big to take to the art area to paint, the paint and brushes can be brought to the cardboard structure for children to paint and decorate.

8. Purchase a piece of unpainted furniture made of natural wood like birch or pine, such as a small rocking chair, a table, or some shelves, and let children participate in the sanding of the furniture to a soft lustre. They will feel a great sense of accomplishment in contributing in this way to their own environment.

The Sewing Table/Textile Art Area

A sewing area in the learning environment introduces children to the pleasures of exploring and creating with fabric, a medium with different properties from those of wood, cardboard, paper, and paint. Although sewing activities are a prevalent play activity in other cultures, particularly in European and Chinese early childhood education programs, it does not have as wide an appeal in North America. The remarkable creations of young children in other countries are proof that children in the early years have the developmental capabilities to play successfully with fabric, wool, and thread.

Like wood, fabric has wonderfully soothing and aesthetically appealing qualities that children are able to appreciate when they are introduced to their expressive and functional properties. Fabric decorations, pretty placemats, handsewn wall hangings, homemade curtains, and bright, patterned cushion covers in the learning environment add to the coziness and friendliness of the setting. When children are

SEWING TABLE

able to make these items themselves, they feel pride in the surroundings that they have had a hand in creating.

As with all other expressive materials, children should be introduced to fabric and sewing supplies gradually and with a view to letting them explore their properties and responsiveness in a variety of ways. Children can spend a long time becoming acquainted with sewing materials simply by cutting out squares, matching fabrics of similar patterns and textures, gluing fabric pieces together, testing the strength and opaqueness of fabric, and even painting or dyeing the fabric long before they ever set to work with a needle and thread.

Teachers can introduce children to sewing by setting out beads and laces in the Quiet Thinking Centre or sewing table and by providing needles, thread, and styrofoam pieces or popcorn for them to string. Simple embroidery activities with printed cotton hopsacking, large needles, wool or thread, and an embroidery hoop to hold the fabric firmly in place are an interesting way for children to begin actually sewing with a thread and needle. In Scandinavian countries it is common to see a sewing machine in the learning environment where the teacher can sew during those times when children are occupied with their own sewing projects. Her presence and involvement with this activity provides an interesting model for children to imitate, especially if she is in the process of making something pretty, like new placemats or cushion covers, to brighten up the learning environment.

Activities for the Sewing Table/Textile Art Area

(for younger children, ages two to four)

1. Set up large needles, thread, and styrofoam "popcorn" pieces for children to string to make decorations for a Christmas tree or a winter tree—a branch in the classroom on which to hang wintertime decorations.

2. Practise lacing leather or plastic strips through holes punched in leather pieces to make pouches or folding cases. Leather lacing kits may be used.

3. Cut remnants of pretty fabrics into attractive, brightly coloured, and patterned squares of fabric. Children can then arrange them on large sheets of kraft paper to make a quilt. Once the pieces have been arranged, the sheet of paper can be carried gently to the art area for pasting, or the paste can be brought to the sewing table. Children paste the fabric onto the paper to make the quilt, which can be hung on the wall when finished.

(for older children, ages four to six)

4. Practise sewing large buttons with large double holes using heavy-gauge thread or wool and darning needles onto fabric pieces made of strong fabric like felt, cotton, or canvas.

5. Stamp simple transfers onto natural cotton hopsacking, arrange the transfer on an embroidery hoop, and let older children practise a simple cross-stitch. Their work could then be joined to other pieces to make a placemat, or simply hemmed by the teacher at the sewing machine to make a doily for a table. Children will need help threading needles, learning to make a cross-stitch, and with other tasks; therefore, a teacher should always be present to assist and support.

6. An interesting project for the sewing area is to have children participate in making curtains for the windows. This is a long-term project with several steps. The teacher would need to purchase natural cotton hopsacking in a bolt large enough to create cafe-style curtains, which are the easiest to make. The cotton fabric could be cut into large pieces approximately 70 cm wide and as long as the window. These cloth pieces should be fastened to a piece of tagboard or cardboard about the same size. Children each paint their own picture on the hopsacking using permanent mixed paint, which will not run or fade in the wash. Once the teacher has collected a painting from each child—more than one attempt may be necessary in some cases—the cloth pieces may be stitched together by the teacher at the sewing machine and hemmed. Rod pocket seams will need to be made in the top of the curtain and deep hems in the bottom. Under the tutelage of a teacher who has sewing experience, the effect of home-made curtains in the room covered in children's artwork is very special. The children take immense pride in contributing to the beauty of their own environment and learn what is possible with fabric, paint, and some imagination and know-how.

7. Cut out felt pieces in a variety of colours for the flannelboard. Older preschool children may make paper templates to place on the felt before cutting out felt pieces. Choose simple shapes at first and then graduate to more complicated templates of characters in stories, or familiar animals or popular heroes.

8. Collect long grasses, reeds, straw, strips of paper, and balls of string and yarn, and let children explore the various ways of weaving these materials together to form a wall hanging.

References

Anderson, H.H. (1975). On the meaning of creativity. In *Creativity in Childhood and Adolescence: A Diversity of Approaches,* ed. H.H. Anderson, pp. 46–61. Palo Alto, CA: Science and Behavior Books Inc.

Anderson, S., and Hoot, J.L. (1986). Kids, carpentry and the preschool classroom. *Day Care and Early Education.* Spring 1986: 12–15.

Beaty, J.J., and Tucker, W.H. (1987). *The Computer as a Paintbrush.* Columbus, OH: Merrill.

Cherry, C., Godwin, D., and Staples, J. (1989). *Is the Left Brain Always Right? A Guide to Whole Child Development.* Belmont, CA: Fearon.

Clemens, S.G. (1991). Art in the classroom: making every day special. *Young Children* 46 (1):4–11.

Gardner, H. (1980). *Artful Scribbles: The Significance of Children's Drawings.* New York: Basic Books.

Gardner, H. (1982). *Art, Mind and Brain.* New York: Basic Books.

Gardner, H. (1989). *To Open Minds.* New York: Basic Books.

Goodnow, J. (1977). *Children Drawing.* Cambridge, MA: Harvard University Press.

Kellogg, R. (1967). *The Psychology of Children's Art.* New York: Random House.

Kellogg, R. (1969). *Analyzing Children's Art.* Palo Alto, CA: National Press Books.

Lasky, L., and Mukerji, R. (1980). *Art: Basic for Young Children.* Washington, D.C.: National Association for the Education of Young Children.

Lowenfeld, V., and Brittain, W.L. (1975). *Creative and Mental Growth.* 6th ed. New York: Macmillan.

MacKinnon, D.W. (1971). Nature and nurture of creative talent. In *Educational Psychology: Readings in Learning and Human Abilities,* ed. R. Ripple. New York: Harper & Row.

McArdle, F., and Barker, B. (1990). *What'll I Do For Art Today?* Melbourne, Australia: Thomas Nelson Australia.

Rubenzer, R.L. (1984). Educating the other half: implications of left/right brain research. ERIC Document, ED150655.

Schirrmacher, R. (1988). *Art and Creative Development for Young Children.* Albany, NY: Delmar.

C H A P T E R 19

THE UNIT BLOCKS
CENTRE

■ IMPORTANCE OF BLOCKS AS A PLAY AND LEARNING MATERIAL

Blocks are one of the most important play and learning materials for children. They have remained a classic fixture in early learning environments from the kindergarten of Froebel on because they provide rich opportunities for play that addresses all developmental domains. Blocks respond and take shape according to children's actions on them. As the blocks respond, they, in turn, elicit from the child further action on the blocks. All types of blocks are highly responsive and dynamic play and learning materials. Unit blocks have special advantages in that they are mathematically precise, large enough to create clear representations, impressive in size and proportion, and handsome to look at.

Blocks grow with the child throughout the toddler, preschool, and middle-childhood stages. They respond to children's sensorimotor play during the sensorimotor period when children delight in their sound, texture, and stacking properties. During the preoperational period, children make enclosures and patterns, and decorate their creations before they build complex structures that represent recognizable structures in the real world.

Blocks can be manipulated in two- and three-dimensional configurations. As a three-dimensional artistic medium, unit blocks play an important role in creative development along with clay, other plastic media, paint, and wood (Gardner, 1980). Block constructions appear to fit the general criteria that apply to creative productions: that is, the production is conceived as a work of art, created by the child for an audience such as the child, his peers, and teachers, and represents an idea that originates with the child (Gelfer, 1990). Creative materials are by definition open-ended, divergent, abstract in design, free-form, and responsive to children's actions on them.

■ TYPES OF BLOCKS

Blocks come in several forms, sizes, and configurations of sets. There are the wooden hollow blocks found in the Active Role Play Centre, tabletop building blocks, which are easy to hold in little hands in the Quiet Thinking Centre, and unit blocks, which constitute a learning centre of their own. There are also interlocking tabletop blocks such as Lego and snap-and-play blocks. For infants, there are foam rubber building blocks and plastic blocks for toddlers. Brick-patterned blocks made of heavy cardboard are often used as props for active role play. Although the play potential of all kinds of blocks is significant, unit blocks are the most responsive and creative of block materials.

■ UNIT BLOCKS

Caroline Pratt invented unit blocks in 1914. They were first used in Harriet Johnson's nursery school in New York and became an established component of the kindergarten at Teachers College, Columbia University in the 1920s under the leadership of Patty Smith Hill (Weber, 1984).

Unit blocks are precise materials, deliberately crafted to promote specific kinds of play and learning, and extend children's symbolic and representational thinking abilities. Abstract in form, well-proportioned, smooth to the touch, and compact to hold, unit blocks are the perfect three-dimensional medium for children's experimentation in the creation of modular structures to represent what they know and understand about their world.

Characteristics of Unit Blocks

Unit blocks have beauty, precision, texture, weight, and sound—physical characteristics that make them endlessly interesting objects of children's sensorimotor exploration. The fact that most unit blocks are made of hardwood, usually birch or alder, adds another dimension of appeal to their natural lustre, smell, texture, and warmth. Beautifully crafted unit blocks that are well maintained and treated with respect add to the overall aesthetic quality of the learning environment in which they should assume a prominent place.

Unit blocks come in sets of approximately 750 blocks or may be purchased in half-sets or individually. Toddlers do well with half a set or a full set, whereas preschoolers and kindergarten children have access to infinitely greater play and learning possibilities with two full sets of blocks. Sets contain blocks of different shapes, which are designed for special interlocking purposes. Some units are multiples of the basic unit and square. A basic unit measures 14 cm by 7 cm by 3.5 cm; each multiple increases in size along the length dimension only to the maximum size, which is a quadruple unit, of 55.5 cm long. Other blocks in a set include pillars (14 cm by 3.5 cm or 7 cm), cylinders (14 cm by 3.5 cm or 7 cm), curves (3.5 cm or 7 cm by 23 cm), arches (3.5 cm by 7 cm by 28 cm), and hardwood planks. They are constructed of solid blocks of hardwood finely sanded and polished.

Figure 19.1   UNIT BLOCKS

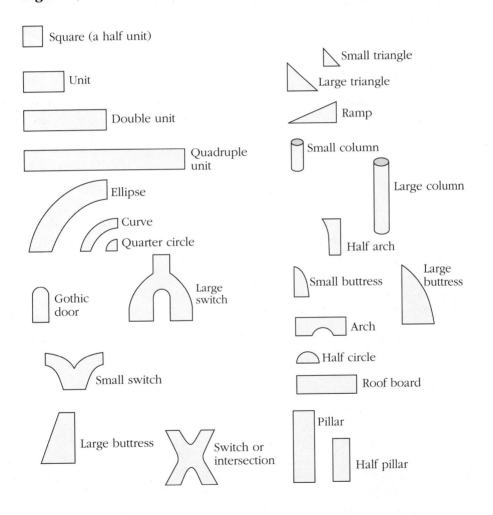

■ UNIT BLOCKS AND CHILD DEVELOPMENT

The usefulness of unit blocks is frequently underestimated. They are far too valuable as developmentally appropriate play materials to be stored out of children's reach. Teachers may be inclined to keep children from playing with unit blocks because they fear the mess that will have to be tidied up. But treating unit blocks as materials to be used only on special occasions reveals a lack of understanding of the developmental potential of these materials to further children's thinking and creative abilities. Unit blocks address developmental objectives in the cognitive, physical, social, and emotional domains and should normally be available for play at all times.

Developmental Stages in Block Play

Hirsch (1984) has described the stages that children pass through in their block play (see Figure 19.2).

Handling Blocks

Toddlers enjoy carrying blocks around and handling them, sliding them together, and sometimes biting them. At this sensorimotor stage in block play, children are simply discovering the properties of blocks without really using them for a purpose. Practice play may occur as a child knocks two blocks together or slides one along the floor repeatedly, but productive play has not yet appeared. For toddlers, one set of unit blocks alone is sufficient for children to explore the materials in a sensorimotor way, stacking them, making towers, and eventually bridging the towers, rubbing and knocking them against one another, sliding them, and examining them from many perspectives. During the first three years, unit blocks are largely sensorimotor play materials that also promote the toddler's motor and manipulative abilities.

Manipulating Blocks

Toddlers begin to place blocks beside one another in a purposeful way before they stack three or four blocks one on top of the other (Reifel, 1984). They may also fill a container with small blocks and try to lift the container. Eventually, toddlers make a small tower by stacking blocks, and they arrange the blocks in rows. More rows and piles of blocks appear about age three. Shortly thereafter, children learn to place blocks in compact, interlocking squares to make surfaces.

Figure 19.2   DEVELOPMENTAL PROGRESSION OF PLAY
WITH UNIT BLOCKS

Making surfaces with interlocking blocks

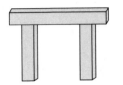

Bridging

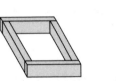

Enclosures

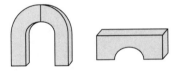

Arches

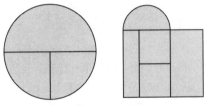

Patterns

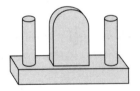

Simple decoration

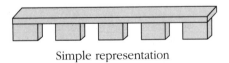

Simple representation

Bridging

The ability to bridge two blocks placed vertically with one placed horizontally signals a significant cognitive step in the child's thinking ability, as the task requires the ability to plan, predict, estimate, and use trial and error (Hirsch, 1984). The ability to place the vertical blocks at a necessary distance from one another—one that enables a third block to bridge the space between them—is an important achievement and deserves recognition.

ENCLOSURES

Enclosures

In their simplest form, enclosures are four blocks placed so that they touch and form an enclosed space. Sometimes children will use arches at this stage as if to designate an enclosure with an entry point.

Patterns

Eventually children begin to connect enclosures, and some elaborate patterns of squares, rectangles, triangles, and pentagons emerge as more and more blocks are used. Often as early as three years of age, children begin to use blocks as symbols, and to attach meanings such as "this is my house" to their block structures. Blockbuilding still remains largely horizontal, with most blocks spread out along the floor in an ever-expanding array of connecting shapes.

Decoration

At this stage, children may make use of the accessories and the more specialized unit blocks such as cylinders, pillars, arches, ramps, gothic doors, switches, buttresses, curves, and quarter circles to decorate their horizontal structures. At this point, structures appear to gain added symmetry and take on realistic configurations even though children are generally not naming them yet.

Representation

Once children begin to name their structures, their blockbuilding generally becomes more vertical and three-dimensional. The structures may assume more life-like forms. A child may call his structure a "condominium" or a "galleria," and practise using new words in the process of representing something she has remembered. Children are generally about five years of age before their structures begin to symbolize real-world structures.

REPRESENTATION WITH UNIT BLOCKS

As play with unit blocks progresses, children revert to previous stages, repeat already-learned skills such as stacking, bridging, enclosing, patterning, and decorating, and elaborate on some of the basic configurations. Children are usually between five and seven years old before they are able to relate the interior space of an enclosure (or room) to its contents; that is, to place blocks representing furniture inside a room and differentiate each piece. Even later, at about the age of seven, children begin to coordinate external features of the structure, such as driveways, garages, streets, and trees, with the structure itself (Reifel, 1984). At some point in the course of mature creative construction play, children will also make use of their block structures as props to elaborate and extend sociodramatic play.

■ FACILITATING PLAY WITH UNIT BLOCKS

Play with unit blocks is largely child-initiated and self-directed. The teachers' principal role is to ensure that the environment maximizes children's uninterrupted play with the blocks and accessories that are available and may be introduced at appropriate times. Teachers supervise the Unit Block Centre to support, encourage, and express interest. They expand children's planning and problem solving by asking questions at the right time and making a suggestion when things seem to be at a standstill for one of the children.

Children should be expected to make progress in their block play. When teachers observe repetitive, practice play, time after time, it is usually a signal that children need help and encouragement to move to the next step with the materials. Hanging attractive posters of block structures, taking photographs of children's block constructions, and tacking them on the bulletin board in the area helps motivate children towards new heights in their block play. It also helps instil a sense of achievement and appreciation of their own creative endeavours. As with clay, the productions are less important than the process involved. There are times, especially for older preschoolers and kindergarten children, when it is important to capture some of their more elaborate structures on film (Clemens, 1991).

Teachers often wonder how to stimulate interest in block play among children who do not readily choose to play in that area. Reading a story about a building or looking at a picture book or photographs from the picture file will sometimes be enough to create the spark of an idea in a child who has had sensorimotor experience with blocks and is beginning to understand their creative potential. No matter how teachers try, some children seem reticent about playing with blocks. It may be useful for teachers to intervene by asking the "regulars" to play somewhere else for a while so that the more reluctant or timid children can have an opportunity to experiment with the marvellous play and learning opportunities afforded by unit blocks.

Children should be encouraged to take from the shelves only the blocks with which they intend to play, and to build slightly away from the shelves so as not to obstruct other children from the shelves as they reach for stored blocks. Protocol for block play should be clarified by the teacher and restated as often as necessary in order to promote care and respect for these materials and for the play of others. Hoarding blocks, knocking down structures, dropping or throwing blocks, banging them together, stepping or sitting on blocks unnecessarily, and touching another child's building structure should be actively discouraged (Cartwright, 1988).

Children generally become so absorbed in their block play that giving a warning about ten minutes before children need to begin the tidy-up process respects children's need to complete their structures to their satisfaction and to disengage themselves gradually from what may have been an intense play experience.

■ USING UNIT BLOCKS WITH OTHER PLAY MATERIALS

The use of unit blocks with other play materials is often debated in early childhood education. There are several schools of thought on the issue. Keeping in mind the design and purpose as conceived by Caroline Pratt, and the unique symbolic quality of unit blocks, some discussion of their use with other play materials may be helpful.

Relatively abstract wooden accessories are compatible with the purity and proportion of the unit block sets and enhance the symbolic and representational nature of children's play with the blocks. When miniature replicas of vehicles, animals, and cultural artifacts like airports, garages, and fire stations are added to unit blocks, they tend to serve as props that introduce role play into the Unit Block Centre. Once children have had ample opportunity to explore the uniquely symbolic and creative properties of the unit blocks alone and have mastered the ability to construct intricate representations using them, they may want to use their structure as a prop to stimulate and enhance role play. At that point in their play, children may request or seek out for themselves the more lifelike artifacts and add them to their structure. It is important to avoid being too quick to suggest or introduce cars, trucks, and artifact toys that tend to distract children from important types of play and exploration with unit blocks alone.

Teachers often have to make a choice about what kind of play is more important than other kinds in the Unit Block Centre. Play with unit blocks may involve highly imaginative symbolic play, as these abstract materials take on whatever characteristics or functions children assign them in their own minds. Unit blocks may also be used with toys and realistic props imported by children from other learning centres for sociodramatic play purposes. When children have reached the stage of representation using unit blocks, they are ready to use their unit block structures as props to stimulate dramatic and sociodramatic play.

Some clear limits have to be established regarding the use of other play materials with unit blocks. Creative arts supplies such as paste, paint, markers, crayons, and other surface-diffusable materials should not be permitted in the Unit Blocks Centre where they may disfigure the blocks. Cardboard, scarves, blankets, or crêpe paper may be brought to the centre and used by the children when they want to decorate their unit block structures.

Teachers who wish to preserve the abstractness of the play materials and to maintain the challenge to children's symbolic thinking should not encourage them to add Tonka trucks, matchbox cars, Fisher-Price people, or other miniatures. The stark realism of miniature domestic and farm animals, vehicles, and doll houses, for example, alters the quality of play with the abstract forms of the unit blocks and their crude wooden accessories. When children build a structure with unit blocks and label it an airport, and then import the Fisher-Price airplane and helicopter and a range of Matchbox cars to put in the parking lot, play loses much of its symbolic and abstract qualities. Teachers should refrain from prematurely setting up props borrowed from other learning centres such as metal trucks and cars, plastic animals, circus artifacts, or steam shovels and tractor-trailers that will also change the symbolic nature of play with the unit blocks. If children themselves decide that they want to import figures, props, cars, or trucks into the Unit Block Centre, however, they should be permitted to do so.

■ EXPLORING THE MATHEMATICAL RELATIONSHIPS OF UNIT BLOCKS

Unit blocks are mathematically precise in that the basic blocks are multiples or fractions of basic units. Teachers may encourage children to note the half/whole and quarter/half/whole relationships of units and half units, and half circles and quarter circles. Children will learn through experimentation that it takes two half units to make a whole unit and that four unit blocks equal the length of a quadruple unit. These mathematical relationships may be reinforced by encouraging children to stack blocks on shelves that have painted outlines designating which blocks are to be placed in that spot. This practice draws attention to the size relationships children readily see when they try to place a half unit inside a painted outline for a unit and find that the dimensions are not the same.

■ LOCATING THE UNIT BLOCKS CENTRE

It is difficult to assign unit blocks to a specific location relative to other learning centres because they are compatible with most of the other centres in the learning environment, depending on the developmental levels of the children in the program. When they are located in the Creative Discovery Zone, they complement the creative, expressive, and manipulative objectives addressed there. When they are within easy reach of the Daily Living Centre, they may be used as props for children's dramatic and sociodramatic play. Some teachers like to locate them close to, but not in, the Active Role Play Centre to promote transfer of learning from the larger and more primitive hollow blocks. An argument may be made for placing unit blocks close to the Science Discovery Centre to further children's exploration of mathematical relationships and concepts. In this context, unit blocks provide another medium for comparing, ordering, estimating, and predicting, as well as performing simple arithmetical operations like adding and subtracting, and developing a basic understanding of fractions. Similar arguments are sometimes made for putting unit blocks near the tabletop activities, which also address number concept, ordering, and measurement.

Given the flexibility of unit blocks as a divergent play material, some teachers store them on wheeled units so that they may easily be moved anywhere in the classroom where they might enhance play. As unit blocks are creative materials that promote symbolic thinking, representation, planning, problem solving, and creative thinking, they are best located close to the creative, discovery-oriented learning centres. The particular rationale used for locating the Unit Blocks Centre is less important than the assignment of an adequate amount of sheltered space and a location that does justice to their exceptional value as a play and learning medium for children from toddlerhood through middle childhood.

■ TIDYING UP THE UNIT BLOCKS CENTRE

At the end of playtime, teachers should help by modelling appropriate tidy-up behaviours and should encourage the children's efforts. Learning shapes, classification skills, task orientation, ordering, making comparisons (such as same/different, larger/smaller), and manipulative abilities are among the many developmental skills involved in the tidy-up process, which is, in itself, a valuable learning activity. The completion of the tidy-up process contributes to children's satisfaction with the total play experience and teaches them that to finish well is as important as starting well. Children who want to keep their structure standing in order to resume play with it later should be allowed to do so when space permits. This practice encourages children to return to their play after an interruption and confirms the value of their play, including the planning and effort that goes into it.

Storage

Unit blocks require considerable storage space. Shelf units must be approximately 1.3 m wide by 1 m high by 30 cm deep (see Figure 19.3). Dividing the shelves into compartments encourages children to stack blocks neatly in the spaces allotted for each type of block, which is designated by a shape painted on the shelf corresponding to each shape of unit block. Unit blocks should be arranged so that the same sizes are together with the long side in view; they should never be stored in tubs or boxes. Unit blocks should be placed in sheltered space, along with appropriately proportioned wooden accessories. Unit blocks are so important as a responsive play material that they should always be available for children's play in a learning centre of their own.

Figure 19.3   A UNIT BLOCKS STORAGE UNIT

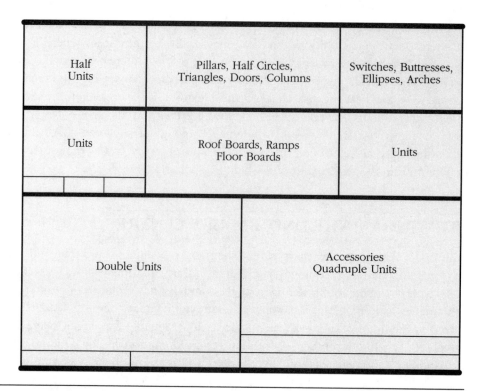

Half Units	Pillars, Half Circles, Triangles, Doors, Columns	Switches, Buttresses, Ellipses, Arches
Units	Roof Boards, Ramps Floor Boards	Units
Double Units	Accessories Quadruple Units	

■ ORGANIZATION AND DESIGN OF THE UNIT BLOCKS CENTRE

The Unit Blocks Centre should consist of a space large enough to accommodate at least four children playing cooperatively, associatively, or in a solitary manner (see Figure 19.4). Cartwright (1988) recommends a minimum of 3 m by 3.5 m for up to eight children. The learning centre should have expandable sides to allow the teacher the freedom to enlarge the area so that when there are more children than usual, they can still play cooperatively. The Unit Blocks Centre should be bounded on three sides to encourage, over time, the child's vertical building with blocks and to define the unit block play area more clearly. It is important to avoid any spillover of unit blocks into pathways or the play spaces of other learning centres. They should be well away from high traffic areas and near neat, clean, relatively quiet activities. They should also be in an area of the learning environment where children will be able to avoid other distractions to concentrate on their play.

The area should be carpeted with unpatterned, smooth, taut, densely woven carpet with a foam underpad. Dividers or storage units surrounding the block play area should be low enough for teachers to observe block play easily.

Figure 19.4   THE UNIT BLOCKS CENTRE

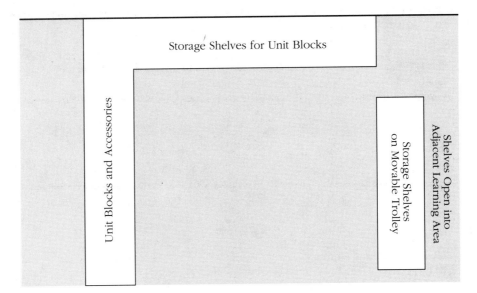

Social contexts of play emphasized in the Unit Blocks Centre

solitary
parallel
associative
cooperative

Categories of play emphasized in the Unit Blocks Centre

functional: practice play
               productive play
creative-constructive play
symbolic: dramatic play
               sociodramatic play

Equipment and Materials

Equipment—shelves for unit blocks; shelves for accessories, trucks, and train set.

Materials—two sets of unit blocks, a wooden train set, and unit block wooden accessories such as cars, trucks, airplanes, animal sets, transportation signs, small trees, and small road signs.

RATINGS OF THE CHARACTERISTICS OF PLAY

The Unit Blocks Centre

noisy	_____	quiet
teacher-centred	_____	child-centred
structured	_____	open
concrete	_____	abstract
clean	_____	
specific-purpose		
materials	_____	open-ended materials
group	_____	individual

(Adapted with permission of the Board of Education, City of Hamilton. *Getting It All Together* (1981).)

References

Cartwright, S. (1988). Play can be the building blocks of learning. *Young Children* 43 (4):44–47.

Clemens, S.G. (1991). Art in the classroom: making every day special. *Young Children* 46 (1):4–11.

Gardner, H. (1980). *Artful Scribbles: The Significance of Children's Drawings.* New York: Basic Books.

Gelfer, J. (1990). Discovering and learning art with blocks. *Day Care and Early Education* Summer: 21–24..

Hirsch, E. (1984). *The Block Book.* Washington, D.C.: National Association for the Education of Young Children.

Reifel, S. (1984). Block construction: children's developmental landmarks in representation of space. *Young Children* 42 (42): 61–67.

Weber, E. (1984). *Ideas Influencing Early Childhood Education: A Theoretical Analysis.* New York: Teachers College Press, Columbia University.

SECTION 7

OUTDOOR PLAY AND LEARNING ENVIRONMENTS

The 1990s have brought renewed interest in playgrounds. For most of this century, the importance attached to the playground as part of the play and learning environment has ebbed and flowed, depending upon the philosophical and practical trends of the time. Teachers should acquire a greater understanding of the potential of outdoor space to promote children's development and learning in all domains. They also need to know the central principles of design and safety which, when taken into account in the planning, increase the usefulness of playgrounds for play and learning.

Section 7 addresses the following topics:

- historical evolution of playgrounds and playground design
- safety concerns in playgrounds
- importance of natural features in playgrounds attached to child care centres and schools
- site design principles
- locating playgrounds for optimal play and learning potential
- playground equipment
- role of the teacher in playgrounds
- playground zones
- play areas in playgrounds
- winter and summer play
- gardening with children

PLAYGROUNDS FOR LEARNING

■ HISTORICAL BACKGROUND

The evolution of the playground in North America has been marked by brief periods of progress and creativity that have frequently been replaced by pressing concerns about the establishment of a network of child care services. North America has been fortunate to have experts and advocates whose philosophical approach and knowledge of children have guided the development of progressive, child-centred playgrounds. Polly Hill added new dimensions to our thinking about playgrounds for children during the 1960s and 1970s. Many of her ideas are now being used and elaborated upon in the design and use of natural features in playgrounds to enhance children's development in all domains.

Esbensen (1987) has traced the evolution of formal playgrounds from the end of the nineteenth century to the present. Public playgrounds and some that were attached to schools began to appear in the late 1800s. During the early 1900s, many municipal jurisdictions were required to provide public playgrounds. The early ones were places with sandboxes, a swing, a slide, and a climbing frame. The "back to nature" focus of the adventure playground in Europe during the 1930s appeared in a few North American playgrounds well into the 1950s and 1960s. The "build your own" thrust of the workyards of the 1960s was followed by the creative playground of the 1970s, and the outdoor classroom concept of the 1970s to the 1980s. The current interest in creating playgrounds that bring children closer to nature to enhance their spiritual, aesthetic, creative, and intellectual development is further evidence of the many cyclical trends that emerge and re-emerge in playground design and early childhood education.

Playground design has evolved from play theory, child development theory, and a more recent preoccupation with physical fitness. The Froebelian kindergarten in nineteenth-century Germany was dedicated to the principle that physical well-being is integral to children's overall growth, health, and psychological development. Froebel's playgrounds were places to foster a sense of wonder about and reverence for nature, and to reach the child's innermost emotions. Early educators believed that outdoor play would vent anxiety, promote self-expression, and provide emotional outlets for children in ways that could not be matched by indoor play.

For much of the past two decades the emphasis on indoor environments and cognitively oriented programs in early childhood education has reduced the role of playgrounds to a place where children can run, be active, and let off steam. Until recently, very little serious attention has been paid to the educational and spiritual importance of the playground as a vital component of the early play and learning environment.

In the 1990s we are witnessing a new trend in playground design that addresses children's need to have close contact with nature, feel a sense of harmony with the natural world, and develop a respect for the environment. Teachers plan activities for outdoor play, but there are many variables outdoors that wise teachers will not attempt to control beyond ensuring children's safety and comfort. Outdoor play, with its opportunities for freedom, exploration, and spontaneity, ultimately affects the quality of children's lives.

■ PLAYGROUND PHILOSOPHY FOR THE 1990S

Many children today live in urban communities, often in condominiums and apartment buildings, and have little access to natural settings. Hazards of many kinds abound in public playgrounds, so children must be well supervised by parents or other designated adults. Very few children run out the back door of their home in the morning to a backyard to play until they are hungry and tired.

Children often live highly regulated childhoods and have limited contact with nature. At the same time, our society wants children to understand and value the environment and to develop conservationist attitudes and habits. Respect for the environment evolves from having experiences in natural surroundings. The notion behind the recent "hug a tree" campaign expresses the intuitive understanding most of us have that in order to really value the environment we must learn to love familiar, natural phenomena. Highly pressured urban living is creating an urgent need to bring children into regular, unstructured contact with the elements of nature, primarily for the enjoyment of children but also as a way to nurture their respect for the environment.

The careful design and location of playground space attached to child care centres and schools could go a long way towards facilitating children's experience of and respect for the natural environment. Playground designers have begun to address this new reality and are creating natural settings and "magical playscapes" that foster hope, wonder, relaxation and a sense of security in children (Talbot & Frost, 1989).

■ OUTDOOR PLAY AND CHILD DEVELOPMENT

The developmental potential of outdoor play is as rich as play indoors. Developmental program planning that addresses physical, social, emotional, and cognitive goals is as important for the outdoor play environment as it is for the indoor classroom. The organization of the playground into play zones is a challenge teachers should address in order to maximize the learning potential of outdoor play equipment, natural areas, open and private spaces, a variety of playground surfaces, and the inevitable delights and richness of the passing seasons and our changing climatic conditions.

Physical Development

Outdoor play has traditionally been thought of as a time for children to develop gross-motor skillls, let off excess energy, build muscles and endurance, and gain control over the various movements of their bodies. Changes in their bodily appearance as they grow and in their competence as they master new physical skills are concrete and observable to children. The progress they make in running faster than before and climbing to the top of the structure today that they were fearful of trying yesterday provides evidence to children of their growth in strength, courage, and competence. The more self-confident children are about their bodies, the easier it is for them to interact with others. They meet the challenges of group play and team endeavours with a stronger sense of having valuable contributions to make and with less reliance on teachers.

Emotional Development

Children's physical growth and increasing competence in using their bodies produce corresponding gains in children's self-esteem and self-concept. Their self-esteem and self-concept do not depend on direct praise, tangible rewards, and coercion (Hitz & Driscoll, 1988). These affective abilities depend largely on children's observations of their own physical competence as well as on feedback they receive from others about their physical attributes and strengths. Important affective characteristics such as emotional control, self-confidence, and self-esteem are acquired by children as a result of their successful experiences in the environment. Praise by teachers cannot replace the child's own experiences of competence. The playground has an instrumental role to play in providing opportunities for children to feel physically competent and proud of their achievements.

Social Development

The quality of children's physical experiences outdoors, as well as those gained in physical programs indoors, will have considerable impact on children's motivation to be active group participants in physical games, exercises, and sports throughout their growing years. In addition to ensuring that the playground provides for spontaneous exploratory play, physical experiences in groups and social play opportunities should be thoughtfully planned and set up or led by teachers and not left entirely to chance. Outdoor play provides more opportunities for large-group activity than indoor play because of the greater space available. The challenge of group projects such as building forts, canals, and making and tending gardens ensures that children will be encouraged to cooperate, rely on one another, function as team members, and communicate.

Spiritual Development

Children's spiritual development is enhanced through outdoor play that brings them into contact with nature. Outdoors, a child's mind may wander more and follow the motivation of the senses to explore and experiment. Sticks, branches, rocks, mud, water, and sand are dependable as well as full of sensuous surprises. Children need to touch the earth just as adults do. Pavement and modern play equipment alone will not address the emotional and spiritual needs of the child to feel close to nature and to be reassured by its beauty, stability, and endless adaptability.

Cognitive Development

Play that is cognitively challenging for children can often be repeated or extended in the outdoor environment. Creative teachers will adapt favourite indoor activities that address perceptual, memory, and logico-mathematical objectives to outdoor play. Many traditional outdoor activities such as obstacle courses, construction projects, and games that challenge the senses and perceptual processes have cognitive as well as physical objectives. I spy, follow the leader, hopscotch, and strategy games such as cooperative parachute activities present many cognitive challenges to children. The variety of problems to be solved outdoors stretches as far as the imagination can reach.

Any teacher who observes children cooperating in the building of a fort with fallen leaves, estimating or measuring the distance between the ball and a hoop, and figuring out how to get from here to there without going through the mud will attest to the variety of divergent thinking skills that are challenged by the endless variations of the natural world. The less structured and rule-bound the playground, the greater the opportunities for exploration, discovery, creative problem solving, and self-expression. All of these are essential prerequisites to healthy cognitive growth.

Language Development

Language often flows more fluently when the child is in the process of performing a physical activity. In the freer environment of the outdoors, children who seldom speak indoors may lose their inhibitions and become quite verbal. Even less verbal children often engage in rich, fluent monologues while attempting to unravel obstacles encountered, for example, when making a tent or filling a stream in the sandbox with water to sail small boats. The freedom, space, and sensory ambience of the outdoors is sufficient to trigger language that is often harnessed by structure and closer living quarters indoors.

■ SAFE OUTDOOR PLAY

Freedom, opportunities to interact with nature in the playground, and opportunities for spontaneous exploration imply preservation of the natural features of the playground and play equipment that is safe and secure. Teachers can trust children to play safely and without constant vigilance when playgrounds are safe. Although they must be present at all times, knowledge that the playground is free of hazards permits teachers to be facilitators of play and learning for children in small groups rather than like sentinels guarding a fortress, fearful of letting down their guard for a moment.

Children also appreciate the feeling of being trusted to play spontaneously, to invent their own play with naturally occurring things outdoors, and to explore without stifling constraints. They feel closer to nature and are able to enjoy its infinite variety and spontaneity. Private spaces outdoors for quiet contemplation and individual exploration allow some seclusion from the bustle of the more active play areas.

A TRACTOR COMES TO THE PLAYGROUND

■ SAFE PLAYGROUND EQUIPMENT

The first North American standards for playground apparatus were developed in the United States in 1928 by the National Recreation Association. Although inadequate, they established a precedent for promoting greater attention to safety concerns in playgrounds. The Canadian Institute of Child Health attracted interest in the need for improved playground standards with their booklet *When Child's Play is Adult Business* (1985). This booklet identifies five major kinds of accidents: falls from heights; shear, pinch, and crush injuries; entanglement; entrapment; and abrasions and burns. In June 1990 the Canadian Standards Association published *A Guideline on Children's Playspaces and Equipment*, which represents the first major attempt in Canada to regulate playground equipment.

According to Esbensen (1984), the greatest hazards to children's safety in playgrounds involve the quality of the equipment, its location in the playground, and the condition of the surfaces in each area. Major problems include the absence of clear boundaries for equipment such as swings and teeter-totters, insufficient protection against falls provided by railings on high equipment like slides and climbing structures, broken pieces or protruding nails, screws or splinters, and small openings just large enough to let a small head or leg through but not out again. Surface areas around high equipment that have lost or have never had sufficient absorptive qualities are often cited as causes of serious injuries in falls.

INSPECT PLAYGROUND FOR HIDDEN HAZARDS

Slides should be checked for sturdy handrails up the ladder and on the landing. The exit ramp on the slide should be gently curved, flattened, and even slightly raised at the end to permit a child to exit easily from a sitting position. A soft landing at the end of the slide cushions a fall or jump off the slide and ensures that the child can walk away quickly before the next child comes down the slide. Tall climbing structures require railings to prevent falls. Apparatus should be checked for openings and fittings that were not engineered with children's body shapes and sizes in mind. It is important to ensure that limbs or heads are not likely to be stuck or clothing caught on awkward protrusions or loose nails. Swings should be separate from other large muscle equipment, and protective barriers should be installed or limits clearly established to prevent children from walking too close to the swing when it is in motion.

■ PLAYGROUND SURFACES

Canada Mortgage and Housing Corporation (1979) recommends that soft surfacing be used in playgrounds. It should be varied in composition and texture to provide clear boundaries between play zones and to add sensory stimulation. The varieties chosen should suit the kind of play anticipated in each zone. Hard surfaces should be reserved for areas at entranceways, adult seating areas, tricycle paths, and under awnings or shelters where children may play out of the rain.

Sand is still regarded as the best organic impact-absorbing surface material to use under play equipment or in any area where children may fall from some height. Sand surfaces should be replenished frequently and raked daily. Most municipalities in Canada require a minimum of 30 cm of sand under climbing structures and swings. Other loose-particled impact surfaces are hazardous because they harbour vermin, other insects, or dust. These hazards pose a serious threat to children with allergies in particular. Some surfaces may scratch or cut, become slippery when wet or too hot under intense sunlight, or freeze into hard, sharp chunks in extreme cold. Very young children frequently put small particles such as pebbles into their mouths and swallow them (Walsh, 1988). Most playground experts recommend that playground surface materials be tested to determine their impact-absorbing qualities before they are used in a playground.

Many kinds of hard surfaces are easily maintained, attractive to the eye, and outline play areas effectively. Patio stones, pavement, concrete slabs, interlocking brick, and inlaid stone slabs with smooth surfaces are widely available and add texture and beauty to the environment. In regions where ground frost is severe, interlocking bricks and patio stones often heave, leaving dangerous protrusions in the hard surface areas, even when care has been taken to lay them on a smooth uniform surface. These surfaces often have to be relaid in the spring to remove bumps and angles that are dangerous and also cause poor drainage. Asphalt is somewhat flexible and elastic: it makes some adjustment to ground frost and returns to a smooth surface in the spring.

Playground surfaces should be monitored daily for dangerous protrusions of stones, pieces of wood, foreign objects like spikes or other building materials, animal contamination, and poor drainage. When playground equipment and surrounding play areas are well inspected for safety, teachers can take a more leisurely approach to supervision in the playground.

■ THE ROLE OF THE TEACHER

The best playgrounds are those that do not require teachers to stand and survey the play areas at all times. Teachers are not able to supervise all play activities even with the best intentions. Safe playground design implies that distinct play zones will be created, play structures securely installed, and sufficient equipment and materials provided to maintain children's interest and ensure their safety without constant vigilance by teachers. Once the daily inspection of the playground for hazardous spots, contamination, or dangerous protrusions has been completed, outdoor play should be relaxed and pleasurable for children and teachers alike. The most important role of the teacher is to facilitate children's play, respond to individual needs, and work with children on specific projects and activities.

The assignment of teachers to specific play zones is as important outdoors as it is in the indoor learning environment. That way, teachers are able to focus their attention on children's play and the activities in a circumscribed area rather than trying to supervise the whole playground or classroom. Activities begun indoors such as water play may also continue outdoors. Seed planting in pots in the Science Discovery Centre continues outdoors with the planting of a garden. Teachers need to be actively involved with children for these kinds of activities. Therefore, they require freedom from the responsibility of supervising the whole playground in order to focus on an activity with one group of children. When there is insufficient staff to safely cover the entire playground, some zones should be closed rather than trying to spread teacher resources too thinly.

Occasionally, teachers become tired and need to sit down. Sitting down does not imply "lying down on the job" or neglect of one's responsibilities. In a professional environment, attractive benches, a picnic table, and lawn chairs permit teachers to rest or engage a group of children in conversation and quiet play. The design of the outdoor learning environment should motivate both children and teachers to realize and enjoy the potential of the outdoor world.

Adult Facilities

Outdoor play periods should offer time for teachers as well as children to enjoy fresh air, greater freedom of movement, and a different pace. Benches at strategic locations allow teachers to sit and still have a clear perspective of the playground. A spot sheltered from the wind permits teachers to conduct an active group activity even on very cold days. Picnic tables provide a working surface for teachers as well as a spot for quiet table activities for children. Comfortable adult facilities raise morale, contribute to teacher effectiveness outdoors, and help make the playground an extension of the indoor classroom. The more appealing the outdoor space for teachers, the more time they and the children will spend outdoors (Esbensen, 1991).

■ SITE DESIGN PRINCIPLES

Under conditions imposed by the hazards and lifestyles of our society, playground design should seek to ensure that playground environments do not encroach on the child's natural tendency to play freely. When children are restricted to going outdoors to play only when supervised and in areas that are fenced to keep children in and intruders out, the quality of their play changes. The challenge for playground designers and early childhood educators is to provide easily accessible outdoor play space that respects children's needs for close interaction with naturally occurring phenomena and the repose that nature offers. The decision about where to locate playgrounds influences all further decisions related to design.

■ LOCATING PLAYGROUNDS

Playgrounds should be located immediately beside the centre or school they serve; preferably there should be direct access to the playground from the classroom (Esbensen, 1990). Locating the playground in the lee of the building provides some protection from harsh winds, excessive sunlight, and severe cold. Some sunlight for both morning and afternoon play periods extends the amount of time and the regularity with which children are able to play outdoors, especially in colder climates.

The Ministry of Culture and Recreation of Ontario (1982) provides detailed plans for constructing sheltered areas, sun shields, and windbreaks that facilitate outdoor play in harsh climates. In inner cities, the installation of a fence to reduce traffic fumes and noises, and to protect children's privacy, is healthier. Fences are more aesthetically pleasing if constructed of wood rather than chainlink or some combination of wood and chainlink.

Playgrounds that have an outlook through a fence to treed, grassy areas are especially well located. Those that can be placed near a row of trees to protect against excessive sun and wind provide a closer link with the natural world and permit children to remain outdoors longer. Variations in topography, such as natural mounds here and there, a natural water source that can be contained, grassy or bushy areas, and sunken levels, add to the natural attractiveness and interest of the playground and should be retained in the design. Terrain should also be well drained and free of dangerous protrusions and hidden holes.

Sun Exposure

The location of the playground should account for the amount of direct sun exposure children will receive during the warm months. Wide overhangs from the roof will add protection from the sun close to the building, and shade trees or gazebos can be added to shelter areas such as sandboxes and construction areas where children may remain for longer periods of time.

Sun exposure poses a significant health hazard to children's playgrounds. The erosion of the ozone layer and our greater knowledge about the long-term ill effects of sun exposure, especially when young, make it imperative that children be protected during outdoor play. In all parts of North America, *children should wear sunhats whenever playing outdoors from early May to late September, except on very cloudy days.* Infants who adjust to wearing sunbonnets outdoors will maintain the practice in early childhood. Centres should have a supply of washable sunhats with brims for children. To facilitate active play, hats should tie firmly under the chin.

The shape, size, and layout of a playground will inevitably depend on the topography of the land available, the size of the lot upon which the centre or school is located, its urban or rural location, and the needs of the children it serves. It is impossible to establish guidelines applicable to all combinations of circumstances, but some general rules of thumb are useful.

Size

The size of the early childhood playground should be based on the number of children who will use the playground at one time. A guideline recommended by Ashmore and Esbensen (1991) is approximately fourteen square metres of space per child for centres with less than thirty children, and nine and one third square metres per child for centres with more than thirty children. Other size-related factors include the proximity of buildings and traffic, and the number and size of play zones to be included.

It is impractical to determine playground size solely by calculating the number of square metres per child. Furthermore, a small playground may foster more social interaction and cooperative play. It is usually easier for teachers to monitor play in a densely organized, compact space. High-density playgrounds effectively reduce the range of play behaviours possible and change the nature of children's interactions. Large open areas may encourage out-of-bounds behaviour and aimless activity, especially when equipment is placed randomly throughout the available space.

■ PLAYGROUND ZONES

Outdoor play space that is attractive, comfortable, natural, and perceptually stimulating for children and adults will ensure that children play outdoors for longer periods in all seasons. The organization of the playground into areas that encourage particular types and social contexts of play promotes positive play behaviours, as does similar organization of space indoors (see Figure 20.1). Esbensen (1987) recommends playground zones for transition, manipulative/creative play, projective/fantasy play, focal/social play, sociodramatic play, physical play, and exploration of natural elements. Walsh (1988) recommends having a quiet area, an open area, and an active area. Canada Mortgage and Housing Corporation (1979) and the Canadian Institute for Child Health (1985) recommend a creative/cognitive area, a social/dramatic play area, a physical play area, a quiet retreat play area, and an adult seating area. Most approaches incorporate landscaped areas and storage facilities.

Experts agree that compatible play zones should be grouped together, that there should be clear pathways in and out of each zone, and that play in one zone should not interfere with play in an adjacent zone. Various playground surfaces define the boundaries of play zones, providing messages about where a certain type of play is to begin and end. Care should be taken to arrange compatible surfaces adjacent to one another; for example, a sand surface placed next to grass rather than asphalt will prevent slipping on sandy pavement.

Talbot and Frost (1989:19) propose the following design features: variation in size of the playground areas and features of the space; open-ended spaces and abstract shapes that assume any meaning the child assigns; the presence of natural elements (earth, fire, air, and water); variation in line quality and shape; sensory stimulation through colour, smell, texture, and sound; novelty; mystery; brilliance; juxtaposition of opposites; richness and abundance; connection with other times and places; loose parts and simple tools; the illusion of risk; and places for doing nothing.

The play zones outlined below may be adapted to incorporate several types of play and social contexts.

Landscaped Areas

Flowers, shrubbery, and trees add aesthetic appeal and a homelike quality to the total environment. Changes in vegetation are also visual markers of the passing seasons in most North American climates. They help children anticipate the signs of seasonal variations such as frost and snow, buds and flowers, birds and insects, and the changing colour of the leaves and grass. Children form attachments to plants and trees in the environment, and the names of flowers, shrubs, and trees become part of their everyday vocabulary. Landscaped areas encourage children to assume some responsibility for their outdoor environment by picking off old blossoms to encourage new growth and by removing weeds. These early outdoor experiences become lifelong reference points that generate a genuine appreciation of nature.

Landscaped areas can be used to preserve natural features such as a small grove of trees for a shady nook, a mound for sliding down in winter, a rocky glen to hide in, or a loamy spot for a vegetable garden. Low wooden fencing, hedges separating play areas, and attractive pathways serve both practical and aesthetic purposes but should not be too dominant.

Private Areas

Small nooks under a tree, in a grove of low bushes, or behind a storage cupboard provide some seclusion for children to be alone for a while to daydream or just rest. These spots, while private enough from the child's perspective, are visible to the teacher who can see over the barriers. A little wooden bench or seat on a tree stump adds incentive for the child to remain in the private spot for a while in order to make designs with a stick in the dirt or gaze at the clouds in the sky. Children need private space, and teachers should respect their need to dream, reflect, imagine, and retreat from active playing (Talbot & Frost, 1989). A private space in the playground may also be a place to erect a tent to serve as a temporary playhouse or to promote sociodramatic play, so long as children have another private area to which they can retreat. Times spent alone in quiet places often spawn ideas and plans that may later be realized in more active play.

Sand Area

The sand play area should be located in a spot sheltered from intense sun and out of the wind. A sand area should be deep enough for children to use pails, sieves, and scoops, and make puddles and moats around castles. Sand areas must be kept clean. Outdoor sand areas usually need to be replenished frequently and inspected daily for signs of domestic animal contamination. The best sand areas are those that can be covered at night, but covers should be removed by day to prevent the formation of mould in the sand, particularly in humid areas. A counter or table placed in the sand area tends to keep sand play inside the area (Esbensen, 1991). As the sand play area often becomes a busy place where conflicts may arise, it is important to set clear limits for play and ensure that they are maintained (Baker, 1966). Sand should never be thrown and should be kept in the sandbox or table.

Sand is most effective outdoors when there is a water source nearby; sand needs water in order to realize its potential as one of nature's most responsive, natural substances. Safe access to water may be facilitated in a number of ways. A simple tap, hose, pump, trickle of a stream, or plastic pool placed adjacent to the sand are all that is needed. Natural or adult-made streams have more creative play value than pools because they can be dammed, bridged, and used for punting boats and wading in the summer months (CMHC, 1978). When streams are specially constructed they are easier to control and can be switched on and off easily. Whenever water is added to the playground, it must be supervised constantly as water is an inherently dangerous element for children. In cold climates, a frozen stream may become a patch of ice for sliding or skating. In fall, the dry basin for the stream collects fallen leaves for building forts.

Loose Materials Area

Outdoors is an ideal place to provide open-ended materials, some naturally occurring and some adult-made. Loose wood or branches, rock piles, a dirt pit, wooden boxes, boards, small ladders, saw horses, old tires, clotheslines, washtubs, and other props borrowed from indoors facilitate creative-constructive play that responds to children's actions on them. The loose materials area may be located at the boundary of a landscaped zone in order to enclose the piles of odds and ends with which children can build.

Open Spaces

Open areas allow for large-group play, organized group activities, sociodramatic play on a grand scale, and a fantasy play area. They may be located in areas contoured with mounds, slopes, and embankments that can be used differently in each season. Children need space for practising basic movements such as running, climbing, jumping, hopping, galloping, rolling, sliding, balancing, and skipping. The topographical variation in this area provides cues to children about the kind of active movements that are possible. In summer, hills, mounds, and gulleys become places to roll down, climb up, hide in, and jump over. Organized, teacher-led, fitness and motor-skills programs may be conducted here in the milder months. Open spaces allow children to run, hide, and spread out without the worry of interfering with large equipment or play in other zones.

An open area that is paved permits children to play with balls, hoops, and tricycles as soon as temperatures allow for less restrictive clothing in the spring. In colder climates, the freezing of a small rink on the paved area provides hours of sliding or skating fun.

Vehicle Trails

Wagons and tractors may be used to transport play materials as long as the vehicles remain on the paved pathways. Wise teachers will set clear limits in this area and ensure that they are upheld. "STOP" and "GO" signs, traffic lights, and signs with directional arrows help clarify limits. The surface of this area may be concrete, asphalt, or compacted gravel, as long as wheeled vehicles can move smoothly.

Figure 20.1 PLAYGROUND DESIGN

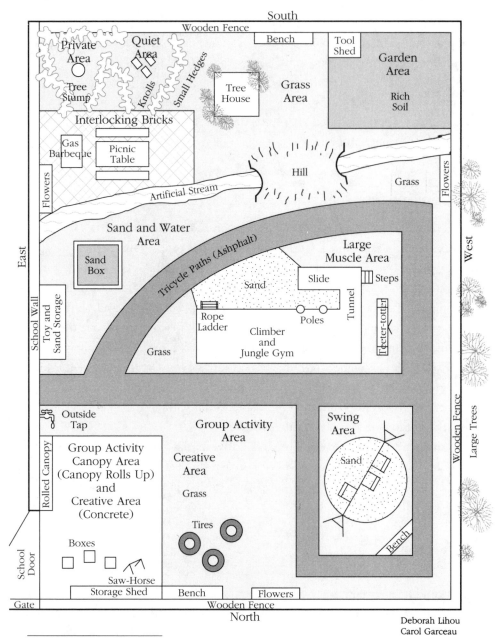

Deborah Lihou
Carol Garceau

Active Play Areas

Playground equipment to promote physical development of the large muscles and motor coordination should address all parts of the child's body and not just the limbs. Climbing equipment such as jungle gyms and climbers with ladders, slides, and poles are obvious choices for climbing and hanging, and for promoting balance and coordination. Slides embedded in a mound of sand, for soft landings, and a chute with a drop-off horizontal to the ground introduce children to height, the sensation of fast movement, and risk taking. Single swing seats promote coordination, muscular development, and a sense of freedom and emotional release. Through learning to pump the swing to gain momentum, children develop a sense of the mid-line of the body. Swings must be located low enough to the ground to permit easy mounting by young children and dismounting by young children. There must be sufficient space to swing without hitting other children and from which to exit without obstructing pathways or risking collision with other children (Esbensen, 1987).

Modular plastic climbing and playhouse equipment that children can construct, take apart, and rearrange themselves provide opportunities for children to be creative and develop physical abilities. Prefabricated wooden climbing structures have the advantage of smooth, well-treated surfaces, and dimensions and scales that are appropriate for children's small sizes. Pressure-treated wood that has been treated with a toxic preservative should be used with great caution in the construction of play structures or any play equipment.

Tree Houses and Playhouses

Playhouses and social/physical play areas built over an impact surface material like sand or pea gravel provide opportunities for climbing, balancing, and gaining some security about heights. Most children dream of having a tree house to play in at some time in their early years. Some tree houses may be set in a sturdy tree at a modest height with easy access by ladder or stairwell. They may also be set on secure wooden frames. In the absence of a tree house, a playhouse on stilts or house frame will also promote sociodramatic play and language skills. Playhouses should be readily visible by teachers but sufficiently removed from quiet play areas to permit children to exercise their imaginations in role play.

■ WINTER PLAY

Winters in some regions of North America present challenges for teachers and children that are not experienced in the same ways outside North America. Teachers of young children often struggle to find ways to maximize the amount of time children spend outdoors, especially during long winters. Open spaces and paved areas that are sheltered from the wind are particularly important during the winter months. Rainy winter weather in some regions poses unique problems for teachers who have to deal with muddy playground areas and wet outerwear on a daily basis.

COOPERATIVE GAMES IN THE WINTER

Pavement areas that can be kept clear of snow buildup are useful in areas where snow accumulation is heavy.

Sturdy vinyl or rubberized outerwear that repels rain effectively and is easily wiped dry is a necessity for children in some regions. A large roof overhanging a paved or well-drained gravel area permits outdoor play during long rainy periods. Cubbies equipped with open slats hold overshoes and rubbers off the floor for easy drying. Electric drying cupboards, where wet snowsuits and nylon shells may be hung to dry quickly, make the wet and cold months of the year more manageable in centres and schools. Such simple amenities make life much easier for children and teachers in many parts of Canada where bulky outerwear is a fact of life for two or three seasons of the year.

Children's clothing plays an important role in determining for how long and under what conditions children will be able to play outdoors during the winter. Teachers need to be warmly dressed themselves in order to sustain long periods outdoors and to appreciate the infinite possibilities for play and learning during the winter months. Hats or hoods, and warm socks and boots are essential for teachers as well as children. Teachers who are not properly dressed for winter play tend to limit children's outdoor play times (Baker, 1966).

Winter offers marvellous play opportunities outside that often make children of warmer climates very envious. When visiting a demonstration child care program in Fort Lauderdale, Florida, in January, a teacher was surprised to see the walls of the centre decorated with hundreds of children's drawings of winter play activities showing children skating, making snow people, sliding, and snowshoeing. Paper snowflakes hung in the windows. In a corner of one playroom was a metre-high snowman made of papier-mâché and decorated with a red wool scarf, black hat, and a carrot for his nose. Temperatures in Fort Lauderdale had been in the high 20s for weeks! Stories like that make us realize that we do not always appreciate the potential of wintertime play to enrich children's lives.

An important part of our mandate as teachers is to help children adapt to our climate, seasonal variations, and geographical realities. Playgrounds should be designed with winter in mind and not just for the fair days of spring, summer, and fall. Children need places to build a slide on a hill for their sleighs and magic carpets, a place for sliding on ice, space to make snow forts and snow sculptures, and open areas to make pathways in the snow, build snowmen, and make snow angels.

Winter also provides opportunities for investigating many natural phenomena such as wind and air currents, freezing and melting, ice buildup, and condensation. Endless science experiences are available outdoors when teachers are observant, aware, and plan ahead. Many creative construction activities are easier in packing snow than with wet sand. Even exploring the various types of snow and discovering why the Inuit have so many words to describe it provides a wealth of concrete, sensory learning for children. Winter is also a time for young children to be introduced to sports such as skating, snowshoeing, and skiing. Children as young as three can be introduced to bobskates on a patch of ice. Plenty of time to simply observe, feel, and explore winter phenomena provides children with endless ideas for art activities in the Creative Arts Centre.

■ INDOOR-OUTDOOR SUMMER PROGRAMS

In order to use precious summer days to their fullest, many teachers plan indoor-outdoor programs, bringing whole play stations and a wide range of activities outdoors to paved areas, open spaces, and loose materials areas. Many art activities can be conducted outdoors more easily than inside because of the space available. Fat chalk on wet pavement provides an interesting new medium for children to explore; large paint brushes and pails of water for "whitewashing" fences, railings, and pavement keep children interested for long periods; hollow blocks used with loose materials allow for the creation of interesting new structures. Messy activities such as dyeing, papier-mâché, and cardboard construction with leftover appliance boxes and crates are often easier to manage outdoors. The list of indoor activities that have interesting new opportunities and effects outdoors grows quickly once teachers turn their attention to planning for indoor-outdoor play. On beautiful days, children should spend as much time as possible outdoors enjoying the greater freedom and sensory stimulation available there as long as they are well protected from the sun.

■ GARDENING WITH CHILDREN

Child Development Opportunities

Gardening provides a wide range of developmental and learning opportunities for young children. Although it requires teacher supervision and leadership and is usually undertaken in groups, gardening also provides occasions for children to work independently. Children's understanding of the concept of time is enhanced by visible seasonal markers such as the sprouting of seeds, the ripening of vegetables, and the clearing of the earth at the season's end. Making seeds grow and watching the stages gardens pass through are activities that allow children to witness visible signs of life, which instil in them a sense of wonder at the regularity of nature. Children acquire factual knowledge about plants, pest control, and life cycles from gardening projects. Physical abilities and coordination skills are practised from planting through to harvesting and fall cleanup. Vocabulary and language fluency is enhanced by gardening projects. Memory, concepts, and problem-solving and attending skills are addressed. All stages of garden projects provide children with visible, concrete results for their efforts. Gardening is possible during three seasons in most regions of North America.

Locating a Garden

The first step in the planning process is to find a suitable location for the garden and then draw a plan. It is best to start with a small, manageable patch of ground and to cultivate it well rather than setting aside more space than one teacher can handle with a group of children. A two-metre-square patch is a large enough area to prepare and tend during the first year of a garden project. A spot with good topsoil, large enough to accommodate a group of about eight children and a teacher working together, located near a water source, and in a sunny area meets the most important specifications. In most North American climates, south-easterly exposure maximizes the amount of sunshine the garden will receive.

Planning the Garden

Planning a garden makes an excellent project for the waning days of winter when seeds may be started in flats with potting soil and jiffy starter sets and placed on sunny window sills or under grow lights. The planning stages are important for they help children acquire a basic familiarity with seeds, soil, and the names of vegetables and other plants. They may also be introduced to tools and supplies for gardening. Plenty of preparatory activities may be undertaken during the early spring months to increase children's anticipation of making a garden, including introduc-

PLANTING A GARDEN BESIDE THE PLAYHOUSE

ing new words and plant names and establishing protocol for planting, maintaining, and harvesting the garden. Children can explore gardening magazines, collect posters, draw pictures, make tags for sticks to use as markers for rows, plan and build a scarecrow, examine seeds, and make a scrapbook for photographs and drawings to document the stages in the garden project from beginning to end.

Tools and supplies have to be purchased, and this provides an occasion for field trips to the local garden centre. The area selected for the garden has to be cleared, filled with good topsoil, and fertilized. A border to separate the garden from adjoining play areas has to be built. A number of planning tasks can be undertaken long before the arrival of the planting season. When teachers in the centre or school collaborate, the garden with its diversity of stages and tasks becomes a cooperative endeavour in which everyone has a role.

Planting and Maintenance Tasks

Once the soil has been prepared, children can help with the planting by raking the earth, creating rows with a hoe, and sowing the seeds. Rubber gloves should be worn when handling seeds to protect hands from the toxic coating on some seeds. Watering, weeding, and staking tasks can also be conducted by preschool and kindergarten children who are usually excited by the "real work" involved in the project. Taking photographs at each stage in the development of the garden provides a concrete record of children's accomplishments.

Harvesting and Cleanup

Right from the earliest harvesting of crops such as radishes and lettuce to the later zucchinis and pumpkins, children take pride in being able to take produce home for dinner with their families and enjoy raw vegetables at snacktime. Some teachers like to have a compost area to promote recycling and conservationist attitudes. Children can also participate in removing old plants from the garden as they finish producing, placing them in the compost bin, removing stakes and markers, turning the soil, and adding natural fertilizer for the following year. There are an abundance of excellent books on gardening with children that make wonderful additions to the learning environment library, especially during the planning stages.

Playground Equipment List

Large Muscle
climbing structure or A-frame
crawl-through tunnels
jungle gym
securely suspended rope to climb and swing on
tire or bucket swings
rope ladder
firefighter's pole
triangular ladder
slide with 15- to 20-cm drop at end
spring-based see-saw
trampoline
ramps for sliding and jumping
bowling set
snow shovels
baseball bat and ball
7," 10," and 18" balls
large hoops
punching ball or bag
skipping ropes and hoops
rowboat
bean bags and target

balance
balance beams or boards that interlock
balance blocks
stilts
pogo stick
skate boards with helmets and shin pads
stationary-spring riding animals
horizontal ladder
simple playhouse or house frame
stick horses
tree house
steering wheel on wooden frame
large, hollow wooden building blocks

Vehicles and Accessories
gas station fuel pump
tricycles
wagons or carts
pedal cars
wheelbarrow
tractor

bicycle pump
hard hats
cargo for wagons and carts

Loose Materials
painted wooden boxes
barrels and kegs
large packing boxes and crates (e.g., appliance cartons)
sawhorses
short wooden ladders
lumber in 2-m and 1-m lengths
rocks and boulders
workbench
softwood supplies
tool kit and tools
tires
logs
tree stump
telephone cable spools
weather-treated large blocks
rope
milk crates

tarpaulins
clothesline and pulleys
large and small paint
   brushes
pails
water-soluble paint
old shirts and drop sheets
surplus building materials

Gardening

hose and tap or pump
rakes
spades
hoes
hand shovels
claws
bags and baskets
sprinkler
watering cans
seed packets
flats for seeds
peat moss
sterilized manure
string or rope
wooden stakes

rubber gloves
gardening gloves for the
   teacher
overalls
old fabric and rags (for a
   scarecrow)
jiffy starter kits
gardening books

Sand and Water

buckets
scoops
shovels
sieves
steam shovels
heavy-duty trucks and
   cars
hose and tap
construction hats
camp stools
fishing rods and nets
tackle box
plastic wading pool
air mattress
diving mask

paddles
small sailing boats
inflatable raft
jugs and plastic pails
funnels and siphons
pup tent
flashlight
sleeping bag
knapsack
tin lunch boxes
canteen
tin pots and pans
saddle bags

Storage and Furniture

storage sheds with locks
benches
picnic table and umbrella
lawn chairs
barbecue or hibachi
firewood and grate
firepit
propbox

Activities for Outdoor Play in Landscaped Areas

1. Plan, design, and maintain a garden of hardy vegetables and flowers. This project can be undertaken during three seasons of the year in most parts of North America and may be begun in the early spring with the selection of seeds and the planting of flats, and concluded in the fall with the garden cleanup. Children should be involved in the project according to their developmental levels. Older preschoolers and kindergarten children will be able to undertake tasks at all stages in the gardening project.

2. Use props from familiar stories and nursery rhymes in the quiet and private landscaped areas with a tent or a simple A-frame structure to stimulate imagination and foster dramatic and sociodramatic play (for three- to five-year-olds).

3. Play with the hose in the sand pit to create streams and waterfalls, and make castles and moats as might be done at the beach. On warm days, children may be dressed in bathing suits and sunhats and pretend that they are having a day at the beach. They will need scoops, shovels, and pails initially, and then will bring other materials from the loose materials area to augment their creations (for three- to six-year-olds).

4. In the adult facilities area on fine days set up specific-purpose materials from indoors such as puzzles, beads and string, Lego, Workjobs, and other activities that can be enjoyed outdoors (for all ages).

5. Plan a barbecue or a picnic lunch with the children that they can help prepare. For example, children can mix their own portion of hamburger meat with chopped onion and seasonings and give it to the cook to cook for them. Let them set the picnic table and spread their own condiments on their hamburgers. This type of activity is best conducted in the early spring before the arrival of insects, wasps, and flies (for four- to six-year-olds).

6. Encourage children to undertake large, ongoing projects in the creative area with the loose materials provided there. Building a clubhouse out of large appliance boxes; making a fort using old logs, planks, rocks, and branches; and constructing a crude wooden planter to sit on top of a tree stump or to hold flowers elsewhere in the playground are just a few of the myriad building and project opportunities children may pursue with the loose materials in the creative area (for older preschoolers and kindergarten children).

Activities for Outdoor Play in Open Areas

(for three- to six-year-olds)

1. The open space and uneven topography of this area allow children to create snow slides in the winter on the hills for their magic carpets. They may make a tunnel system of snow, make angels in the snow, and build snowmen in the greater space available.

2. Organize group activities, such as follow the leader, activities with balls for catching and throwing games, parachute activities, exercises, and motor-skills activities, that provide practice in basic fundamental movements, both locomotor and non-locomotor, such as running, hopping, jumping, galloping, marching, skipping, leaping, swaying, twisting, turning, balancing, bending, and stretching.

(for older preschoolers and kindergarten children)

3. Build a snowblock house using simple connected enclosures and then subdividing the enclosures to make rooms and hallways.

4. Begin a game of cross over by having the children form a large circle. Children should look at the children standing on each side of them. On a signal from the teacher, all children must try to cross through the circle to the opposite side of

the circle without bumping into one another or touching one another. Children then check to see if they are standing beside the same children on the opposite side of the circle. (The game aids spatial awareness, directionality, agility, dodging, predicting and anticipating another's movement, and relative distance.)

5. Play human obstacle course. Older preschoolers and kindergarten children pick a partner and find a place within a defined part of the open area to make an obstacle using their bodies (connecting arms, bending over to make bridges, lying down with toes together to make a diamond shape for children to jump in and out of, etc.). Then the teacher selects the first pair to walk, skip, or gallop through the human obstacle course. Each pair of "obstacles" will prescribe how the oncoming pair is to go through their obstacle. The oncoming pair must listen carefully to hear the instructions. It may be that they are to go "over legs," "through a hole made by the arms," or "hop through a web of arms and legs." Between obstacles, each pair must remember to hop, skip, gallop, or follow whatever movement the teacher has called out at the beginning of the course. When the pair reaches the end of the course, they form an obstacle and the next pair called by the teacher begins the course. The pairs that are in position as obstacles may alter their obstacle between pairs or they may simply call out different instructions on how to pass them. The game is over when each pair has completed the obstacle course.

6. Play mirroring. The teacher demonstrates by facing the group and going through a series of moves in slow motion that the children are asked to duplicate as the leader moves. The children then take partners and, facing each other, stand about four feet apart from each other leaving room between pairs. One child in each pair is the leader and begins moving slowly. The other child is to mirror the leader's actions with her own body. After a while, children switch roles. (The game helps promote body awareness, body image, spatial awareness, balance, coordination, directionality, and laterality.)

7. Read or tell stories with a playhouse or tree house as the central feature of the story. Even stories like *The Swiss Family Robinson* will stir children's imaginations to create sociodramatic play around the plot of the story they have heard. Provide props to use as reference points in their sociodrama.

References

Ashmore, P. and Esbensen, S. (1991). Guideline from a telephone conversation between Esbensen and Ashmore in June 1991. Reported by Esbensen in August 1991.

Baker, K.R. (1966). *Let's Play Outdoors*. Washington, D.C.: National Association for the Education of Young Children.

Beckwith, J. (1985). Equipment Selection for

Modern Playgrounds. In *When Children Play*, ed. J.L. Frost and S. Sunderlin. Wheaton, MD: Association or Childhood Education International.

Canada Mortgage and Housing Corporation. (1978). *Play Spaces for Preschoolers* (advisory document prepared by P. Hill, S. Esbensen, and W. Rock). Ottawa: CMHC.

Canadian Institute of Child Health. (1985). *When Child's Play is Adult Business: A Consumer Guide to Safer Playspaces*. Ottawa: CICH.

Canadian Standards Association. (1990). A guideline on children's playspaces and equipment (CAN/CSA-Z614-M90).

Children's Environments Advisory Service. (1975). *Adventure Playgrounds*. Ottawa: Central Mortgage and Housing Corporation.

Children's Environments Advisory Service. (1975). *Creative Playgrounds*. Ottawa: Central Mortgage and Housing Corporation.

Esbensen, S.B. (1980, March/April). Legislation and guidelines for children's play spaces in the residential environment. *Ekistics* 281:123–25.

Esbensen, S.B. (1984). *Hidden Hazards on Playgrounds for Children*. Hull, Quebec: Université du Québec à Hull.

Esbensen, S.B. (1987). *The Early Childhood Playground: An Outdoor Classroom*. Ypsilanti, MI: HighScope Press.

Esbensen, S.B. (1988). Play Environments for Young Children: Design Perspectives. In *Playgrounds for Young Children: National Survey and Perspectives,* ed. S.C. Wortham and J.L. Frost. American Association for Leisure and Recreation.

Esbensen, S.B. (1990). Designing the early childhood setting. In *Child Care and Education: Canadian Dimensions*, ed. I. Doxey, pp. 178–92. Toronto: Nelson.

Esbensen, S.B. (1991). Let's play outdoors: getting back to nature. Nova Scotia: Child Care Resources.

Hitz, R., and Driscoll, A. (1988). Praise or encouragement? New insights into praise; implications for early childhood teachers. *Young Children* 43(4):6–13.

Lovell, P., and Harms, T. (1985). How Can Playgrounds Be Improved? A Rating Scale. *Young Children* 40 (3): 3–8.

McCracken, Janet Brown. (1990). *Playgrounds Safe and Sound*. Washington, D.C.: National Association for the Education of Young Children.

Ministry of Culture and Recreation, Ontario. (1982). *A Guide to Creative Playground Equipment*. Toronto: Government of Ontario.

Sunal, D.W., and Szymanski Sunal, C. (1990). Helping young children appreciate beauty in natural areas. *Day Care and Early Education*. Fall, 1990: 26–29.

Talbot, J., and Frost, J.L. (1989). Magical Playscapes. *Childhood Education*. Fall, 1989: 11–19. Adapted with permission.

Vergeront, J. (1988). Places and spaces for preschool and primary (outdoors). Washington, D.C.: National Association for the Education of Young Children.

Walsh, P. (1988). Early childhood playgrounds: planning an outside learning environment. Melbourne: Martin Educational in association with Robert Andersen and Associates.

Wardle, F. (1990). Are we taking play out of playgrounds? *Day Care and Early Education*. Fall, 1990: 30–34.

References on Gardening with Children

Hack, K., and Flynn, V. (1985). Green Beans: Gardening with Two's. *Day Care and Early Education*. Fall, 1985: 14–17.

Jelks, P.A., and Dukes, L.V. (1985). Promising Props for Outdoor Play. *Day Care and Early Education*. Fall, 1985: 18–20.

Miles, Arlene B. (1989). Cultivate a Budding Gardener. *Parents*. April, 1989: 78–79.

Waters, M. (1987). *The Victory Garden Kids' Book. A Beginner's Guide to Growing Vegetables, Fruits and Flowers*. Boston: Houghton-Mifflin.

COMBINING ALL ELEMENTS OF THE PLAY AND LEARNING ENVIRONMENT

Section 8 (Chapter 21) summarizes the steps involved in planning the learning environment. This textbook has emphasized the role of the environment in contributing to the richness of play, promoting child development, and facilitating developmentally appropriate learning in early childhood.

Teachers have to make connections between planning the environment to support play and learning, and planning curriculum for two- to six-year-olds. The approach adopted in this textbook assumes that child care programs and kindergartens will take responsibility for the education of children at the early end of the continuum. A play-based, child-centred approach that promotes development in all domains ensures that children will acquire important learning skills and lays the foundation for formal, academic learning later on. Early childhood educators are obligated to engage in informed, purposeful planning of environments, resources, and learning experiences.

Chapter 21 addresses the following topics:

- summary of steps in planning the learning environment
- recognition of individual learning styles
- curriculum planning
- developmentally appropriate practice in early childhood education

PUTTING THE PIECES TOGETHER

The design of the play and learning environment in early childhood education involves seeing the indoor and outdoor classrooms as complex networks of mutually complementary and interdependent parts. This textbook has led the reader through the steps involved in creating child-centred environments that emphasize developing and learning through play. This chapter will summarize these steps and link them to the design of developmental curriculum and programming. Appendix B lists developmental goals and objectives that may serve as a guide to curriculum planning and programming.

■ STEPS IN PLANNING THE PLAY AND LEARNING ENVIRONMENT

1. Observe and assess children's developmental levels, needs, and interests

Planning environments and programs for young children begins with an understanding of child development and the particular developmental levels, needs, and interests of the children in our programs. Although child development theory is not the only theoretical foundation upon which to plan early childhood education programs, it is generally accepted today as the best approach for ensuring the developmental appropriateness and overall quality of programs for young children (Kessler, 1991). When programs are planned without accounting for the developmental levels, needs, and interests of young children, children suffer (Bredekamp, 1991).

Knowledge of children's developmental levels, needs, and interests is acquired largely through formal and informal observation and careful record keeping. Although observation methods and assessment are not addressed in this textbook on play and learning, the role of regular observation cannot be overstated. It is the teacher's way of knowing who their children are and how best to make an appropriate fit between the needs of the individual child and the environment in which they play and learn. Observations generally reveal children's developmental levels and abilities in all domains. Information from observations is reflected in individual assessment reports for each child. These reports form the basis for planning environments and programs. There are many excellent textbooks on observation in early childhood education that will help the student develop these necessary skills.

2. Use play theory

Play theory explains the important relationships between children's behaviours with things and events in their environments, and their physical, cognitive, social, and emotional development. A solid understanding of play theory and the importance of play as an agent of development and learning is essential to planning learning environments. Children learn through play that is hands-on, sensory-based, freely chosen, undertaken for its own sake, responsive to their own actions, meaningful, and relevant to their daily lives.

Children learn through play; it is growth-enhancing, therapeutic, healing, and reassuring. Play nourishes and fulfils children in that it promotes feelings of success and mastery over the environment. When children believe that they can make a meaningful impact on their surroundings and that the environment is responsive to their needs and behaviours, they feel valued and powerful.

3. Plan space

Organized play space provides non-verbal messages to children about the types of play and behaviour that are encouraged in each part of the environment. When space is well planned, children can be more independent and self-directed in their play and spend less time guessing at what is expected of them or trying to decipher choices that are not obvious.

Teachers have to know what the legal space requirements are, the relationship between the contents of play space, and the amount of space available. Space planning should provide for pathways and open space that guide behaviour and movement from one learning centre to another. Juxtaposing learning centres that are complementary and creating groupings of learning centres and play stations that involve similar types of play provide cues to children about what they are to do and learn in each learning centre.

Pathways should lead children into and out of learning centres, and all centres should be accessible from the main pathways. No pathway should flow through an

PROJECTS—LEARNING TOGETHER

area designated as play space for any piece of equipment. Pathways should go around learning centres, not through them.

Dead space is a trouble spot where children tend to lose their motivation for play and become confused about what is expected of them. Densely organized space promotes a high level of social and interactive play; loosely organized space encourages individual play and small group, project-oriented, activity-centred play.

A child-centred learning environment means that the equipment is child-sized; play materials are accessible to children; and there is enough space to play with materials without intrusion from other activities. The organization of play space based on the identified developmental levels, needs, and interests of the children who will be using the space is an essential element in the successful learning environment. Many factors have to be considered in order to ensure that environments promote children's self-directed play in settings that respond to their actions (Kritchevsky & Prescott, 1977).

The contents of the play and learning environment are the play equipment, materials, and supplies. The contents may be set up as simple, complex, or super units, designations that are defined according to the capacity of the unit to interest children for a period of time and the number of children who would normally play with the unit. Simple units appeal to one child playing at a time; complex units usually support four children at a time; and super units are combinations of complex units or units with many subparts that allow for small-group and cooperative play for up to eight children at a time (Kritchevsky & Prescott, 1977). The calculation of the complexity of the environment at any given time is based on the total number of play spaces available at the various units of play in the playroom. It is important that the number of play spaces be optimal for each age level.

The variety dimension of the play and learning environment relates to the number of kinds of play that each unit of play invites. Even though an environment may have sufficient complexity, if the types of equipment and play materials all provide for similar kinds of behaviours and learning, children's interest may wane quickly and restless behaviours will emerge. It is important to ensure that the number of different kinds of things for children to do be sufficiently broad to address the needs and interests of all children in the group for the time they will be playing in an area.

4. Locate and design learning centres

Learning centres provide the frameworks for play and learning in the environment, and should be organized and located so that they complement one another. Each learning centre generally promotes certain types of compatible play. Learning centres promoting similar types of play and social contexts should be placed close to each other to permit children to transfer the learning and skills acquired in one centre to another centre. The careful juxtaposition of centres with similar goals also allows for organization of the environment according to the dimensions of messiness/tidiness, noise/quiet, active/passive, and individual versus group-oriented play behaviours. The equipment, materials, and supplies in each learning centre influence the kinds of play and social configurations that occur there and the specific activities that can be planned and set up for that centre.

When learning centres are set up with no rational plan for their organization, children have to rely heavily on teacher direction and intervention. A high level of teacher involvement in guiding, intervening, and leading children's play activities not only exhausts teachers and detracts from their roles as facilitators of learning, but also reduces children's freedom and ability to be self-directed.

5. Choose equipment, materials, and supplies

Equipment, play materials, and supplies should be matched to the developmental priorities of each learning centre. In order to make effective matches, teachers have to know the play and learning potential inherent in each play material. There is a wide range of play materials available for young children in today's market. Some have excellent play and learning potential, as they have been created by designers who are knowledgeable about child development and early learning styles. Others can be inappropriate, mindless, and sometimes harmful. Knowing the tools of the trade in our profession means that early childhood educators have to know the purposes, value, function, and inherent quality of play materials. When teachers are sure of the quality and purpose of play materials they have selected, they can make astute links between materials and learning centres, and between materials and the developmental objectives of activities. It is also important to have a keen sense of the time it takes for children to explore materials fully and to master the inherent skills and learning potential embedded in each type of material. This understanding helps teachers gauge how long to leave materials and activities set up in a learning centre.

6. Establish a climate for learning

Children learn when they feel psychologically safe and physically comfortable. Their psychological health depends on their physical well-being and their sense of being nurtured, valued, and protected. Children need to know that what they do really matters to the adults in their lives (Katz, 1974). When they are anxious, afraid, hungry, unloved, abused, tired, suffer from low self-esteem, or are unwell, children do not have the courage or the initiative to venture, take risks, lose themselves in absorbing activity, choose, or follow through on tasks and challenges. Play demands children's full attention, interest, and willingness to let go. When children lack these basic capacities and a sense of wholeness and safety in their lives, it is difficult for teachers to help them overcome these deterrents to their ability to play.

Environments can be designed to promote feelings of effectiveness, self-worth, and mastery in even the most anxious and timid children. Play and learning opportunities can be planned to help children overcome some of the emotional, social, and psychological barriers to play. Establishing an effective climate for play involves awareness of individual needs and capabilities, choosing activities that interest children, recognizing their efforts, however tentative or faltering, and respecting their feelings. All children need a chance to find their own space, and play and work in their individual ways and at their own levels, alone or with others. It is important to establish a climate that allows each child the time needed to gain confidence, reach out, and tackle new and challenging experiences.

7. Design curriculum

An organized learning environment provides a solid foundation upon which to plan and implement developmental curriculum. First of all, teachers have to know the developmental levels, needs, and interests of their children. They should also understand the play and learning potential of each learning centre. Each learning centre should be dedicated to promoting particular developmental goals and types of play.

Curriculum design requires that teachers identify the play and learning priorities for the young children in the program. This step relies on information about individual children based on observation and assessment of children's developmental levels and needs.

Developmental goals for curriculum for the early years are based on child development theory. A range of developmental goals and objectives for each domain are listed in Appendix B. The selection of specific developmental goals for a program depends on assessments of individual children and on the abilities that parents and teachers believe that their young children should acquire and the knowledge they should be exposed to. For example, in some programs, safety, hygiene, street-proofing, and cultural awareness may influence the choice of developmental goals and knowledge requirements for children. In other programs, more emphasis may be placed on children's acquisition of literacy and numeracy skills. Choices of which developmental goals a program will emphasize are value-laden and relevant to geography, socio-economic conditions, and culture, to name just a few factors.

When the developmental goals that will drive a curriculum have been identified by parents and teachers, the next step is to articulate the developmental objectives relevant to each goal. These objectives will be the short-term steps children will follow towards mastery of the longer-term goal. Learning centres and activities can then be planned to address the range of developmental objectives identified. The developmental goals and objectives form the backbone of the curriculum for the program.

Activity planning should be related to the children's developmental abilities, previous experience, and interests. Activities should address the individual needs of children. They should be implemented in a learning centre or playground zone where the type of play involved in the activity is compatible with the goals, types, and social contexts of play associated with the learning centre. Appendix B will assist teachers in linking developmental goals and objectives for the children in their programs with specific learning experiences that promote practice and mastery of developmentally appropriate abilities.

8. Consider individual learning styles

Some children learn better from visual stimuli and need to be able to see a concept demonstrated before they are able to understand. Other children are auditory learners for whom listening, interpreting, and acting upon auditory messages comes easiest. Tactile learners have to touch, feel, and interact physically with things in order to form concepts that endure. These children like to test, experiment with, and manipulate materials in all manner of ways. Some children are more inclined to be observers and relatively passive in their learning. Many enjoy learning in social contexts by observing, imitating, interacting, and collaborating with others. Other children may prefer solitary learning experiences in an environment where they are able to pursue their own objectives while playing alone, follow their interests, and reach their own understandings at their own pace. Some children learn easily in a quiet, orderly environment where activity and noise are kept to a minimum and they are able to remain at a task for long periods of time. Other children need plenty of activity, room to move, frequent breaks, and many opportunities to change from one activity to another. Activity planning for each learning centre should account for a wide variety of learning styles.

This textbook makes frequent references to the work of Howard Gardner on the development of multiple intelligences in young children. According to Gardner, individuals have different blends and levels of intelligence in each of seven areas: linguistic, logical-mathematical, musical, spatial, bodily-kinesthetic, interpersonal, and intrapersonal intelligences (Gardner, 1983). Providing environments and learning experiences that promote active, self-directed learning and respect children's individual abilities, aptitudes, and interests, acknowledges the existence of a wide range of learning styles and differing types of intelligence.

In early childhood, it is important to determine where children's particular talents lie by exposing them to a wide range of experiences. A central task of early childhood education is to find the agents of "crystallization" for children (Gardner, 1989). Later on, when children enter elementary school, programs and curriculum should guide them to courses and activities for which they have special aptitudes.

PROBLEM SOLVING

Children not only differ from each other in their dominant learning styles, but also employ different learning styles depending on the nature of the task in which they are engaged. Choosing teaching and learning methods for activities that are self-directed and active respects children's individual learning styles. They will generally ask for direction, assistance, and leadership when they need it.

Gardner (1989) believes that in this kind of environment, teachers of young children should be "laid back" within a structured physical environment. Teachers, he believes, have to "cue in" to the child's interests, aptitudes, and learning styles. When materials and tasks are clear, children can be free to pursue them in an open, easy-going atmosphere in which the teacher is a resource person and facilitator. Teachers should be able to match materials and children wisely, and be ready to switch materials when children are not making progress with them. When activities and materials are clearly planned, whether or not they are open-ended or specific-purpose, it is easier for teachers to assess children reliably and guide them profitably.

9. Plan activities

Activity planning addresses the developmental objectives children are ready to address. Learning experiences should build upon skills and tasks that children have mastered in previous experiences and take them one step further. Planning for learning involves understanding the components or steps necessary in acquiring new skills and concepts. Teachers then have to break new learning tasks into bite-sized chunks to help children deal with manageable amounts of new knowledge or skills at any given time.

Effective planning of learning experiences also involves making knowledgeable and effective matches between the developmental objectives each activity addresses and combinations of play equipment, materials, and supplies.

Knowing the "tools of the trade" for an early childhood educator is mostly a matter of understanding the play and learning potential of a vast range of equipment, materials, and supplies.

10. Select teaching and learning methods

Developmental approaches to early childhood education assume that children learn primarily through their active interaction with concrete objects and experiences in their environment. The more active, hands-on opportunities children have to explore materials and supplies, and to learn about the properties and actions of things under a variety of conditions, the more likely they are to build a solid foundation of mental structures and concepts upon which later academic learning can build.

Early childhood is a time for informal education, when children should engage in "structure forming" activities that are largely child-initiated and self-directed. Teacher-directed activities are referred to as "structure utilization" activities (Elkind, 1979:108). The essential characteristics of active, informal methods are that they "inspire children's interest, play, experimentation and cooperation" (DeVries &

Kohlberg, 1987:41). Freedom to choose from clear alternatives is an essential element of informal teaching and pedagogy. The early childhood period is the prime time for building an intellectual foundation of concept formation, habits, skills, and positive attitudes towards discovery and learning that supports later learning.

11. Evaluate

Evaluation gathers information about the value of programs, often for the purpose of comparing programs and making decisions about their adoption, continuation, or elimination. Evaluation also collects data about programs in order to assess their strengths and weak areas, and determine objectives for improvement and revision. Both types of evaluation are appropriate and necessary within early childhood education at different times and for different purposes. Improvement-oriented evaluation procedures should be continuous and used by teachers and administrators to monitor the effectiveness of teaching practices in programs, determine children's participation and progress in the program, ferret out weak areas that can be strengthened, maintain the relevance of programs, and assist teachers in understanding their professional roles and improving their performances.

ACTIVE LEARNING

Evaluation has sometimes been mistakenly associated with intimidation and threat. People often fear that evaluation will expose the weak elements in organizations, programs, and strategies for the purpose of eliminating the programs or reassigning people. In the past two decades or so, evaluation has become a sophisticated discipline and has reversed some of the negative connotations previously associated with it. Evaluation is now seen more often as a positive force for renewal, support, and improvement. Evaluation of all components of early childhood education is essential if the profession is to make progress in the interests of children. Teacher training programs should instil confidence in teachers, who will appreciate the value of using regular and systematic evaluation procedures and instruments in order to gain a better understanding of what they do, how they do it, and how to make informed changes in the planning and implementation of programs that work for children and society.

Evaluation techniques and instruments for early childhood education programs are few and far between at present. The components of evaluation that should be addressed include: activity evaluation, curriculum evaluation, program evaluation, analysis of play space, evaluation of the physical and affective characteristics of the play and learning environment, and teacher evaluation.

■ DEVELOPMENTALLY APPROPRIATE PRACTICE

Developmentally appropriate practice has been clearly defined for American programs (Bredekamp, 1987). A great many of the concepts apply equally to programs for Canadian children. However, Canada is a nation of enormous size and complexity, with tremendous diversity among regions and the people who populate them. It also holds many values and interests that are different from those held in the United States. Canada also has a history to be proud of, and to preserve and pass on to its children.

Canadian early childhood educators hear a great deal about anti-bias curriculum and multiculturalism in society. Multiculturalism in Canada implies openness to and genuine acceptance of the diverse cultures and ethnic groups that make it one of

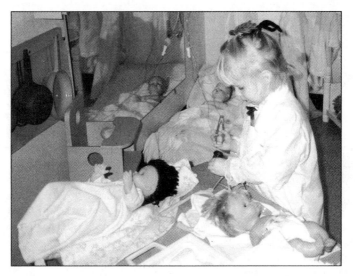

DEVELOPMENTALLY APPROPRIATE PLAY

the best nations in the world in which to live. It is important that the positive values that have made Canada unique and strong are supported. What Canadians seek to eliminate are prejudice, intolerance, illiteracy, innumeracy, and poverty. Canadians have values and ideals that the systems of education should endeavour to instil in children without prejudicing them against the different ones of other nations. Canadian early childhood educators need to assess and evolve their own understanding of the values the country represents and of what constitutes developmentally appropriate practice and effective early childhood education for Canadian children.

There is still considerable distance between the good intentions that prevail in the early childhood profession and present practices. These distances have to be bridged by teachers who possess the will, human qualities, knowledge, and skills needed to meet children's individual needs and build a strong foundation for their later years. Many teachers have a good deal of will and the necessary human qualities of compassion, warmth, ability to care and nurture, dedication, and openness to learning themselves. Sophisticated, well-honed teaching skills and knowledge of children are also needed to link proven theory with acceptable and relevant practice.

This textbook has attempted to provide a step-by-step approach to planning play-based environments and curriculum that will help children build a strong developmental foundation for lifelong learning. Achieving their optimal development in all domains is empowering for children; they are more likely to be successful and interested learners as they grow and mature, and to feel a heightened sense of mastery in their own lives and environmental contexts. Teachers of young children play a crucial role in children's lives during the childhood years and beyond.

References

Bredekamp, S. (1987). *Developmentally Appropriate Practice in Early Childhood Programs Serving Children From Birth Through Age 8*. Washington, D.C.: National Association for the Education of Young Children.

Bredekamp, S. (1991). Redeveloping early childhood education: a response to Kessler. *Early Childhood Research Quarterly* 6 (2):199–210.

DeVries, R., and Kohlberg, L. (1987). *Constructive Early Education: Overview and Comparison with Other Programs*. Washington, D.C.: National Association for the Education of Young Children.

Elkind, D. (1979). *The Child and Society*. New York: Oxford University Press.

Gardner, H. (1983). *Frames of Mind*. New York: Basic Books.

Gardner, H. (1989). *To Open Minds*. New York: Basic Books.

Katz, L. (1974). *Talks with Teachers*. Washington, D.C.: National Association for the Education of Young Children.

Kessler, S.A. (1991). Alternative perspectives on early childhood education. *Early Childhood Research Quarterly* 6 (2):183–98.

Kritchevsky, S., Prescott, E., and Walling, L. (1977). *Planning Environments for Young Children: Physical Space*. 2d ed. Washington, D.C.: National Association for the Education of Young Children.

DEVELOPMENTAL GOALS AND OBJECTIVES FOR CHILDREN AGED TWO TO SIX

COGNITIVE DOMAIN

Goal: everyday living skills

(*Note:* The objectives of this goal are grouped together because they reflect basic skills that young children need in their daily lives. These concepts contain elements of perceptual, language, and logical thinking skills and concepts that overlap and blur the boundaries between the domains.)

Objective: colour

recognize/perceive colour

match colour

label colour

attach meaning to colour

sort objects according to colour

discriminate colour groupings (shades, tones, etc.)

sequence colour by shades/tones in one colour group

use colour to form patterns

Objective: shape

recognize/perceive shape

match same shapes

label geometric shapes

attach meaning to shape

sort objects according to shape

alter shapes—create a new shape from another shape

discriminate embedded shapes

use shapes to form patterns

alter shape-retaining outlines, boundaries (topology)

Objective: size

recognize/perceive size

differentiate sizes (big/little, tall/short, etc.)

match sizes

use size labels

attach meaning to size

order objects by size

sort objects by size

seriate objects by size

use ordinal words for size (small, medium, large, etc.)

link size to length, width, height

measure objects/record size/make comparisons

Objective: space

differentiate part/whole

put things together and take them apart

observe things from different perspectives

know words related to position (here/there, in/out)

recognize relative positions (beside, across from, inside)

move in space

imitate the movements of others

know words related to direction (over/under, around/through)

locate things in the playroom, school, neighbourhood

recognize representations of things in pictures

recognize distances between things some of which went further than others

create things in space (using construction materials or other concrete objects—e.g., furniture and blankets)

represent and describe things in terms of position and direction

Objective: time

remember the actions of others over time

recall events not associated with time

recall events related to past and present

predict events

place events in the order they happened

associate numbers with time (e.g., the clock-face)

know that time passes in constant and measurable units

estimate amount of time a task will take

use time well (i.e., plan time)

understand relationship between age and time

understand relationships among speed, distance, and time

tell time (seven years and up)

Objective: family relationships

know own family members

know that one's own family is important

recognize similarities among families

recognize differences among families (e.g., size, culture, habits, customs)

know that families live in different ways

know that we have immediate families and extended families

Goal: memory skills

Objectives:

remember past events—short-term, then long-term

recall details and events of stories

repeat simple finger plays, songs, and rhymes

identify various concepts from memory (e.g., colour, shape, size, family)

recall what was previously seen or heard from memory

repeat verbal messages

follow verbal instruction

role play remembered events from everyday life

maintain social roles in a sociodramatic play context

Goal: cognitive-perceptual abilities

Objective: visual-perceptual skills

identify/label objects

discriminate similarities and differences

match objects according to observable similarities

classify objects according to observable similarities

recognize something after seeing only part of it

perceive small details

concentrate on small details in a visual field

Objective: auditory-perceptual skills

identify/label sounds

discriminate similarities and differences

match similar sounds

classify sounds

recognize something after hearing only part of it

concentrate on a sound

interpret sounds

identify direction from which a sound is coming

link what is heard to its source

differentiate between musical sounds

follow sounds to their source

listen actively

follow verbal instructions

Objective: cognitive perception related to haptic, olfactory, and gustatory skills

identify/label according to touch, smell, taste

discriminate differences/similarities according to touch, smell, taste

match according to touch, smell, taste

classify according to touch, smell, taste

Goal: attending abilities

Objective: task-orientation skills

choose an activity

define the task

begin the activity

follow through/persist

finish the activity

communicate that one is finished

Objective: attention skills

return to an activity after an interruption

block out distractions

voluntarily focus on an activity when requested to do so by the teacher

use time well

attend to a task for a reasonable period of time

Goal: critical thinking

Objective: problem-solving skills

link cause and effect

make comparisons and draw conclusions

anticipate and think ahead (plan)

estimate

develop creative thinking skills (i.e., originality, flexibility, elaboration)

predict

try alternative methods to solve a problem

overcome obstacles in a task and try alternative routes to a solution when needed

ask questions

use resource persons effectively

communicate/report what one has done

Goal: logical concepts

Objective: order

order by size

order by temporal sequence

order by ordinal relationship: first, second, third

order by length, height (seriation)

Objective: classify

sort according to one observable attribute

sort according to two observable attributes

sort according to knowledge-based attribute(s)

sort according to abstract attribute(s)

sort according to hierarchies of classes

Objective: understand number

know sight and sound of numbers (recite)

know social significance of number

label number symbols

create sets using one-to-one correspondence

recognize equal sets

count meaningfully (understand quantity)

retain constancy of quantity in spite of properties of objects counted (number constancy)

conserve number (know that number is constant in spite of changes in the configurations of objects)

Goal: language and literacy

Objective: visual-perceptual abilities

recognize abstract shapes and symbols

discriminate letter symbols

identify/label letters

move eyes in left-to-right direction

move eyes together—tracking, pursuit, scanning

focus—near/far

scan a page

remember pictures, symbols

reproduce correct directional positioning of letter and number symbols

Objective: auditory-perceptual abilities

identify gross sounds

identify less obvious sounds/tones

recognize significant phonemes in words

link sound to its source

differentiate syllables—know that words are made of distinguishable sounds

clap according to syllables in words

know that beginning sounds are the first ones we say in a word

know that ending sounds are the last ones we say in a word

recognize words with similar beginning and ending sounds

use words that rhyme (e.g., fish, dish)

imitate sounds

Objective: receptive language abilities

listen actively/attend

differentiate consonant sounds and blends

understand the speech of others

follow one-, two-, and three-step instructions

Objective: expressive language abilities

label concrete objects

use words in correct context (meanings of words)

use language that can be understood by others

combine words into sentences

link words and phrases into longer passages

deliver messages

describe events

tell a story

Objective: link language and physical abilities

speak while physically active (describe actions)

use words that describe physical actions or sensations

follow verbal instructions in physical activities

represent a verbal instruction physically

pantomime stories or experiences

Objective: use language creatively

use descriptive words

describe experiences verbally

play with words—rhymes, nonsense rhymes, riddles

use words to convince/persuade/influence

recite chants

use words in song

make up new words

learn words from other languages

use words associated with feelings

use props to enhance and support language

tell stories

Objective: appreciate language

choose favourite words

find new words in stories and rhymes

match similar words according to sound and other properties

repeat favourite stories, rhymes

experiment with other languages and modes of communication (pantomime)

experiment with creative elements of language (e.g., cacophony, onomatopoeia, alliteration, simile, metaphor)

Objective: socialized speech

articulate clearly—pronounce correctly

ask and respond to questions

engage in conversation

observe pragmatics of conversation—speak in turn, listen to speaker, respond to others

memorize poems, rhymes, songs

Objective: read

recognize own name printed

recognize familiar words/names in print

read simple signs

read directions in computer software programs

tell stories from illustrations in books

read simple stories

Objective: print

trace letters, numbers, and other symbols

copy symbols/words using mouse on computer screen or using koala pad

print own name

print letters and numbers

print simple words

AFFECTIVE DOMAIN

Goal: psychological health

Objective

form attachment/bonds

separate from family members successfully for brief periods

trust others

act independently

appreciate own achievements

value self (exhibit self-esteem)

express needs verbally

express feelings using drama, art
media

express emotions/feelings verbally

accept one's own negative feelings

find acceptable outlets for fear, anger,
anxiety, and other powerful negative feelings

clarify and express feelings by using
creative play materials, props, et cetera

Goal: social relations

Objective

care for others/help others

respect others—family members,
peers, teachers

initiate contact with others

function successfully in groups at
appropriate times

respond to environmental and social
demands appropriately

Goal: social perceptions

Objective

form reliable concept of self based on
feedback

understand role in group/social play

demonstrate ease in social situations

imitate remembered events

maintain role in sociodramatic play

respect social norms/rules/conven-
tions

adapt to changing demands

feel positively about one's own gender

feel positively about one's ethnic heritage

feel sense of belonging to group

appreciate humour and fun

Goal: moral behaviour and understanding

Objective

observe limits/rules

control/channel emotions appropriately

restrain inappropriate impulses

get what one wants in socially acceptable ways

delay gratification

PHYSICAL DOMAIN

Goal: body awareness

Objective: body image

recognize body parts

name body parts

move body parts on command (in a
song or game)

recognize differences between one's
own body and those of others (e.g.,
colour of eyes, height, hair colour)

recognize own individuality and that
of others

Objective: spatial awareness

move body in a confined space

make body smaller to fit into a small
space

project and control the body in space
without colliding with others

locate objects in space in relation to
oneself

locate objects in space without reference to oneself

follow direction and path of objects in space

print letters and symbols that maintain a consistent direction in space

Objective: laterality

move both sides of the body simultaneously and equally (bilaterality)

move each side of the body consecutively, first one side then the other (alternating laterality)

perform cross-lateral patterns of movement (move left arm and right leg forward, then right arm, left leg, and so on, in creeping, walking, marching) (cross-laterality)

perform one action with one side of the body and a different action with the opposite side (integrated laterality)

Objective: directionality

move own body in specific directions or positions

move objects in specific directions or positions

follow directional signals on command: forward, backward, sideways, left, right

recognize and follow symbols indicating direction

recognize and copy correct direction of numbers and letters

Objective: temporal awareness

move own body to various tempos, rhythmical patterns, and intensities

perform fundamental locomotor and non-locomotor movements

sing and clap rhymes

perform simple folk dances

manipulate objects (tossing and catching) to rhythm or music

combine bouncing, tossing, catching, or juggling to music or rhythm

Goal: basic fundamental movements

Objective: locomotor skills

crawl
creep
walk
run
jump
hop
gallop
march
skip
climb

Objective: non-locomotor skills

bend
curl
stretch
sway
turn
twist
swing
reach
lift
push
pull
twirl

Objective: manipulative abilities

propulsive movements:
  roll
  throw
  kick
  punt
  strike
  bounce
  volley
absorptive movements:

catch

trap

ball handling

Objective: fine-motor skills

finger dexterity

pincer movements

hand control

trace

grasp

crush

arrange objects

shape and mould

fill and pour

bend and fold

Goal: sensory-perceptual abilities

Objective: visual perceptual skills

form discrimination

depth perception

figure-ground perception

ocular-motor skills: accommodation, fixation, pursuit, tracking

Objective: auditory perceptual skills

listen

discriminate

respond

integrate movements and commands

Objective: spatial awareness and kinesthetic discrimination

make physical adjustments to one's body in the environment

slow down and speed up on cue

make physical adjustments to space by crouching, balancing, stretching

Objective: physical abilities

physical fitness:

muscular strength

muscular endurance

flexibility

cardio-vascular endurance

circulatory-respiratory endurance

motor fitness:

balance

speed

agility

power

coordination

Objective: healthy habits and attitudes

exercise daily

enjoy physical activity

eat healthy food

avoid harmful substances

Glossary of Terms Used in This Book

accommodation - the revision that takes place when children alter their existing mental structures to fit what they already know with the new learning or experience that challenges their present understanding.

activity - an event circumscribed by a time frame, context, or specific setting that includes materials that may be used flexibly or whose use is prescribed; activities may be pre-planned or spontaneously selected and initiated by the child.

activity-centred methods - direct teaching or supervision by an adult to ensure children's safety and success with the activity in which a specific outcome is intended.

affective development - the social and emotional development of the child.

assimilation - the change that children make in an object, event, or phenomenon to try to fit a new learning experience to already existing mental structures.

associative play - loosely organized play in which children participate in a similar activity but do not subordinate their individual interests to those of the group.

attention span - the amount of time a child will attend to a task or activity assuming that it is interesting to the child.

auditory discrimination - the ability to hear differences and similarities in sounds and tones.

auditory-motor integration - the ability to move the body according to sounds on command of the auditory stimulus.

child-centred education - refers to learning in settings where children select activities themselves, pursue them in their own ways, set their own goals, decide when they have finished, and sometimes communicate what they have done. Children are encouraged to assume responsibility for their own learning within the planned environment with a teacher who facilitates learning.

classification - the ability to group objects according to similar attributes that may be defined or selected by the teacher or chosen by the child.

climate - the social and emotional mood or tone prevalent in an environment.

cognitive development - the child's intellectual and perceptual development; development of the mind and senses.

competitive play - play in which two or more children in a group or two or more groups of children compete to win.

complexity - the measure of the capacity of the learning environment to keep children interested for reasonable periods of time. Complexity is calculated by determining the potential of each play unit for active participation by one or more children.

complex unit - a play unit with subparts or a juxtaposition of two essentially different play materials that enable the child to manipulate or improvise. Four play spaces are attributed to a complex unit.

concept - an idea or understanding of the relationships that exist between objects, people, or events.

concept formation - the learning process involved in being able to classify or order ideas or things according to the principles that comprise the concept.

concrete operational period - the developmental stage in which children have the ability to apply simple logic to solve problems and to perform simple mathematical operations using numerals, by relying on concrete objects. This period applies to children between the ages of seven and eleven approximately.

conservation of number - the ability to understand that the quantity or number of objects in a set remains the same in spite of transformations or changes in the configuration of the set.

constructive play - productive play in which children interact with materials in ways that produce results the child intends.

constructivist early childhood education - refers to programs that provide self-directed play and learning opportunities with materials that respond to the child's actions on them and lead to concept formation.

contents - the play units available within the play space.

cooperative play - group social play involving children with common goals who assume different roles or tasks. Play often persists for a relatively long time and at high levels of complexity.

creative-constructive play - play in which children interact with the play materials for their own purposes, often without any plan or strategy to produce a specific outcome.

dead space - a large amount of empty space roughly square or circular in shape often in the centre of a room or play area with no visible boundaries.

developmentally appropriate practice - refers to the provision of programs and learning environments for young children in which the individual developmental needs and capabilities of children constitute the basis upon which activities and programs are planned.

developmental domain - an area of development dominated by the child's cognitive, physical, social, or emotional capacities.

developmental goals - long-term aims for the development of children based on the normal tasks of development in the cognitive, physical, social, and emotional domains.

developmental objectives - short-term steps towards the achievement of long-term developmental goals. Objectives are usually expressed as skills, tasks or behaviours to be practised and mastered by the child.

developmental tasks - abilities/skills that children normally acquire at specific stages in their development.

diagnosis - the teacher's assessment of which objectives children are able to meet successfully and which require more practice.

dramatic play - sustained pretend play in which one child persists in acting out a role using gestures, props, or movement.

early childhood curriculum - an outline of the developmental goals and objects that are considered to be developmentally appropriate for children at specific stages. The curriculum approach is interactionist and includes a statement of goals and objectives, activities that address objectives, a description of teaching and learning methods that will facilitate children's largely self-directed mastery of the objectives, and a plan for evaluation of the activities, environments, and program.

ecology - the study of the interrelationships of living things with the environments in which they exist.

equilibration - the motivational factor for learning that occurs as a result of the joint processes of *assimilation* and *accommodation*.

equipment - the furniture, storage containers, and large items of play equipment that are often used to define the boundaries of a learning centre and the type of play that is encouraged there.

evaluation - the systematic appraisal of the effectiveness of an activity, program, or curriculum in promoting developmental progress and learning for young children.

exploratory methods - children's active manipulation of concrete objects in the environment for the purpose of examining them, discovering their properties, and acquiring physical knowledge using the senses.

facilitator - a person whose role it is to make something easier for others to do, say, think, or feel.

fantasy play - a form of symbolic play in which children imitate characters and events from stories, television programs, rhymes, verse, and other dramatizations.

figure-ground perception - the ability to select a limited number of stimuli (figure) from a visual field or mass (ground); the figure and the field may keep changing; the stimuli which are to be selected form the figure; the rest forms a background or field.

fine-motor skills - usually refers to the use of the fingers and hands in tasks that require manipulation of objects. These skills may also include hand, eye, and foot coordination.

formal education - education in which activities are usually initiated or suggested by the teacher, often for some sort of reward. Formal education usually refers to more traditional schooling. This term may also refer to education that makes use of already formed mental structures.

free-form materials - surface-diffusable materials that flow rather than fit together to make the whole.

free play - play in which children make their own choices and decisions, and are free to express their own feelings and representations in play.

functional play - simple, repetitive movements with or without concrete objects; usually dominant during the sensorimotor period. Functional play is usually found in the play of the infant and toddler who explore objects physically, using their senses.

games-with-rules play - play in which children begin to accept certain external limitations on their play such as rules made by someone else. Children also begin to make their own rules and to question existing rules.

guide - an aspect of the teacher's role which is to help the child make the most of the play and learning environment.

hands-on learning - activity in which children learn largely through their active, physical interaction with concrete objects in the environment.

imitative play - an early form of symbolic play that begins during the first year of life and refers to the child's simple imitation of the parent or other caregiver.

informal education - educational activities used for the purpose of structure formation (i.e., to form mental structures) and are generally initiated by children for their own sake.

learning centre - a well-defined area of a playroom or playground with boundaries. Includes specific equipment, materials, and supplies related to promoting children's development and learning of particular concepts and skills.

learning style - the approach to learning favoured by a child. For example, children may prefer social learning contexts or solitary learning endeavours, or may require visual or auditory stimulation, frequent feedback, or considerable independence in order to learn effectively.

left-brain thinking - thought that originates in the left hemisphere and governs analytic, logical, temporal, sequential, linear, verbal, abstract, factual, computational, concrete, and practical processes.

logical concepts - seriation, classification, and number concepts, which, in early childhood, include a range of thinking abilities that lead children progressively towards mastery of abilities relating to concepts of order, class, quantity, and conservation.

logical-mathematical knowledge - understanding of universal concepts and principles and of the largely abstract relationships that exist between them.

malleable materials - soft, pliable substances that can be moulded by the child and take the shape the child intends. Includes clay, plasticene, wet sand, and playdough. Sometimes referred to as plastic materials.

materials - the concrete objects and toys that appear in the foreground of the play and learning environment for children to play with, manipulate, explore, test, and transform.

methods - the strategies or techniques teachers use to implement play and learning experiences for children that emphasize learning opportunities in which children are active learners.

modular materials - materials that have many pieces or multiple units, usually of uniform shapes and sizes that are made to fit together in specific ways.

number constancy - the ability to understand that quantity does not change according to the properties of the objects being counted.

one-to-one correspondence - matching two sets of objects when each set contains the same number of objects.

onlooking play - play in which a child is observing children playing but does not physically participate.

open-ended materials - materials with an indefinite number of outcomes and a maximum amount of flexibility in the ways in which these materials may be used by children.

ordering - a complicated form of comparing based on a particular relationship between two objects.

ordinal number - the forming of relationships based on what comes first, second, third, and so on in a series.

parallel play - play in which two children play side by side, each with her own activity and do not interact, although they may talk in monologues.

pathway - a broad, elongated, unobstructed space that is visible at children's eye levels and helps to separate and define learning centres. Pathways lead children into and out of learning centres.

physical knowledge - sensory-perceptual learning about the concrete, physical properties of objects. It refers to learning about colour, shape, size, texture, and other observable characteristics of things.

play - behaviour with no external goals, undertaken more for the process involved than for any purpose or end. Play is freely chosen, spontaneous, non-literal, enjoyable, and valued in itself. It involves children's attempts to fit new experiences with what they know already.

play station - an area or equipment within a learning centre dedicated to play with materials that address specific developmental and learning objectives.

potential units - empty spaces in a play area surrounded by visible or tangible boundaries to which can be added play equipment and/or materials.

practice play - an early functional play that is exploratory and usually involves the repetition of physical behaviours that have already been mastered. It is characterized by the infant's sucking on objects, making sounds, gazing and other repetitive, largely sensorimotor behaviours.

prescription - the teacher's analysis of the child's developmental needs to which she attaches specific plans designed to help the child make developmental progress.

pretend play - play in which children practise their own versions of adult behaviours rather than imitating only what they have seen; it is usually very simple and somewhat predictable.

productive play - play in which the outcomes are increasingly recognizable to adults; play outcomes and products become more lifelike and recognizable.

props - materials that children may use to support their symbolic play particularly in dramatic and sociodramatic play or sociodrama.

repetitive play - a form of functional play usually involving the repetition of physical behaviours that have already been mastered.

representation - the ability to engage in symbolic behaviours using standard symbols, words, drama, visual art, or music to evoke images, ideas, or to substitute for something else.

reproductive play - play in which children represent remembered events, images, and actions. This type of play is increasingly representative of what children understand or want to understand about their environmental experiences.

responsive play materials - materials such as blocks, clay, and Lego that respond to children's physical exploration and manipulation by taking the shape the child intends.

right-brain thinking - thought that originates in the right hemisphere of the brain, such as intuitive, spontaneous, random, holistic, nonverbal, visual, spatial, sensory, and symbolic processes.

sensorimotor play - largely physical and sensory play as children gain control over their movements and gather information by way of the senses. It is play that involves the child's physical interaction with concrete objects in the environment in order to discover the physical properties of things.

seriation - the arrangement of objects based on a graduated order, in which there is a common baseline and equal gradations in the size of successive objects in a series.

set - a group of objects with at least one common attribute.

simple unit - a play unit with one primary purpose in play, generally used by one child at a time for the purpose intended. Simple play units do not usually have subparts; simple units are attributed one play space.

social-conventional knowledge - facts and information that are socially and culturally transmitted and often arbitrarily assigned such as rules, proper names, conventions, and customs.

sociodrama - the enactment through play of a story or another dramatic production; it is usually externally motivated and limitations are imposed on roles and behaviours by the story or by another drama.

sociodramatic play - play in which two or more children collaborate in dramatizing experiences from their own physical and social environments. It involves representations of remembered events which are common to the children playing. Children assume related roles and follow each other's cues in acting out an event or social context.

solitary play - play in which one child plays alone, although he may be in a room where other children are playing.

specific-purpose materials - means-ends materials that have an internal structure that often mandates the outcome of play as well as steps to be followed in reaching the outcome.

superhero play - symbolic play that may be dramatic, sociodramatic play, or sociodrama, in which children assume roles associated with fictional, often fantastical, characters from stories or television programs. The superheroes are generally endowed with superhuman qualities, and the play often has a rough-and-tumble quality.

super unit - a complex unit that has one or more play materials added to it (i.e., three or more play materials are juxtaposed). Eight play spaces may be attributed to super units, which means that they usually occupy a large space and are fairly elaborate.

supplies - the consumable items in the play and learning environment that need to be replenished frequently.

symbolic play - play in which objects and actions are used to represent other objects or actions.

teacher-demonstration - a teaching method in which the teacher demonstrates, with or without the help of the child, how to perform a specific movement or skill.

teacher-directed methods - planning and teaching strategies in which the teacher decides in advance of the learning experience what objectives will be addressed, how they will be addressed, and guides the implementation of the activity to its anticipated outcome.

temporal order - refers to the relationship among events according to the order in which they took place.

testing play - a form of functional play characterized by motor testing, crawling into and out of small places, or challenging one's physical abilities.

three-dimensional materials - lifelike representations or whole objects having length, width, and depth such as an actual apple or a car.

two-dimensional materials - materials that have length and width but very little depth.

variety - the potential of the play unit to accommodate different kinds of play activity such as digging, pouring, building, stacking, and twirling.

Bibliography

Alexander, D. (1983). Children's Computer Drawings. ERIC Document, ED 238562.

Almy, M. (1984). A child's right to play. *Young Children* 39 (4). Washington, D.C.: National Association for the Education of Young Children.

Althouse, R. (1988). *Investigating Science with Young Children*. New York: Teachers College Press, Columbia University.

Anderson, H.H. (1975). On the meaning of creativity. *Creativity in Childhood and Adolescence: A Diversity of Approaches,* ed. H.H. Anderson, pp. 46–61. Palo Alto, CA: Science and Behavior Books Inc.

Anderson, S, and Hoot, J.L. (1986). Kids, carpentry and the preschool classroom. *Day Care and Early Education*. Spring: 12–15.

Anselmo, S., and Zinck, R.A. (1987). Computers for Young Children? Perhaps? *Young Children* 42 (2):22-27.

Ariès, P. (1962). *Centuries of Childhood*. New York: Knopf.

Arnett, J. (1989). Caregivers in day care centres: does training matter? *Journal of Applied Developmental Psychology* 10: 541–52.

Austin, E.M. (1986, November). Beyond superheroes: constructive power play in the preschool. Paper presented at the Annual Conference of the National Association for the Education of Young Children.

Axline, V. (1947). *Play Therapy*. New York: Ballantine.

Baker, K.R. (1966). *Let's Play Outdoors*. Washington, D.C.: National Association for the Education of Young Children.

Baratta-Lorton, M. (1972). *Workjobs: Activity-Centred Learning for Early Childhood Education*. Menlo Park, CA: Addison-Wesley.

Barnes, B.J., and Hill, S. (1983). Should young children use microcomputers: LOGO before LEGO? *The Computing Teacher* 10 (9):11–14.

Beatty, J.J., and Tucker, W.H. (1987). *The Computer as a Paintbrush: Creative Uses for the Personal Computer in the Preschool Classroom*. Columbus: Merrill.

Beckwith, J. (1985). Equipment selection for modern playgrounds. In *When Children Play*, ed. J.L. Frost and S. Sunderlin. Wheaton, MD: Association for Childhood Education International.

Behrmann, M.M., and Levy, S.A. (1986). Computers and special education. In *Computers in Early Childhood Education,* ed. J. Hoot, pp. 104–27. Englewood Cliffs, NJ: Prentice-Hall.

Bender, J. (1971). Have you ever thought of a prop box? *Young Children* 27 (1): 164–69.

Bereiter, C., and Engelmann, S. (1966). *Teaching Disadvantaged Children in the Preschool*. Englewood Cliffs, NJ: Prentice-Hall.

Berko Gleason, J. (1989). Studying language development. In *The Development of Language,* 2d ed, ed. J. Berko Gleason, pp. 1–34. Columbus, OH: Merrill.

Berrueta-Clement, J.R., Schweinhart, L.J., Barnett, W.S., Epstein, A.S., and Weikart, D.P. (1984). Changed lives: the effects of the Perry Preschool program on youths through age 19. Monographs of the High/Scope Educational Research Foundation. Ypsilanti, MI: High/Scope Press.

Bettelheim, B. (1987). *A Good Enough Parent*. New York: Random House.

Bettelheim, B. (1987). The importance of play. *The Atlantic* 262 (3).

Birk, L. (1985). Relationship of caregiver education to child-oriented attitudes, job satisfaction and behaviors toward children. *Child Care Quarterly* 14 (2): 103–29.

Bohannon, J.N., and Warren-Leubecker, A. (1989). Theoretical approaches to language acquisition. In *The Development of Language,*

2d ed., ed. J. Berko Gleason, pp. 167–223. Columbus, OH: Merrill.

Brady, E.H., and Hill, S. (1984). Young children and microcomputers: research issues and directions. *Young Children* 39 (3):49–59.

Bredekamp, S. (1987). *Developmentally Appropriate Practice in Early Childhood Programs Serving Children From Birth to Age 8*. Washington, D.C.: National Association for the Education of Young Children.

Bredekamp, S. (1991). Redeveloping early childhood education: a response to Kessler. *Early Childhood Research Quarterly* 6 (2): 199–210.

Bruner, J. (1960). *The Process of Education*. Cambridge, MA: Harvard University Press.

Bruner, J. (1983). *Child's Talk: Learning to Use Language*. New York: W.W. Norton.

Bruner, J., and Anglin, J. (1973). *Beyond the Information Given: Studies in the Psychology of Knowing*. New York: W.W. Norton.

Burg, K. (1984). The microcomputer in the kindergarten: a magical, useful, expensive toy. *Young Children* 39 (3):28–33.

Burns, M.S., Goin, L., and Donlon, J.T. (1990). A computer in my room. *Young Children* 45 (1): 62–67.

Butler, A.L., Gotts, E.E., and Quisenberry, N.L. (1978). *Play as Development*. Columbus: Merrill.

Campbell, S. (1984). *Facilities and Equipment for Day Care*. Ottawa: Health and Welfare Canada.

Canada Mortgage and Housing Corporation. (1978). *Play Spaces for Preschoolers* (advisory document prepared by P. Hill, S. Esbensen, and W. Rock). Ottawa: CMHC.

Canadian Institute of Child Health. (1985). *When Child's Play Is Adult Business: A Consumer Guide to Safer Playspaces*. Ottawa: CICH.

Canadian Standards Association. (1990). A guideline on children's playspaces and equipment. (CAN/CSA-Z614-M90).

Canadian Toy Testing Council. (1990). *1990 Toy Report*. Ottawa: Canadian Toy Testing Council.

Cartwright, S. (1988). Play can be the building blocks of learning. *Young Children* 43 (4): 44–47.

Casey, B. (1990). A planning and problem-solving preschool model: the methodology of being a good learner. *Early Childhood Research Quarterly* 5 (1): 53–68.

Casey, B, and Lippmann, M. (1991). Learning to plan through play. *Young Children* 46 (4): 52–58.

Cass-Beggs, B. (1974). *To Listen, To Like, To Learn*. Toronto: Peter Martin Associates Ltd.

Cazden, C. (1981). Language development and the preschool environment. In *Language in Early Childhood Education*, ed. C. Cazden, pp. 3–16. Washington, D.C.: National Association for the Education of Young Children.

Cech, M. (1990). *Globalchild*. Toronto: Addison-Wesley.

Charlesworth, R., and Radeloff, D. (1991). *Experiences in Math for Young Children*. 2d ed. Albany, NY: Delmar.

Cherry, C. (1983). *Please Don't Sit on the Kids*. Belmont, CA: Pitman.

Cherry, C., Godwin, D., and Staples, J. (1989). *Is the Left Brain Always Right? A Guide to Whole Child Development*. Belmont, CA: Fearon.

Children's Environments Advisory Service. (1975). *Adventure Playgrounds*. Ottawa: Central Mortgage and Housing Corporation.

Children's Environments Advisory Service. (1975). *Creative Playgrounds*. Ottawa: Central Mortgage and Housing Corporation.

Christie, J.F., and Wardle, F. (1992). How much time is needed for play? *Young Children* 47 (3):28–32.

Clemens, S.G. (1991). Art in the classroom: making every day special. *Young Children* 46 (1): 4–11.

Clements, D.H. (1986). Logo programming in the early grades: research and implications. In *Computers in Early Childhood Education:*

Issues and Practices, ed. J. Hoot. Englewood Cliffs, NJ: Prentice-Hall.

Coburn, P., Kilman, P., Roberts, N., Snyder, F.F., Watt, D., and Weiner, C. (1985). *Practical Guide to Computers in Education.* 2d ed. Reading: Addison-Wesley.

Coles, R. (1990). *The Spiritual Life of Children.* Boston: Houghton-Mifflin.

Communications Directorate, Environment Canada. (1990). *What We Can Do For Our Environment: Hundreds of Things to Do Now.* Ottawa: Minister of Supply and Services.

Cruikshank, D.E., Fitzgerald, D.L., and Jensen, L.R. (1980). *Young Children Learning Mathematics.* Boston: Allyn & Bacon.

Davidson, J.I. (1989). *Children and Computers: Together in the Early Childhood Classroom.* Albany, NY:Delmar.

DeMause, L. (1974). *History of Childhood.* New York: Psychohistory Press.

DeVries, R., and Kohlberg, L. (1987). *Constructivist Early Education: Overview and Comparison with Other Programs.* Washington, D.C.: National Association for the Education of Young Children.

Dickson, W.P., and Vereen, M. (1983). Two students at one microcomputer. *Theory Into Practice* 22 (4):296–300.

Doherty, G. (1991). *Factors Related to Quality in Child Care: A Review of the Literature.* Toronto: Ontario Ministry of Community and Social Services—Child Care Branch.

Donaldson, M. (1978). *Children's Minds.* London: Fontana.

Duckworth, E. (1973). The having of wonderful ideas. In *Piaget in the Classroom,* ed. M. Schwebel and J. Raph. New York: Basic Books.

Duckworth, E. (1987). *The Having of Wonderful Ideas and Other Essays on Teaching and Learning.* New York: Teachers College Press, Columbia University.

Duckworth, E. (1991). Twenty-four, Forty-two, and I Love You: Keeping It Complex. *Harvard Educational Review* 61 (1):1–24.

Elkind, D. (1977). The early years: the vital years. *Journal of the Canadian Association for Young Children.* 3 (1): 20–21.

Elkind, D. (1981). *The Hurried Child.* Reading, MA: Addison-Wesley.

Elkind, D. (1987). *Miseducation—Preschoolers at Risk.* New York: Knopf.

Elkind, D. (1988). Play. *Young Children* 43 (4):2.

Elkind, D. (1989). Developmentally appropriate education for 4-year-olds. *Theory into Practice* 28 (1):47–52.

Elkind, D. (1989). Developmentally appropriate practice: philosophical and practical implications. *Phi Delta Kappan* 71 (2):113–17.

Ellis, M. (1973). *Why People Play.* Englewood Cliffs, NJ: Prentice-Hall.

Erikson, E. (1968). *Identity, Youth and Crisis.* New York: W.W. Norton.

Esbensen, S.B. (1980) Legislation and guidelines for children's play spaces in the residential environment. *Ekistics* 281: 123–25.

Esbensen, S.B. (1984). *Hidden Hazards on Playgrounds for Children.* Hull, Quebec: Université du Québec à Hull.

Esbensen, S.B. (1987). *The Early Childhood Playground: An Outdoor Classroom.* Ypsilanti, MI: High/Scope Press.

Esbensen, S.B. (1988). Play environments for young children: design perspectives. In *Playgrounds for Young Children: National Survey and Perspectives,* ed. S.C. Wortham and J.L. Frost. American Association for Leisure and Recreation.

Esbensen, S.B. (1990). Designing the setting for the early childhood program. In *Child Care and Education: Canadian Dimensions,* ed. I. Doxey. Toronto: Nelson.

Fein, G. (1985). The affective psychology of play. In *Play Interactions: The Role of Toys and Parental Involvement in Children's Development,* ed. C.C. Brown and A.W. Gottfried, pp. 19–28. Skillman, NJ: Johnson & Johnson.

Fein, G., and Rivkin, M. (1986). *The Young Child at Play.* Washington, D.C.: National Association for the Education of Young Children.

Fields, M., and Lee, D. (1987). *Let's Begin Reading Right: A Developmental Approach to Beginning Literacy.* Columbus, OH: Merrill.

Forman, G.E., and Kuschner, D.S. (1988). *The Child's Construction of Knowledge: Piaget for Teaching Children.* Washington, D.C.: National Association for the Education of Young Children.

Fowler, W. (1980). *Infant and Child Care: A Guide to Education in Group Settings.* Toronto: Allyn & Bacon.

Freud, A. (1946). *The Psychoanalytical Treatment of Children.* London: Imago.

Furman, E. (1990). Plant a potato—learn about life (and death). *Young Children* 45 (6): 15–20.

Gallahue, D.L. (1982). *Understanding Motor Development in Children.* New York: Wiley.

Garbarino, J. (1989). An ecological perspective on the role of play. In *The Ecological Context of Children's Play,* ed. M.N. Bloch and A.D. Pelligrini. Norwood, NJ: Ablex.

Gardner, H. (1980). *Artful Scribbles: the Significance of Children's Drawings.* New York: Basic Books.

Gardner, H. (1982). *Art, Mind and Brain.* New York: Basic Books.

Gardner, H. (1983). *Frames of Mind.* New York: Basic Books.

Gardner, H. (1989). The study of intelligences. Speech delivered to the Annual Conference of the Canadian Association for Young Children. Kingston, Ontario: October 13, 1989.

Gardner, H. (1989). *To Open Minds.* New York: Basic Books.

Garvey, C. *Play.* Cambridge: Harvard University Press.

Gelfer, J. (1990). Discovering and learning art with blocks. *Day Care and Early Education.* Summer: 21–24.

Gesell, A. (1940). *The First Five Years of Life.* New York: Harper and Row.

Gesell, A., and Ilg, F. (1943). *Infant and Child in the Culture of Today.* New York: Harper.

Gilmore, J.B. (1966). Play: a special behavior. In *Current Research in Motivation,* ed. R.N. Haber, pp. 343–55. New York: Holt, Rinehart & Winston.

Ginsberg, H., and Opper, S. (1969). *Piaget's Theory of Intellectual Development: An Introduction.* Englewood Cliffs, NJ: Prentice-Hall.

Glenn, J.A., ed. (1977). *Teaching Primary Mathematics: Strategy and Evaluation.* London: Harper & Row.

Grover, S. (1986). A field study of the use of cognitive-developmental principles in microcomputer design for young children. *Journal of Educational Research* 79 (4): 325–32.

Hendrick, J. (1988). *The Whole Child.* 4th ed. Columbus: Merrill.

Hill, D.M. (1977). *Mud, Sand, and Water.* Washington, D.C.: National Association for the Education of Young Children.

Hirsch, E. (1984). *The Block Book.* Washington, D.C.: National Association for the Education of Young Children.

Hitz, R., and Driscoll, A. (1988). Praise or encouragement? New insights into praise: implications for early childhood teachers. *Young Children* 43 (4): 6–3.

Hofmann, R. (1986). Piaget and microcomputer learning environments. *Journal of Learning Disabilities* 19 (3): 181–84.

Hohmann, M., Banet, B., and Weikart, D. (1979). *Young Children in Action.* Ypsilanti, MI: High/Scope.

Holt, B. (1989). *Science with Young Children.* Rev. ed. Washington, D.C.: National Association for the Education of Young Children.

Houle, G.B. (1987). *Learning Centres for Young Children.* 3d ed. West Greenwich, RI: Tot-lot Child Care Products.

Howell, R.D., Scot, P.B., and Diamond, J. (1987). The effects of "instant" LOGO computing language on the cognitive development of very young children. *Journal of Educational Computing Research* 3 (2):449–60.

Hungate, H. (1982). Computers in the kindergarten. *The Computing Teacher* 9 (5): 15–18.

Hunka, S. (1987). The role of computers in Canadian education. In *Contemporary Educational Issues: the Canadian Mosaic,* ed. L.L. Stewin and S.J.H. McCann, pp. 69–81. Toronto: Copp Clark Pitman.

Isaacs, N. (1972). *A Brief Introduction to Piaget.* London: Agathon Press.

Javna, J. (1990). *50 Simple Things Kids Can Do to Save The Earth.* Kansas, MO: The Earth-Works Group, Andrews and McMeel, A Universal Press Syndicate Company.

Jipson, J. (1991). Developmentally-appropriate practice: culture, curriculum, connections. *Early Education and Development* 2 (2):120–36.

Johnson, J.E. (1985). Characteristics of preschoolers interested in microcomputers. *Journal of Educational Research* 78 (5): 299–305.

Jorde-Bloom, B. (1989). *The Illinois Directors Study.* Report submitted to the Illinois Department of Child and Family Services. Evanston, Illinois: National College of Education. ERIC Document, ED 305 167.

Kamii, C. (1972). An application of Piaget's theory to the conceptualization of a preschool curriculum. In *The Preschool in Action,* ed. R. Parker. Boston, MA: Allyn & Bacon.

Kamii, C. (1982). *Number in the Preschool.* Washington, D.C.: National Association for the Education of Young Children.

Kamii, C. (1985). *Young Children Reinvent Arithmetic: Implications of Piaget's Theory.* New York: Teachers College Press, Columbia University.

Kamii, C., and DeVries, R. (1978). *Physical Knowledge in Preschool Education: Implications of Piaget's Theory.* Englewood Cliffs, NJ: Prentice-Hall.

Kamii, C., and DeVries, R. (1980). *Group Games in Early Education.* Washington, D.C.: National Association for the Education of Young Children.

Katz, L.G. (1974). *Talks with Teachers.* Washington, D.C.: National Association for the Education of Young Children.

Katz, L.G., and Chard, S.C. (1989). *Engaging Children's Minds: The Project Approach.* Norwood, NJ: Ablex.

Kellogg, R. (1967). *The Psychology of Children's Art.* New York: Random House.

Kessler, S.A. (1991). Alternative perspectives on early childhood education. *Early Childhood Research Quarterly* 6 (2):183–98.

Kessler, S.A. (1991). Early childhood education as development: critique of the metaphor. *Early Education and Development* 2 (2): 137–52.

Kimes, B.K., and Maurer, K. (1987). Teaching with less talking: learning centres in the kindergarten. *Young Children* 42 (4):20–27.

Kimmel, S., (1981). Programs for preschoolers: starting out young. *Creative Computing* 7 (10): 50–53.

Klein, P.S. (1988). Children's feelings toward computers: a phenomenological view of some developmental aspects. *International Journal of Early Childhood* (OMEP) 20 (1): 52–60.

Kohlberg, L., and Mayer, R. (1972). Development as the aim of education. *Harvard Educational Review* 42 (4):449–96.

Kostelnik, M.J. (1992). Myths associated with developmentally appropriate programs. *Young Children* 47 (4): 17–23.

Kostelnik, M.J., Whiren, A.P., and Stein, L.C. (1986). Living with he man: managing superhero fantasy play. *Young Children* 41 (3): 3–9.

Kritchevsky, S., Prescott, E., and Walling, L. (1977). *Planning Environments for Young Children: Physical Space.* Washington, D.C.: National Association for the Education of Young Children.

Lasky, L., and Mukerji, R. (1980). *Art: Basic for Young Children.* Washington, D.C.: National Association for the Education of Young Children.

Laurendeau, M., and Pinard, A. (1968). *Les Premières Notions Spatiales de L'enfant.* Montreal: Delachaux & Niestle.

Lewin, A.W. (1981). Down with green lambs: creating quality software for children. *Theory Into Practice* 24 (4): 277–80.

Lind, K.K. (1991). *Exploring Science in Early Childhood: A Developmental Approach.* Albany, NY: Delmar.

Lindauer, S.K. (1987). Montessori education for young children. In *Approaches to Early Childhood Education,* ed. J.L. Roopnarine and J.E. Johnson, pp. 109–26. Columbus, OH: Merrill.

Lipinski, J.M., Nida, R.E., Shade, D.D., and Watson, J.A. (1984). Competence, gender and preschoolers' freeplay choices when a microcomputer is present in the classroom. ERIC Document, ED 243609.

Lovell, K. (1971). *The Growth of Basic Mathematical and Scientific Concepts in Children.* London: University of London Press.

Lovell, P., and Harms, T. (1985). How can playgrounds be improved? A rating scale. *Young Children* 40 (3): 3–8.

Lowenfeld, V., and Brittain, W.L. (1975). *Creative and Mental Growth.* 6th ed. New York: Macmillan.

MacKinnon, D.W. (1971). Nature and nurture of creative talent. In *Educational Psychology: Readings in Learning and Human Abilities,* ed. R. Ripple. New York: Harper & Row.

Malka, M., and Schulman, S. (1986). Microcomputers in special education: renewed expectations for solutions to chronic difficulties. *The Exceptional Child* 33 (3): 199–205.

McArdle, F., and Barker, B. (1990). *What'll I Do For Art Today?* Melbourne, Australia: Thomas Nelson Australia.

McCracken, J.B. (1990). *Playgrounds Safe and Sound.* Washington, D.C. : National Association for the Education of Young Children.

McGarvey, L. (1986). Microcomputer use in kindergarten and at home: design of the study and effects of computer use on school readiness. ERIC Document, ED 272275.

Ministry of Culture and Recreation. (1982). *A Guide to Creative Playground Development.* Toronto, ON: Government of Ontario.

Ministry of Education, Ontario. (1991). *The Early Years.* A consultation paper. Toronto: Ministry of Education.

Mock, K. (1984). Multicultural education in early childhood: a developmental rationale. In *Multicultural Early Childhood Education,* ed. K.A. McLeod. Toronto: Guidance Centre, University of Toronto.

Moomaw, S. (1984). *Discovering Music in Early Childhood.* Boston, MA: Allyn & Bacon.

Morrow, L.M. (1989). Designing the classroom to promote literacy development. In *Emerging Literacy: Young Children Learn To Read and Write,* ed. D.S. Strickland and L.M. Morrow. Newark, DW: International Reading Association.

Myers, B.K, and Maurer, K. (1987). Teaching with less talking: learning centers in the kindergarten. *Young Children* 42 (4): 20–27.

Nash, C. (1989). *The Learning Environment: A Practical Approach to the Education of the Three-, Four- and Five-Year-Old.* Toronto: Collier-MacMillan.

National Association for the Education of Young Children (1985). *Toys: Tools for Learning.* Washington, D.C.: NAEYC.

National Association for the Education of Young Children (1991). Position Statement: Guidelines for Appropriate Curriculum Content and Assessment in Program Serving Children Ages 3 Through 8. *Young Children* 46 (3):21–38.

Nault, M. (1991). *William, Won't You Wash Your Hands?* Ottawa: Canadian Institute of Child Health.

Neumann, E. (1971). *The Elements of Play.* Unpublished Doctoral Dissertation. University of Illinois.

Newell, A., Shaw, J.C., and Simon, H.A. (1962). The processes of creative thinking. In *Contemporary Approaches to Creative Thinking,* ed. H.E. Gruber, G. Terrell, and M. Wertheimer, pp. 65–66. New York: Atherton.

Nichols, W., and Nichols, D. (1990). *Wonderscience: a developmentally appropriate guide to hands on science for young children*. Palo Alto, CA: Learning Expo Publishing.

Olson, C.P., and Sullivan, E.V. (1987). Beyond the mania: critical approaches to computers in education. In *Contemporary Educational Issues: The Canadian Mosaic*, ed. L.L. Stewin and S.J.H. McCann, pp. 95–106. Toronto: Copp Clark Pitman.

Paasche, C., Gorrill, L., and Strom, B. (1990). *Children with Special Needs in Early Childhood Settings: Identification, Intervention, Mainstreaming*. Toronto, ON: Addison-Wesley.

Papert, S. (1980). *Mindstorms: Children, Computers and Powerful Ideas*. New York: Basic Books.

Pelligrini, A.D. (1980). The relationships between kindergartners' play and reading, writing and language achievement. *Psychology in the School* 17: 530–35.

Pelligrini, A.D. (1984). Children's play and language: infancy through early childhood. In *Child's Play and Play Therapy*, ed. T.D. Yawkey and A.D. Pelligrini, pp. 45–58. Lancaster, PA: Technomic Publishing Co. Inc.

Pelligrini, A.D. (1991). A longitudinal study of popular and rejected children's rough-and-tumble play. *Early Education and Development* 2 (3): 205–13.

Pence, A., and Goelman, H. (undated). Can you see the difference? Regulation, training and quality of care in family day care. Unpublished manuscript, Victoria, BC: University of Victoria.

Perry, G., and Rivkin, M. (1992). Teachers and science. *Young Children* 47 (4): 9–16.

Piaget, J. (1969). *The Psychology of the Child*. New York: Basic Books.

Piaget, J. (1970). *The Science of Education and the Psychology of the Child*. New York: Viking Compass.

Piaget, J. (1972). *To Understand Is to Invent*. New York: Grossman.

Piel, J.A., and Baller, W.A. (1986). Effects of computer assistance on acquisition of Piagetian conceptualization among children of ages two to four. *AEDS Journal* 19 (2–3): 210–15.

Plummer, B. (1974). *Earth Presents*. Washington, D.C.: A & W Visual Library.

Postman, N. (1982). *The Disappearance of Childhood*. New York: Delacorte Press.

Ragsdale, R.G. (1985). Response to Sullivan on Papert's "Mindstorms." *Interchange* 16 (3): 19–36.

Ragsdale, R.G. (1987). Computers in Canada: communications and curriculum. In *Contemporary Educational Issues: The Canadian Mosaic*, ed. L.L. Stewin and S.J.H. McCann. Toronto: Copp Clark Pitman.

Ramsey, P. (1982). Multicultural education in early childhood. In *Curriculum Planning for Young Children*, ed. J. Brown. Washington, D.C.: National Association for the Education of Young Children.

Reifel, S. (1984). Block construction: children's developmental landmarks in representation of space. *Young Children* 42 (2):61–67.

Rogers, C. (1969). *Freedom to Learn*. Columbus, OH: Merrill.

Rogers, C.S., and Sawyers, J.K. (1988). *Play in the Lives of Children*. Washington, D.C.: National Association for the Education of Young Children.

Rubenzer, R.L. (1984). Educating the other half: implications of left/right brain research. ERIC Document, ED150655.

Rubin, K.H. (1980). Fantasy play: its role in the development of social skills and social cognition. In *New Directions in Child Development: Child's Play*, ed. K.H. Rubin, pp. 69–84. San Francisco: Jossey-Bass.

Rubin, K.H., Fein, G.G., and Vandenberg, B. (1983). Play. In *Handbook of Child Psychology, Volume 4: Socialization, Personality and Social Development*, ed. P.H. Mussen and

E.M. Hetherington, pp. 693–774. New York: John Wiley & Sons.

Ruopp, R., Travers, J. Glantz, F., and Coelen, C. (1979). Children at the centre. Final Report of the National Day Care Study. Cambridge, MA: ABT Associates.

Sauvy, J., and Sauvy, S. (1974). *The Child's Discovery of Space.* Middlesex, England: Penguin.

Schermann, A. (1990). The learning child. In *Child Care and Education: Canadian Dimensions,* ed. I. Doxey. Toronto: Nelson.

Schickedanz, J.A. (1986). *More Than the ABC's: the Early Stages of Reading and Writing.* Washington, D.C.: National Association for the Education of Young Children.

Schirrmacher, R. (1988). *Art and Creative Development for Young Children.* Albany, NY: Delmar.

Schwartz, S.L., and Robison, H.F. (1982). *Designing Curriculum for Early Childhood.* Boston, MA: Allyn & Bacon.

Schweinhart, L.J., and Weikart, D.P. (1984). *Changed Lives: The Effects of the Perry Preschool Program on Youths Through Age 19.* Ypsilanti, MI: High/Scope.

Scriven, M. (1967). The methodology of evaluation. In *Perspectives of Curriculum Evaluation,* ed. R. Tyler, R. Gagné, and M. Scriven, (AERA Monograph Series on Curriculum Evaluation). Chicago: Rand McNally & Co.

Shade, D.D. (1985). Will a microcomputer really benefit preschool children? A theoretical examination of computer applications in ECE. ERIC Document, ED264951.

Siann, G., and Macleod, H. (1986). Computers and children of primary school age: issues and questions. *British Journal of Educational Technology* 17 (2): 133–44.

Sigel, I.E., and Cocking, R.R. (1977). *Cognitive Development from Childhood to Adolescence: A Constructivist Perspective.* New York: Holt, Rinehart & Winston.

Sime, M. (1973). *A Child's Eye View: Piaget for Young Parents and Teachers.* London: Thames & Hudson.

Simon, T. (1985). Play and learning with computers. *Early Childhood Development and Care* 19 (1–2): 69–78.

Smilansky, S. (1968). *The Effects of Sociodramatic Play on Disadvantaged Preschool Children.* New York: Wiley.

Smilansky, S. (1971). Can adults facilitate play in children? In *Play: The Child Strives Toward Self-Realization,* ed. S. Arnaud and N. Curry. Washington, D.C.: National Association for the Education of Young Children.

Smilansky, S., and Shefatya, L. (1990). *Facilitating Play: A Medium for Promoting Cognitive, Socio-Emotional and Academic Development in Young Children.* Gaithersburg, MD: Psychosocial & Educational Publications.

Smith, R.F. (1982). Early childhood science education: a Piagetian perspective. In *Curriculum Planning for Young Children,* ed. J.F. Brown, pp. 143–50. Washington, D.C.: National Association for the Education of Young Children.

Smith, R.F. (1987). Theoretical framework for preschool science experiences. *Young Children* 42 (1): 34–40.

Sponseller, D. (1974). *Play as a Learning Medium.* Washington, D.C.: National Association for the Education of Young Children.

Steffin, S.A. (1986). Using the micro as a weapon: fighting against convergent thinking. *Childhood Education* 59 (2): 251–58.

Stipek, D.J. (1982). Work habits begin in preschool. In *Curriculum Planning for Young Children,* ed. J.F. Brown. Washington, D.C.: National Association for the Education of Young Children.

Streibel, M.J. (1984). An analysis of the theoretical foundations for the use of microcomputers in ECE. ERIC Document, ED248971.

Strom, R.D. (1981). *Growing Through Play: Readings for Parents and Teachers.* Belmont, CA: Brooks/Cole.

Sullivan, E.V. (1985). Computers, culture and educational futures—a meditation on "Mindstorms." *Interchange* 16 (3): 1–8.

Sunal, D.W., and Szymanski Sunal, C. (1990). Helping young children appreciate beauty in natural areas. *Day Care and Early Education.* Fall, 1990: 26–29.

Suskind, D., and Kittel, J. (1989). Clocks, cameras, and chatter, chatter, chatter: activity boxes as curriculum. *Young Children* 44 (1): 46–50.

Suter, A.B. (1977). A playground—why not let the children create it? *Young Children* 32 (2): 19–24.

Talbot, J., and Frost, J.L. (1989). Magical playscapes. *Childhood Education* Fall, 1989: 11–19.

Teale, W.H., and Sulzby, E. (1989). Emerging literacy: new perspectives. In *Emerging Literacy: Young Children Learn to Read and Write,* pp. 1–15. Newark, DW: International Reading Association.

Tisone, M., and Wismar, B.L. (1985). Microcomputers: how can they be used to enhance creative development? *Journal of Creative Behavior* 19 (2): 97–103.

Torrance, P. (1966). Torrance Tests of Creative Thinking. Norms Technical Manual Research Edition. Princeton: Personnel Press.

Turkle, S. (1984). The intimate machine: eavesdropping on the secret lives of computers and kids. *Science.* April: 41–46.

Vergeront, J. (1988). *Places and Spaces for Preschool and Primary (Outdoors).* Washington, D.C.: National Association for the Education of Young Children.

Vietch, B., and Harms, T. (1981). *Cook and Learn: Pictorial Single Portion Recipes.* Menlo Park, CA: Addison-Wesley.

Vygotsky, L. (1962). *Thought and Language.* Cambridge, MA: Massachusetts Institute of Technology Press.

Walsh, D.J. (1991). Extending the discourse on developmental appropriateness: a developmental perspective. *Early Education and Development* 2 (2): 109–19.

Walsh, P. (1990). *Early Childhood Playgrounds: Planning an Outside Learning Environment.*

Melbourne: Martin Educational in association with Robert Andersen & Associates.

Wardle, F. (1990). Are we taking play out of playgrounds? *Day Care and Early Education.* Fall: 30–34.

Weber, E. (1984). *Ideas Influencing Early Childhood Education: A Theoretical Analysis.* New York: Teachers College Press, Columbia University.

Weikart, D.P. (1971). *The Cognitively-Oriented Curriculum: A Framework for Preschool Teachers.* Urbana: IL: University of Illinois.

Weininger, O. (1979). *Play and Education: The Basic Tool for Early Childhood Learning.* Springfield, IL: Chas. C. Thomas.

Whitebrook, M., Howes, C., and Phillips, D. (1990). Who cares? Child care teachers and the quality of care in America. Final report of the National Child Care Staffing Study. Oakland, CA.

Whitehurst, K.E. (1971). The young child: what movement means to him. In *The Significance of the Young Child's Motor Development,* proceedings of a conference sponsored by the American Association for Health, Physical Education and Recreation and the National Association for the Education of Young Children.

Wood, D. (1988). *How Children Think and Learn.* Oxford, England: Basil Blackwell Ltd.

Wortham, S.C. (1984). *Organizing Instruction in Early Childhood: A Handbook of Assessment and Activities.* Boston, MA: Allyn & Bacon.

Wright, M. (1983). *Compensatory Education in the Preschool: A Canadian Approach.* Ypsilanti: MI: High/Scope Press.

Yardley, A. (1989). *Young Children Learning.* Oakville, Ontario: Rubicon Press.

Zeece, P.D., and Graul, S.K. (1990). Learning to play: playing to learn. *Day Care and Early Education* 18 (1): 11–15.

Index

To the owner of this book

We hope that you have enjoyed *Empowering Children* and we would like to know as much about your experiences as you would care to offer. Only through your comments and those of others can we learn how to make this a better text for future readers.

School _____ Your instructor's name _____

Course _____ Was the text required? _____ Recommended? _____

1. What did you like the most about *Empowering Children?*

_____

_____

_____

2. How useful was this text for your course?

_____

_____

_____

3. Do you have any recommendations for ways to improve the next edition of this text?

_____

_____

_____

4. In the space below or in a separate letter, please write any other comments you have about the book. (For example, please feel free to comment on reading level, writing style, terminology, design features, and learning aids.)

_____

_____

_____

_____

Optional

Your name _____ Date _____

May Nelson Canada quote you, either in promotion for *Empowering Children* or in future publishing ventures?

Yes _____ No _____

Thanks!

MAIL ⇒ POSTE

Canada Post Corporation / Société canadienne des postes

Postage paid	Port payé
if mailed in Canada	si posté au Canada

Business Reply | **Réponse d'affaires**

0107077099   01

Nelson

0107077099-M1K5G4-BR01

Nelson Canada
College Editorial Department
1120 Birchmount Rd.
Scarborough, ON M1K 9Z9

PLEASE TAPE SHUT. DO NOT STAPLE.